I0528094

GRASPING SASQUATCH

PREPPING FOR SCIENTIFIC FIELD RESEARCH

JOHN S. BARANCHOK, PH.D.

THE REVIEWS ARE IN AND THEY ARE...
WELL,... MIXED!

"What will you do with your Bigfoot experience? In his book *Psychological Horizons*, Dr. Baranchok has stepped out of the norm and has written a book which will help you develop personal knowledge and scientific processes needed to gather and analyze data related to the mystery known as Bigfoot. He motivates you to re-evaluate how you approach the subject and how to deal with past and future experiences. The book is written ... to educate the novice and challenge those who have been interested in the subject for many years. You will learn and relearn concepts which will help your own research techniques, contribute to the advancement of gathering data, and how to process your experiences. This is a must read for any Sasquatch researcher or those simply looking for a Bigfoot experience!"

Shelia Johnson, M.Ed. Counseling Psychology, Bigfoot Researcher,
Conversations with Shelia TJ Facebook Page

"Insights from a professional psychologist; a novel approach ... His comedic self-depreciating approach is endearing ... and ... his sarcasm is fun ... Really!"

Rick Reles, BFRO Investigator

"For fans of Sasquatch research comes this guidebook filled with personal encounters and laden with tools to improve skills and outcomes in your own fieldwork."

Gary Strobl, Bigfoot Researcher

"What an unhelpful, POS! A boring, repetitive, and mostly irrelevant Bigfoot book! Only a few insights into Bigfoot or Bigfoot fieldwork techniques. The author is a conceited, "know-it-all" ass trying to impress the reader with his training, experience and knowledge of science and psychology, despite lacking the decades of Bigfoot field experience possessed by other writers, researchers, and investigators on the subject!"

(Anonymous)

"Dr. Baranchok has done the Bigfoot world a huge favor in the writing of this book. His background in neuropsychology offers insight that very few in the community can offer. His chapter on how to control your fight-flight response during a Bigfoot encounter is a must read for any and all serious researchers."

C. Wayne Totherow, Founder of Mannimal Research
and Southeastern Sasquatch Investigations

DEDICATIONS AND THANKS

Dedicated to my parents John Baranchok and Evelyn M. Baranchok: Thank you for my life, your love, and wisdom. I grow to appreciate them more with each passing day! May you rest in peace.

Dedicated to My Beloved Daughter Sedona Ann Baranchok: Thank you for your ongoing presence in my life. You continue to light my life with the glow of your beauty and the caring warmth of your spirit! Always remember, you are the purveyor of your own reality!

Thanks to Anne and Ferris Maloof: Thank you for teaching me unconditional love and acceptance. I hope to master them one day!

Thanks to Lori Copeland Wade: Thanks for taking me under your wing and in doing so inspiring much contained in this book.

Thanks to Jeff Carpenter: We met when you saved my ass on my first expedition. I can't begin to say how much you have taught me about Bigfoot research. Thank you!

Thanks to: Lori Wade, Jeff Carpenter, John Eaves, Rick Reles, George Wrigley, Glenn Williams, Mark Ogilbee, Greggory Craddock, and Charlie Raymond: You have been my Bigfoot research professors at the Bigfoot University located in Northern Georgia, Southern Tennessee, and God-only-knows-where in Kentucky. Thank you so much for your time, patience, and tolerance.

Thanks to D. Jeff Meldrum, Ph.D. for the personal communication, publishing guidance, and expressed interest in my efforts herein. Your work is part of the bedrock foundation and a pillar of the scientific exploration of the Sasquatch species. You remain a beacon to the few pursuing the scientific exploration of the species.

Thanks to Ron Morehead for the use of his photo. Your pioneering work in Bigfoot Field Research set a standard in sonic research into the species. You remain on the cutting edge of theory and thought in the field.

Thanks to Matt Moneymaker for guiding me through the Bigfoot Field Research Organization's (BFRO's) NDA to find a path for sharing my own and others' expedition experiences. Thank you for forming BFRO making Bigfoot accessible to the masses and allowing me access to BFRO's internal documents.

Thanks to Janice Carter for setting a living example of strength and courage in sharing her story (through her own words and those of Mary Green) so that others might do the same. Your ongoing fieldwork, insights, and openness continue to be a source for very critical topics Bigfoot science needs to further explore.

Special Thanks to Terry Thomas for his incredible cover artwork reflecting my own biases concerning the needs for and direction of future Bigfoot research. I greatly appreciated your enthusiasm in integrating my own and other's conceptualizations of Bigfoot into your art. Pablo Picasso and Salvador Dali were not available and likely would not have "taken notes" in as open fashion as yourself!

Special Thanks to my Copy and Content Editors: John Kuczma, Sheila Johnson, Kerry A. Cosby, Michele Ice, Gary Strobl, and Rick Reles. Your generous donation of time, effort, and feedback was invaluable to the final product of this book.

Thanks to the Crew at MedPsych Services, PC: Greg Lovell, M.A., Marcie McElroy, Tonya Davis, and Kieffer Collum. You know and have had to deal with "the good, the bad, and the ugly" in me. Your steadfast support and professionalism allowed this book to come to fruition. Thank you!

Thanks to the Primary Supporters of MedPsych Services, PC: William Naguszewski, MD; Robert Naguszewski, MD; Carl Billian, MD; Anne Groover, MD; Johnathan Beckner, MD; Brian C. Hard, MD; David Hale, MD; Marc Wall, MD; Jay Schecter, MD; Jeffrey Glass, MD; Anne White, MD; Dennett Gordon, Ph.D.; Debbie Gordon, B.A.; Shereef Girgis, MD; and Richard Donadio, MD.

Without your interest in and support of my work in Neuropsychology, Pain Psychology, and General Clinical Psychology, I could have not remained living in the Southeastern United States and discovered my awesome hobby of looking for Bigfoot. (Debbie Gordon: Please catch yourself before you fall on the floor laughing.)

Thanks to Great Personal Friends and Playmates: Greg Lovell, Michael Cummings, Amanda Reisner, Dennett Gordon, Sedona A. Baranchok, Lucian Seth Turner, and Jay Kuczma. We've had a lot of good times together and hope we can have many more!

Thanks to: Sheila and TJ Johnson, Kevin Zorc, Garrett Strobl, Rebecca Strobl, and Sedona A. Baranchok: Thank you for your unwavering enthusiastic encouragement and support of me writing this book. Others didn't discourage, but none have been as unconditionally strong and unwavering in their support as you guys! You have greatly helped me make it happen! Thank you!!

Thanks to you all!! I wish you peace, health, wellness, prosperity, happiness, and love. Mostly, I wish you Love, as the rest means nothing without it!

Sincerely,
John S. Baranchok, Ph.D.

DISCLAIMERS

CONCEPTUAL AND CONTENT DISCLAIMER: Although the word "Bigfoot" is in the title of this book twice and is the most frequently used word in this book, *THIS IS NOT A BOOK ABOUT BIGFOOT!* It is a book about *PROCESSES, PROCEDURES, AND TECHNIQUES TO ENHANCE SCIENTIFIC BIGFOOT RESEARCH!* These are offered as an adjunct avenue to prove the existence of the species and minimize the potential need to "harvest" and dissect a member of the species to achieve that goal.

This book is intended to provide "self-help" information on how the dedicated researcher can regulate his or her fight-flight response to move forward and pursue their quarry, should they want to take that potential risk. It is intended to educate the researcher on key psychological and scientific definitions, processes, and phenomena that influence their ability to become less biased about themselves, their observations, interpretations, and conclusions of research data. Indeed, it is intended to teach the dedicated researcher the strengths and weaknesses of different types of evidence and others' research findings for their value, meaning, and relevance to Bigfoot. It is meant to teach basic experimental designs and statistical analysis concepts so that the researcher can develop their own research protocols in a more scientifically sound and objective fashion. In the opinion of this writer, these topics represent the fundamental prerequisite knowledge needed by any researcher dedicated to providing the SCIENTIFIC PROOF OF THE EXISTENCE OF BIGFOOT AS SPECIES IN ORDER TO BENEFIT THE SPECIES!

Although on one level, this book represents a "How To Capture Bigfoot" book, that topic is described from a **SCIENTIFIC**

THEORETICAL PERSPECTIVE. The reader seeking concrete "How to" geographical/topographical, logistical, mechanical, and/or otherwise apparatus-based procedures and traps to "capture" Bigfoot will likely be disappointed in this book. The book does contain examples of that pragmatic ilk but is not written from the experiential/phenomenological research perspective.

That perspective, while needed and extremely valuable in scientifically proving Bigfoot's existence has also proven itself insufficient to the task. Consider the plethora of credible evidence amassed through the phenomenological/experiential approach over the past 60+ years of modern Bigfoot research history. Credible audio, video, and photographic evidence of the creature exists. One can pay low to modest to exorbitant expedition fees to possibly versus probably have a Bigfoot experience. This might include "tree knocks," roars, whoops, screams, cries, growls, limb breaks and twists, tree structures, eyeshine, footprints, bluff charges, fleeting glimpses of shadows, fleeting glimpses of creatures, zapping, and psychic/paranormal activity (to name few) all genuinely attributable and often attributed to Bigfoot. The rarer expeditioner may catch a brief glimpse of a Bigfoot. The much rarer and the extremely lucky one may experience an extended, multi-second view. None of these awesome experiences and evidence have been found sufficient to scientifically prove the existence of Bigfoot.

Explanations for this failure have been advanced and increasingly include government intervention/interference and conspiracy. It therefore pains me to point out a more practical explanation. *Impressive as the aforementioned evidence may be, it simply fails to rise to the "standard required" by "Science" to allow it to constitute "Scientific Evidence" and proof of the species.* It remains primarily anecdotal, subjective, and as such often biased. It typically lacks scientific control of extraneous influences and a tight experimental design. Most frequently, it lacks statistical data analysis answering an a priori (in advance of exploration) hypothetical question. The databases are guarded for the purposes of commercial and financial gain. Results are rarely publicly published for peer review and replication versus refutation. In short, although often using elements of the scientific method, the phenomenological/experiential approach fails to stringently follow the complete scientific method and process. As such, phenomenological/experiential evidence serves the very necessary and critical function of representing the **foundation** for scientific discovery. It has not, and will never, however, rise to the level of objective scientific proof! Don't accept it. Disagree with it and reject it. Cry foul, dig in your heels, yell, scream, and protest. It remains a basic scientific fact. Phenomenological/experiential expeditions represent a good start toward "science" but are not the end point on that scientific path.

It also remains a basic fact that for humanity to assist the species in a broad and official capacity (protecting its habitat, for example), scientific proof is the standard demanded. Phenomenological/experiential proponents have given us the **foundation** for that proof. But for a few exceptions, research efforts continue to pour footer on top of footer, foundation on top of foundation, without moving on and upward to **frame up a scientific structure** to form "The House of Bigfoot."

It is with that in mind that I labored to write this book. As such it does include a wide variety of "Scientific How To" processes and techniques, but nonetheless fails to provide many concrete geographical, topographical, and apparatus-based techniques or processes. **Some** examples of those are in here, but they do not predominate these writings.

The content of these writings is also not primarily of the "show and tell," anecdotal ilk. In short, the primary goal of this book is not to tell first or second-hand "Bigfoot Encounter Stories," be they objectively narrated or of the sensationalized variety. No offense is intended to the writers of those books when I say that it is my opinion such books have been overdone ad nauseam. No surprise there; hell, they sell! Nonetheless, those sales primarily benefit the fortune of the publisher and the fame and celebrity status of the writer. Rarely do they benefit the species! Again, this book *does contain a few personal and second-hand examples of such stories,* but this is not primarily that kind of book. It is not intended to be. Those stories are advanced with a broader intent.

LEGAL DISCLAIMER: WARNING: Please note, it is the opinion of the author that any person who enters the woods (or any other location) looking for Bigfoot (or on any cryptid, extra-terrestrial, or paranormal investigation or experience) puts themselves at an increased risk for psychological and/or physical harm, injury, or death. From a scientific perspective, the existence of Bigfoot remains unproven. From an experiential/phenomenological perspective, however, I have little doubt that there is an inadequately understood creature in existence that has the **potential** to harm, injure, dismember, destroy, or kill any human being, at will. This is not to say I believe or promote the view that this creature is inherently evil (or good), dangerous (or benign), predatory (or protective), avoidant (or social and cooperative), aggressive (or warm and cuddly), terrestrial (or extra-terrestrial), paranormal (or normal), instinctually reactive (or sentient and considerate), inter-dimensional/intra-dimensional (or four-dimensional) or anything else. I am simply saying: WE (HUMAN BEINGS) DON'T KNOW OR UNDERSTAND THIS CREATURE OR PHENOMENA WITH ANY DEGREE OF CERTAINTY! AS SUCH, WE CANNOT TRULY KNOW ITS POTENTIAL RISK (OR LACK THEREOF) TO OURSELVES!

Additionally, the range of reported locations of alleged Bigfoot evidence/sightings contain inherent risks. Swamps, bogs, forests, mountain ranges throughout the world; high and low deserts; glaciers; interstate highways and other super highways; local and city streets; suburbia; rural country forest and wilderness roads; abandoned dwellings; and even tunnels and city subways have been cited in Bigfoot sightings. Each of these locations/environments has inherent physical and psychological risks and dangers associated with them. An abbreviated list of organic creatures would include venomous and non-venomous spiders; venomous and non-venomous snakes; other venomous or non-venomous insects and bugs; disease-carrying species such as rats, mice, and mosquitoes to name a few. Here live household/domesticated cats, feral cats;

household/domesticated dogs, feral dogs; coyotes, wolves; bears; big cat species; venomous and toxic plants; venomous and toxic fish; corral, microscopic viruses; bacteria, and disease. *Most critically, here lives the most dangerous organic species on earth: humans, well-meaning and vicious, predatory and deadly.*

There are road hazards; power tools dangerous to operate without adequate training; potentially dangerous manually manipulated tools; rocks; tree stumps; branches; unseen holes or gullies; cliffs or simply unseen unlevel surfaces over which to trip when you are walking. There are rivers and lakes to drown in; water pools (stagnant or fresh in appearance) to get sick drinking from or simply being nearby. Food poisoning, dehydration, hypothermia, hyperthermia, sunburn, and freezing to death are possible. This list fails to mention unimagined and unknown accidental occurrences that can hurt, injure, maim, or kill.

The potential for psychological trauma or injury abounds and is not limited to witnessing the harm, injury, death, or dismemberment of a friend or stranger or the same to oneself. Anxiety, fear, nightmares or terrors, insomnia, sleep deprivation, humorously intentioned hoaxes, or practical jokes turned bad can and do happen. Alternatively, you might encounter toxic, hysterical, borderline, overly controlling, inordinately helpless and needy, sociopathic, and psychopathic human personalities that are very real risks and potentially harmful, dangerous, and even life-threatening.

When you go on a solo or multi-person hunt or expedition for Bigfoot, the above represents only a partial list of risks you take and the dangers you may encounter before, during, or after that experience. THIS AUTHOR CANNOT AND WILL NOT BE HELD LEGALLY RESPONSIBLE AND BEARS NO LIABILITY FOR ANY PHYSICAL, PSYCHOLOGICAL /EMOTIONAL TRAUMA, HARM, INJURY, OR DEATH INCURRED TO ANY READER OF THIS BOOK OR ANYONE ELSE SEEKING BIGFOOT ON ANY LEVEL (PHYSICAL, PSYCHOLOGICAL, OR INTELLECTUAL). THIS REMAINS TRUE EVEN IN THE EVENT THEY ARE UTILIZING KNOWLEDGE, TECHNIQUES, OR ADVICE LEARNED FROM

AND CONTAINED IN THIS BOOK. WHEN YOU LEAVE THE SAFETY AND SECURITY OF YOUR BEDROOM OR HOME TO VENTURE OUT INTO THE WORLD TO SEEK BIGFOOT OR ON ANY OTHER ADVENTURE (LOOKING FOR CRYPTIDS, UFOs, GHOSTS, OR JUST GOING TO THE CORNER GROCERY STORE, FOR EXAMPLE); YOU RISK YOUR PHYSICAL AND PSYCHOLOGICAL INTEGRITY AND WELFARE. YOU TAKE THEM "INTO YOUR OWN HANDS," AND BEAR TOTAL RESPONSIBILITY FOR THESE. I HAVE STRIVEN IN GOOD FAITH AND WITH PERSONAL AND PROFESSIONAL INTEGRITY TO PROVIDE INFORMATION OF VALUE AND UTILITY TO THE BIGFOOT ENTHUSIAST AND/OR FIELD RESEARCHER WITHIN THESE WRITINGS. HOW YOU CHOOSE TO USE IT IS UP TO YOU, AND YOU DO SO AT YOUR OWN RISK.

It is also the opinion of this author that the person reading this book is likely to be offended by some written statement(s) in this book. I address some controversial issues and theories within the Bigfoot community. Many people have strong opinions and allegiances concerning these. I make some categorical statements that many might take exception to or find offensive. I make statements/comments about certain individuals or groups that may offend those people or those involved with those organizations. Although not on a pornographic level, I use verbiage that many consider offensive, vulgar, and inappropriate. I make bad and, at times, offensive jokes using potentially offensive language. In short, if you are thin-skinned, extremely "politically correct," hyper-religious, or hyper-conservative, you **will be** offended when you read this book.

There is a good chance that even if you are none of these, you may be offended by something in this book. Please take the offensive comments in this book in the spirit in which they are intended: provocation of alternate forms of thinking/concepts, critical thinking, and as literary humor. Nonetheless, forewarned is forearmed!

NDA DISCLAIMER: It is my genuine intent and legal responsibility in these writings to comply with my Bigfoot Field

Researchers Organization (BFRO) and Mannimal Research Non-disclosure Agreements (NDAs). As of this writing, I am a member of the "Mannimalresearch.com group" and have attended and will attend BFRO expeditions. Both of these groups require NDAs of participants. In these writings, I strive to honor those and believe I have been successful in doing so (in both the spirit and letter of these agreements).

One only needs to enter "Bigfoot research organizations" or "Sasquatch research organizations" into a Google or Yahoo search engine to discover just a partial list of individuals and/or organizations conducting Bigfoot/Sasquatch research. These groups have various degrees of scientific integrity and various primary motivations (mission statements notwithstanding). Most are open to the public or offer private membership for field expeditions.

I ran such searches and examined information found on pages one and two from each search. The list below is what I discovered. They are posted in the order that I discovered them during my search. The order in no way reflects which falls into the categories of: "The Good, The Bad, and The Ugly." I assure you that all three types are out there (contained in my list or not). I leave it to the informed reader to make those determinations.

The list included: Bigfoot Research Organization (Passim), Blue Mountain Bigfoot Research, North American Wood Ape Conservancy (NWAC), Sasquatch Washington USA (the Squatchateers), Upper Peninsula Bigfoot/Sasquatch Research Organization, National BigFoot Research Organization, Native Oklahoma Bigfoot Research Organization, Alberta Sasquatch Research and Investigation Organization, Criptid Brothers Investigations, Bigfoot Research Center, The Gulf Coast BigFoot Research Organization, Cascades Sasquatch Research Organization (CSRO), (KBRO), The Sasquatch Research Association, Rocky Mountain Sasquatch Organization, Washington Sasquatch Research Team (WASRT), Sasquatch Investigations Of The Rockies, Sasquatch Canada, British Columbia Sasquatch Organization, and Alberta Sasquatch. I would add Mannimal Research to this list for their scientific dedication and goals. This latter name was not a "hit" on the first two pages of my search.

I include this partial list in my NDA DISCLAIMER page *to highlight that there is not a shortage of individuals and organizations readily available to the aspiring Bigfoot researcher.* This is also true of books on the subject (*Squatchin 101* by Charles Kimbro & Monongahela[1]; *The Locals* by Thom Powell [2003][2], Published simultaneously by Hancock House Publishers, LTD, & Hancock House Publishers] are two of the best in my opinion). *From these, one can learn specific locations, procedures, and techniques to find Bigfoot.* Indeed, the World Wide Web and a recent surge in publications on Bigfoot suggest that NDAs sometimes aren't worth the paper they are written on in terms of protecting habituation areas and other locations where concentrations of the creatures might reside. Additionally, television shows such as *Mountain Monsters* and *Finding Bigfoot* and The History Channel and The Learning Channel Bigfoot specials also provide guidance and information on how to conduct Bigfoot Field Research (BFR).

Despite the "public domain" nature of television shows like *Finding Bigfoot* (which in my opinion provides an excellent formula/structure/process/algorithm on "how to" conduct Bigfoot field research), non-disclosure agreements (NDAs) still abound. But to prove my point on the informative nature of TV on Bigfoot research, let's use *Finding Bigfoot*[3] as an excellent example it represents. How does that show go about "Finding Bigfoot"?

1. **Gather Information:** "Hot spot" information based on recent Bigfoot sightings is readily available from a number of sources (to the detriment of harassing the species, in my opinion). On the World Wide Web, sites such as the BFRO Main Page and Expedition Bigfoot's page (a North GA Bigfoot museum) regularly report specific locations of Bigfoot sightings in a timely fashion. The relatively recent surge of books on the subject also provides general procedures to find likely Bigfoot habitats, as well as specific locations.

Finding Bigfoot, however, gathers this information primarily from town hall meetings. During these, individuals both of the brave and attention-seeking ilk tell their Bigfoot encounter stories. They are asked to point out on a map the exact area where these occurred. This makes for an efficient search strategy and saves leg work. The reader, however, does not need to hold a town hall meeting. One only need announce to family, friends, and new acquaintances that they are looking for Bigfoot. The information (along with some snickers, laughs, and ridicule) will be forthcoming. It is left up to the receiver of this information to weigh its authenticity and value/prioritize the locations to go looking. Never fear, *Finding Bigfoot* once again teaches a vetting process through their in-depth interviews and site visits with selected witnesses.

2. **Develop Your Search Strategy and Deploy the Troops**: Using their local map, based on vetting of witnesses and geographic/topographic considerations, the stars of the show divide and conquer. They establish their individual and group "base camps" and further discuss night-time investigation strategies. The reader only need rinse and repeat these processes.

3. **Conduct Nighttime (or Daytime) Investigation Using Various Provocation Techniques**: *Finding Bigfoot* highlights their teams' nighttime investigations. This fits what I find a puzzling assumption versus bias within the BF community: "Bigfoots are more active at night than during the day." I'm not really sure how or if this has been scientifically proven. It may be that supporters of evolutionary Bigfoot theory (e.g. Dr. Grover Krantz, Dr. Jeff Meldrum) "reasonably" extrapolated from parallel or potentially similar species concerning this behavior. Despite anecdotal whispers and shouts, however, I was unable to uncover statistical analysis showing significantly more nighttime than daytime sightings. It does, nonetheless, seem to be the consensus of most versus many researchers I have encountered. It also flies in the face of more than a few credible daytime sightings. I personally would suggest investigating any time of day until issues of "peak activity levels" are systematically investigated above and beyond subjective accounts. I would also add, that it's a lot easier to see footprints and the creature itself during the day than at night. So, take a hike in the woods. Look, listen, feel, and smell your way

through the forest with or without some form of recording equipment. You are doing Bigfoot field research!

4. Return to Base Camp or Otherwise Regroup and Debrief: After investigations in respective areas have been completed, the team reconvenes and compares notes. What they discover is then used to inform and plan subsequent investigations. The reader, once again, only needs to rinse and repeat!

There you go! You are now a bona fide Bigfoot Field Researcher! I haven't violated a single aspect of any NDA I have ever signed revealing how to become one. I have done so to demonstrate how information on Bigfoot that might appear relevant under NDAs, can be sourced legally (at no risk) as they fall under the category of "public domain."

I have also taken other steps to ensure I respect my NDAs. I do not reveal specific investigation locations. I also don't divulge specific strategies unique to the expedition organizations that I participated in. As such, any similarity to or resemblance of information, comments, concerns, practices, and procedures noted, discussed, or employed in this book to other established research organizations (named or un-named above) or individuals (named or un-named in this text) is completely unintended and coincidental. When appropriate, based on public statements/claims, research publications, and information dissemination, I have named specific organizations and/or individuals and provided appropriate citations.

In general (with the exception of my DEDICATION AND THANKS page), I have obtained permission to use private individuals' names or altered their identity and initials to maintain confidentiality and protect the innocent (and the guilty). The use of persons' or organizations' names does not constitute an endorsement of the writings in this book. Indeed, some of those might wish I hadn't named them.

A final note revolves around clarifying and differentiating the identities of two names in the Bigfoot community used in this text: **Jeff Carpenter and Scott Carpenter.** These names represent two different individuals. I consider **Jeff Carpenter an** outstanding woodsman, Bigfoot investigator, and a personal friend. He is a BFRO

Investigator. On expeditions, he was our "go-to guy" for differentiating identified/classified nature sounds and phenomena from those possibly created by Bigfoot. He considers Sasquatch a flesh and blood creature.

Scott Carpenter is also a Bigfoot researcher. He has penned multiple books on the subject that are, in my opinion, "must reads." I met Scott when he was a guest speaker at a BFRO expedition I was attending, but I am unclear if he has any formal relationship with the BFRO organization. We also exchanged a brief private message over Facebook regarding some little-discussed topics related to Melba Ketchum's DNA study on the species. I do not know him personally or well enough to definitively speak for his theoretical beliefs regarding Sasquatch (beyond those mentioned in his book in which he characterizes them as Nephilim). Given that characterization, some might argue that he is of what is commonly called the "Woo" theoretical orientation. This may or may not be the case. I would point out, however, that his belief that Sasquatches are Nephilim is not necessarily inconsistent with or preclusive of them being flesh and blood creatures.

Thank you for your understanding in these matters.

John S. Baranchok, Ph.D.

A BIGFOOT SCIENTIFIC RESEARCH JOKE?

A policeman sees a drunk man searching for something under a streetlight and asks what the drunk has lost. He says he lost his keys and they both look under the streetlight together. After a few minutes, the policeman asks if he is sure he lost them here, and the drunk replies, no, that he lost them in the park. The policeman asks why he is searching here, and the drunk replies, "This is where the light is."

FOR YOUR CONSIDERATION

"The eye sees only what the mind is prepared to comprehend."

— ROBERTSON DAVIES

"One of the biggest problems with the world today is that we have large groups of people who will accept whatever they hear on the grapevine, just because it suits their worldview—not because it is actually true or because they have evidence to support it. The really striking thing is that it would not take much effort to establish validity in most of these cases...but people prefer reassurance to research."

— NEIL DEGRASSE

"To raise new questions, new possibilities to regard old problems from a new angle, requires creative imagination and marks real advance in science."

— ALBERT EINSTEIN

"To increase our objectivity, we must learn to switch off the mini-movies. Objectivity requires us to be mindful, present in the moment, and experience what is happening without judgment. "

— ELIZABETH THORNTON

"In order for sensation to accede to the objectivity of things, it must itself be changed into a thing. The agent of change is language: the sensations are turned into verbal objects."

— OCTAVIO PAZ

"Science is based on the possibility of objectivity, on the possibility of different people checking out for themselves the observations made by others. Without that possibility, there is no empirical principle capable of deciding between different arguments and theories."

— JOSE PADILHA

"Through awareness of self and science, we can only hope to approach objectivity. Through self-knowledge, scientific psychologic experimentation, replication, and dissemination of information, we can hopefully achieve a scientific discovery!"

— JOHN S. BARANCHOK, AUGUST, 2020

CONTENTS

APPENDICES

INTRODUCTION

This is a primer text written for the aspiring and the already practicing Bigfoot Field Researcher. It is intended to enhance their scientific and psychological knowledge base and skills **in preparation** for their search for Bigfoot in the fields and woods of the continental United States. The fields of counseling and neuropsychology are replete with knowledge including general psychology theory and principles, counseling and behavioral change techniques, the scientific method, experimental design and statistical analysis, and anatomy and physiology (the structure of the body and its nervous system). These need to be brought to bear in the search for Bigfoot. These are all **exceedingly relevant** to doing Scientific Bigfoot Research (SBFR) and fieldwork. As such, this book presents these concepts and knowledge with specific Bigfoot anecdotes and examples highlighting their relevance.

It is my goal to share key points, theories, and issues as well as other information from the field of psychology and science; giving the aspiring Bigfoot field researcher the fundamental knowledge to **PREPARE** to enter the field and inform their research. For the already practicing and experienced field researchers, it is my hope that this information will better inform, develop, and enhance your existing skills. It should make your research more systematic and objective. This will benefit not only the Bigfoot community but the sorely lacking "scientific evidence" that so many clamor to achieve to "preserve the species."

At the time of completing this writing, I have attended nine Bigfoot Field Researchers Research Organization (BFRO) expeditions and several "private" or personal ones. These were done solo or with dear friends, I have met through the BFRO community. I have personally heard a tree knock, seen "red eye shine" and wood structures, heard a howl, heard a growl, saw two footprint castings, and experienced a "landslide." These of course were all purportedly or potentially Bigfoot related. I have heard other's stories of being "zapped" and "bluff charged," as well as fleeting and extended, distant and up-close sightings that have included "mind speak" and vanishing. *I have not had a personal definitive visual encounter where I have clearly witnessed the species with my own eyes.* I continue this field research on a regular basis as I hope to learn more about field techniques and have such an encounter. *As such, I am NOT a field research expert. This is not a book primarily detailing concrete methods about how or where to find Bigfoot.* If you purchased this book for that purpose, I would refer you to other texts including *Squatching 101* by Charles Kimbro and Monongahela[1], who have covered this topic in an expert fashion that I can only aspire to. Despite already being addressed in my Conceptual and Content disclaimer, *this is a book on how to enhance your psychological and scientific knowledge base and emotional reactions IN PREPARATION FOR conducting "objective and scientifically based research" into the species.* Due to this goal, it will include field research examples that speak to how and where to find the creature, but addressing those subjects is not the primary goal of this book. *If you hope to become a more objective or objective scientific field researcher of Bigfoot, please read on.*

To the professionally trained zoologist, veterinarian, physician, physical scientist anatomist/physiologist, anthropologist, archaeologist, psychologist, therapist/counselor, lawyer, statistician, theologian, writer/editor/publisher, etc., I will first say that I am very impressed with the fact that you are open-minded enough to have bought or are considering buying this book. At the risk of offending, however, you are not the primary target audience for this book. It is unlikely you will find this book written to the standards and practices within your field of expertise. You will most certainly be offended by some of my comments therein. Furthermore, to those educated at the doctoral level, you shouldn't find much new within these pages (beyond self-help techniques) as your education should have covered many or most of them. It has been decades since I published an academic paper or abstract. Although I had expertise in a few of the topics discussed here, I am currently an expert in none or maybe one of them, with that expertise being experiential, rather than academic or hardcore scientific. I am certainly open and will appreciate feedback clarifying unintentional misunderstandings, errors, and factual mistakes on my part. I am not perfect. But please spare me indignant rages, diatribes, as well as verbal and written assaults on my character based on your expertise in your field of study.

The primary intent of this book is to entertain and educate the Bigfoot research enthusiast less informed on scientific and psychological information; ideas and principles relevant to the study and understanding of the Bigfoot and Bigfoot phenomena. It is not to be a professional or academic treatise or tome. As such, I use my sometimes dark and/or vulgar, often sarcastic sense of humor in these writings. If you are hypersensitive or easily offended by such, please spare me the grief!

I have simplified the writing process by frequently using and citing "online" resources; not always sourcing original materials for ideas, thinking, and writings on all topics. I have relied heavily on texts in my admittedly ancient psychology, science, and statistics library. I have long forgotten the fine details of the American Psychological Association's writing style format. I work full time, just turned 61 years of age (at the time of the original writing), and hoped to complete this manuscript before I die. Please forgive me for these admitted shortcuts. In all cases, however, when I knowingly borrow or directly use ideas and words/writings of others, I have given appropriate credit and citation. I may be a sarcastic jerk, but a plagiarist I am not!

My writing style also reflects a duality in myself and (I suspect) others with serious interests in Bigfoot: phenomenological/experiential versus scientific priorities. My writing style at times takes on a conversational tone and at others, a scientific/academic tone. Rather than forcing my writing into one style or another, I have chosen to allow those styles to remain and reflect that duality. *I think it highlights an important and at times conflicting nature of Bigfoot research and fieldwork.*

It was suggested I would be wise to divide this lengthy book into two separate books. A large part of me (not my belly) agreed with this suggestion. Longer books cost more money to produce and sell. By publishing one long book during a time when finances are tight for most folks, I run the risk of hurting sales of the book. Written with the intent of passing on critical information to improve Bigfoot research, that intent would be lost if it didn't sell.

Long books are also a "turn-off." Just looking at the thickness of a lengthy book makes me not want to read it, even when written by one of my favorite authors! I am referring to Stephen King, not myself. I lose interest, become exhausted just picking it up, and ultimately don't read it or won't buy it! Another good reason to divide my manuscript into two books.

The first "half" of this book is "more accessible" than the second half. The first half is frankly less boring and technical, more colorfully written, easier to digest, and probably more relevant to your "typical" Bigfoot research enthusiast than the next half. The second half mostly involves types of evidence, research design, and statistics. Only so much can be done to make the last two topics interesting. It is admittedly written in a dryer/more "academic" fashion. It will likely be of greater interest and value to the more serious and dedicated researcher than the causal hobbyist. Another good reason to divide this book into two; give people a relevant choice in their purchase.

Despite these and other very valid reasons to divide the

manuscript into two books, I have kept it one book. This does run the risk of "not getting the word out" to and not benefiting a larger audience. Such a division, however, would compromise the dissemination of what I consider the most valuable and important information contained in the manuscript: that information in the second half of the book.

For the most part, Bigfoot Fieldwork has followed the same process and pattern for at least 60+ years without resulting in scientific proof of the species acceptable to the broader scientific community. Continuing to do the same for another 60 years is unlikely to yield a different result. The information contained in the second half of this book is of critical importance to the serious investigator/fieldworker and Bigfoot scientist. *It represents requisite core knowledge to increase the scientific validity, reliability, and ultimately the scientific value of future research efforts. Without beginning to apply this knowledge and processes to our Bigfoot fieldwork, it seems highly unlikely that we will achieve our scientific aspirations to benefit the species.*

If I had divided the manuscript into two books, the second book would most certainly not sell due to the nature of the material. The important information contained therein would therefore go primarily unnoticed and unread and have little to no potential to advance the field. By keeping this information linked to the more accessible information in the first half of the book, I hope to have maintained **accessibility** to information in the second half. This should also preserve its potential to be of benefit to the field. *In effect, the price you pay for the more easily consumable and digestible information in the first half of the book is having access to the information contained in the second half.* If you are the casual Bigfoot researcher, you might ignore the second half initially. As you develop a desire for your research to have a true scientific impact, you may then wish to wade through the second half of the book.

As such, I have divided the manuscript into a two-part book. PART ONE covers the basics of belief, bias, and other fundamental knowledge. It also concretely details lessons on how to modulate emotional and behavioral self-control (the fight-flight response). It is best suited for the casual or new Bigfoot researcher. It also remains important to the experienced fieldworker who may not be familiar with psychological self-regulation techniques and the other critical knowledge contained therein.

PART TWO covers more advanced concepts/knowledge, as well as research and statistical techniques. I consider this information more scientifically relevant and critical to improving the scientific value of future Bigfoot research. It represents the knowledge and processes that we need to use to strive to achieve more scientifically rigorous and objective scientific research and research findings. Through such applications and results, we should have a greater likelihood of scientific acceptance. This should ultimately benefit the species.

Additional introductory comments revolve around terminology that I will use liberally throughout this book. You will note I will refer to Bigfoot as an animal, beast, creature, hominid, being, spirit, demon, target species, stimuli, independent and dependent variable. I use terms like intra or inter-dimensional creatures, entities, or phenomena. I also use a variety of other terms and nomenclature depending on the context of the discussion at hand. *Many of these terms carry the weight of particular theoretical underpinnings and belief systems that I do not necessarily believe or disbelieve; subscribe to or not.* I will often use some of these terms interchangeably and without regard for these theoretical underpinnings. *It is not the purpose of this book to define, debate, or resolve the merit and often conflicting nature of these terms and their associated theories. At the time of this writing, I have not personally adopted nor do I subscribe to a particular bias beyond emphasizing the role of science and psychology in trying to prepare one's knowledge base and "self" to explore these issues for your own edification/enjoyment and knowledge.* By using the principles discussed herein, you should find yourself in a much better position to make some decisions about your own beliefs and be better prepared to settle these sticky wickets for yourself. It is not my intent or job in this text to do this for you! That will hopefully be your own journey and adventure! Good reading!

PART I

THE BASICS: BELIEF, BIAS, FUNDAMENTAL KNOWLEDGE, AND SELF-CONTROL

1

YES!! THERE IS A SANTA CLAUS AND I BELIEVE IN BIGFOOT: THESE ARE MY BIASES!

Upon embarking on my journey and interest in Bigfoot, I quickly learned to anticipate a wide variety of reactions from people with whom I shared my interest. They ranged from surprised laughter of the disbelieving individual who thought I was joking. There was the reaction of the "professionally trained logical skeptic" woman who had to politely cover her snickering mouth and grab a nearby piece of furniture to stop herself from falling onto the ground, rolling about in hysterical laughter. I got the blank stare and dropped jaw of a professional colleague who knows me to be a serious neuropsychologist and couldn't quite be sure if what I was saying was serious or an attempt to lighten the weight of a case of Alzheimer's disease we were discussing. Then there was the genuine, "Oh really! That's interesting" of the open-minded curiosity seeker who proceeded to ask questions. I've also observed the embarrassed facial expression of the reluctant person who had a face-to-face encounter with Bigfoot as they muster the courage to share their story. Then there was the "Wow! Me too!! I belong to a research group and go on expeditions!"

For myself, however, the most infuriating response was the pompously over-confident ass, who in response to my declaration that "I believe in Bigfoot" retorted "Yeah sure!! And I used to believe in Santa Claus when I was 4 years old, too!" If you represent that person, I'm torn between begging you to just put down or return this book versus insisting you read on. If you read on, please use the most open-minded attitude you can muster so that you might extricate your soul from burning in the depths of hell!!!

Yes! To an emotionally hardened and calloused adult, a belief in Santa Claus may seem like a silly, infantile lie we tell children. The Christian Church supports it to keep enrollment up and the offering plates full. "Madison Avenue" continues to promote him for sales and profit. To even the indifferent working-class Joe, St. Nick can represent either a day or two off from work (with or without pay) or an opportunity for overtime. But to continue to believe in his existence??!! Come on!!

I nonetheless believe in Santa Claus for more than one reason! First, secular history reveals there was an actual, physically endowed "St. Nick." "Saint Nicholas" was born circa 280 in Patara, Lycia; an area that is part of present-day Turkey. He lost both of his parents as a young man and reportedly used his inheritance to help the poor and sick. A devout Christian, he later served as Bishop of Myra, a city that is now called Demre."[1] For better or worse, profit and greed, or happiness and time off, the Christian Church and Madison Avenue have undeniably propagated the character and the season.

Secondly, you only need to open your heart long enough to look into the awe, wonder, and amazement in a child's eyes seated in Santa's lap at the mall or on Christmas morning to see the reality living on within them. As corny and sentimental as it may seem, do it, or remember when you could or have done it, and Santa's existence will become undeniable.

Finally, a physical being or not, a childish fantasy or not, Santa represents the spirit of giving and caring for the poor and sick and lives on in our society today. Priests, social workers, nurses, physicians, psychologists, counselors, therapists, firemen, police, and teachers on some level at some time (no matter how jaded they become) had a desire to help and heal others when they chose their profession.

So, Santa at one time was a corpuscular being, whose spirit lives on within a variety of professions, the eyes of children, and the spirit of giving during the holiday seasons or at other times. I believe in Santa Claus!

I also believe in Bigfoot! Mary Green and Janice Carter (2002) have written and published *50 Years with Bigfoot: Tennessee Chronicles of Co-Existence*,[2] a remarkable account of a Tennessee family's relationship with a Bigfoot clan. It includes detailed descriptions of Bigfoots' appearance, behaviors (including observing tree knocking), and close relationships/friendships with that family. Dr. Jeff Meldrum's excellent book, *Sasquatch: Legend Meets Science* nicely reviews and summarizes Bigfoot's existence in Native American culture through their oral tradition, totems, and other concrete symbols (masks, stone foot carvings, tracings, just to name a few).[3] It also details scientific research and evidence of the animal. Nick Redfern's book, *The Bigfoot Book: The Encyclopedia of Sasquatch, Yeti, and Cryptid Primates* also highlights Bigfoot occurrences in other locations and cultures under the same and similar names.[4] He also documents other creatures sometimes resembling Bigfoot (the Yeti) and others bearing no resemblance (Aliens interacting with Bigfoot). Stan Gordon' Book *The Silent Invasion* documents extensive sightings of Bigfoot and UFOs.[5] Scott Carpenter's Book *The Nephilim Among Us Updated* highlights Christian and Jewish texts referencing creatures potentially Bigfoot-related.[6] It also advances his hypothesis that they represent one of a variety of Nephilim (the offspring of humans and the fallen angels cast out of heaven by God). There have also been thousands of credible and "professionally" vetted sightings that cannot be dismissed as hoaxes.

Much more "concrete evidence" (incorrectly characterized pun intended) of their existence can be found in authenticated casts of Bigfoot prints with the original ones often made from Plaster of Paris, Bakelite, or Hydrocal. Dr. Meldrum once again draws kudos on this topic.[7] He is generally considered and recognized in Bigfoot circles as one of the foremost experts in debunking hoaxed and misidentified prints and authenticating genuine Bigfoot prints and print casts. He reportedly owns and maintains one of the largest collections of these, with other icons in the field (e.g., Grover Krantz, for one) contributing to that collection.

Finally, the Patterson Gimlin film (1967) was initially deemed a hoax, but later repeatedly authenticated and currently stands as the "Gold Standard" of video evidence of Bigfoot.[8] (Although, at the time of final editing of this book, there are authenticity challenges being mounted.) The interested reader/viewer need only search the World Wide Web for additional Bigfoot video evidence. Such a search (with almost any search engine) on "Best Video Evidence of Bigfoot" produces a variety of videos left for the observer to vet and authenticate. They are nonetheless astonishing (and in some cases) convincing. Nonetheless, if you remain closed-minded after understanding the trials and tribulations associated with the Patterson Gimlin film and viewing it, these later examples will be a waste of your time.

My point here is I believe in Bigfoot because there is substantial evidence consistent with its existence, some of which I have personally witnessed and experienced on BFRO Expeditions. Indeed, although Dr. D. Jeff Meldrum (2006) asserts that "the question of belief is simply not at issue" ... [in that] ... "it connotes acceptance of something that is true in the absence of objective evidence or conclusive proof... ."[9] Nonetheless, even the hard-core scientific proponent that he is has commented: "... that a respectable portion of the evidence ... suggests ... the existence of an unrecognized ape known as Sasquatch."[10] He later adds "For me, it now seems more incredible to suggest this matter could be dismissed as mere stories, misidentifications, and spurious hoaxes than it is to at least rationally entertain the well-founded suggestion that the legend of Sasquatch possibly has its basis in a real animal and may eventually prove to be among the most astounding zoological discoveries ever."[11] In a personal email to the current author, he wrote, "The sheer number of credible witnesses reporting remarkably consistent observations strongly indicates there is something out there unacknowledged."[12] I think those statements contain many qualifiers that go to great length to avoid saying, "I believe in Bigfoot," despite him writing 276 pages of text on the subject. I believe he would be quick to point out, however, that there is a big difference between saying one "believes" in the existence of Bigfoot and personally or professionally "knowing it exists" and/or "proving scientifically" it exists!

I personally will never claim to **know** Bigfoot exists unless I see one fairly up close and can unequivocally determine it is not a man in a suit. I state this despite my unequivocal belief and certainty of the experiences of many of the investigators in the GA/TN/KY BFRO and KBRO that have had such encounters and in the face of mounting observational/phenomenological evidence.

The more formidable task for the Bigfoot community remains **scientifically proving** *it exists*. Although debated, I continue to believe we need to rise to a higher scientific level in order for government agencies and organizations to take steps to protect the species and their habitat. Currently, an internet search reveals Skamania County, Washington, passed a law in 1969 deeming the "slaying of Bigfoot to be a felony and punishable by 5 years in prison."[13] The law was later amended, designating Bigfoot as an endangered species. California keeps a record of non-game mammals in the California Code of Regulations. If any animal is missing from that list (as is the case with Bigfoot), that means it can't be hunted legally. Oregon follows a similar policy to California's in that any animal not classified under Oregon wildlife laws is considered "prohibited." Like the rest of the Pacific Northwest, Oregon has a long history of alleged Sasquatch encounters. "[We] receive periodic reports of Bigfoot sightings," [says] Michelle Dennehy, wildlife communications coordinator for the Oregon Department of Fish and Wildlife.[14] "It would appear that scientific proof is needed before the broader scientific and zoological communities accept its existence and list it on a national register of endangered species. Such a designation is reportedly necessary to receive federal funding to [protect the species and its habitat]."[15]

Producing such evidence will not be easy. Despite multiple books touting the "scientific" evidence of Bigfoot, the bulk of the cited evidence contained therein is phenomenological in its nature (analogical, anecdotal, demonstrative, digital, forensic, physical, or testimonial; see "Evidence" definitions in Chapter 7). Such evidence is apparently insufficient for the broader scientific communities and powers that be. *As such, it may be that experimental evidence will be required.* Given the rarity of confirmed sightings of the beast relative to the number of those looking/researching, such experimentation will indeed be a formidable and long-drawn-out process.

A broader acceptance of Bigfoot is both plagued by and enhanced by the challenge of reconciling the *phenomena* of Bigfoot and the *science* of Bigfoot. This "split personality" may be an outgrowth of the individuals involved in the process and/or the economic reality of life. Using myself as an example, I did not set out to write a book on Bigfoot research. I originally "joined" the BFRO expedition because I needed to see a Bigfoot up-close and personally to KNOW they exist rather than simply believe that they do. In short, I was seeking a phenomenological Bigfoot experience, nothing else. This desire grew out of my initial guilty pleasure of watching a TV show entitled *Mountain Monsters.*[16] No offense intended to the stars or producers of that show, I found it both interesting (interviewing, tracking, trap building) and funny as hell (getting all fired up for the hunt while toting shotguns, and then running like hell soon after the heated action gets started). This led me to another TV show (*Finding Bigfoot*[17]) that appeared less hysterical (in production approach and content, as well as belly laughs). It introduced me to BFRO through Matt Moneymaker's participation in the show. Participating in a BFRO expedition therefore seemed an ideal step to achieve my phenomenological aspiration.

Expeditions: Trained as a psychologist but naive as I was about Bigfoot, I was and remain thoroughly impressed by Lori Wade's (the Georgia BFRO expedition group leader) vetting approach to determining if I would be allowed to attend an expedition. You see, BFRO takes your money, but it's up to the individual group leader to decide if you would be a "good fit" in the expedition group and process. (While I can't speak for all BFRO groups, I found that this was not just paying lip service to a sham process to make money, but was a genuine concern and a very real process for her. If you ever have a chance to meet her, take it! She is an awesome expedition organizer/leader, has a genuine, deep, and abiding interest and knowledge base in Bigfoot, and has a heart of gold. Most importantly she is an incredible human being!)

I spent a little over a year with BFRO, doing six of Lori's official BFRO expeditions. During that time, I also ventured out on five personal expeditions with friends met through the group. I was surprised and impressed by the professionalism and "scientific" foundation of these official events. Pre-scouting to identify target trails and sites, and ensuring access was safe to these is but one example. Having a medic at base camp at all times. Pre-expedition group meetings to designate group leaders and members for the night's expedition are done. Of great value and importance, mapping what areas each group will target is done to avoid overlap engendering iatrogenic (self-produced) experiences by one group unintentionally producing a "Bigfoot experience" for another group. Enhancing this step, walkie-talkie and phone communication (when possible) are used for real-time communication and coordination during the actual outings. Notes or other forms of record keeping are done during outing activities. These notes include group-initiated provocations versus target species-initiated experiences by the occurrence's type and time. If an encounter occurs, "on-trail" efforts to explain, understand, and/or debunk occurrences before attributing them to Bigfoot are rigorously pursued. Group debriefings following outings summarizing results on a daily and full expedition-length time frame are kept and posted. Guest speakers/lectures from experts in the field are also part of her expeditions. This represents just a partial list of the exhaustive (and likely exhausting) attempts to utilize systematic professional and scientific principles and processes to enhance the likelihood of having a fabulous phenomenological Bigfoot experience.

The longer I participated, the more I realized: 1) My Class A experience wasn't going to come immediately if ever, as these are elusive creatures and there simply are no guarantees; and 2) The scientific and psychological side of my training rekindled a deep itch to do more systematic scientific and experimental research. This should result in numeric data that could be analyzed to prove hunches, hypotheses, and experiences. A phenomenological experience was no longer enough. I had to make some kind of scientific or research contribution to the broader process.

Speaking for myself, however, applying systematic and scientific principles to hunting or tracking Bigfoot does not make hunting and tracking "science" or "scientific." For me, identifying an independent variable (a tree knock, for example) and dependent variable (Bigfoot responding to that knock), then developing an experimental design (a research study/experiment) around which a hypothesis (notion, idea, theory, or educated guess) can be tested is what makes "science." I hypothesize that "Bigfoot responds to one tree knock more frequently and reliably than two consecutive tree knocks."

Next, consistently and systematically manipulating (testing) the independent variables (one versus two tree knocks) influence on the dependent variable (Bigfoot's response to those knocks) and recording these results are part of what makes "science." For me, taking those experimental results, and converting (encoding) them into a numeric database for statistical analysis to test and answer the hypothesis is what turns a fun fieldwork expedition into Scientific Bigfoot Research (SBFR). Those processes are what can subsequently prove or disprove the **mental and behavioral correlational or causal hypotheses** related to Bigfoot. Those processes are what scientifically prove Bigfoot uniquely reacts to tree knocks. In my opinion, that is the "scientific" way of doing research and fieldwork. That is what transforms profit and fun-driven commercial expeditions into "scientific" Bigfoot research.

While an expedition can be conceptualized as an experiment, the primary independent variable is most typically the presence of human beings looking for Bigfoot in a variety of ways. These ways are not necessarily monitored or controlled for in type, frequency, consistency, and repeatability. Despite all the organized and structured steps that are taken, no hypotheses are being developed beyond the tracking and hunting hypothesis (e.g., making a tree knock will provoke a tree knock from a Bigfoot in the area). Those are not officially being investigated, let alone systemically controlled for in frequency, numbers, material used, force exerted or applied, and spacing/timing of knocks (among other things). The dependent variable is almost always a Bigfoot encounter, the face-to-face nature of which rarely happens in a sustained or extended fashion that can be objectively verified. *These ARE NOT meant as criticisms of Lori, any other BFRO expedition leader, or the BFRO organization itself. These are the realities of an expedition mounted for the primary purposes of making some form of contact with a scientifically unproven species and gathering data for the primary purpose of having more expeditions and more encounters.*

For most individuals who have put in hours in the field, *we see, hear, feel, and smell things that convince most people with a phenomenological agenda that Bigfoot exists.* That does **not**, however, make it **scientifically validated or proven**. In short, again, applying systematic and scientific principles to hunting or tracking Bigfoot and calling it "field research" does not make that hunting and tracking "scientific research." For myself, even when such field research generates scientific observations, those observations need to be transformed into numeric data and analyzed to answer specific hypothesized, scientifically based, or generated questions (other than "Where do we need to mount more expeditions?"). *Indeed, the database to prove the empirical scientific existence of the species may already exist.* But if used primarily for the purposes of planning more "research expeditions" to generate more income, *such a database serves little, if any scientific value. It also does little to nothing additional to prove the existence of the species scientifically than what has been done for decades.*

As such my need to contribute scientifically to the species seemed to represent a challenge within existing BFRO structures and protocols. Thus, I chose to write this book instead. While it hopefully will generate a few dollars to keep me on the hunt, *the information contained here is primarily put forth in the hopes of educating field researchers on scientific and psychological principles that can be used to enhance, "tighten up" or fine-tune their own research efforts.* I hope that the knowledge gained can be applied to benefit both the field researcher and their attempts to identify and preserve the species and its habitat.

Again, the above paragraphs in no way represent a criticism of Lori Wade's expeditions or the BFRO organization. They were written to highlight the occasionally **conflicting duality of values** I wrestle with every time I go on the search for Bigfoot. Do I go with the phenomenological flow, enjoy the experience, and uncritically accept what comes my way? Or, do I screen the experience through experimental scientific lenses? The latter may be most beneficial to the species, but also likely detracts from the phenomenological aspects of the experience. *At times, it also bruises egos and disrupts the established and accepted group agenda and process.* I believe, however, that I am not alone in my "split personality" when it comes to a Bigfoot encounter.

Belief vs Faith vs Knowledge

A final comment about "believing" in Bigfoot revolves around the concept of "faith." Faith is defined as "complete trust or confidence in someone or something" or "strong belief in God or in the doctrines of a religion, based on spiritual apprehension rather than proof."[18] Again, Dr. Meldrum similarly asserts that "the question of belief is simply not at issue" ... [in that] ... "it connotes acceptance of something that is true in the absence of objective evidence or conclusive proof."[19] To "believe in" Bigfoot requires a leap in faith at this point in time for many people (myself included). As such, that belief represents a potentially significant theological dilemma (at least for me).

As a Christian, not only do I believe in God, but I KNOW (with absolute certainty) that God exists. Ironically some of the biggest skeptics regarding Bigfoot's existence would unhesitatingly agree with and accept my knowledge of God while denying any belief in or knowledge of Bigfoot. Think about that. You know God exists, but refuse to believe in Bigfoot. You believe in God and can cite a variety of phenomenological evidence to support that belief. Yet, there is a large body of phenomenological evidence to support believing in Bigfoot as well, but many God-fearing Christians would scoff at the idea. *It is not my intention to be blasphemous. It is my intent to point out that both beliefs require a similar "leap in faith" process. Many are willing to take one and not the other.* Yet, similar to Dr. Meldrum, I am not prepared to say "I KNOW Bigfoot exists," and will not make such a statement until I closely and clearly see one (or prove it scientifically). Call me a hypocrite. On this topic, I am (as just described above).

Yes, I believe in Bigfoot, and this book is written acknowledging the bias in that belief. Indeed, it assumes that Bigfoot does exist (without debating its origins), but remains scientifically unproven to the degree necessary for the wider adoption of its existence by the "Scientific Community." It is my sincere hope the writings herein better educate the novice and dedicated field researcher to inspire them to use better scientific reasoning, logic, and experimentation in their field research.

The Bigfoot Self-evaluation Scales

Before you read further, take the time to place an "X" on the below scales to begin to explore your beliefs and attitudes (biases) about Bigfoot and its existence. These are advanced as an initial foray into creating instrumentation to measure certain aspects of people's biases about Bigfoot. They do not represent comprehensive or even final measures of that phenomenon. Feel free to think about these and modify them accordingly!

The first of these "Likert Scales" is the most simplistic and basic (the purest). Such purity is often ultimately of the greatest value.

Simply place an "X" anywhere on the **bold dotted line** below the scale to represent where your beliefs in Bigfoot lie.

The Bigfoot Belief Scale (BBS)

I am 100% Certain That Bigfoot Does NOT Exist	I am Not Sure If Bigfoot Exists Or Does Not Exist	I am 100% Certain That Bigfoot DOES Exist

☐– – – – – – – – – – – – – – – – ■ – – – – – – – – – – – – – – – ☐

One of these continua ranges from 100 percent certainty that they don't exist to 100 percent certainty that they do exist. Belief in Bigfoot may or may not necessarily predict bias toward potential Bigfoot evidence. It may, however, inform how far you are willing to go to potentially risk your life to have a Bigfoot experience. This in turn might inform the degree to which you might wish to countercondition your fight-flight response.

Be honest in your assessment as self-deception will not serve you well in the Bigfoot community (unless you don't care about objectivity). It leads to inappropriate interpretations of sights, sounds, feelings, smells, and other experiences that may or may not be Bigfoot-related. That perceptual interpretation will likely influence your reaction to the same. Simply place an "X" anywhere on the **bold dotted line** below each scale that best reflects your Bigfoot beliefs.

The Advanced Bigfoot Belief Continuum (BFBC)

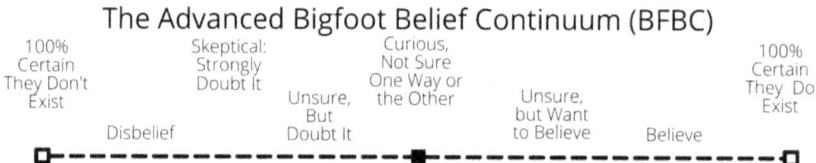

The Bigfoot Research Attitude Scale (see below) might better serve as a screening tool for expedition leaders to assess potential expedition participants' motives for coming on an expedition. I **can't** imagine an expedition leader who would want a participant with a "hoaxing attitude" on an expedition. I **can** imagine that some would not wish to screen out individuals who just want to have some camping fun. Of course, that would be up to organizations' and leaders' policies. These scales could serve as dependent or independent variables in future research studies. It might, for example, be of interest or value to examine the relationship between these scales and the likelihood of reporting a Bigfoot experience. Does our belief in Bigfoot or our attitude toward Bigfoot research in fact have a relationship with us having a Bigfoot experience?

The Bigfoot Research Attitude Scale (BFRAS)

Again, I have introduced these scales merely as an example of a way to assess your **beliefs** concerning Bigfoot and your **interest** in Bigfoot research. I think these two factors will influence your desire or willingness to counter-condition your fight-flight response using the techniques I will teach below. Logic would suggest that the closer you get to the "100% Certain" end of the **belief** continuum, the more likely you'd want to remain calm during a Bigfoot encounter. This likely increases your willingness to counter-condition your fight-flight response. Similarly, as you develop a more serious **interest** in participating in Bigfoot research, you may again be more likely to have the desire to counter-condition your fight–flight reaction to Bigfoot. This counter-conditioning would then allow you to move forward with further research during or after a Bigfoot experience. On to the main goal of this book!

2

SCIENTIFIC AND PERSONAL OBJECTIVITY VS. BIAS? THE BODY DICTATES THE ANSWER!

A dmitting my hypocrisy and sensational enjoyment of phenomenological Bigfoot experiences, I also promised the reader increased scientific and personal objectivity in Scientific Bigfoot Research (SBFR). As such, the terms **science**, **objectivity**, and **bias** must be discussed.

Merriam-Webster's Online Dictionary defines "**science**" as: "knowledge or a system of knowledge covering general truths or the operation of general laws especially as obtained and tested through the scientific method."[1] They define the **scientific method** as: "principles and procedures for the systematic pursuit of knowledge involving the recognition and formulation of a problem, the collection of data through observation and experiment, and the formulation and testing of hypotheses."[2]

For our purposes, I will borrow a more psychologically oriented definition in that much fieldwork attempts to capture Bigfoot behaviors and inform attitudes, thoughts, and emotions from the same. As such, a psychological definition of the scientific method seems particularly suited to our studies. The scientific method is "a general set of procedures for gathering and interpreting evidence that limits sources of errors ... yields dependable conclusions ... and demands special attitudes and values of the scientist. These special attitudes and values include but are not limited to: motives driven by a curiosity about the unknown and uncertain in which we seek to discover lawful, orderly patterns of relationships in the target phenomena, remain critical and skeptical of all conclusions while simultaneously maintaining a necessary open-mindedness that makes truth provisional, ready to be modified by new data, and never absolute. Respect for data as the ultimate arbitrator of disagreements and as the cornerstone of basic knowledge is also a basic value ... Secrecy is banned so that all data may be publicly verifiable - open to inspections, criticism, and replication by others. Scientific knowledge is built on the basis of empirical evidence obtained by observation and measurement, rather than solely on the basis of "authority" beliefs and data-less "experts." Data is collected using methods to eliminate or correct the subjective influences of the researchers, increasing their objectivity. Inferences and conclusions about the meaning of the evidence are kept distinct from the description of the data and methods for collecting them."[3]

"Basic to such research ...is... (a) reliance on empirical methods of investigating the mysteries of ... nature; (b) systematic attempts to measure and quantify aspects of behavior and processes of the mind; (c) adoption of procedural safeguards to increase objectivity and reduce the ever-present danger of personal biases; (d) the keeping of complete records of observation and data analysis in a form that other researchers can understand and evaluate; and (e) communication of one's findings and conclusions in ways that allow independent observers to replicate (repeat) the findings - or to reject the conclusions."[4]

"Such research seeks to discover the structure of behavior and psychological processes, as well as their causes and determinants (current author's emphasis).[5] *To find* **structure** *and* **inter-relationships**, **correlational methods, and analysis** *should be used; to discover answers about* **causality, experimentation** *must be used"* (current author's emphasis). "This is achieved within a framework of functional analysis (internal organismic factors/contributions versus external environmental/contextual influences/factors) and using techniques to enhance objectivity (defining variables operationally, standardizing procedures to eliminate unwanted variability, and

avoiding bias). Our research should build reliability and validity into it, differentiate between Coincidence, Correlations, and Causality, and provide ethical safeguards for the subjects, data, and results and their use."[6] These issues will be discussed in more detail later in this and other chapters on scientific knowledge as it relates to Bigfoot research.

If a Tree falls in the woods, …

In many ways, these issues as they relate to Bigfoot are captured by the old philosophical conundrum: "If a tree falls in the woods and there is no one there to hear it, does it make a sound?" Of course, the logical conclusion is, "Yes, of course, you freaking idiot! We see the fallen tree; we know from our own experience that trees make sounds when they fall. As such, logic dictates it made a sound when it fell (or was pushed over by Bigfoot)!" Such a response may indeed be sufficient for the Bigfoot researcher whose main goal is to gather subjective phenomenological personal data and experiences on Bigfoot.

If you see what looks like a very large, barefoot print in the snow (miles from where human activity would be expected and in the freezing dead cold of winter when no sane human would be out walking in their bare feet), it indeed seems reasonable to assume it was made by a Bigfoot. This point seems both reasonable and difficult to refute except on two issues: Such reasoning is not scientifically sound or provable as it is weak in the above-defined scientific methods. Secondly, past Bigfoot history has taught us there have been, and always will be hoaxers seeking fame, fortune, or other agendas such as Mr. Ray Wallace.

Coincidence, Correlation, and Causality

Speaking to the science first, the possibly versus probably correct (but unscientifically proven) notion of "if you find a very large footprint in the snowy woods in the dead of winter … it must have been made by a Bigfoot." The scientific problem/weakness of this conclusion is based on our definition of science and the scientific method: the issues of **coincidence**, **correlation**, and **causality**. The possibly reasonable hypothesis that a Bigfoot made the track, speaks to causality. The Bigfoot caused or made the footprint; therefore, the footprint is evidence that Bigfoot exists. *Causality in science can only be proven through repeated and replicated experimentation, not by solely relying on coincidence or correlation.*

Causality cannot be proven by a **coincidental** event (the first time you saw a Bigfoot you were wearing your pink-polka-dotted underwear, so every time you go out in search of Bigfoot you wear that same underwear and eventually see a Bigfoot again). "A coincidence is a chance or random association of events, often relegated to the realm of superstition."[7]

Causality cannot be proven by **correlational** events. You can easily define and remember what a correlation is by considering the root structures of the word: Co-relationship. "Co" refers to "together" or "with." According to Webster's Online Dictionary, "Co" means "with, together, joint, jointly associated in an action with another."[8] "Relationship" is intuitively understood by most people, but can be defined as "the way in which two or more concepts, objects, or people are connected, or the state of being connected."[9] "A relationship between two or more variables or events."[10] *Correlation* is a co-relationship; a together relationship. Anyone who has been married and subsequently divorced (about 50% of USA adults), however, knows that not all relationships remain or constantly occur together!

I used to believe that rising temperatures "caused" ice cream to melt. It seemed reasonable to me. I became incensed when my statistics professor suggested it was a correlational relationship, not a causal one. In the summer, as the heat/temperature goes up, ice cream will melt faster, I argued! "Ah yes!" countered the sagely wizened professor, "but what about in below-zero freezing weather? When the temperature/heat rises from minus twenty degrees Fahrenheit to zero degrees Fahrenheit, does the ice cream melt?" **Causality** *requires a co-occurrence to exist or happen 100% of the time! It is not until the temperature rises above freezing that ice cream begins to* *melt, therefore rising temperatures and ice cream melting is a correlational relationship, not a causal one.*

Correlations can be "positive" whereby as one variable increases or decreases in frequency or occurrence, so does the second in the same fashion. For example, the number of Bigfoot researchers may be "positively" correlated with the amount of reported evidence of Bigfoot. As the number of Bigfoot researchers going into the woods increases, the evidence of Bigfoot (including anecdotal evidence and actual sightings) goes up. This does not necessarily mean that the Bigfoot population is increasing (but can easily be misinterpreted as such)!

Correlations can also be "negative," whereby as one variable or event increases in frequency, the second variable goes down or decreases in frequency. An example can be seen in human population growth and Bigfoot habitat. As humanity grows in numbers, we need more space to live in and more forest and other Bigfoot habitat is converted to habitat for human beings. Thus, as the human population increases, available Bigfoot habitat decreases. This in turn can "**interact**" with my example of increased "sighting" evidence of Bigfoots as they (Bigfoot) have fewer places to hide from humanity. Such "**interactions**" of variables or events will be discussed later in the statistics section of this book.

So, for causality to exist, a 100% relationship between variables/events needs to be proven. This is a challenge to scientifically prove or objectively achieve without experimentation. "In order to identify cause-and-effect relationships scientifically, certain conditions must be met. First, the targeted behavior, variable, or event (the dependent variable) can be started or stopped by presenting or withholding the variable or event we believe will influence our dependent variable. That 'influential' variable is defined as the independent variable" (current author's emphasis).[11]

The second necessary condition to be met to prove a *causal* relationship is that "the changes in the behavior of the dependent variable occur only within the context of or following the manipulation of the independent variable. When a causal relationship between an independent and dependent variable has been demonstrated, we can conclude only that changes in the first have caused changes in the second."[12]

Here is the Bigfoot example. Jeff Carpenter is one of the best Bigfoot Field Researchers I have met. A true woodsman, he was raised and has worked in and around the woods his entire life. He is an expert in nature sounds and events that often can be mistaken as Bigfoot evidence. He has developed a camera trap system/set-up (the location of which I will not divulge to respect his propriety) to capture images of Bigfoot. *His phenomenological goal is to obtain photographic evidence.* In this system, however, he is **experimenting** with different objects to attract Bigfoot to his trap and be photographed. Toys, balls, and fruit are but a few examples. In this intended versus unintended experimental design, Bigfoot (coming within photographic distance of the camera) represents the dependent variable. He's trying to influence/target Bigfoot behavior. The independent variable(s) are the different "baits" used to draw or entice Bigfoot in. Is he more likely to get a successful picture of Bigfoot when he leaves an orange (the fruit) than if he leaves a child's orange toy ball? The fruit versus the ball are the independent variables. *Only when the orange toy ball draws Bigfoot to it 100% of the time and the orange fruit is ignored 100% of the time can he conclude the causal relationship between the orange* **ball** *and Bigfoot.* What if the color of the ball is changed to yellow? This could then be used to generate hypotheses about Bigfoot's color perception, but only if the two balls were identical in size (controlling for a possible extraneous variable of size). Get it? *Establishing a causal relationship is rarely as simple as it would appear. It needs to account for a variety of possible influences or other relationships "correlated" with the independent variable. This accounting thereby controls* **extraneous variables** *that could influence the correlational versus causal relationship.*

Hoaxing

On to Mr. Wallace as the second example of how it is not safe or sound to declare with "scientific certainty" Bigfoot made that print in the snow!": Hoaxers (and other sources of misidentification). Nick Redfern (2016) in his excellent book highlights the "controversial life and career" of Ray Wallace.[13] By way of my own short summary of Mr. Redfern's treatment of Mr. Wallace, he was a contractor on a road construction project based in Bluff Creek, California at the beginning of 1957. In 1958, Mr. Wallace was apparently running a Korbel, California Mad Rivers construction site, where enormous footprints were found. This occurred at the same time that enormous footprints were also found around Gerald Crew's bulldozer at Bluff Creek. Upon Mr. Wallace's death in 2002, his family claimed he had engaged in "widespread fakery" including case reports and footprints.[14] They related that Mr. Wallace disseminated numerous footprint molds to other friends and family and encouraged them to create tracks in isolated areas where they might be mistaken as genuine Bigfoot tracks.

In 1968, Andy Warhol's prediction: "In the future, everyone will be world-famous for 15 minutes" appeared in the program for an exhibition of his work at the Moderna Museet in Stockholm, Sweden.[15] In Ray Wallace's life, we have an account of an individual (predating that statement) so bent on fame and notoriety, that he falsified the footprints of Bigfoot. He propagated further hoaxing by encouraging others to also create fake Bigfoot trails. Nonetheless, his false evidence and actions still ended up figuring prominently in the Humboldt Times Newspaper writer, Andrew Genzoli, coining the term "Bigfoot."[16] It should be far from inconceivable in this modern era of the World Wide Web and other forms of electronic media that more individuals than ever are bent on achieving their 15 minutes of fame. One only need look to "Facebook Challenges" for evidence of the lengths people will go to achieve this fame (witness the COVID-19 toilet seat licking challenge, among many). As such, it should not be inconceivable that some needy, attention-seeking soul would go to great and previously inconceivable lengths to fake Bigfoot prints in the snow. *They cannot be trusted or considered as scientific evidence of Bigfoot in and of themselves without further study and cross-validation.*

Experimental Evaluation of Hoaxing

The good news is however, such prints are not inconceivably beyond the reach of possible scientific investigation and at least partial validation. An experiment could be designed in which casts of authenticated Bigfoot prints could be placed in the snow next to recently discovered "possible" Bigfoot prints matched for length, breadth, and other physical characteristics. Weight estimates could be calculated and controlled pneumatic pressure applied to approximate the required depth of the "replica" imprint. Video and computerized metric monitoring could be used to track the rate of decay, melting distortion, and other factors to create/generate data that could then be analyzed to evaluate for similarities. This could move us toward an even more scientific forensic analysis process of authenticating Bigfoot prints than exists today. *My point being, scientific experimentation can conceivably be applied to such phenomena to move us closer to scientific data about Bigfoot, even without capturing and studying multiple examples of the species.* Such technically burdensome and awkward procedures do indeed seem like overkill when experts in footprint identification already exist in the field. *I offer it up simply as a brief highlight that experimental procedures could be brought to bear on the topic as part of the evaluation process to* **prove**, *rather than* **opine** *Bigfoot causality.*

Organismic Perceptual Bias: You've Got It, Like It or Not!

By addressing the definition of science and the scientific method, I have highlighted a path to move towards or approximate "**objectivity**." Some define **bias** as the opposite of or lack of **objectivity**. A variety of types of bias exist, many of which will be addressed in this book. To speak to the title of this chapter, however, I will next discuss what I refer to as "**organismic perceptual bias**." This is an unavoidable form of bias in us all by nature of the fact that we exist in our physical bodies. *Our body, with its central and peripheral nervous system, makes it literally impossible for us to be consistently* *objective or unbiased. RESEARCHERS OF ALL FIELDS NEED TO LET THE IMPLICATIONS OF THAT LAST SENTENCE REALLY SINK IN!*

The Anatomy and Physiology of Bias

We have two broad divisions in our body's nervous system: The **central** nervous system and the **peripheral** nervous system. Our central nervous system consists of our brain and spinal cord (which connects to the base of our brain). Our peripheral nervous system consists of our musculoskeletal nervous system (the nerves running to and through our bones and muscles) and our autonomic nervous system (ANS). Our ANS is the nerves running to our organs that control the automatic processes/responses in our body. Such automatic processes/responses include but are not limited to blood flow, water distribution in our body, hair growth, our heart beating, constriction or dilation/expansion of our blood vessels, breathing/respiration, digestion, urine (pee), and fecal (poop) elimination, and adrenalin release. *The ANS is also a primary modulator of a factor very relative to Bigfoot hunting:* **the fight-flight response.** *This happens when frightened or threatened with harm, our body's organ systems get ready to make us run away from the threat or danger or to fight the threat or danger.* You don't have to consciously or intentionally think to make your heart beat or blood flow or digest your food, or breathe, or make your hair grow, etc. All these functions are on "automatic pilot" or "cruise control;" they are controlled by your autonomic nervous system.

In his chapter on Sensation in *The Psychology of Life*, Zimbardo (1988) defines sensation as "the process of stimulation of a receptor that gives rise to neural impulses resulting in an 'unelaborated,' elementary experience of feeling or awareness of conditions outside or within the body."[17,18] He then adds, "*The elaboration, interpretation, and meaning given to a sensory experience is the task of* **perception**" (my emphasis).[19]

In his chapter on **perception**, *he further defines perception as the stage after sensation "in which an internal representation of an object is formed,* *and an experienced percept of the external stimulus is developed. The representation provides a working description of the perceiver's external environment. Information from lower-order detectors is organized and modified by higher-order brain processes to convert stimulus features and elements into patterns and forms that are recognizable" (my emphasis).*[20] *Sensation involves the stimulated receptors (nerves) of our senses (vision, hearing, the feelings of our body [touch, pain, balance, proprioception, and kinesthesia], as well as our smelling and tasting abilities.) Perception is what happens when these sensations are processed by our brain. Perception is influenced by our upbringing/raising and current environmental factors.*

Again, relating it to Bigfooting: Perception is what we hear, see, smell, taste, or feel when signals from our sensory nerves are processed by our brain. Perception is informed and subsequently experienced as a result of environmental conditions interacting with the things we've learned, performed, and otherwise experienced throughout our lives. Let that really sink in! Think about what that means about bias when squatching, interpreting possible Bigfoot signs, or reading Bigfoot research! Sensation and perception are hard-wired into our bodies by the very nervous system that allows us to stay alive, but perception is informed and influenced by our current surroundings (often the dark woods when squatching) and all the living we've done in our life. AS SUCH, THIS MEANS BIAS IS HARDWIRED INTO OUR BODY AND CANNOT BE CONSISTENTLY AVOIDED BY ANY PERSON LIVING INSIDE AND THROUGH THEIR BODY, NO MATTER HOW OBJECTIVE THEY MAY TRY TO BE!!! Thus, the title of this chapter.

Again, **let that really sink in.** Think about what that means about YOUR bias when squatching, interpreting possible Bigfoot signs, or reading Bigfoot research. Were you raised in the southern United States Bible Belt, attending an Orthodox/Old Testament Baptist church? Should you then be surprised if you perceive/interpret Bigfoot signs and research to mean they are a spiritual, demonic, or angelic presence? Were you raised in and spent most of your life working in the deep woods; enjoying hunting, trapping, and fishing your entire life? Should you then be surprised that you perceive Bigfoot as a flesh-and-blood creature of the woods? Did you pull yourself away from the roots of your northeastern United States, middle-class upbringing, get overly educated, and travel across the US working and learning? Should you then be surprised you don't know what the hell to perceive Bigfoot as, but know darn well you need to write a book on the subject?

Our nervous system and our life create an UNAVOIDABLE organismic bias in us, which then informs and influences how we experience (see, hear, smell, taste, and feel) Bigfoot. This is why any experientially-based field researcher is at risk for misinterpretation and/or prematurely jumping to conclusions about anything Bigfoot. This is why using scientific methods and principles in Bigfoot field research is so critical in attempting to approximate objectivity in that field research. It doesn't mean that fieldwork observations or conclusions are wrong, but they ARE nonetheless, at greater risk of being inappropriately biased. This is another reason why it may not be safe to conclude that a tree made a sound when it fell. This is yet another reason why it may not be safe to conclude a Bigfoot left that print in the snow (or dirt) in the woods.

Other Forms of Bias

Having defined organismic perceptual bias (organic or physiological bias), the reader should note there are **other** forms of bias that come to bear on our perception and understanding of all things Bigfoot. The "**experimenter expectancy bias effect**" also known as "**demand characteristics**" is but one example. In studies involving human subjects (or at least, comprehending and thinking subjects), "subtle communication cues from the experimenter (through word emphasis, tone, manner, or gestures)" and/or assignment of tasks and responsibilities and queries of an expedition leader "can lead to self-fulfilling prophecies."[21,22,23]

For example, you do a night investigation with a lead investigator who believes Bigfoot is an inter-dimensional being. Your four-person group is tied or hitched to a fifty-foot rope to ensure "no one gets sucked into another dimension on the expedition, or if you do, to ensure that we can pull you out of that dimension." The group establishes an "observation circle" (each observer sitting facing one direction point on the compass; North, East, South, and West) in a "cleared" meadow. The nearest surrounding tree line is 400 yards in the distance. Suddenly, seemingly literally out of nowhere, an object flies past the group then circles back toward its original path from which it appeared and disappears. All four people get a fleeting glimpse of it. "We know it was something because we all saw it, but don't really know what it was. Well, one thing is for sure, though; it came out of and disappeared into nowhere, didn't it? Did anyone see from where it originated or where it disappeared to? No, nothing but the thin air!!" On the way back to base camp, the conversation between the four genuinely perplexed people continues, and by debriefing time the report becomes: "We didn't see any Bigfoot, but are pretty sure one threw something out of an inter-dimensional portal and retrieved it back into the same portal." *The lead investigator's genuine belief that the targeted subject is inter-dimensional was further reinforced in other participant's minds by being tied together with a rope. When an unexplainable experience happened, their final explanation was similarly tied together to the lead investigators' belief system. The situation* **demanded** *that a conclusion be reached without any overt intentional persuasion or pressure being applied by the leader to convince the rest of the group.*

The next night, another group of four goes to the same location with the woodsman, who believes Bigfoot is a flesh and blood creature. Although not connected to each other by a rope, they otherwise position themselves the same as the group from the previous night. Lo and behold, they have the same experience. Suddenly, seemingly literally out of nowhere, an object flies past the group, then circles back toward its original path from which it appeared and disappears. All four people get a fleeting glimpse of it. By the time this group returns to base camp, the report is: "We had no activity whatsoever. A bat circled us once in the meadow and then flew off." Same event, different conclusion based on **experimenter expectancy bias** and the **demand characteristics** of the situation.

Who was right? While the bat explanation seems appealing as it seems more grounded in consensus reality, we can't truly know for sure. Sufficient scientific controls or protections from bias were not instituted to make that determination. The experience is reduced to people's personal opinions also known as "personal bias." You've had a Bigfoot phenomenal experience. MAYBE!

If you encounter a Bigfoot, up close and personal, will you remain calm or run like hell? Consider a special kind of bias in medicine known as the "**placebo effect.**" "This happens when a patient improves after taking a treatment substance, thought to be a therapeutic drug (for example) for the cure of their ailment even though the substance is chemically inert (without any medicinal or curative value; a sugar pill). *This clinically significant response to a stimulus or treatment that occurs independent of its actual physiological (physical) effect is called the placebo effect*" (my emphasis).[24] *In a more general sense, it occurs whenever a behavioral response is influenced by a person's expectations of what to do or how to feel, rather than by the specific independent variable (the substance or treatment) employed to produce the response.* If around the campfire, you are taught that Bigfoot encounters are going to be scary, potentially violent, or dangerous interactions with a "monster or beast that can tear you to shreds and kill you," you are more likely to subscribe to and act according to the "Run like hell" school of bias. If on the other hand, Bigfoots are defined as friendly and relatively harmless creatures (witness the movie Harry and the Henderson's)[25] that can be "our friends and protectors; stewards of mother nature and protectors of the forest," you will more likely subscribe to "remain calm" school of bias. In reality, you must always remember that **these are biases** and that depending on the beast in front of you (especially if not a Bigfoot, but a human, bear, big cat, wolf, or other predatory creature), **either biased reaction** could be the wrong reaction. *We need to know with reliability and validity what we are experiencing, preferably before we act.*

The good news is that we can program ourselves to use this bias to stay calm in the face of Bigfoot activity (when appropriate) and even move forward to learn more about the source of the activity. It's called "Stress Inoculation," a psychological technique used in the treatment of Post-Traumatic Stress Disorder (PTSD) and other forms of anxiety. You will learn how to use it for your own benefit in Chapter 5 of this book.

The final **accepted** form of bias to be discussed in this chapter is the "**Hawthorne effect.**" "Simply put, the very act of studying a group or behavior, influences and changes that group or behavior. Factory workers' productivity increased as a result of them simply knowing they were being observed/studied, not because of any experimental manipulation or intervention to increase productivity."[26]

In physics, the parallel is the "**Heisenberg Uncertainty Principle.**" According to Merriam Webster's Online Dictionary this was "Introduced first in 1927 by the German physicist Werner Heisenberg ... [and]... states that the more precisely the position of some particle is determined, the less precisely its momentum can be predicted from initial conditions, and vice versa."[27] Studying one aspect of molecular activity interferes with another aspect of its activity.

The Hawthorne Effect and NAWAC Tag 7

"The Hawthorne Effect." As applied to Bigfoot, I recently listened to the North American Wood Ape Conservancy (NAWAC) Tag 7 Podcast Show[28] and reviewed their apparently self-published paper on the same.[29] I must first say they are to be congratulated on the achievement reflected in this podcast and paper. The creative and inventive technology developed and employed for this study should be noted by other researchers and considered for their own tracking research studies of Bigfoot. The sheer financial investment, planning, fluidity of conceptualization and goals, not to mention the countless man/woman hours in the field over years of study to achieve POSSIBLY tagging a North American Wood Ape (commonly known as a Bigfoot) is mind-boggling by any scientific research standard, likely even in the field of zoology. In my opinion, it should stand as a historic landmark and milestone in Bigfoot field research.

Having stated the above, it pains me to also point out that it (like all scientific investigations) is not without its limitations. I hope to point some of these out throughout my text, not to criticize or berate their Herculean efforts. This is done to highlight certain psychological principles, experimental design issues, and data interpretation issues so that my readers can enhance their own understanding of these through this excellent research example. These issues are primarily related to the Hawthorne effect and its influence on data interpretation.

In their paper, they note, "There is no way to know if the distribution of location data points documented by NAWAC teams over a ten-month period for the Tag 7 animal are representative of the behavior of other members of the same species."[30] During their "Apes Among Us" podcast[31] round table discussion on the subject at approximately 1:20:25, they begin to discuss the implications of the movement of the tagged animal and how "we did establish some home range calculation estimates ... that varied depending on method ... of 20 to 70 ... square miles."[32] After discussing how seasonal variations seem to affect movements "of the species," at 1:21:11, they highlight one member's "previous assumption was that their range was actually quite small or that they operated in a relatively small area ... [until] ... we started to get hits over two mountain ranges ... away ... the distance ... how far they were moving north and south, east and west, was really incredible."[33] They then further discussed how this "has caused us to redefine our concept of what Area 'X' was."[34]

Having earlier discussed the influence of seasonal variations on movement, at 1:21:56, they proceed to consider other factors such as the type of ape and where in their social hierarchy or group the tagged creature stood could influence movement. "If we in fact tagged a wood ape ... the thing here we don't know is what type of individual animal in any sort of hierarchy this individual stands ... it's very general information for us ... different types of apes have different social groups and social constructs ... and we have no idea of what types of different social constructs of the wood ape would be ... some animals remain relatively local and don't move, but if looking at a gorilla model, there are rogue males that range all over the place and so potentially we tagged one of those but to your point, we just don't know."[35] *Awesomely accurate scientific objectivity there!* (I am being serious, not sarcastic, in that last statement.)

My points here are multiple. Although acknowledged in the discussion, they don't even know with sufficient scientific certainty (due to limitations in their experimental design) if they tagged a wood ape. If they had included video recordings at the site of the tags, they **might have** obtained convergent (it is consistent with a Bigfoot) or divergent (it is consistent with another animal) validity data of the tagged beast. They then might have been able to either prove with near 100% certainty they tagged a wood ape with video or photographic evidence or some other animal. Or they could have greatly increased the likelihood of knowing they tagged a wood ape with an "auditory signature" (footfalls, breathing). Such auditory evidence would have eliminated the apparent Bigfoot deterrent qualities associated with infra-red modulated cameras.

To the point of the Hawthorne effect currently being discussed, they consider type of ape, that ape's role within the type of social structure, and seasonal factors. *They didn't seem to consider or debate how their own research group's presence in "Area X" might be influencing such a greater range of movement than previously assumed. They also apparently failed to consider the more specific Hawthorne influence of whatever creature was tagged with.* This may have contributed to the possible Bigfoot "knowing" it was tagged/being studied due to the potentially uncomfortable versus noticeable "burr" nature of the tags themselves. In and of itself, this could have an influence on its wide-ranging movements.

More simply applied to a human model, when you are walking in the woods and get a burr attached to you that irritates your skin, it **would** be considered normal for it to affect your movement. *As such, the 'burr' nature of the tracking device itself clearly also needs to be considered as a potential influence on movement.* It therefore potentially contaminates any naturalistic conclusions about and changes their assumptions about the true range of the unidentified creature! Like

Heisenberg said of atomic and sub-atomic particles, "When we study ... [a Bigfoot,] ... the more precisely the position of ... [a Bigfoot] ... is determined, the less precisely its momentum ... [and movement] ... can be predicted from initial conditions, and vice versa."[36] *Studying one aspect of Bigfoot activity interferes with other aspects of its activity!!!* As such, while the hypotheses during their roundtable discussion are certainly of theoretical interest, they **may be** premature in their scientific consideration, discussion, and conclusions, in my opinion.

As Bigfoot researchers, the actual act of studying and observing Bigfoot behavior likely influences and changes their behavior; potentially biasing the results and conclusions of our study. This is why naturalistic field studies of animals viewed from hidden "blinds" for habituation purposes are so critical. Habituation increases the likelihood we are observing the natural behavior of the animal, unimpeded by the influence of humans. If our presence is known to Bigfoot, we cannot be confident we are observing their natural behavior. Therefore, any conclusions about their behavior run the risk of being incorrectly biased.

We would be mistaken, however, to limit this principle to Bigfoot's awareness of us through our physical presence or scent. What if Woo theorists are correct? What if Bigfoots have psychic or at the least extremely sensitive intuitive instincts? We may then be "sunk" on this subject, blind or no blind. Nonetheless, we must also extend our considerations to our research tools such as cameras, microphones, heat-seeking and night vision scopes/cameras, infrared lights, drones, two-sided tape, bait, and other tools used to gather data (including, in this case, the nature of the telemetry device). *They all represent a potentially unnatural presence in the Bigfoots' environment and can influence their behavior and any conclusions we draw from the same.*

Incredulity Bias

Finally, I'd like to advance what I believe to be a new characterization for a form of bias: "Incredulity Bias." The notion of the concept of something being "incredible" stands at the root or core of the word

"Incredulity." Many may be familiar with an "incredulous reaction" (i.e., "WTF!!!!!! That is so far-fetched and out of any realm of a realistic possibility, that it can't possibly be true!!!! I can't, don't, and won't believe it!!!!) Synonyms include "... disbelieving, unbelieving, doubtful, dubious, unconvinced, distrustful, distrusting, mistrustful, mistrusting, suspicious, questioning, lacking trust, cynical, skeptical, ... [and] ... wary."[37] Incredulous, however, "is stronger than skeptical; if you're incredulous of something, you refuse to believe it, but if you're skeptical, you're doubtful but you haven't ruled it out"[38] ... [Incredulity is] ... "the state of being unwilling or unable to believe something."[39] **As such,** *"Incredulity Bias" is a belief or opinion driven by one's sense of righteous incredulity. It is refusing to believe a concept or idea because it seems inconceivable (based on your emotional reaction to it being beyond your concept of consensus reality).*

Even the most objective scientist, perhaps because of that very objectivity, is vulnerable to this form of bias. At a recent conference during the closing panel discussion, I witnessed an otherwise scientifically objective and open cryptozoologist evidence this bias when asked about "mind speak" or telepathy in the Bigfoot species. He made a joke of it by sitting up in silence for several seconds, and then quipped, "I just answered your question!! Did you get it?" This got the appropriate laugh and he went on to basically state that such phenomena are so far out of the realm of possibility, it is impossible in his mind. Unfortunately for him and other disbelievers, ESP and telepathy in humans does exist and has been scientifically studied (outside of the USA), and used in warfare and to solve crimes. If it happens in humans, why can't it be a possibility with Bigfoot? Perhaps even more germane to this bias: WE'RE RESEARCHING AND TRYING TO PROVE THE EXISTENCE OF **BIGFOOT;** COULD A BIGFOOT (WITH TELEPATHY) BE THAT MUCH MORE FAR-FETCHED THAN THE BASIC CONCEPT OF "BIGFOOT" ITSELF?

Can we truly call ourselves "objective scientists" when we off-handedly dismiss an idea or concept because it simply goes beyond our own conceptualization of reality? Where would the medical science of infectious disease (the concept of unseeable organisms that can make us sick), or molecular science (molecules, atomic structures so small we can't see them with the naked eye even though they actually exist) be if such a bias predominated these fields of scientific investigation? *The incredulity bias: we need to guard against it and actively resist it in ourselves if we hope to objectively and scientifically study Bigfoot phenomena!!*

By way of a brief summary, we are inherently biased by the central and peripheral nervous systems in our body. Raw sensation hits the brain where it is processed into possibly biased perception, which then informs our opinion and reality. Without a scientific framework and techniques to control such bias, our Bigfoot field research is at risk for a variety of types of bias inaccurately informing our conclusions. *This will create false knowledge and lore rather than facts about the species.* That serves neither the species, our attempts to preserve their shrinking habitat, nor other attempts to protect their longevity and existence in the future.

3

ILLUSIONS: IF IT LOOKS AND SOUNDS LIKE BIGFOOT, IT MAY NOT BE A BIGFOOT!

G iven that our central and peripheral nervous systems represent a hard-wired bias system within our body, our senses can deceive us in a biased fashion via illusions. I am not suggesting that every Bigfoot experience is an illusion, but that illusions need to be "**ruled out**" as the cause of an experience. This needs to be done prior to "**ruling in**" Bigfoot as the cause of the experience.

An illusion is "a thing that is or is likely to be wrongly perceived or interpreted by the senses."[1] Also defined as "When your senses deceive you into experiencing a stimulus pattern in a manner that is demonstrably incorrect."[2] "It contrasts with hallucinations (auditory and visual) which are 'a false perception' [generated by the brain through a mental illness] and delusions which are 'a falsely held belief/distorted idea that resists change despite evidence refuting or contrary to this belief' [generated by the brain though mental illness]. Self-deception was defined as a reality distortion coming from the mind's tendency to filter out information that is threatening to one's self-esteem."[3] Bigfoot researchers or believers are not infrequently accused of these by friends and acquaintances when they are brave (or foolish enough) to "share" with them.

Optical illusions: There are currently three types of optical illusions: literal illusions ("when the image you see is different from the images that make it up"),[4] cognitive illusions ("a result of our conceptions and assumptions about the world, which we impose upon visual stimuli"),[5] and physiological illusions ("are the effects on the eyes and brain of excessive stimulation of a specific type-brightness, tint, color, movement."[6] Each of these illusions tricks our brain into misunderstanding what we see in various ways. "A cognitive illusion happens when the brain perceives an object based on prior knowledge or assumptions."[7]

A visual illusion "is an incorrect perception of what you are seeing. What we see does not fit the properties of the object we are viewing."[8] Below are two differing visual illusions I have chosen for their relevance to the Bigfoot phenomenon.

Without measuring it in any fashion, which straight line below is longer? "a" or "b"?

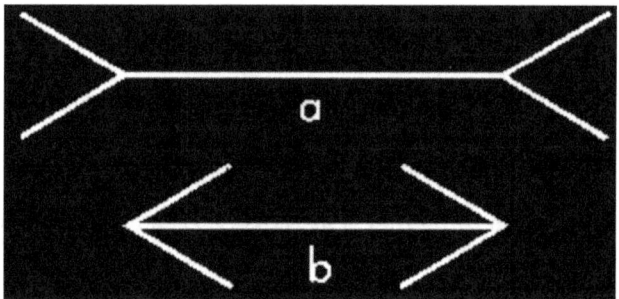

Source: www.merriamwebsterdictionary[9]

"Known as (a variation of and the most common form in which it is seen today) the Müller-Lyer illusion, it consists of a set of arrow-like figures. Straight line segments of ... length comprise the 'shafts' of the arrows, while shorter line segments (called the 'fins') protrude from the ends of the shaft. The fins can point inwards to form an arrow 'head' or outwards to form an arrow 'tail.' The line segment forming the shaft of the arrow with two tails is perceived to be longer than that forming the shaft of the arrow with two heads."[10] In short, the answer is ... they are equal in length despite their visual appearance.

Another (more commonly known) but equally relevant visual illusion to Bigfoot phenomena follows below.

Source: www.britannica.com[11]

Known as "figure-ground phenomena," you may see two faces "facing" or "looking at each other" or you may see a "chalice"/"vase" depending on whether you focus on the figure (the white chalice) or the ground (the black "facial" background). Furthermore, your upbringing and/or experiences also likely influence and inform which of the written descriptions of the images "make the most sense" to you! When I was growing up, we put our daises in vases, not chalices!

Representing the core process activated during a psychological "ink blot" test, **Pareidolia** "is a type of illusion or misperception involving a vague or obscure stimulus being perceived as something clear and distinct. For example, in the *discolorations of a burnt tortilla, one sees the face of Jesus.* Or one sees the image of *Mother Teresa in the folds of a cinnamon bun* or *Vladimir Lenin in the soap scum of a shower curtain.*"[12] "Common examples (of pareidolia) are perceived images of animals, faces, or objects in cloud formations, the *Man in the Moon,* the *Moon rabbit,* and other *lunar pareidolia.*"[13] A "Face on Mars" pareidolia in a photograph of the Cydonia region of Mars is shown below.

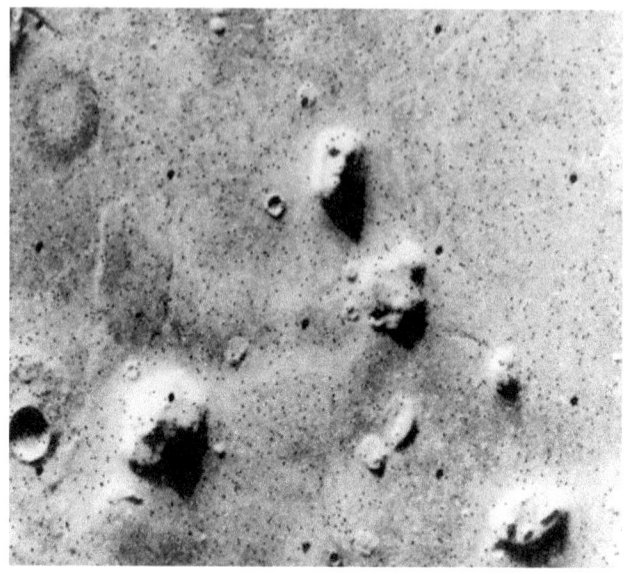

Source: www.space.com[14]

"It is often contrasted with apophenia ... [which] ... is the spontaneous perception of connections and meaningfulness of unrelated phenomena. The term was coined by German neurologist and psychiatrist Klaus Conrad (1905-1961). Conrad focused on the finding of abnormal **meaning** or **significance** in random experiences by psychotic people. The term has found a place outside of psychiatry and is used to describe the natural tendency of human beings to find meaning and significance in random, coincidental, or impersonal data. Apophenia may be described as the tendency to find personal information in noise, or other activity e.g., happening upon an open safety pin and seeing the arms as a sign indicating the **time** [my emphasis] your son committed suicide."[15]

"Apophenia and pareidolia can occur simultaneously as in the case of seeing a birthmark pattern on a goat as the Arabic word for Allah and **thinking** (my emphasis) you've received a message from God. Likewise, not only seeing the Virgin Mary in tree bark but **believing** (my emphasis) the appearance is a divine sign, brings together apophenia and pareidolia. Seeing an alien spaceship in a pattern of lights in the sky is an example of pareidolia, but it becomes apophenia if you **believe** (my emphasis) that the aliens have picked you as their special envoy. Seeing *Satan in the smoke of a burning building* slips from pareidolia to apophenia when the viewer starts **thinking** (my emphasis) that Satan is giving the world a sign that he is alive and well."[16]

Source: Pareidolia: Coincidence or Meaningful Coincidence.[17]

Pareidolia is the visual sensory image. Apophenia is the cognitive interpretation (thinking, believing) assigning meaning or significance to the visual image or stimulus.

R. T. Carroll (2012) elaborates writing "Under ordinary circumstances, apophenia provides a **psychological** explanation for many delusions based on sense perception. For example, it explains many *UFO sightings*, as well as the hearing of sinister *messages on* *records played backward.* Pareidolia explains Elvis, *Bigfoot*, and *Loch Ness Monster* sightings. Pareidolia and apophenia explain numerous religious **apparitions** and visions. And they explain why some people see a face on a building."[18]

Wow! First of all, I must thank Ken Gerhard (2019) for bringing this concept to my attention in his book *The Essential Guide to Bigfoot.*[19] Despite my training in psychology, it was a term I was not aware of or of which I lost awareness.

I must also state that I disagree with Dr. Carroll's (2012) assertion that "Pareidolia explains Elvis, *Bigfoot*, and *Loch Ness Monster* sightings. Pareidolia and apophenia explain numerous religious **apparitions** and visions."[20] While I cannot and will not speak to Elvis (we all know that The King lives on in the hearts of all true rock and roll enthusiasts) or the Loch Ness Monster (not the focus of this writing), I do **disagree** that it explains "Bigfoot sightings." This is an untenable statement from my perspective unless if by "sightings" he is referring to **SOME** of the **errant** visual perceptual processes leading to misidentifications of Bigfoot. He leaves such exceptions little space for such a consideration, however, through the verbiage in his sentence. Indeed, it is accepted and sometimes proven that misidentifications do occur. But to contend or suggest that it explains **ALL** Bigfoot sightings is once again an untenable hypothesis.

For one thing, many such sightings are associated with the alleged creature leaving footprints and hair samples. I needn't point out that pareidolia or apophenia can't leave footprints (castable or not) or tissue samples!! If that perceptual process can leave footprints or tissue samples, he has discovered a truly mind-boggling phenomenon that clearly warrants further investigation! It remains a distinct possibility that such a perceptual process (in concert with apophenia) could explain some footprint evidence and even the association between visual Bigfoot sightings and hair samples later revealed to be bear, horse, or some other identified species. *But to contend it explains them all is simply preposterous in my opinion!*

To give Dr. Carroll the benefit of the doubt, I will note that this contention is made in writing that would now be considered "dated"

(2012). Indeed, much has changed within the Bigfoot community and knowledge base since 2012. But at the risk of playing psychologist, I cannot help but wonder about his sentence: "Pareidolia and apophenia explain numerous religious apparitions and visions." Please note his use of the word "numerous." It denotes "many but not all" and could have easily been used as a qualifier in his previous sentence concerning Bigfoot *if he didn't have a conceptual bias against the existence of Bigfoot*. In my opinion, the bias monster seems to be rearing its ugly head and possibly reflecting the underlying philosophical issues of Dr. Carroll. The two sentences combined within his writings suggested the possibility that he conceptually allows for the genuine existence of some (albeit not "numerous") religious visions, but not even for the **remote** possibility of genuine Bigfoot sightings (i.e., "Pareidolia explains ... Bigfoot ... sightings").

Hopefully, these illusions' relevance to Bigfoot phenomena is self-explanatory, but I will nonetheless briefly highlight this relevance. The straight line (Müller-Lyer) illusion highlights the pitfalls of simply "eyeballing" the estimated size of a Bigfoot. The objects surrounding the creature create a visual context which can lead us to misperceive the creature as bigger or as smaller than its actual size. This is of course holding other influential factors of size perception constant. The distance from the object, the position of the object, the terrain on which the object is seen, the terrain on which the observer is positioned, as well as the discrepancy between the observers and observed respective terrains all influence this perception. The figure-ground phenomenon hearkens to the experience *most researchers participating in nighttime expeditions have on a regular basis.* We will sit at or near the base of a ridge, looking to the top of that ridge. The ridge top is silhouetted against the night sky. Typically, the ridge is topped with trees of a variety of sizes and shapes. *The trees represent the ground in the illusion above, while the night sky between them becomes the figure, which then can be misperceived as a Bigfoot head or body.* Sometimes, however, it may be a Bigfoot! *We may misperceive or correctly see a Bigfoot!*

Pareidolia **could** explain a variety of Bigfoot sightings. *Leaves,* *various grasses, brush, trees and tree limbs, sun and moonlight, shadows, stumps, etc., can interact together or singularly to produce visual illusions resembling Bigfoot.* While I disagree with the assertion it explains the totality of Bigfoot sightings, it certainly is an undeniable influence in some, if not many known/unknown **errant sightings.**

Illusions exist in every sensory modality. Our hearing of sounds may represent the next most commonly encountered sensory modality leading to the misperception of natural or non-Bigfoot stimuli as being Bigfoot related. For example, we often infer the number of Bigfoots present in the surrounding area by the number and apparent directional source of sounds in evidence. Problematic is the "**Binaural Beats**" illusion.

Binaural Beats Illusion: This is an auditory illusion in which "the two ears receive slightly different auditory information [sounds], and this results in the perceptual experience of a different, third, sound. In the example we have here, two audio channels play sounds with slightly different hertz. The hertz is a unit of time that measures frequency. Frequency is a measurement of how often something happens. A frequency of 1 hertz means that something happens once a second. In this example, the left audio channel continuously plays at 100 hertz, with the right channel gradually moving up one hertz in frequency at a time (101, 102, 103, etc.). The difference between the sound coming from the left channel and the sound coming from the right channel creates an experience of a third type of sound, which has a beat, or a rhythm. But there is no actual beat or rhythm."[21] *TWO simultaneous sounds (one registering on our right ear, the other on our left ear) produce the illusion of a separate THIRD sound. Just how many Bigfoots are actually in the area?* The example can be heard at https://www.illusionsindex.org/i/binaural#mp-pic-1-mod.[22]

There are a variety of other examples to review. These are examples, but not a comprehensive list of auditory illusions described in Wikipedia, the free encyclopedia:

The constant timbre melody: "... is defined as a constant pitch ... characterized by a **spectrum.** Along a piece of music, the spectrum measured within a narrow time window varies with the melody and the possible effects of instruments. Therefore, it may seem paradoxical that a constant spectrum can be perceived as a melody rather than a stamp."[23] *In effect, a constant melodic sound is perceived despite it actually being a discrete/time-limited "stamped in" sound!* "When did that Bigfoot stop or start its howl?" Source and example are at https://commons.wikimedia.org/w/index.php?title=File%3AConstantSpectrum Melody.org.[24]

The **Deutsch's scale illusion**: "Discovered by Diana Deutsch in 1973, Deutsch's 'scale illusion' is an **auditory illusion** in which principles of grouping by frequency, proximity, and spatial location are put into conflict and in which frequency proximity wins out. It is produced by simultaneous ascending and descending major scales beginning in separate stereo channels with each successive note being switched to the opposite channel. With the left channel: C'-D-A-F--A-D-C'; and the right: C-B-E-G-E-B-C; the ear hears both: C'-B-A-G--A-B-C'; and: C-D-E-F--E-D-C. The tones are equal-amplitude sine waves, and the sequence is played repeatedly without pause at a rate of four tones per second."[25] In effect, we hear the directional location of a sound based on the source closest to us. *Misdirection!* "Where exactly did that Bigfoot cry or scream come from?" Source and example at https://en.wikipedia.org/wiki/ File: Deutsch_scale_illusion.ogg.[26]

The **Franssen effect**: "The Franssen effect is an **auditory illusion** where the listener incorrectly localizes a sound. It was found in 1960 by Nico Valentinus Franssen (1926–1979), a Dutch physicist and inventor. There are two classical experiments, which are related to the Franssen effect, called Franssen effect F1 and Franssen effect F2. In the F1 case, you should hear a sudden noise appear at one loudspeaker and then "jump" to the other loudspeaker, where the source of the sound remains for the rest of the five seconds." In the F2 effect "you hear the tone coming from a loudspeaker that is no longer presenting any sound. However, the location that you perceived as the sound's source is the loudspeaker that presented the sound first, and thus its location seems to dominate your perception of the sound's location."[27] *We hear a sound originating from a directional source no longer producing a sound! "Is that Bigfoot on the left or right side of us?"* Go to https://web.archive.org/web/20080704172543/http://www.parmly.luc.edu/parmly/franssen.html for a demonstration of this effect.[28]

Glissando illusion: The glissando illusion was first reported and demonstrated by Diana Deutsch in Musical Illusions and Paradoxes, 1995. "An **auditory illusion**, it is created when a sound with a fixed pitch, such as a synthesized **oboe** tone, is played together with a **sine wave** gliding up and down in pitch, and they are both switched back and forth between **stereo** loudspeakers. *The effect is that the oboe is heard as switching between loudspeakers while the sine wave is heard as joined together seamlessly, and as moving around in space in accordance with its pitch motion.* Right-handers often hear the **glissando** as traveling from left to right as its pitch glides from low to high, and then back from right to left as its pitch glides from high to low."[29] *We're hearing ourselves being surrounded by multiple sound sources when only one of two sources is making the sound at any given time! "Damn! We were surrounded by at least four or five Bigfoots!! Let's get the hell out of here!!!!!"*

Illusory continuity of tones: The illusory continuity of tones is "the **auditory illusion** caused when a tone is interrupted for a short time (approximately 50 ms or less), during which a narrow band of noise is played. The noise does, however, have to be of a sufficiently high level to effectively mask the gap. Whether the tone is of constant, rising or decreasing pitch, the ear perceives the tone as continuous."[30] *We hear a continuous and static level sound irrespective of whether the sound is rising, falling, or remaining constant! "Nah, that couldn't have been a Bigfoot because its roar didn't rise or fall!"*

Discontinuity: "is an **auditory illusion** in which a continuous ongoing sound becomes inaudible during a brief, non-masking noise. The illusion is perceived only by some listeners, but not by others, reflecting individual variation in hearing abilities. ... The most susceptible listeners describe their sensations in terms of the sound actually containing a physical gap."[31] *We're hearing a single sound as* *being discretely interrupted or temporarily stopped despite it actually being constant. Be careful how you interpret a sound that seems to stop and start when you are around a second sound source like a "non-masking" (not drowning out the other sound) waterfall, "babbling brook," or rushing stream!*

Hearing a missing fundamental frequency given other parts of the harmonic series: "A harmonic sound is said to have a missing fundamental, suppressed fundamental, or phantom fundamental when its overtones suggest a fundamental frequency but the sound lacks a component at the fundamental frequency itself. The brain perceives the pitch of a tone not only by its fundamental frequency but also by the periodicity implied by the relationship between the higher harmonics; we may perceive the same pitch (perhaps with a different timbre) even if the fundamental frequency is missing from a tone."[32] *Our brain fills in a tone in a vocalization pattern that isn't actually being produced! "Did you hear that Bigfoot growl when all those Coyotes started going off?"*

McGurk effect: "a perceptual phenomenon that demonstrates an interaction between hearing and vision in speech perception. The illusion occurs when the auditory component of one sound is paired with the visual component of another sound, leading to the perception of a third sound. The visual information a person gets from seeing a person speak changes the way they hear the sound. If a person is getting poor-quality auditory information but good-quality visual information, they may be more likely to experience the McGurk effect. Integration abilities for audio and visual information may also influence whether a person will experience the effect. People who are better at sensory integration have been shown to be more susceptible to the effect. Many people are affected differently by the McGurk effect based on many factors, including brain damage and other disorders."[33] *"Did you hear him say those words or make that wail? That had to be the Bigfoot's voice, I saw his mouth moving!!"*

Octave illusion/Deutsch's high–low illusion: "The octave illusion is an **auditory illusion** discovered by Diana Deutsch in 1973. It is produced when two tones that are an octave apart are repeatedly played in alternation ("high-low-high-low") through stereo headphones. The same sequence is played to both ears simultaneously; however, when the right ear receives the high tone, the left ear receives the low tone, and conversely. Instead of hearing two alternating pitches, most subjects instead hear a single tone that alternates between ears while at the same time its pitch alternates between high and low."[34] *"I couldn't tell one Bigfoot adult was on one side and a juvenile was on the other side or what?"*

Auditory Pareidolia: "In sounds, hearing indistinct voices in random noise." Remember Beatles' albums where many became convinced if you played it backward, you heard messages to the effect that "Paul is dead"? That's it! From a broader perspective than the auditory sense it "is the tendency for incorrect perception of a stimulus as an object, pattern or meaning known to the observer, such as seeing shapes in clouds, seeing faces in inanimate objects or abstract patterns, or hearing hidden messages in music. Pareidolia can be considered a subcategory of apophenia."[35] (*You're camped next to a "babbling" brook and are certain you hear some creature whispering to you.*) I actually had this experience on my first expedition laying by myself in my enclosed tent, not knowing a soul from the expedition group. *It kept whispering, "Come out, come out, come out and play; come out, come out, come out and play!"* It was only the regularity and persistence of the illusion that tipped me off it wasn't some animal or person messing with me. Against all my instincts, I got out of my tent and discovered I was camped 20 feet from a water culvert pipe I hadn't previously noticed! *Damn, son!!*

The concept of pareidolia may extend to include **hidden messages** in recorded music played in reverse or at higher or lower-than-normal speeds, and hearing indistinct voices in random noise such as that produced by air conditioners or fans."[36] "Pareidolia was at one time considered a symptom of human psychosis, but it is now seen as a normal human tendency."[37]

The **Shepard–Risset tone or scale:** "...named after MK Roger Shepard, is a sound consisting of a superposition of sine waves separated by octaves. When played with the bass pitch of the tone moving upward or downward, it is referred to as the Shepard scale. This creates the auditory illusion of a tone that continually ascends or descends in pitch, yet which ultimately seems to get no higher or lower."[38] *"Was that howl getting higher or lower?"*

The Deutsch Tritone paradox: "is an **auditory illusion** in which a sequentially played pair of **Shepard tones** separated by an interval of a tritone, or half an octave, is heard as ascending by some people and as descending by others."[39] *See "The Shepard–Risset tone or scale" above.*

Speech-to-song illusion: "The speech-to-song illusion is an **auditory illusion** discovered by Diana Deutsch in 1995. A spoken phrase is repeated several times, without altering it in any way, and without providing any context. This repetition causes the phrase to transform perceptually from speech into song."[40] *"It had to be a Bigfoot singing! The only other sound was the trees and leaves blowing in the wind!"*

Yanny or Laurel: "'Yanny or Laurel' is an **auditory illusion** of a re-recording of a vocabulary word plus added background sounds, also mixed into the recording, which became popular in May 2018. In the brief audio recording, 53% of over 500,000 people answered on a Twitter poll that they heard a man saying the word 'Laurel,' while 47% reported hearing a voice saying the name 'Yanny.' Analysis of the sound frequencies has confirmed that both sets of sounds are present in the mixed recording, but some users focus on the higher frequency sounds in 'Yanny' and cannot seem to hear the lower sounds of the word 'Laurel.' When the audio clip has been slowed to lower frequencies, then the word 'Yanny' has been heard by more listeners, while faster playback loudens 'Laurel.'"[41] *Given the number of people involved, I found this just plain interesting!*

My inclusion of computerized creations of auditory illusions is not accidental. Some Bigfoot researchers have found/believe that these creatures can imitate car fobs and other artificially created tones. It is with this in mind that such artificially generated illusions have been included in this list. *Nonetheless, do we have any idea how many of these phenomena can be naturally produced or produced in conjunction with a man-made object like a metal water pipe or a soda can with rainfall hitting it? That turned out to be my "Bigfoot fob experience."* It does not suggest any endorsement or refutation of Bigfoot attributions or theories but represents my scientific bias of remaining open to all theories and data on the creature.

My main point, however, remains that sounds create illusions and can influence the "reality" of what we are hearing. Monongahela (2020) in his "How to search for Bigfoot through sounds" chapter in Charles Kimbro's book Squatchin' 101 highlights the importance of ruling out other animal and nature sounds prior to concluding it was a Bigfoot.[42] *I wish to simply add to that point that the Bigfoot audio researcher and recorder should have a comprehensive knowledge and understanding of the wide variety of auditory illusions before concluding they have just heard and recorded a Bigfoot if proposing to use that (sonic/auditory evidence) as evidence of Bigfoots existence.*

In summary of illusions, I have focused primarily on visual and auditory illusions as a confounding source of conclusive evidence of Bigfoot when in the field. I believe the visual examples provided remain glaringly self-evident if you've been on even a one-night expedition.

While more obscure, and difficult to understand and experience, the sonic illusions described are of equal relevance. *Is the sound rising or falling in pitch, tone, or volume?* This is important in distinguishing its animal source, number, and location. They reveal that a single source of sound can create the illusion of two sources of sound and that two sources of sound can produce the illusion of a third source (or more). Remember that the next time you hear "a large pack" of coyotes cutting loose in the night. *Can you really be sure, how many there are? Can you be sure that was a Bigfoot howling with them?* In the field, we often identify the number of Bigfoots present by their sounds, yet these illusions highlight that this may not always be a safe assumption. *We would do well to further verify those independent sources. We also use sound to decide a direction in which to pursue our quarry.* Again, appropriate consideration needs to be taken. *This is not to suggest that such sources are never a valid or reliable measure. It does, however, highlight that the possibility of illusions needs to be carefully considered and ruled out.* It also highlights the challenge presented to proponents that insist purely phenomenological or experiential evidence should suffice as scientific proof of Bigfoots' existence as a species.

4

MORE "CRITICAL" DEFINITIONS AND DISCUSSION

A fterimages: "A visual illusion in which [eye] retinal impressions persist after the removal of a stimulus ... [It is] ... believed to be caused by the continued activation of the visual system. ... A common afterimage is the spot of light one sees after a camera flash has been fired."[1] Examples of afterimages can be found in the Psychology and Mental Health section on www.britannica.com.[2] The interested reader can pursue these phenomena further through a variety of psychological texts. A brief explanation, however, highlights "colors opposite each other on the color circle are [known as] complementary colors. Each hue gives its complementary hue, as a color or black and white afterimage."[3] "Afterimages may be negative or positive. Negative afterimages are the opposite or the reverse of the original experience and are more common and longer lasting. Positive afterimages are caused by a continuation of the receptor and neural processing following stimulation; they are rare and brief. An example is continuing to see the light of a flash bulb."[4]

Relevance to the Bigfoot phenomena revolves around red or green "eye shine" often attributed to Bigfoot(s) and the mysterious lights often associated with or seen in known Bigfoot habitat. In order to maintain our night vision during expeditions, we regularly use flashlights or head-band lights that produce red or green light. When using white lights that are then turned off, our eyes require a great time span to achieve a type of sensory adaptation known as "dark adaptation." This is our eyes adjusting to the dark until we can see details in the dark. Red and green lights eliminate this adaptation time span and allow us to immediately see in the dark. Nonetheless, we often walk for hours "in the dark" partially illuminated by our red and green lights. We look down, shining those lights on the ground, or look forward into the dark night illuminated by our lights. Polite and considerate expedition protocol requires the researcher to turn off their red or green headlamps when facing each other or conversing so the light does not shine directly in each other's faces. Should it then be surprising that, when we turn off our red or green lights and stare into the forest, we see "red or green eye shine" peeping out from behind or next to the trees?

Before you indignantly assault me for pointing out this phenomenon as a potential eye shine explanation, please understand I am not suggesting that it explains all instances of red or green eye shine attributed to Bigfoot. I do believe there are scenarios where this would not explain such visual experiences. I offer and explain this psychological illusion to the researcher who wishes to be better informed as to possible explanations that need to be considered when debunking or ruling out such phenomena. Again, this should be done prior to concluding that it is indeed "Bigfoot eye shine."

Similarly, "dark adaptation ... the process which results in an increased sensitivity to low levels of light ... explains ... noticing that when you first go out of a brightly lit ... [area] ... on a dark moonless night you see very few stars; then as you watch the sky, the sky begins to fill with more and more stars. The reason for this is not that the stars get brighter, but that your eyes get more sensitive to the light that is already there ... [like] ... when your eyes 'adjust to the dark' in a movie theater."[5]

The combination of afterimages and dark adaptation might explain my own and others' experience of seeing twinkling dull white lights on a "Bigboy trail" in the Georgia woods. A "Bigboy trail" is a path or "game trail" in the woods whereby it appears the trees next to the path have the branches broken or stripped off below a height of 12-15 feet. It is hypothesized that this is done by Bigfoots so their passing down that path is not inhibited by such obstructions. Given this particular location's proximity to a graveyard, these lights have been also attributed to spirits, ghosts, and "mini orbs," not to mention "fox fire" (glow-in-the-dark tree lichen) by other field researchers more experienced than I. Again, I am not saying the psychological explanation carries greater validity to explain the specific events in that specific area. *I am highlighting this psychological phenomenon to inform the researchers wishing to educate themselves of factually studied and scientifically proven psychological phenomena that might come to bear when investigating, debunking, and explaining phenomena possibly being attributed to Bigfoot.*

Alcohol: A distilled spirit (not an ethereal ghost, but a liquid substance). It is best used to calm one's nerves around a campfire after an up-close and personal encounter with a Bigfoot (or a predatory non-target species such as a bear, big cat, wolf, coyote, fox, wild pig, human being, etc.). Xanax works well too! Such an encounter might include, but is not limited to: a blood-curdling scream, growl or howl, or bark. Also included is a "gruff or snuff" (you'll know it when you hear it); a bluff charge; and a dank or rotting meat, dog, or other putrid aroma where nearby bushes are rustling. Tree falls, landslides, tree breaks, tree knocks, sticks, stones, rocks, nuts, and tree branches or trees being thrown at you. It may also include a face-to-face encounter including red or green glowing eyes. I advise against using this substance before going out as **it distorts perception** and can make stumbling through the woods in the dark a dangerous experience. Nonetheless, liberal quantities might be consumed by some or many after such encounters.

Please be aware that one beer, one glass of wine, one mixed drink (cocktail or hot toddy), and most wine cooler and hard cider drinks have the same amount of alcohol in them as a single one-and-one-half ounce shot of "hard" liquor. If used in more than moderate quantities, you will not need to look up the definition of a "hang-over" because you'll be experiencing it in person on a phenomenological level!

Anthropomorphism: The attribution of human characteristics or behavior to a god, animal, or object.[6] Obviously, for our purposes, we need to be concerned about this process as it applies to Bigfoot, be they objects, animals, gods, or demons, inter or intra-dimensional or not. It is indeed rare to meet a Bigfoot researcher who does not anthropomorphize.

A glaring example revolves around the often-repeated statement, "Bigfoots are curious." Really? How do you know? Can you read their mind or feel their intrinsic curiosity? For the true psychics, the mind reading question may be answered "Yes," but for the average Bigfoot field researcher, we have clearly long inferred such "curiosity" based solely on their behavior.

"Well, they follow us when we come into the forest; that proves they're 'curious.'" "They hang out near children and watch them play because they are 'curious' about children." "Because they are so 'curious' about what we are doing, they come to investigate us and know we're in the woods long before we know they are there." *Well, if curiosity killed the cat, there would apparently not be any Bigfoots alive today if curiosity drives all these and other behaviors!!* Such ideas and statements are intuitively appealing and seem supported by logical reasoning on a personal/phenomenological level based on behavior. *Nonetheless, they remain uninvestigated and unproven from a scientific perspective.*

If you've been in the woods long enough, you've had other animals follow you in a parallel course. Possibly worse, they may have followed just behind you or just ahead of your course. Bears, wolves, and big cats do this when "**stalking**" their prey!! They are not doing it because they are "curious" about you. They are doing this because you are lunch! *Curiosity (an intellectual cognitive process) has* **nothing** *to do with it; instinctual stalking behavior programmed into them on a cellular level could have* **everything** *to do with it.* You might also just notice the napkin tied around their necks!

"Well, there is no record of Bigfoot killing children or adults. So many are seen watching kids, there would most certainly be a record of child abductions or deaths from Bigfoot if stalking was the case." Really? How many unexplained disappearances from the woods has David Paulides documented in his "4ll Missing" books?" (April 3, 2012, for example).[7] "Well, you don't know those were done by Bigfoot!" Absolutely correct! Just like you don't know that they weren't done by Bigfoot; that's what makes them "unexplained."

Then there are the cases of Albert Ostman and Joseph Edwin Leffler.[8] Ostman lived to talk about being abducted by Bigfoot and having to live with them for weeks before his successful escape. Three-year-old Joseph Leffler was reportedly cared for by Bigfoots and escorted back to personnel looking for him after his disappearance.

If you frequent nature websites, you may have seen videos of a large Polar Bear "petting" a chained-up dog,[9] and others of Polar bears "playing" with huskies.[10] Yes! The narrators on these videos and I may be anthropomorphizing with that statement. My point is apex predators are known to "play with" their prey prior to killing and eating them. If you doubt it, watch a cat play with a mouse, dead or alive. *This is an inbred, hard-wired, species-specific behavior, not a thought-out yearning for fun, recreation, or curiosity.*

Additionally, there are more or equally logical explanations for these Bigfoot behaviors. How about "vigilance?" According to the Oxford Languages Online Dictionary, vigilance is "the action or state of keeping careful watch for possible danger or difficulties."[11] Merriam-Webster Online Dictionary defines "Vigilant" as "*alertly watchful, especially to avoid danger.*"[12] This is species-specific, hard-wired/atavistic fight-flight behavior, **NOT** curiosity. Curiosity is "*a strong desire to know or learn something;*"[13] or "*inquisitive interest in others' concerns; interest leading to inquiry.*"[14] Is Bigfoot watching children or following us because it wants to inquire or ask us a question so it can learn something from us? "Hey human, what is the square root of pie; you got a piece I could eat?" We have no way of knowing or proving this with scientific certainty!

How about "pursuit **predation** in which predators give chase to fleeing prey."[15] "The chase can be initiated either by the predator or by the prey, should the prey be alerted to a predator's presence and attempt to flee before the predator gives chase. The chase ends when either the predator captures and consumes the prey, or the prey escapes. Pursuit predation is typically observed in carnivorous species within the kingdom Animalia, with some iconic examples being cheetahs, lions, and wolves."[16]

It stands In contrast to "ambush predation."[17] "While pursuit predators use a detection and pursuit phase in order to obtain prey, ambush predators use stealth to capture prey. Strength and speed are important to pursuit predators, whereas ambush predators ignore these in favor of surprise from a typically concealed location. While the two patterns of predation are not mutually exclusive, morphological (structural anatomical) differences in body plan can create a bias in an organism towards each type of predation."[18]

It seems to this researcher that Bigfoot has the detection abilities, body, and speed for either form of predation. My point remains; however, *these are genetically inbred, hard-wired, species-specific behaviors that don't involve the intellectual prowess or grey matter brain abilities required for curiosity.* Are these not likely or just as likely explanations for Bigfoots' behavior as the intellectual pursuit of "curiosity?"

Asshole: What you call someone who, during a night excursion, tries to scare the shit or piss out of you. Also, what you call someone with whom you get into a heated debate on the origins of the Bigfoot species. Both the former and the latter are strongly discouraged on expeditions. Assholes make poor hiking and camping mates, strange bedfellows, not to mention smelly porta-potties and latrine sites, especially when positioned up-wind of base camp.

Awareness: "perception or knowledge of something. Accurate reportability of something perceived or known; is widely used as a behavioral index of conscious awareness. However, it is possible to be aware of something without being explicitly conscious of it ..."[19]

Self-Awareness: "self-focused attention or knowledge. There has been a continuing controversy over whether nonhuman animals have self-awareness. Evidence of this in animals most often is determined by whether an individual can use a mirror to groom an otherwise unseen spot on its own forehead. A few chimpanzees, gorillas, and orangutans have passed this test."[20]

Like my below definition of "Knowledge," I include this definition for your consideration and philosophical reflection rather than as a factual or conclusive definition of the word. Please see my discussion under "Knowledge" for further reflections on this.

Awe: The emotion inspired by a close encounter with Bigfoot.

Awe Shit!: What a Bigfoot researcher says (and sometimes does in their shorts) during a close encounter with a Bigfoot.

Confabulation: In neurological science, the brain's tendency to "fill in the blanks" with information that may or may not be factually accurate when the person cannot remember or accurately recollect what has happened. This is at the core of nationwide court decisions ruling that hypnotically retrieved memories are inadmissible as evidence. In effect and affect, the brain makes something up (information, memories, images, sounds, etc.) to reduce the dissonance (discomfort due to inconsistencies in recollections or behaviors associated with the blank spots in consciousness).

In stroke (cerebral vascular accidents; "CVAs"), pathological confabulation is often seen in patients who have suffered a right-middle-cerebral artery embolic stroke (clogged artery). Depending on the exact location within the right middle cerebral artery, the loss of blood flow and neuronal (brain cell) death associated with that stroke can be distributed across most (medial/middle, posterior/back, and anterior/front) of the right cerebral hemisphere. This constitutes a surface of most of the entire right side of the brain. Such widespread damage creates quite a few "blank spots" in an individual's consciousness/awareness, driving the brain to fill in the gaps with information. This information can range from factual/accurate to just close enough to factual and accurate as to appear so, to totally inaccurate/made up/confabulated and implausible (not possible or grounded in consensus reality to others; delusional).

Relevant to Bigfoot phenomena, brain damage or abnormal brain function are not required for this phenomenon to occur. *Blank spots can also be associated with autonomic arousal, traumatic experiences, quasi-hypnotic experiences, or altered brain activity during dreaming.* That's true even if you insist "I Don't Dream!!" If you didn't dream, you'd be hallucinating and not able to read this book!!!!

Sometimes we just plain forget. We can appear forgetful to ourselves and others. "Executive skills" (attention, concentration, working memory, flexibility in thinking, impulsivity regulation) interact with each other to make a person feel and appear forgetful. Neuropsychologic memory tests, however, reveal memory functioning to be perfectly appropriate for their respective age, education, and gender cohorts (peer group). They might be diagnosed with a "pseudo-dementia."

Hypnotic levels of awareness, as well as trance behavior/experiences, are normal parts of everyday consciousness for all human beings. Every night when we go to sleep and every morning when we wake up, we pass through hypnotic trance levels of consciousness. When falling asleep, the hypnotic level of awareness is referred to hypnogogic phenomenon. When awakening from sleep, the same phenomena are referred to as hypnopompic phenomena. These phenomena can include hallucinations in most sensory modalities including vision (visual hallucinations), hearing, (auditory hallucinations), smells (olfactory hallucinations), tastes (gustatory hallucinations), and bodily sensations (kinesthetic hallucinations e.g., pain, spinning, floating, falling, suffocation, etc.). These can be short/transitory or extended in duration. These also produce "memory gaps." Confabulation fills in those gaps.

By definition, a hallucination is indistinguishable from

consensus reality to the person experiencing it. But again, mental illness is not a necessary condition to experience hallucinations. I am not suggesting the possibility of "mind speak" (or telepathic communication) between Bigfoot and humans doesn't genuinely occur. Nor am I suggesting the bodily sensations and real physical experiences attributed to "Zapping" don't occur. *They nonetheless have their hallucinatory counterparts.* As such they offer a possible explanation for or alternative to such reality-based phenomena.

To emphasize my lack of making light of, criticizing, or discounting the possibility of mind speak, I will unequivocally state that telepathic communication has been proven in laboratories outside the USA (Russia for example). Another psychic phenomenon known as remote viewing has been weaponized and utilized by a variety of countries during warfare.

In remote viewing, subjects go into a trance and observe activities going on at a remote location, elsewhere in the world, or even in the "future." I (with others) have personally participated in a remote viewing exercise where we stole test questions for an impending "tough test." We later "fessed up" and discovered that at the time we were doing the remote viewing, the test had been "made up" in the professor's mind, but not yet typed or put down on paper in any form or fashion. Insert "Twilight Zone" music here.[21]

Confabulation also occurs as a result of and during trauma. I have met more than one researcher who has lost visceral control of their bodily functions during an "up close and personal" (aka "Class A" encounter in BFRO nomenclature) Bigfoot encounter. In short(s) (and sometimes when not wearing any), they've shit or pissed themselves. The point being, that such an encounter can not only activate your fight-flight response but can also be traumatizing. It would then not be surprising for the person to have either a trauma-induced hypnotic experience or a trauma-induced confabulation experience that could include mind speak. *Again, this does not mean mind speak does not exist, but also begs the question as to the generating source thereof. Is the Bigfoot or the human the actual source or* *confabulatory source for the phenomena?* I speak to how to answer that question later in this book (see Chapter 8).

Confabulation will also occur as a result of daydreaming, eyewitness testimony under interview stress (police or military interrogations), and courtroom testimony and is exploited in "brainwashing procedures." The reader must keep in mind that in all of the aforementioned scenarios, this is a brain-driven and unconscious (not intentional) process or phenomenon. When it is done consciously or intentionally, it is then termed "a lie or lying."

Expedition Debriefing Considerations to Increase Accurate Reporting

Tying this concretely into my own Bigfoot experiences, this begs the question of the validity of and how much we can trust any group expedition eyewitness testimony of Bigfoot encounters. It also suggests some important possible protocol procedures for "within group" expedition discussions and "individual and/or group debriefings" after Bigfoot encounters. It would be advantageous to field research and scientific study of Bigfoot phenomena to minimize confabulation and other forms of bias. But think about what happens on a Bigfoot expedition.

Before the expedition begins, you begin planning your trip thinking about Bigfoot. You pack and drive hours ... thinking about seeing or hearing Bigfoot. If taking a companion, you talk and think about Bigfoot on the drive to base camp. At base camp, people are talking about ...? Bigfoot. Have any been seen or heard in the area? In preparation for the evening's activities, we divided into groups and discussed strategies based on possible Bigfoot signs and activities. We are already primed to experience Bigfoot before we leave camp!

In my experience, a group of three or more go into the night in the hopes of finding Bigfoot. As of this writing, I have not been part of a group that has had a Class "A" encounter (meaning I haven't nor have any of the group members I've been with definitively seen a Bigfoot during one of our

*outings). We have heard roars, "tree knocks," Bipedal-like footsteps, tree
falls, and landslides. We've also seen footprints and objects being thrown
towards us. All of these were attributed to the possibility of Bigfoot being the
source of the event phenomena.*

I have also heard stories of people on the same expedition as
myself, but in a different investigative group, being zapped and
suffering nose bleeds, arm paralysis, and having hairs standing on
end or "at attention." Highly experienced investigators I know
reported the feeling of being punched in the stomach so strongly that
the investigator doubled over and vomited. Another highly
experienced investigator had the feeling of being hit in the chest with
a baseball bat with such force that they (sic) were propelled onto their
(sic) back onto the ground. *What happens either after experiencing the
events or retreating to safety after these events?*

*BFRO and Scientific Protocol demands that as soon as possible after
such experiences (if not immediately) we try to further investigate,
understand, or debunk the experience as some form of a natural
phenomenon before assigning/attributing it to possible Bigfoot phenomena.
A procedure I applaud and condone! But think about how this is
accomplished.*

***Through interpersonal dialogue, monologue, and other discussion
immediately following the unusual event a conversation occurs.*** *Topics
typically covered include what just happened, what it seemed like, what it
could have been, and "settling on a consensus" of what happened. This
happening so soon after the event is both potentially beneficial and
potentially detrimental. Immediately after the event, your brain is possibly
the most accurate and objective, but paradoxically, it is also at that very
time when the participants within the group are most vulnerable to
confabulation, suggestion, or story conformity/regression to the mean. The
latter occurs by all participants settle on the same story despite
disparate/different perceptions of the event. I am not therefore suggesting
that such an investigative or debunking conversational process should not
take place. It does, however, need to be done with great vigilance for the
possibility of confabulation and to simultaneously guard against*

interpersonal or group pressures for undue conformity. A tough combination!

An example of interpersonal and group conformity occurred to me. On a nighttime investigation, you go out to explore pre-scouted sites. The lead investigator and I witnessed an injured lightning bug falling in a highly unusual, divergent, and rapid descending flight pattern toward the ground. Upon landing on the ground, it "blinked its last blink" creating the optical illusion of "disappearing into the ground." I saw a lightning bug. The lead investigator saw a mini-orb floating from the sky and eventually descending into the earth.

I, the neophyte researcher (it was during my first outing on my first expedition) after a minor debate that it was not an orb but an injured lightning bug, was easily pressured by the more experienced (more than 10 years as a Bigfoot researcher) investigator's demands to record what we both just witnessed. I was told to record it as a "mini-orb descending from the sky and entering the ground." Minutes later (fortunately, but purely coincidently) we simultaneously glanced at the ground where the "orb" entered the earth and saw the lighting bug begin to faintly blink in the throughs of death. To the investigator's credit, he then agreed it was a lightning bug, rather than a mini orb.

Typically, after the on-site debunking or problem-solving conversation, we rehash or once again talk about experiences on the hike back to the car or base camp. *I believe this to a be detrimental process.* Although potentially not feasible to achieve, I would encourage official expedition protocols to **discourage** this from happening. At this point, the group members are **goal-directed and focused** on either returning to camp or moving on to the next site to be investigated. *Through this goal-directed, focused cognitive state, the "bias stage" is already set.* It is then natural to continue the discussion of the event as they are leaving the site. *Through the process of this communication, along with diverted and divided focus, however, information (your data) can begin to morph or change in a few critical ways.*

1. Observations and opinions that are shared typically become even more similar and alike. *This is once again known as regression of the mean.*

2. *Detrimental in the process is the fact that diverging details, observations, and information can lose their salience (value or strength of importance) to the observer.* This can happen either through processes like confirmation bias, hypnotic or social suggestion, conformity (see confirmation bias definition), or confabulations (see confabulation definition).

3. *This "down-graded" information can then be discussed and become shared amongst group members. By the process of the **group's individuals' minds** being focused on returning or moving on, they are simultaneously "distracted" by that focus. Due to that focus, they become and remain more receptive or open to social or hypnotic suggestions and/or confabulation of degraded information.*

4. Furthermore, if phenomenological differences in data do not regress/conform to the mean or drop out of consciousness and context, *they may strengthen in their salience (value/importance) to the observer.* Such strengthening also engenders a bias of "I am right in my observations."

5. Such a "righteousness bias" engenders a degree of certainty when results are later communicated through an official debriefing back at base camp. This can result in data being included in the final data set irrespective of its validity.

6. Such inclusion, however, occurs often as a function of the force of the individual's exclamations of certainty in their observations (not to mention the sheer force of their will and personality within the larger group). *In short, the squeaky wheel gets oiled even when the squeak is inconsequential to the bigger picture. This further potentially produces errant data!*

At least in the expeditions I have attended, returning to base camp after a nightly expedition typically occurs between 12:00 AM and 4:00 AM. An informal debriefing then happens, planned or not. Members commonly share their experiences with others lingering around the campfire (while awaiting the return of all groups deployed). They then go to bed or to further chats with friends around individual campfires.

The formal group investigative debriefing is then held the following morning after breakfast. Guess what is discussed over breakfast? Again, I appreciate the practical logistical reasons for the schedule/routine. I nonetheless believe such conversations and delays to be ultimately detrimental to the purported scientific process involved in the expedition.

*Such conversations and delays are also potentially harmful to expedition members who are occasionally traumatized by frightening Class B or A experiences leaving them shaking and "looking white as a ghost." The process of sleep and time delay associated with formal debriefing allow further time for confabulation to set in. For the potentially traumatized participant, they are put in a position where they might seek out individual group members to informally debrief them. The often-chosen option of **avoiding traumatic events** might cause the person to get to bed, hoping **to avoid further discussion of the event**. This avoidance allows time for self-induced hypnosis or dreaming and therefore confabulation of data (information) to occur. It also allows the process of avoidance to set the stage for the development of Post-traumatic Stress Disorder (PTSD).*

A more psychologically appropriate process, albeit considerably more inconvenient **could be** employed. It would first need to involve the process of developing a specific debriefing protocol. These are admittedly offered in a hypothetical or "ideal" scenario. Matt Moneymaker has already developed a good start on such a protocol which can be found in BFRO policies and procedures on interviewing.[22] Multiple people could be trained as official "debriefers" and create multiple debriefing teams. *Upon returning to camp, the individuals traumatized and/or with salient scientific data would be debriefed separately from each other (out of hearing range of each other)* *by the trained debriefers. This is documented using video and/or audio recordings.*

During this individual debriefing procedure, each storyteller should be allowed *to tell their story uninterrupted by any questions from the debriefer.* Once the person is given this chance to "get their story off their chest," the debriefer would have them tell it a second time and ask appropriate **non-leading** and open-ended questions to clarify the individual's experience. Once each group member had been individually debriefed, a recorded group debriefing could be led by the debriefing team and observed silently by other expedition group members. After that third pass at the story (the first done as a larger investigative group), the story would be told one final time in a "free for all" question and answer debriefing by the entire expedition group (also moderated by a debriefing leader and recorded).

Why so many repetitions? For the traumatized expedition member, *avoidance is the enemy and sets the stage for the trauma to set in.* The longer the delay between the traumatizing event and their opportunity to tell the story in their own way and at their own pace, the more likely it is to create trauma and lead to PTSD. This is one reason the first formal debriefing is done individually (in private) and uninterrupted. Individually holding these separate from each other's debriefings is done to minimize regression to the mean and other forms of distortion and cross-contamination of the scientific information. It also preserves disparate details that might otherwise disappear. It is also done to avoid embarrassment or emotional decompensation in front of multiple individuals.

Subsequent recitations individually and in the group format represent repeated social exposure (rather than avoidance) to the trauma. This gives the teller repeated immediate opportunities to resolve and integrate aspects of the trauma in an objective and healthy fashion. It also allows them to begin to develop coping strategies (other than avoidance) to integrate the information into their cognitive and emotional worlds.

The old adage: "If you get bucked off a horse, you've got to get right back on it, or you'll never learn to ride" applies. The more time given for the fear of "getting thrown a second time" to set in, the less likely it becomes that the person will be successful in learning to overcome their fear. The fear will gain strength through avoidance as the person deprives themselves of the opportunity to learn that not all horses will throw or buck them. *This is how anxiety develops into anxiety disorders. Avoidance of the fearful stimulus deprives the person of opportunities to learn to cope with the anxiety-producing event and the anxiety builds and gets more permanently implanted.*

Why recordings? *Objectivity of analysis and the ability to capture either embellishment or diminishment of facts and information (data).* By being able to observe and monitor this process, the data preserved for analysis is most likely to remain objective and undistorted by numerous potential contaminating sources (confabulation, suggestion, confirmation bias, demand characteristics, group pressure/influences, etc.).

Why even tell the story in front of a group? Aside from the repetition issue discussed above, the telling in front of the group allows for the "**normalization**" of the experience for the tellers. It also gives them a chance to **receive support and empathy for their experience.** By normalization, I mean "to make it normal" within the context of the larger expedition group. It is one of the main reasons many if not most attend an expedition. *They want to experience Bigfoot because they know they're not crazy. They believe or even may know Bigfoot exists!*

By being monitored and led by the trained debriefer, it serves to build a tighter positive group process. It also ensures the **building of empathy and support within all group members** as they realize that they could be the ones telling the story.

*It also allows for the **group process** to identify facts missed by the debriefers who will be more focused on the debriefing process and impact. Two heads are better than one for identifying important facts and information. It also makes the entire group more invested in any science coming out of the expedition group. The entire group shares in the* *witnesses' phenomenological experience, becomes part of that experience and knows they are contributing to the research project through their participation. Here the "Hawthorn effect" becomes the "Hawthorn phenomena" productive on another level; a scientific level.*

Confirmation Bias: "... the tendency to look for information that supports, rather than rejects, one's preconceptions, typically by interpreting evidence to confirm existing beliefs, while rejecting or ignoring any conflicting data."[23]

Confirmation bias has the potential to run rampant in Bigfoot field research, especially that which seems to take the quantum leap from observation to theory creation, bypassing the very necessary step of hypothesis testing. "Do you agree or disagree with woo phenomena?" In my opinion, it is theoretically feasible but scientifically untested. I personally believe that confirmation bias played and continues to play a role in the development of some of the woo theories.

"How can they possibly disappear and reappear so quickly?" "Well by changing their molecular vibratory qualities, they can mask or cloak." Or "they can shift into another dimension and appear to disappear right before our eyes." *Such explanations dismiss any number of established parsimonious possibilities known to occur in nature (chameleon effects and other natural camouflage, being two).*

*Given our lack of "**scientific research**" into any of these explanations, they simply speak to the confirmation bias of the speaker when "one disappears right before your eyes." This does not in any way preclude genuine Woo experiences but highlights how an "observation" can create a theoretical leap. This is done without ever testing hypotheses via a data analysis that would support or refute the newly derived theory. We develop theories to confirm our pre-existing biases but do so without formally testing the hypothesis in a systematic fashion.*

Control: For the purposes of this book, control can be used as a noun or a verb and has two broad meanings within each of those semantic classifications. As a noun, it can mean:

1. "The power to influence or direct people's behavior or the course of events."[24]

2. "A group or individual used as a standard of comparison for checking the results of a survey or experiment."[25]

As a verb, it can mean:

1. "Determine the behavior or supervise the running of."[26]
2. "Take into account (an extraneous factor that might affect results) when performing an experiment."[27]

Let's talk about control as an influencing or determining factor (a controlling factor)! It's mostly an illusion versus a delusion, depending on how rigidly you try to hold on to it! Cup your hands and scoop up some water in your hands. Hold tightly, squeeze your hands tightly together, and watch the water disappear through your attempt to control it. Relax and gently support the water in your hands and you will hold it long enough and benefit by drinking from its sustenance!

I am a cognitive-behavioral psychotherapist. This means I believe that how and what we think and behave drives how and what we feel. That philosophy arguably developed out of widespread dissatisfaction with Freudian psychoanalytic theories of psychotherapy. Nonetheless, there isn't much in the world of psychology that Sigmund Freud didn't cover in his writings. He was a neurologist by training and the founding father of psychiatry by thought, theory development, reputation, and practice. He hypothesized that we resolve our **control conflicts/dynamics** during the **anal stage of psychosexual development**. Oh, good! SEX!

These psychosexual stages of development involved "successive ways of satisfying instinctual biological urges through stimulation of different areas of the body: the mouth, the anus, and the genitals."[28] The successes and failures of resolving those urges form the foundation for personality development.

In the anal stage of development (approximate age range of 2-3 years old), "the primary source of gratification comes first from the elimination of feces [thus the term 'anal expulsive;' the smearing, messy, untidy, disorganized, and unstructured side of an obsessive-compulsive coping and personality style] ... and/or then from the retention of them [thus the term 'anal-retentive:' the neat, tidy organized and clean side of obsessive-compulsive coping and personality style]."[29] **Both sides of this coin involve control:** loss of it or maintenance of it and is indeed (hopefully) one of the few things in our lives we can learn to control!

We all know perfectionists, "Type A"/driven personality styles, and "control freaks." We also all know messy people, "sloppy" drunks, not punctual, unstructured, carefree, and completely disorganized "airheads." These characterizations are not meant to offend, but do in fact represent varying degrees of control issues in personality dynamics. They are most likely someone in your life or someone you know or are at least familiar with. They highlight the illusion versus delusion that we can or can't control ourselves and our environment, when, in fact, a balance of these extremes in behavior is arguably one model of satisfactory mental health.

As a tracker of or trekker towards mental health, one of the first and most valuable lessons one must learn is: **WE CAN'T CONTROL ANYTHING OUTSIDE OF OURSELVES!** "A bird in the hand is worth two in the bush;" "We can't have what we can't hold;" "That's why it's called fishing, not catching;" "When it rains, it pours;" "Life is like a box of chocolates ...;"[30] and, "The only two things certain in life are death and paying taxes;"[31] all speak to the uncertainty and illusiveness of trying to control things. We certainly can't control others! All we can do is learn to control ourselves!

Control Group: See "Experimental Group."

Decision Making: I will not insult the reader with a formal definition of the word "decision," the word "making" nor the term "decision making." I will assume these words are inherently understood by most, if not all English-speaking people. We make decisions on a daily basis and have done so even before we had an awareness of ourselves, let alone our capacity to make decisions for ourselves. We decide when to get up or go to sleep. We decide what foods to eat, what clothes to wear, what friends to socialize with, who are our enemies, who we want to get to know and who we don't, etc., etc.

Although lost to many, if not most of us, we also **decide** how to react emotionally and behaviorally. Witness the infant in its first hours or days of learning to stand, wobble, and fall; eventually toddling and walking. The close observer will note that early (the first several times) in this process, when infants fall on their behind they look around the room at the reactions of the adults therein to "**decide**" how to react to the fall. Initially, they don't cry or laugh. They look and **decide** how to react to the reactions of the adults in the room. They are learning.

When adults consistently respond to such a fall with: "Oh, you poor baby, that hurt!!" and adopt a painful, injured, fearful, or shocked expression on their face; the baby will learn and quickly "**decide**" to cry. When the adults say: "Oops! You go boom-boom," and react with a big smile on their face, laugh pleasantly, make silly faces, or otherwise make light of the fall; the infant learns and quickly "**decides**" to laugh about the fall. *As those responses reoccur, the infant's decisions on how to emotionally or behaviorally react to that situation are repeatedly made and eventually become automatic, over-learned emotional reactions that no longer require conscious thought or decision. Their emotions and behavior in effect are switched to "automatic pilot."*

*Once "automatic," these become unconsciously produced. Thus, most of our emotional reactions are learned, but we lose sight of the fact that at some point **we decided** to react that way. The good news is that what is learned can be unlearned!*

Important to Bigfoot sightings, phenomena, and experiences, however, are the *three broad classes or types of decision-making conflict processes we face*: **Approach versus Approach**; **Approach versus Avoidance**; and **Avoidance versus Avoidance**. An "Approach versus Approach" conflict occurs when we must choose between two highly appealing or enjoyable options. Do we summer in the Hamptons or Martha's Vineyard, Darling? Blonde or brunette? Corvette or Viper? Back rub or foot rub? Glock or Kimber? Lemon or lime? Vanilla or vanilla with sprinkles? Fishing or Bigfooting? Do I get the prime rib or the lobster? We LOVE both options and are torn over which to choose! Surprisingly, not always an easy decision to make. Because we want both, our desires or preferences allow us to "**approach**" choosing both, but we can only choose one! Fortunately, we often can order surf and turf or go on a Bigfoot expedition that also gives us lake or stream fishing options.

The "**Approach versus Avoidance**" decision is typically the easiest decision to make, but not always! One option we want, desire, or love (**approach**), and the other we find repulsive, distasteful, unpleasant, or anxiety-producing (**avoidance**). A tenderloin steak or liver? An ice cream cone or a tablespoon of cod liver oil? Mercedes or Kia, when you can afford either? Easy-peasy for most people.

But what about going on a Bigfoot expedition after just having had a terrifying encounter with a Bigfoot? Part of you wants to go because you love being in the outdoors, you love the people in the research group, and you need to see a Bigfoot to validate for yourself what just happened (**approach**). On the other hand, it literally scared the piss and shit out of you. You're having nightmares and intrusive memories of the event. You just want to put it behind you, forget it, and move on with life (**avoidance**).

Finally, the "**Avoidance versus Avoidance**" decision is typically the toughest to make. Both options are distasteful, repulsive, painful, or otherwise unpleasant or anxiety-producing. Death by hanging or electrocution? Intravenous injection or drawing blood? Dentist or waterboarding? Shovel elephant shit or rhino shit all day? Eat Limburger cheese or Durian fruit? Hickory switch or Dad's belt? In each case, if you find either option unpleasant (**avoidance**), don't want to choose either, but must choose one! Very highly stress-producing and all you want to do is avoid both, but you can't! Danger! Will Robinson! Danger!!!! Run away!

Of fundamental importance to the objective field, a researcher is to think about and understand the type of decisions you face on an expedition. By maintaining this awareness, you can account for the context under which you are making a decision and allow it to better inform that decision.

I have presented those examples within the context of **conscious intent** for illustration. Not all decisions during expeditions are as straightforward as the above examples as not all decisions are made with **conscious** intent. Some are made with **subconscious** intent or are **unconsciously** influenced! For example, you've just been bluff-charged by a Bigfoot. Do you move forward in the face of your fear attempting to change what would typically be an avoidance situation into a literal **approach** situation? Or, do you take the original **avoidance** option and retreat tactfully?

When you've been longing for a Class A sighting, but have a fleeting, partial sighting of something that **could be** a Bigfoot, what is your decision in reporting it? Do you unconsciously or subconsciously report it as a Class A (**approach**)? This often results in you getting swept up in the expedition group process of excitement, congratulations, praise, and esteem of your peers which serves to erase any original uncertainty. Or do you admit and maintain that uncertainty in the face of the group process and chalk it up to "just one of many" Class B, C sightings, or maybe have it identified as "not even" a Bigfoot sighting (**avoidance**)? The resulting consolation from your group adds to the disappointment.

Similarly, and perhaps a more commonly encountered decision conflict during expeditions: You are in an expedition group of four when three of the four see or hear something that you did not. Do you go along with the group and say you did too (**approach**), or do you become the "odd man or woman out" and say you didn't (**avoidance**)? *On-the-spot interpersonal rewards, gains, and warm fuzzies can often be more powerful than any chance of national fame.* During my relatively brief time doing Bigfoot Field research, I have repeatedly seen uncertainty and peer pressure/the group process change the descriptive qualities and certainty of encounters.

When Glenn Williams and John Eaves (or similarly identified "occasional" camp cooks) prepare their canned pantry camp stew: do you eat it knowing your stomach will be growling and in pain on the evening outing (**avoidance**) or do you eat cold canned beans, knowing your stomach will be grumbling and that you'll be farting all that evening's expedition (**avoidance**)? Please note, in either situation, you know you'll be regretting it on the porta-pottery or compost toilet the next morning, but won't be able to avoid using that stinky thing (**avoidance vs avoidance**)!!! Group expedition sponsors and leaders beware; any of the above examples can have a disastrous effect on the overall expedition group process and experience!!!! (LOL)

Dissonance (Cognitive Dissonance Theory; Leon Festinger, 1957): "an unpleasant psychological state resulting from inconsistency between two or more elements in a cognitive system.[32] It is presumed to involve a state of heightened arousal and to have characteristics similar to physiological drives (e.g., hunger). Thus, cognitive dissonance creates a motivational drive in an individual to reduce the dissonance ... first described by Leon Festinger."[33]

Dissonance reduction: "the process by which a person reduces the uncomfortable psychological state that results from inconsistency among elements of a cognitive system. Dissonance can be reduced by making one or more inconsistent elements consistent with other elements in the system, by decreasing the perceived importance of an inconsistent element, or by adding new consistent elements to the system. Finally, **self-affirmation theory** postulates that merely affirming some valued aspect of the self, even if it is not directly relevant to the inconsistency, can reduce dissonance.[34]

At its root, it might be argued that dissonance is the source of all forms of bias and problem-solving. Dissonance (out of whack, out of balance, uncomfortable notions, ideas, or behaviors inconsistent with our typical "self" or experience of the world) creates a **psychological imbalance** within us that we strive to *rebalance or create a new state of equilibrium. We therefore solve the problem in the most expedient fashion.* This often takes huge leaps in logic and reasoning and often leads to forms of bias discussed elsewhere in the text (confirmation bias, incredulity bias, biased interpretation of results, and justification for behaviors and studies).

Phenomenologically, in Bigfoot fieldwork dissonance is consistently evoked, experienced, and resolved, be that resolution accurate or inaccurate scientifically. "What was it I just saw?" "What was that sound?" "Did you

hear (see, feel, smell) that?!" "Why are the animals in the woods so quiet?"
Our psyche drives us forward to answer these questions. Potentially
problematic as a form of bias, those answers will often be generated,
produced, or informed by our perception. Our perception is informed and
influenced by our life experiences, many of which are not shared by others.
As such they may not be universal or universally accepted in consensus
reality. Of course, such perceptual solutions or answers, irrespective of
other's phenomenological field of experience, may or may not be the correct
solution or answer.

My firefly story once again is relevant here. On my first
expedition, I was sent out with two highly experienced investigators.
We positioned ourselves facing three of the four points on the
compass and then adjusted seating to split the difference in the
fourth. While looking out I observed what I was sure was a lightning
bug flying a zig-zag and looping irregular pattern down out of the air
towards myself and the sub-group leader. It moved with a zig-
zagging, erratic, and relatively more rapid speed than one would
expect. I pointed to the unusual trajectory of descent for a lightning
bug. They are typically very slow, and steady but more of an ethereal
floating and hovering, rather than erratic descent. The most
experienced of the group acknowledged seeing this and proceeded to
hypothesize that it might not be a lightning bug, but a mini-orb
instead. I insisted "No, it's a lightning bug" as it continued its injured
and erratic descent towards us. The experienced investigator insisted
more strongly it was a mini-orb. The light hit the ground right
between our chairs and went out, igniting the investigator's now more
definitive insistence that it was a mini-orb "that was just absorbed
into the ground" (when the light blinked out). He insisted that I
needed to record it as such. Being the rookie of the group, I dutifully,
but skeptically did so.

Five minutes passed and we coincidently looked down to the ground
between us simultaneously where we had seen the "mini-orb disappear into
the ground." This time, we saw the dying lightning bug's light flash on
again!! It turns out the lead investigator had recently had a close up, Class
A encounter that left quite an impression and that began to influence his

perception about what was and was not Bigfoot-related. Our perception in any sense is always potentially informed by and therefore potentially biased by our past experiences. We then rely on that perception to resolve our dissonance, sometimes correctly, other times incorrectly.

Empirical: "... derived from or denoting experimentation or systematic observations as the basis for conclusion or determination, as opposed to speculative, theoretical, or exclusively reason-based approaches. Many forms of research attempt to gain empirical evidence in favor of a hypothesis by manipulating an **independent variable** and assessing the effect on an outcome or **dependent variable** ... based on experience."[35] This is then called an experiment.

To the current author, the two definitions of empirical highlight the schism or conflict between what I call "Bigfoot Science" and "Bigfoot Scientific Research (BFSR)." In the field, most fieldwork ends at the point of recording the experience. Since empiricism (see below) is associated with science, I guess technically fieldwork that ends with recording observations and/or using them to inform the next investigation is a "scientific process." I don't think it should be called "science," but the definitions are undeniable. As such I would characterize it as "weak science." It is not my intention to offend field researchers but the work begs the question: What is it going to take to come full cycle or circle with the data gathered and begin to statistically analyze it so we can go from assumption to tested hypotheses to theory to proven scientific results?

It seems to me we get so caught up in the experience, the possible personal and commercial benefits and gains from the fieldwork, that the additional steps to create more "definitive" Bigfoot Scientific Research (BFSR) are rarely or never pursued. Yes, the results are summarized on a daily basis. Yes, that information is shared. Those whiteboards are posted along with other pictures on organizations' selected pages on the web. The expedition witnesses are asked to "write up" their experiences/raw data. From there, however, I've yet to see the data numerically encoded beyond for the purpose of creating advertisements for the organizations' next expeditions. Why then bother calling it "science" or "scientific"? It boils down to marketing research.

Empirical Knowledge: "... in the sciences, knowledge gained from experiment and observation rather than from theory. See **empiricism.**"[36]

Empirical Method: "any procedure for conducting an investigation that relies upon experimentation and systematic observation rather than theoretical speculation. The term is sometimes used as a vague synonym for **scientific method.**"[37]

These definitions highlight my argument and belief that *what is needed to enhance Scientific Bigfoot Research (SBFR) to a level acceptable to the broader scientific community is "experimentation."* It appears to me we have spent decades doing "systematic observation" but such observation has in fact driven and resulted in "theoretical speculation" rather than moving us toward hypothesis testing via experimentation. *Without this later shift or move toward, or into experimentation, the species' existence is unlikely to be proven scientifically.* I will not debate the pros and cons of that happening!

Empirical Validity: "the degree to which the accuracy of a test, model, or other construct can be demonstrated through experimentation and systematic observation (i.e., the accumulation of supporting research evidence) rather than theory alone."[38]

Based on my readings, it would appear there are multiple massive databases in existence consisting of years, if not decades of accumulated evidence. It is also my perception that these are closely guarded territories that remain highly restricted in their access and use to the broader scientific Bigfoot research community. The most frequent use I have observed appears to be for purposes of personal and commercial gain. This does not promote true scientific knowledge. Have I beaten that horse enough?

Empiricism:

1. "An approach to **epistemology** (a philosophy concerned with the nature, origin, and limitations of knowledge) holding that all knowledge of matters of fact either arises from experience or requires experience for its validation. In particular, empiricism denies the possibility of **innate ideas,**

arguing that the mind at birth is like a blank sheet of paper (see **tabula rasa aka "blank slate"**). During the 17th and 18th centuries, empiricism was developed as a systematic approach to philosophy in the work of John Locke, George Berkeley, and David Hume. These thinkers also developed theories of **associationism** to explain how even the most complex mental concepts can be derived from simple sense experiences."[39]

"Although there is a strong emphasis on empiricism in psychology, this can take different forms. Some approaches to psychology hold that sensory experience is the origin of all knowledge and thus, ultimately, of personality, character, beliefs, emotions, and behavior. **Behaviorism** is the purest example of empiricism in this sense. Advocates of other theoretical approaches to psychology, such as **phenomenology**, argue that the definition of experience as only sensory experience is too narrow; this enables them to reject the position that all knowledge arises from the senses, while also claiming to adhere to a type of empiricism."[40]

2. "The view that experimentation is the most important, if not the only, foundation of scientific knowledge and the means by which individuals evaluate truth claims or the adequacy of theories and models."[41]

At this point, it should be needless for me to point out that I am biased toward the second of these two definitions. Not so much because the first is irrelevant or of no value, but because the systematic observation associated with field research has clearly proven itself inadequate to the task of generating substantial scientific "facts" that could be used to prove the existence of Bigfoot. Not meant as an insult or slap in the face. I think of it as an undeniable objective observation. It's time to move on and try something different by using field research as the foundation to inform "experimental" investigation rather than the phenomenological end unto itself as it seems to have become the norm for many field researchers. I guess that horse ain't dead yet!

Experimental Group: "A group of participants in a research study who are exposed to a particular manipulation of the independent variable (i.e., a particular treatment or [experimental manipulation or test] ...) ... An **independent variable** (my emphasis) is the variable in an experiment that is specifically manipulated or is observed to occur before the dependent, or outcome variable, in order to assess its effect or influence. *Independent variables may or may not be causally related to the dependent* (my emphasis). .... A **dependent variable** (my emphasis) is the outcome that is observed to occur or change after the occurrence or variation of the independent variable in an experiment. It is the effect that one wants to predict or explain in **correlational research.** *Dependent variables may or may not be related causally to the independent variable* (my emphasis). ... *The responses of the experimental group are compared to the responses of a* **control group,** *other experimental groups, or both* (my emphasis).

The **control group** is "a comparison group in a study whose members receive either no intervention [manipulation] at all or some established intervention [manipulation]. The responses of those in the control group are compared with the responses of participants in one or more experimental groups that are given the new treatment, [manipulation or test] being evaluated."[42]

Knowledge: "... the state of being familiar with something or aware of its existence, usually resulting from experience or study. ... The range of one's understanding or information. In some contexts, the words *knowledge* and *memory* are used synonymously."[43]

I include this definition for your consideration and philosophical reflection rather than as a factual or definitive definition of the word. It somewhat equates "knowledge" with awareness which in my mind are two different concepts. Awareness for me is a state of fully living in the millisecond with all of one's senses fully activated and functioning. We may become aware of a subtle sound or odor as we sit in a room or in the woods. To know or have knowledge of that sound or odor requires more complex cognitive processing and association with other senses, as well as past experiences.

The definition states knowledge and memory are synonymous. I also disagree with this. In order to remember something, an intentional, conscious cognitive process or "recollection" is typically required.

It has recently been shown that you can condition a single cell to behave in a specific fashion. Extrapolating from that, such conditioning might represent the foundation for concepts such as Jung's (1916) "collective unconscious" and genetic memories."[44] The collective unconscious is the part of the **unconscious** that, according to Carl Jung (1916) "is common to all humankind and contains the inherited accumulation of primitive human experiences in the form of ideas and images called **archetypes** and manifested in myths as well as other cultural phenomena (e.g., religion) and in dreams."[45] "It is the deepest and least accessible part of the unconscious mind."[46] "A genetic memory is a memory present at birth that exists in the absence of sensory experience, and is incorporated into the **genome** over long spans of time."[47]

Given my disagreement with equating knowledge and memory, it should not surprise the reader that I consider the use of the word "memory" in the phrase "genetic memory" misnomers. "**Genetic behavior**" or "**genetic conditioning**" *would be more accurate in my opinion*. So many of the manifestations of so-called "genetic memories" or the collective unconscious are **behavioral manifestations**. Even those that apparently reflect past knowledge (from a previous life, for example) don't arise out of a conscious recollection but typically are **spontaneously** displayed or known.

Irrespective of such philosophical debate or perhaps more accurately through such philosophical debate, I leave the reader to draw their own conclusion and then to consider the implications of that conclusion on paranormal activity, Woo phenomena and theory, and the possible factual existence of Bigfoot.

Norms: "something that is usual, typical, or standard ... a standard or pattern, especially of social behavior, that is typical or expected of a group."[48] In statistics, it is represented by the "normal distribution." Remember when everyone in class [even the smart kids] failed a test and the teacher said "I'm going to have to grade the test on a curve?" That "**bell-shaped**" curve is the "normal distribution" (of numeric scores showing test results, and other data representing phenomena and experience).

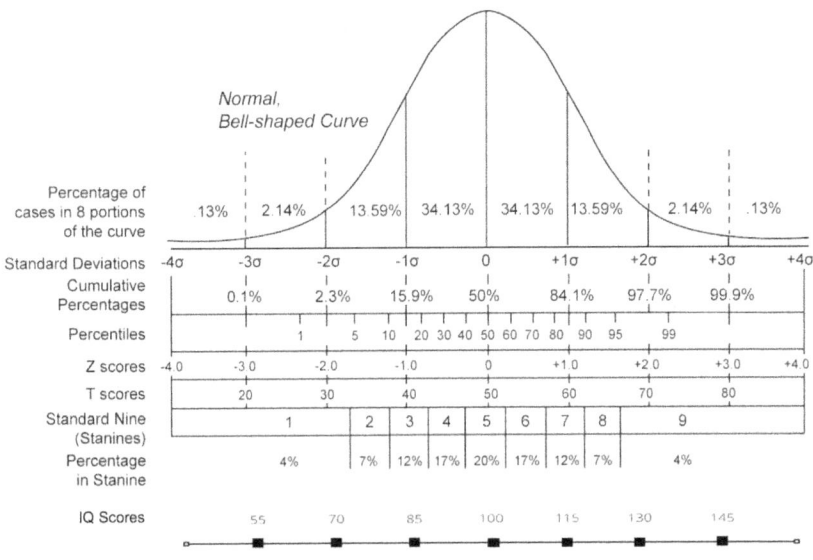

Adapted and modified from Wikipedia.[49]

It defines what is "normal" or "average," as well as what is unusually ("abnormally") "strong" or "weak." The focus here is mathematical, and statistical issues. They describe a *normal distribution of qualities* that exist in the species homo-sapiens. Height, weight, shoe size, intelligence. There is no philosophical "anti-science" or "pro-science" debate or revolutionary ideals here. Nor are there elitist, condescending, authoritarian, or uncompromising values. *For the current writer, it is the process that comes closest to objectivity.* Furthermore, it's a "**process.**" *This process is neither malevolent nor benign in and of itself. We need to beware, however, of the intent of the minds and hands wielding them.*

This is also in no way a judgment or condemnation of groups with a phenomenological /experiential process of "logical" acceptance of an event and the associated sensational (sights, sounds, odors, tastes, and somatic/tactile) experience. I am frankly not sure why the experiential and experimental philosophies seem to be so oppositional or preclusive. You've got to start and experiment with your independent (the expedition) and dependent variables (Bigfoot phenomena) variables hopefully with Class "A," Class "B," or Class "C" experiences. Might they be normally distributed? In order to understand the answer to that last question, you need to understand the normal curve. Onward to Appendix A ... if you dare!

PICKING UP FROM APPENDIX A:

Now you've read Appendix A and understand the concepts of average, mean, standard deviations, percentiles, t-scores, z-scores, and sample. Yes! Read on. You Pass Go. You collect your reward and trek further down the path equipping your Bigfoot Scientific Research tool bag to assist in scientifically proving the existence of Bigfoot.

You answered "No" to understanding those concepts. No worries!!!! If you want to similarly equip your Bigfoot tool bag as those above, reread Appendix A paying more attention to those terms, and the Covid and 2020 Presidential Race examples. Although not exemplified "in Bigfoot," they highlight the scientific importance of being able to objectively read journals, and papers, and hear news shows and how they may or may not inform your own research. Without such knowledge, you might as well be using a Bigfoot Inkblot test to inform your research.

You answered "Hell No!" to your understanding of those concepts. Additionally, you don't want to have to learn concepts like "population," "sample," "standard deviation," and "statistical tests"? You don't want to understand how *to test for scientific statistical differences* between groups? For example, is there a "scientifically, statistically significant difference" between a group of "Bigfoot tree knocks" and a group of tree knocks made by a Human). If being part of that study and the possibility of *"creating an auditory signature"* to distinguish Bigfoot from other creatures doesn't appeal to you? No worries!! Don't force yourself to read "Appendix A."

You may not be invested enough right now to take the time and effort to understand those concepts. Again, no worries! You will be better served to continue to focus on Part One of this book and maybe the "Chapters on Evidence" (Chapter 7), "Zapping" (Chapter 8), and the final chapter (Chapter 11) in Part Two of this book.

Right now, you don't have to provide that type of evidence or answer those questions requiring that knowledge! Value remains in gathering purely subjective, verifiable experiential data! "Firm up the foundation," while others "frame up scientific house of Bigfoot proof." *All are needed and valued.* Doing one should not preclude the other. All ultimately contribute to the end result. Different strokes for different folks!

Moving on with more on the normal curve and understanding scientific research. When discussing the normal curve and "**change**" (**significant** decreases or increases) one standard deviation (one step) difference or change is required to be considered "statistically significant." *A "statistically significant" change is a "real change" not attributable to random effects or error.*

Let's say you took a Bigfoot IQ test (pre-test) and then studied hard, reading every book in existence on Bigfoot. After that extensive reading/studying, you take a second Bigfoot IQ test (post-test). Was your last score on your Bigfoot IQ test (118) significantly higher than the one before it (108)? "Well, it went up 10 points so it must be true (real) improvement, correct?" You'd need only to plot that IQ score on the above Bell-shaped illustration and note if it improved (or declined) a full standard deviation. *If it hadn't or even only came close to a one-step (standard deviation) improvement, scientifically (statistically) that would not be considered a true or "real" change. It would represent normal variability or other factors contributing to the change in the numeric value (which is a* **symbol** *of your Bigfoot IQ). If it had* **improved a full step** *then your studying would have truly paid off.*

As to the best of my knowledge, a standardized (normed) Bigfoot IQ test does not exist (there's a project for an aspiring scientific BF researcher); we'll use the existing concept of an Intelligence Quotient

(IQ) and existing tests of same (IQ) for this example. Hang with me on this one!

IQ scores have a mean or average score of 100 and a standard deviation (step up or down) of 15 points. Plotting your 108 BFIQ score on the IQ line of our illustration reveals it falls in the average range of intelligence (between "0" and "1" standard deviation on the normal curve). Plotting your apparent higher score of 118 reveals it to be in the high-average range in the next step (standard deviation) higher than your 108 score. Yes, it's a significant improvement or change, correct? Wrong!!!!! *Even when two scores exist or fall in two different step ranges (standard deviation ranges), those two scores are not considered statistically significantly different unless there is a full (complete) step in between the two numbers! For IQ scores, a full step is 15 points.* The difference between 118 and 108 is 10 points, **not** fifteen. As such, even though 108 falls in the average range of intelligence and 118 falls in the high-average range of intelligence; *these two scores representing your Bigfoot intelligence are not statistically significantly different from each other.* Although the 118 score appears to represent a higher score than the 108 score, *that 10-point improvement falls short of a full standard deviation (one full step) improvement.* As such, the 118 score **does not** represent a significant improvement!! The improvement is attributed to random error and change.

It (the symbolic number) certainly appears bigger. But it only **represents/reflects** the underlying **concept** of your Bigfoot intelligence. Your Bigfoot intelligence **score** has not increased significantly in spite of all your reading and studying. In "scientific reality," you are **not** significantly smarter about Bigfoot than before you read and studied! What a bummer! You can still console yourself if you remember, *numbers are symbols representing IQ scores, not the intelligence itself! It seems highly likely that the depth and breadth of your Bigfoot knowledge increased, but was not being measured or appropriately measured by the test!* Back to the drawing board! "Science," she is a frequently disappointing bedfellow!

Occam's razor: "... also spelled **Ockham's razor,** also called the **law of economy** or **law of parsimony,** a principle stated by the

Scholastic philosopher William of Ockham (1285–1347) that '*pluralitas non est ponenda sine necessitate,*' 'plurality should not be posited without necessity.' ... The principle gives precedence to simplicity: of two competing theories, the simpler explanation of an entity is to be preferred. The principle is also expressed as 'Entities are not to be multiplied beyond necessity.' .... *Occam's razor is the principle that, of two explanations that account for all the facts, the simpler one is more likely to be correct* (my emphasis). It is applied to a wide range of disciplines, including religion, physics, and medicine ... The validity of Occam's razor has long been debated. Critics of the principle argue that it prioritizes simplicity over accuracy and that, since one cannot absolutely define 'simplicity,' it cannot serve as a sure basis of comparison. They cite as an example the competing theories of creationism and evolution, in which relative 'simplicity' depends on temporal and cultural context."[50]

This scientific ideal remains a large stumbling block in the path to scientific acceptance of Bigfoot and Bigfoot phenomena. The species Bigfoot itself arguably represents an outlier whose explanation may not be readily available and accessible through principles of parsimony. Note, the definition above (when speaking to the validity of the principle) cites issues of creationism and evolution as a potential challenge to the parsimony concept based on the temporal and cultural context within which it is being considered. Given that one of the predominating theories for the existence of Bigfoot (a flesh and blood hominid) finds its very roots firmly entrenched in the creationism versus evolutionary debate. It should be no surprise that many argue that Occam's razor and other principles of parsimony cannot be validly applied to Bigfoot or Bigfoot phenomena. This, of course, opens the door to any number of theories or explanations of Bigfoot and Bigfoot-related phenomena. "It's not that simple. It's a complex phenomenon!" *(All the more reason in my mind to bring scientific principles described herein to bear!)*

Woo phenomena are defined below and (to many Bigfoot philosophers) represent the proof that Occam's razor needs to be applied to explanations of Bigfoot. They suggest that some Woo claims are so complicatedly theoretically fantastic and beyond consensus reality that they can't possibly be true [see incredulity bias]. Therefore, Woo phenomena are better explained by simpler notions and theories when Occam's razor philosophies are applied.

Remember, however, razors cut both ways!! Woo phenomena also stand as the foundation for arguments against applying parsimony to Bigfoot and related phenomena!! It's an outlier, unusual, out of the realm of the ordinary, averse to traditional scientific experimentation methods (have we really applied them?) and techniques, yet theoretically supported by quantum physics and other physical sciences and theories. Therefore, Occam's razor or the principle of parsimony can't be applied; it is simply **too complicated** of a phenomenon to be reduced to a single theory or principle.

Hmmmm!? Like so many Bigfoot issues, you're damned if you do and you're dammed if you don't! The reading researcher must wrestle with these issues themselves as the current author sees no value in resolving this issue for them based on his own biases. To do so would skew and bias the readers' reasoning.

Outliers: "an extreme observation or measurement, that is, a score that significantly differs from all others obtained. For instance, assume a researcher administered an intelligence test to a group of people. If most individuals obtained scores near the average IQ of 100, yet one person had an IQ of 200, the latter score would be an outlier. Outliers can have a high degree of influence on summary statistics (e.g., the mean and standard deviation can be pulled severely toward outliers)[51] and on estimates of parameter values ... (population of scientifically sampled ranges of characteristics),[52] ... and they may distort research findings if they are the result of error."[53]

Statistical outliers: When an outlier is discovered in a series of scores or in a database or conceptually representative numbers preparing to be statistically analyzed.

Phenomenological/Behavioral Outliers: Extreme phenomena or behaviors identified in the field or under other experimental conditions during passive observation, active observation, or experimental manipulation.

I would draw the reader's attention to the influence of outliers on summary statistics and parameters. Parameters are "a characteristic of a population, such as the mean or standard deviation that is described or estimated by a statistic obtained from sample data. For example, the mean score on a national exam for a sample of colleges provides an **estimate** of this parameter in the population of colleges ... any of the variables in a statistical model that is studied or used to explain an outcome or relationship."[54] Terms like "high degree of influence" and "distorts research findings" highlight how outliers can create inaccurate or errant observations, statistical results and conclusions based on same. This produces error and bias if not understood!

When occurring in a scientific study database, statistical outliers are removed from the database or otherwise not included in the statistical analysis to protect the "accuracy" of the results and the reality the results reflect. Think about that and let it sink in. "... *not included in the statistical analysis to protect the 'accuracy' of the results and the reality the results reflect.*" In general, removing such data is considered a perfectly acceptable process to employ and is in fact often encouraged or demanded prior to statistical analysis to avoid having an inaccurately skewed or biased data set. "Garbage included on the front end of the analysis produces garbage out the back end!" That makes perfect sense in the bathroom and during statistical analysis! But do the results then accurately reflect the true consensus reality?

I am not sure about your world, *but the world I live in is replete with outliers.* The abnormal, unusual, errant, freakish, and unexplainable feelings, events, people, places, and things we encounter throughout our lives all represent potential outliers. If you're reading this book, you are interested in an outlier: Bigfoot! You may be an outlier yourself... so much for book sales!

So, when excluding an outlier from a database, we are in fact manipulating the true accuracy of the "reality" we are analyzing! "Heisenberg Principle!" Anyone!!!? Anyone? Heisenberg? Party of three... no maybe .... party of two ... one!? Yes One!"

We are excluding that part of that reality that is not convenient, we don't like, can't explain, and don't want to influence our results ... that which we don't want to influence the resulting scientific picture of consensus reality! Hmmmmm. *Kind of like what other people do when we tell them of our interest in Bigfoot and they immediately dismiss it out of hand. Kind of like what "hard" scientific Bigfoot researchers do when the Woo phenomenon is brought up and they dismiss it!*

Outliers! Their inclusion potentially distorts our database, but their exclusion denies the reality of what we measured. When those outliers represent an error or are errant, their exclusion is absolutely required. But when they are not errant and excluded because they don't conveniently fit our study or experimental model/design or our perception of reality, that exclusion then creates a biased and inaccurate picture of our outcome.

Pareidolia: See Chapter 3 for a discussion of Visual Pareidolia, Auditory Pareidolia and their relevance to Bigfoot phenomena.

Reason: "...consecutive thought, as in deduction or induction. Although at one time reason was considered a mental faculty, this meaning is typically not intended in current usage.; ... in philosophy, the intellect (or nous) is regarded as the source of true knowledge: ... a statement offered to justify an action or decision or to explain the occurrence of an event. ...."

Reasoning: ... thinking in which logical processes of an inductive or deductive character are used to draw conclusions from facts or premises ..."[55]

Inductive reasoning: "the form of reasoning in which inferences and general principles are drawn from specific observations and cases. Inductive reasoning is a cornerstone of the scientific method ... in that it underlies the process of developing hypotheses from particular facts and observations ..."[56] Arthur Cannon Doyle built his popular fame on inductive reasoning through his creation of Sherlock Holmes, although it is often incorrectly characterized as deductive reasoning.

Deductive reasoning: "the form of logical reasoning in which a conclusion is shown to follow necessarily from a sequence of premises, the first of which stands for a self-evident truth ... or agreed-upon data. In the empirical sciences, deductive reasoning underlies the process of deriving predictions from general laws or theories ..."[57]

In this author's opinion, Bigfoot field research has utilized too much deductive reasoning. While inductive reasoning was initially used to develop hypotheses, rather than testing those hypotheses, we have allowed them to morph into theories unto themselves. The deductive reasoning process has subsequently taken over and allowed raw experiential and phenomenological observation to be twisted to support one's theoretical bias. Confirmation Bias Anyone!? Anyone!!? .... Confirmation Bias!!?? Anyone!? ... Anyone? No!!!! No!!! "Confirmation Bias Anyone?" "Confirmation Bias!"

I recently attended a conference where a panelist actually dismissed "Woo Phenomena" because he "just doesn't see it as feasible." So much for unbiased objectivity driving hypothesis testing. I am not suggesting that the Woo phenomena and theories are valid (or invalid). I am, however, suggesting they should not be dismissed out of hand and not systemically investigated simply because they see "too far-fetched" to some of the current "big names" of the Bigfoot Community. *To me, that is the epitome of unscientific bias and closed-minded thinking!*

You may pay hundreds to thousands of dollars to go on a Bigfoot expedition. Not only do you want, but based on fees, may grow to expect a "Bigfoot experience" even though the paperwork you signed explicitly stated that there are no such guarantees. Your response bias has already been established before your first outing and before we take into consideration your habits. **Both expedition leaders and serious expedition researchers/participants should deeply dwell on this for some time and fully appreciate its implications.**

Sentient: "Able to perceive or feel things."[58] In other definitions, sentience is defined as "able to experience feelings," "responsive to or conscious of sense impressions," and "capable of feeling things through physical senses."[59] "Sentient beings experience wanted emotions like happiness, joy, and gratitude, and unwanted emotions in the form of pain ..."[60]

Sentient Beings: "Declaring consciousness." Non-human

animals, including all **mammals** and birds, and many other creatures, including **octopuses**, also possess these neurological substrates. They could also have included fish, for which the evidence supporting sentience and consciousness is also compelling."[61]

Non-sentient Beings: "First, we would include here those beings that do not have a nervous system, such as Porifera (the phylum that includes sponges), and those who do have a nervous system which is not centralized, such as echinoderms and cnidarians. Non-sentient animals would then include sponges, corals, anemones, and hydras."[62]

Sentient vs. Self-aware: "sentient, adjective: able to perceive or feel things. Self-awareness is the capacity for introspection and the ability to recognize oneself as an individual separate from the environment and other individuals.[63] "It is not to be confused with consciousness in the sense of qualia (the internal and subjective component of sense perceptions, arising from stimulation of the senses by phenomena)."[64]

Wow!! Maybe it's just me, but these were surprising definitions to apply to Bigfoot. Aside from the basic question of if it (Bigfoot) exists, *I thought its sentience would be debatable.* That would appear not to be the case as "sentience" seems to be related to having a nervous system and sensing. While I guess Bigfoots surviving close range, high-power rifle fire might question its ability to feel pain, *most other data seems consistent with it having some form of a nervous system through which it senses its environment and would therefore be considered sentient.*

Self-awareness, however, in Bigfoot seems a little less clear-cut. *Can Bigfoot introspect?* Revisit my anthropomorphism discussion where I advance other species-specific/atavistic behaviors to account for "curiosity" on BF. Certainly, my own words challenge such introspection and higher-order reasoning! Although we all have met humans who similarly challenge the theory that introspection and higher order reasoning exist in humans!! It seems to me this is a topic to reflect on more closely in the future and through experimentation rather than philosophical debate. Jean Piaget's theories on when children develop their own sense of self separate from other people and objects (object permanence) should be a good place to start theoretically and for guidance on experimental design.[65]

Sight: Your sense of vision or your ability to see.

Sightings: Seeing or in some other sensory modality experiencing Bigfoot evidence or an actual encounter with a Bigfoot. In its definition, BFRO explicitly limits such encounters to the visual and auditory (hearing) senses. During an actual or real-life phenomenological/experiential level, field reports of "sightings" include olfactory (smells), gustatory (tastes), and tactile/kinesthetic (touch/bodily feelings) sensations.

BFRO defines three types of "reports of sightings/encounters:" "**Class A,**" "**Class B**" and "**Class C.**"[66] "The difference between the classifications relates to the potential for misinterpretation of what was observed or heard. A given witness might be very credible but could have honestly misinterpreted something that was seen, found, or heard. Thus, for the most part, the **circumstances** (my emphasis) of the incident determine the **potential** (my emphasis) for misinterpretation, and therefore the classification of the report."[67]

Class A

"Class A reports involve clear sightings in circumstances where misinterpretation of the animals can be ruled out with greater confidence. For example, there are several footprint cases that are very well documented. These are considered Class A reports because misidentification of common animals can be confidently ruled out, thus the **potential** for misinterpretation is very low."[68]

Class B

"Incidents where a possible Sasquatch was observed at a great distance or in poor lighting conditions and incidents in any other circumstance that did not afford a clear view of the subject are considered Class B reports..."[69]

"For example, credible reports where nothing was seen but distinct and characteristic sounds of Sasquatches were heard are always considered Class B reports and never Class A, even in the most compelling "sound-only" cases. This is because the lack of a visual element raises a much greater **potential** for misidentification of sounds."[70]

"Class B reports are not considered less credible or less important than Class A reports; both types are deemed credible enough by the BFRO to show to the public. For example, one of the best-documented reports ever received by the BFRO is a Class B report from Trinity County, California. It involved a very credible witness who backpacked into a remote area that has a history of Sasquatch-related incidents. He described various occurrences around his camp at night that are strongly suspected to be Sasquatch-related. The report is still considered Class B though because there was no clear visual observation to confirm what was heard outside the tent."[71]

"Almost all reports included in the (BFRO) database are first-hand reports. Occasionally a second-hand report is considered reliable enough to add to the database, but those reports are never Class A, because of the higher potential for inaccuracy when the story does not come straight from the eyewitness."

Class C

"Most second-hand reports, and any third-hand reports, or stories with untraceable sources, are considered Class C because of the high potential for inaccuracy. Those reports are kept in the BFRO archives but are very rarely listed publicly in this database. The exceptions are of published, or locally documented incidents from before 1958 (before the word 'Bigfoot' entered the American vocabulary), and sightings mentioned in non-tabloid newspapers and magazines."[72] "The BFRO's report classification system rates the **circumstantial potential for misinterpretation** (my emphasis), not the credibility of the witness or how interesting the report is. If you are checking the Recent Additions page periodically for new reports, or to steadily gain a better understanding of behavior and geographic range, you should pay attention to **both** (my emphasis) Class A and Class B reports."[73]

First and foremost, thanks to BFRO for advancing this **report** classification system. This represents an important initial step towards creating a common understanding and nomenclature to use to discuss sighting/encounter reports for their phenomenological and scientific relevance. Thank you! The BFRO also reports this publicly on its web page to the benefit of a scientific and commercial spirit. Bravo!

Additional kudos to BFRO for placing phenomenological/experiential research into its proper foundational scientific context. On the same web page describing the classification system, BFRO states: "The use of subjective evaluation is what separates the legal perspective of witness testimony from the scientific perspective. Witness reports are considered 'anecdotal evidence' by science, mainly because they are not testable. Yet many scientists are wise enough to understand that anecdotal evidence always precedes and leads to the collection of scientific evidence. In the history of science, scientific evidence has never been collected or even pursued until there has been enough anecdotal or indirect evidence at hand to merit an effort to collect testable evidence. Thus, without the collection and evaluation of **anecdotal evidence or indirect evidence**, *there would be no scientific discoveries at all* (my emphasis). This is the intrinsic relationship between the two types of evidence. *Sighting reports by themselves are not scientific evidence, but they are what lead us to the scientific evidence*" (my emphasis).[74]

The content of the information, however, remains anecdotal (by its nature and design) and phenomenological/experiential. More foundation! The foundation doesn't, however, build the structure itself. It has to be framed up! A research process shift is needed to begin framing up the house. Experimentation can be that "causal" frame.

To prove "Causality," an "a priori" hypothesis needs to be established. Next, an experimental design built around that hypothesis is created. It needs to produce numeric data. That data is next subjected to **descriptive** and **inferential** statistical analysis. Results are reported in a paper format for peer review, replication, or refutation. If desirable or inspirational, that experiment is replicated by other scientists.

Secondly, like this book and any other work or research on the subject of Bigfoot, the classification system suffers from the paradoxical irony of attempting to discuss information related to a factually experiential/phenomenological entity that remains a scientifically unproven species. *This is unavoidable, but nonetheless relevant to note given the primarily* **subjective** *nature of most of the "data" gathered and analyzed to date.*

Along similar lines, the careful and astute reader will note that it is **the report** of the encounter, not **the encounter** itself, which is being rated. This correctly (in my opinion) *separates the* **consensus reality** *of the occurrence from the* **perceptual experience** *and report of the individual(s) having the encounter.* This is an important distinction on a scientific level. A report (using words) represents a symbolic expression of a subjective perceptual (phenomenological) experience; *it is not the actual consensus reality itself!*

"With respect to the pursuit of an unclassified species, the collecting of credible sighting reports is an essential part of the scientific process."[75] *Unfortunately, although an essential part of the scientific process, it appears that (for many if not most) it has become* **equated** *with the end game of the scientific process. Fieldwork on the topic has now been ongoing for decades (indeed generations). Yet, there have been relatively few statistical forays into "scientifically" analyzing the data based on an a priori hypothesis. There have been even fewer experimentally designed ventures that stay the course through data analysis and publication. I would respectfully suggest that the empirical, but nonetheless subjective/phenomenological approach to Sasquatch Fieldwork has sufficiently proven (in and of itself) to be inadequate in its efforts to scientifically* **prove** *the existence of the species (as it should be by BFRO's own words above). Such fieldwork* **has** *established a firm foundation for further scientific exploration. It also seems primarily stuck in its ability to move onward and upward in beginning to build the*

structural framework for the scientific experimentation and statistical
analysis needed to rise to the level of acceptance of the broader scientific
community!

We could and should (at some point) debate some of the possible
reasons for this inertia. There remains a lack of comprehensive
training of thousands of truly astute and dedicated field researchers
in the scientific method, experimental design, and statistical analysis.
There is a lack of funding for the more time-consuming,
mundane/non-sensational, redundant, and tedious experimental
research processes. Commercial ventures and gains (and the literal
and metaphorical territorialities and jealousies associated with the
same) seem to have supplanted scientific priorities. Additionally, the
illusiveness and relative rarity of the species represent another
contributing factor, among others. Such a debate, however, is not the
purpose of this book.

Given the subjective nature of field research experiences, the
classification system itself is understandably non-specific and lacks
operationalized details. For example, "Incidents where a possible
Sasquatch was observed at a great distance or in poor lighting
conditions and incidents in any other circumstance that did not
afford a clear view of the subject are considered Class B reports."[76]

In my opinion, however, to move forward from the subjective
toward "approaching" the objective, further **operationalizing** some
of the verbiage in the classification system and *providing more specific*
examples would be of benefit to the process. What for example constitutes
"a great distance"? Seventy-five feet on a crystal-clear day in a
meadow unobstructed by trees and brush? One hundred and fifty
feet under the same circumstances? Three hundred feet, a quarter
mile, half mile, a mile? There is also a difference between "a great
distance" on a crystal-clear day in a meadow unobstructed by trees or
brush and a "great distance" in a densely foliaged forest shrouded in
mist. This both acknowledges the need for general terminology but
simultaneously highlights the need for more specific examples to
assist in operationalized definitions.

"Poor lighting" could be further **operationalized** by speaking to the number of lumens associated with the lighting. Clearly, the lamp/lighting industry has realized this by including lumen ratings, in addition to their "bright vs dim" light descriptors in their packaging and advertising. Additionally, photographers have long utilized technology to monitor and adjust their cameras for light brightness. "... incidents in any other circumstance that did not afford a clear view of the subject" could be further operationalized through concrete examples of those "circumstances."

Finally, as noted above, the classification system focuses on visual and auditory sensations. Sasquatch encounters are not limited, however, to these two senses. "Dead dog, rotting meat, or sulfur or sewage smells" have repeatedly been reported. The taste of that smell in your mouth or the taste of bile or stomach acid and nausea from fight-flight kicking in is also reported. The feeling of "being watched or observed or stalked" is often reported. "Being zapped" and telepathic and bodily sensations associated with this is a subject unto itself associated with Bigfoot encounters. All of these *are subjective perceptual experiences* (some more reliable than vision and hearing) that should be incorporated into the classification system, in my opinion.

The above review and suggestions are not advanced as a condemnation of the BFRO classification system. I strongly support it. Even if I did not, however, it has proven useful enough to be commonly adopted within the Bigfoot community including groups competing with BFRO for consumer recognition and money. *I am simply suggesting the need to update the contents therein to be more inclusive and specific in definitions.*

Site: Where you pitch your tent or park your trailer. Also known as a "campsite." Not to be confused with the word "cite" meaning to acknowledge or identify the source of a quotation. This latter "cite" is the root word in "citation" as in "I have over three hundred citations in this damn book's citation list."

Woo phenomena: Loosely defined by the current writer's limited experience as spiritual, paranormal, inter-dimensional, extra-terrestrial, or otherwise extraordinary phenomenological experiences, concepts, and theories **correlated** with the Bigfoot phenomena. It includes but is not limited to the belief, theory, and/or experience of Bigfoot entering an area through an inter-dimensional portal. Reports of Bigfoot appearing and disappearing literally in the blink of an eye via inter-dimensional portals exist. Alternate theories include "altering their molecular structure or vibration" and other "cloaking" phenomena. Also included are Bigfoots being observed leaving, entering, and even piloting UFOs, as well as mind speak or other telepathic, paranormal, and mystical capabilities in the Bigfoot species.

Dr. John Stamey (May 15, 2019) wrote a brief, but nonetheless thought-provoking commentary on Woo phenomena (that I will somewhat echo here as it reflects my current perspective on this subject).[77] When I "joined" BFRO to begin going on Bigfoot expeditions, I shared my decision with family friends, and professional colleagues (physicians and psychologists) alike. While I received some accepting and surprised support, the majority of the responses I received ranged from that of incredulity to vain attempts to hide the laughter, as people attempted to "catch themselves" before falling to the floor in hysterical laughter.

Imagine my surprise, when during my second expedition, I heard whispers of "Woo groups" or "believers in Woo phenomena" around the campfire. The general reactions to these groups were not infrequently dissimilar to the "majority of responses" just described above. Ok, let's get this straight. We're criticized and laughed at by the broader scientific community and the general public. (This occurs in the face of undeniable and mounting evidence consistent with a Bigfoot species.) Yet we treat a subgroup of Bigfoot fieldworkers/enthusiasts with the same derision through the similar or arguably same process that is used to criticize and mock us. What is wrong with that picture?

Speaking for myself (I am not a BFRO representative), we can't consider ourselves true "objective" scientists exploring the phenomena and/or species known as Bigfoot, but then eliminate, ignore, or minimize frequent observations associated with the phenomena/species simply because they fall outside of the range of our personal or scientific belief system/framework. Through such incredulity bias, we are then conducting highly biased science!

For many, the Woo phenomenon is simply dismissed as outlier data and disregarded in analyses as if it doesn't exist. If we are being "unbiased and inclusive in our objective or scientific observation," I would suggest we are doing a poor job at that when we ignore the Woo phenomena. Whispers and shouting in the Bigfoot community have contended that traditional/orthodox scientific methods may not be up to the task of proving the existence of Bigfoot. "New or non-traditional techniques may need to be employed!!" While I agree wholeheartedly with that contention, I would argue that given the biases reflected in many fieldworkers' receptivity (or lack thereof) to Woo phenomena, *we may have self-sabotaged traditional science's ability to accomplish the task by limiting the scope of the investigation.*

Don't get me wrong! I appreciate the perspective that: "We can't even scientifically prove Bigfoot's existence as an unidentified terrestrial species, so how can we expect to prove they are inter-dimensional beings?" Nonetheless, given physics theories of parallel universes and black holes, not to mention the US government's recent admission that UFOs (not extraterrestrial spacecraft) do exist, it seems to me we do the species a phenomenal disservice in dismissing Woo phenomena out of hand. Telepathy and ESP do exist in our consensus reality and have been weaponized and exploited by less rigid nations (Russia for example). Our own general disbelief in such phenomena, in my opinion, is as much a cultural phenomenon as a scientific fact. Bias, this culturally based, rears its ugly head.

Don't get me wrong on this point either. I am not suggesting that if during a field expedition, an investigative group or group member reports: "I saw a cloaked Bigfoot exit a square inter-dimensional portal and using mind speak, we discussed shaking hands, which we then did," that it should automatically be entered into the database as a Bigfoot experience. I am arguing, however, that *such a Woo phenomenon should be treated like any other Bigfoot phenomenon that cannot be objectively verified.* Think about it! Phenomenologically experienced (without an observed source) tree knocks and/or distant vocalizations, footprints, wood structures, tree twists, tree snaps or push-downs, landslides, and bluff charges are relatively readily accepted as and attributed to Bigfoot or Bigfoot phenomena. *They are all unseen!!!* Orbs, eye shine, and even zapping due to infrasonic sound waves are less readily accepted. All of these phenomena should be systematically investigated, if possible debunked or confirmed, prior to being accepted or rejected as a Bigfoot experience. *As such, I would argue we need to remain open and receptive to the Woo phenomena if we are to truly and in an unbiased fashion conduct "scientific" Bigfoot research.*

5

HOW TO CONTROL YOUR FIGHT-FLIGHT RESPONSE DURING A BIGFOOT ENCOUNTER

(BE CAREFUL WHAT YOU WISH FOR; YOU JUST MIGHT GET IT!)

The field of counseling psychology is uniquely poised to assist aspiring or well-seasoned (Mmmm, tasty with salt and pepper!) Bigfoot researchers/field workers. Some not only wish to have an up-close encounter with Bigfoot but also remain "calm enough" (or at least not scared shitless) to move forward to further pursue that encounter. *In this chapter, we will review a few techniques to recondition our fight-flight response to accomplish this.* Please be aware, however, that our fight-flight response includes **hard-wired**, species-specific behavior designed to protect us from threat, danger, and physical and emotional harm. There is no thought or reasoning involved. *Many would and should argue that deconditioning or reconditioning this response could be counterproductive and should not be done or done only after considerable consideration!* Forewarned is forearmed!

The reader would do well to review the initial portions of Chapter 8 on the fight-flight response. *Be sure that you understand the role of the sympathetic and parasympathetic divisions of our autonomic nervous system prior to reading this chapter.* A fundamental understanding of the same is essential for appreciating what we are attempting to accomplish in this chapter.

At the **core** of this response is **sympathetic nervous system arousal** in response to a threat or danger, be it real or imagined. **Sympathetic arousal** gets us ready to fight or flee. Our bodies prepare to defend against assault, advance our own assault, or run like hell!

When confronted by a Bigfoot, many people prefer the latter option and run like hell, or at least get out of the area. These are apex creatures in the woodlands and other environments *they dominate*. By accounts, although often avoidant and benign, it would appear they certainly have the physical prowess to totally intimidate, scare, decimate, and destroy the toughest and largest of the human species carrying their wits and a weapon or two. It is a natural and arguably adaptive/self-preserving response to get the hell away from these creatures as quickly as you can if you happen upon one. "Most" people would! "Many" versus "Most" do and are better off for it!

If you are reading this book, however, you may not be "Most" people. Like myself, you may be brave (or foolish) enough to want to experience these creatures in their natural habitat, at close range, in the hope of proving to yourself they exist. You may wish to study and document their behavior to understand their role and function in our world. Alternately, you may be seeking fame and fortune or at least your 15 minutes of fame by exploiting your experience.

There are a variety of other motives to experience these magnificent beasts up close and personal and you would do well to understand your motives for doing so. These will inform to what degree you would or should learn to control or attempt to override your fight-flight response. Do you really want to stand fast and steady in the face of an ear-piercing cry? How about an earth-shattering roar or a guttural, teeth-baring growl that vibrates in your stomach? Are you prepared for a ground-shaking, tree-breaking, bluff charge? How about an accidental close encounter that can literally scare the shit or piss out of you, lock you into a frozen position, and/or immobilize your ability to flee. You may even wish to be brave enough to want to move forward and closer toward the beast (ill-advised in my opinion) or follow its fleeing tracks in pursuit (after changing your underwear)!

The techniques discussed below represent counseling techniques I have used with my pain management and post-traumatic stress disorder patients to learn to counter the fight-flight reactions to physical pain and traumatic stress. *Prior to doing so, however, I ask the reader to place a mark on the Advanced Bigfoot Belief Continuum (BFBC) scale in Chapter 1 to further explore your motives for finding Bigfoot.*

Counter - Conditioning Fight-Flight:

The autonomic nervous system (ANS) along with the hypothalamus (a part of your brain) serve a central role in our body's fight-flight response. Generally speaking, the **sympathetic division** of the ANS is the "Excitatory or Activating" division or the "On switch." The **parasympathetic division** of the ANS is the "Calming" or "Off switch." These are **involuntarily** driven/maintained and as such are on "**automatic pilot.**" We don't have to consciously think to regulate our heart speed, natural respirations or blood flow, hair growth, eye blinks, digestion, urinary retention or expulsion, pupil dilation or constriction, etc. These are "unconsciously" or automatically modulated by the autonomic nervous system. *It is possible to gain voluntary control over these functions, however, by using the relaxation response.*

Relaxation Response allows voluntary modulation of ANS activity

In 1976, Herbert Benson, a Harvard cardiologist discovered that relaxation and meditation techniques could give us voluntary control over the automatic aspects of our autonomic nervous system. He coined the term "The Relaxation Response." "The Relaxation Response is essentially the opposite reaction to the 'fight or flight' response ... The fight-or-flight stress response occurs naturally when we perceive that we are under excessive pressure, and it is designed to protect us from bodily harm. Our **sympathetic nervous system** becomes immediately engaged in creating a number of physiological changes, including increased metabolism, blood pressure, heart and breathing rate, dilation of pupils, and constriction of our blood vessels, all of which work to enable us to fight or flee from a **stressful** or dangerous situation. It is common for individuals experiencing the fight-or-flight response to describe uncomfortable physiological changes like muscle tension, headache, upset stomach, racing heartbeat, and shallow breathing. The fight-or-flight response can become harmful when elicited frequently. When high levels of stress **hormones** are secreted often, they can contribute to a number of stress-related medical conditions such as cardiovascular disease, GI diseases, adrenal fatigue, and more."[1]

There are many methods to elicit relaxation or the "Relaxation Response" including visualization, progressive muscle relaxation, energy healing, acupuncture, massage, breathing techniques, prayer, meditation, tai chi, qi gong, and yoga. True relaxation can also be achieved by removing yourself from everyday thought and by choosing a word, sound, phrase, prayer, or by focusing on your breathing."[2]

A colleague who previewed my manuscript suggested that all of life (not just Bigfoot encounters) is stressful. He added that some people even have "euphoric" encounters with Bigfoot. So where is the value in learning to relax and counter-condition your fight-flight response in that situation? Life is stressful! It gives you positive and negative experiences! Why learn to relax especially if you've had a euphoric Bigfoot encounter?

Some of those points warrant further consideration. It may be that some people have had euphoric Bigfoot encounters! My admittedly limited experience in the field and volumes of anecdotal reports and books suggest these would be the exception, rather than the rule. I personally have never heard of an uplifting euphoria associated with a Bigfoot encounter. Nonetheless, such an encounter may have occurred. I have witnessed a Native American researcher describe seeing a cloaked Bigfoot exit a rectangular inter-dimensional portal, and communicate telepathically with the researcher resulting in them shaking hands. This was undeniably an exciting and positive experience for the researcher and probably most of his investigative group! I have also seen expedition members return to base camp excited and optimistic after hearing tree knocks, vocalizations, or finding footprints. *I've yet to see a positive euphoria.*

On the contrary, I have repeatedly seen experienced seasoned investigators and researchers returning to base camp frightened out of their wits, unable to speak calmly, and looking "white as a ghost." Experienced BFRO Investigators who evaluate eye-witness reports of encounters frequently comment that "you can tell when a witness is genuine in their report when you see the telling of their story rekindle signs of arousal, discomfort, or fight-flight symptoms. These witnesses become 'uneasy,' seem 'on edge,' develop 'goose flesh' and chills, and sometimes get emotional. They may cry or get notably anxious as they relate their tale. They don't want to or are reluctant or uncomfortable with requests to 'return to the scene' of the encounter." *I suspect these and worst visceral experiences are the more common reactions to a Class A, visual, or face-to-face encounter with a Bigfoot.*

Giving my admittedly more experienced colleague the benefit of the doubt, however, let's assume euphoria is a common occurrence. Have you ever seen someone in a euphoric state? My own experiences revolve around witnessing individuals in a drug-induced, delusional, hyper-religious, or manic euphoria. Confused dementia patients can work themselves into a euphoric frenzy. *It's needless to say that heightened rationality, logical reasoning, and a razor-finish objectivity are not the hallmarks of such a level of arousal. As such, using relaxation to calm oneself or reduce euphoria might be of benefit to scientific objectivity! Yes?!*

Let's give my (maybe no longer a) friend in Bigfoot research further "benefit of the doubt." Let's eliminate his contention of euphoria and just focus on the admitted positive and uplifting excitement from a "safe" encounter. Even these are associated with autonomic arousal and stress reactions in our bodies. He was absolutely correct when he stated that "life is stressful!"

Stress reactions occur not only during negative, overwhelming, or traumatizing events, but also during positive, uplifting, and potentially euphoria-producing events!! The sympathetic division of the ANS is activated during these events as well!! Marriage, the birth of a child, buying a house or car, winning the lottery, having a milestone birthday, giving a keynote speech, going on vacation, holidays, getting a loan, passing that big final exam, graduating from high school or college, etc., have all been shown to produce significant stress reactions in our bodies due to autonomic arousal!! *Need I go any further to justify why learning to relax and counter-condition your autonomic nervous system's sympathetic arousal for a positive or negative Bigfoot encounter would be beneficial?* **Relaxation** is the first step in that counter-conditioning process.

Learning to relax is the first step in counter-conditioning or reconditioning your fight-flight response. It is how you gain temporary control over and begin to change the reaction of your autonomic nervous system. There are literally entire books written on how to relax and we do not need, nor is it my goal to review or summarize those. I will teach you four simple relaxation techniques: **Pursed Lip Breathing (PLB)**, **Autogenic Relaxation (AR)**, and **Differential relaxation**. Finally, we will perform what is called **Progressive Relaxation (PR)** but is more accurately characterized as **Progressive Differential Relaxation (PDR)**. The latter stands in contrast to another relaxation technique known as PBR (Pabst Blue Ribbon!).

Pursed Lip Breathing (PLB), as suggested by its name, is breathing slowly and deeply through "pursed lips," ... you know, the shape you formed your lips into when you "smooched" your first sweetheart at the age of eight or nine. If you are "sweet sixteen and never been kissed" or 45-year-old a virgin (or a cloistered monk), you can learn to form pursed lips by remembering the last time you drank sweet tea (for you Southerners) or Soda or Pop (for you Northerners) or a Soft Drink (for you left coast folks) through a straw. The tight little "O" you shaped your lips into is called pursed lips!

During pursed lips breathing (PLB), you take a deep breath in (inhale) through your mouth, nose, or mouth and nose at the same time. Hold that breath to the count of "One" or "Two" and then slowly exhale through pursed lips. If you haven't already tried it, let's do it now! (It's as simple as breathing!)

Take a deep breath in whatever way you naturally deeply inhale. Hold that breath to the count of "One or Two." Now slowly exhale through pursed lips until the air naturally empties out of your lungs without forcing the extra air out (no need to become an airhead!) *Your exhale should be twice as long or longer than your inhale.* Breathe in to the count of two, exhale to the count of four; breathe in to the count of four, exhale to the count of eight; breathe in to the count of eight, exhale to the count of sixteen. I am **not** suggesting doing this in sequence for the time lengths specified above. I am just doing the math for the mathematically challenged! *You simply want your exhale to be at least twice as long as your inhale (obviously, without hyperventilating).* Why is that you might ask?

"*I want our exhale to be twice as long or longer than our inhale because we're learning to relax!*" I would answer. **NOTICE** what happens when you take that deep breath in ... our body and muscles take on tightness and tension. **NOTICE** what happens when we slowly exhale ... *we slowly release or let go of the tension from the muscles of our body!* It's that simple! We are forcing ourselves *to spend twice as much time getting rid of/letting go of tension as we are taking on tension* through PLB. Can you imagine living a life with twice as much comfort and relaxation as you have tension and tightness!? It would be amazing, wouldn't it?

Personally, I start every relaxation induction by prepping my body (preparing or "priming" my autonomic nervous system) by beginning relaxing with three deep pursed lip breaths. You can and may want to, however, simply set a timer for five minutes and simply sit or lay with your arms and legs uncrossed (to avoid reducing blood flow) and do PLB until the alarm sounds.

Why only five minutes? You'll only need to try it once to realize how much of a challenge it is to sit quietly for five minutes and simply focus on breathing deeply via PLB. Your breathing and body slow down, but for the beginning breather (ironic to be a beginner at breathing, isn't it), time, the world, or your mind may not ... slow down. For many of my clients, especially those with perfectionistic, controlling, driven, or obsessive-compulsive tendencies, five minutes of PLB feels like an eternity. It can be a challenge in which case you may need to reduce your alarm or time to three minutes. Can you give yourself three minutes a day to allow your "self" time to relax?

Autogenic Relaxation

Now that you know how to breathe, it is time to **re-learn how to relax.** I say **re-learn** as there was probably a time in your life when you did this effortlessly, without having to think about it or make it a priority or task or something you have to do before you go out looking for Bigfoot. For many of us, that time was our childhood. If you are fortunate, that time was last night when you fell asleep! On to autogenic relaxation!

Autogenic relaxation simply involves *repeating a relaxing phrase, in the present tense, that focuses you on relaxing the major muscle groups in your body.* Because we use our arms and legs on a daily basis, we typically have them under good voluntary control. As such, I prefer to focus on relaxing these. You simply sit or lay in a chair, couch, or recliner with your arms and legs uncrossed. You take three deep pursed lip breaths and then simply repeat a relaxing phrase that focuses your awareness on the muscles of your right arm (4-8 times). Next, the muscles of your left arm (4-8 times). Then the muscles of your right leg (4-8 times), then the muscles of your left leg (4-8 times). Next the muscles of both your arms (2-4 times) and then the muscles of both your legs (2-4 times). One of the phrases I was taught to use and frequently do use when teaching others is: *"Now I'm relaxing my right arm... it's feeling more calm ... and ... feeling more peace."*

But for me, the image of my arms being so relaxed that they flip-flop around like a limp piece of cooked spaghetti also has particular relevance and meaning to me because I LOVE TO EAT (as my waistline suggests). So sometimes I will sit in a chair that allows me to dangle my arms beside the chair and my upper body, take three deep pursued lip breaths and then say out loud: *"Now I'm relaxing my right arm, it's dangling limp and loose like a piece of cooked spaghetti" for 4-8 repetitions on my right arm, 4-8 repetitions on my left arm, 4-8 repetitions on my right leg, 4-8 repetitions on my left leg, 1-3 repetitions on both my arms and 1-3 repetitions on both my legs.*

I attended a workshop put on by a therapist who used this technique with his clients who happened to be hysterical women. He found the phrase: *"Now I am relaxing both my arms, they are dangling limp and loose, flapping like a rag doll."* He felt they could relate to that image much better than other images.

The arms and legs of one of my clients began to feel "warm and heavy" as he began to relax. Thus, we used the phrase: *"Now I am relaxing my right arm, it is getting warm and heavy, feeling more calm and peace."*

I am encouraging you to use any phrase that has a relaxing meaning to you, not just the phrase I used above. *"My arms are dangling limp and loose like two floppy rubber bands."* Evoke and create whatever image or thought or sensation you naturally associate with a calm peaceful state of relaxation, quiet, or tranquility. It doesn't matter as long *as it's said in the present tense* and *focuses you on those major muscle groups* you voluntarily use on a regular basis.

*The phrasing should always be stated in the **present tense** as if it is happening right now or currently. Not "Now I'm going to relax my arms" (future tense) or "Now I've relaxed my arms" (past tense). Only the present tense should be used in the phrasing.*

I have also always focused on the arms and legs. The larger the muscle group and the more we consciously use it in our daily lives, the easier it will typically be to relax. Trying to relax the muscles connecting the vertebral bodies of your back and spine, for example, will not be easy. They are smaller muscles that we are not consciously aware of very frequently as we go through our day.

You should also **not** get rigidly tied to the number of repetitions on each limb. If your arm(s) or leg(s) get relaxed by the second or fourth or sixth repetition, then move on to the next step or targeted limb. Alternatively, if they aren't beginning to relax after the eighth repetition, do more repetitions until they begin to relax. Each person relaxes at a different pace and you'll have to experiment and learn what works best for you. It's not a race or a competition. Let go and let it happen.

I also enjoy *combining the relaxing phrase with deep breathing.* Take a deep breath in and as you slowly exhale, say *"Now I'm relaxing my right arm."* ... Another deep inhale or deep breath in and on the slow exhale ... *"feeling more calm and feeling more peace."* By the end of the relaxation induction, I may only get out *"Now I'm relaxing"* with one exhale. Inhale ... *"My right arm"* on the exhale ... Inhale ... *"Feeling more calm"* on the exhale ... Inhale and ... *"Feeling more peace"* ... on the exhale. Alter the rhythm even slower as you get better at relaxing and controlling your deep breathing.

Practice this at a minimum of three times a week for fifteen to thirty minutes each time. The more you practice, the better you will become at relaxing and the quicker you will relax. You need to learn to achieve a deep state of relaxation and comfort. *The depth of that state will be* **imperative** *for the inoculation process.* In an ideal world, I would ask you to practice this twice a day, every day. Imagine taking 30 minutes to an hour every day to relax yourself. What a great life it could be!

There are times when doing relaxation that people have certain experiences that they wonder about. "What happens if I fall asleep?" You fall asleep and will eventually wake up.

"Is it good or bad if I fall asleep?" Yes! It's good in that it is a sign you are being successful in relaxing. Success! Celebrate it! It's not so good in that when you fall asleep, you fail to complete the entire exercise and don't get as deeply relaxed as if you had stayed awake through the entire exercise. You can practice staying awake by using the word "Now" as your signal to check your awareness. If you notice yourself getting tired or falling asleep, pick up the pace of the relaxation procedure or move parts of your body. You could also practice relaxing on a less comfortable couch or chair.

For our purposes of reconditioning your fight-flight reaction, *you will want to maximize your ability to get and stay deeply relaxed.* The more relaxed the better, as that will make it easier to stay calm and relaxed as you confront increasingly threatening and stressful scenarios of Bigfoot encounters during the inoculation process.

Unless absolutely necessary, do not practice relaxation in bed. Keep your bed available exclusively for falling asleep and having sex. *It is important that you remain awake during relaxation exercises.* As such, if you are practicing relaxing in bed, you are training or conditioning yourself to remain awake in bed. This can lead to increasing difficulties lying down and quickly going to sleep in bed.

If your bed is the only place in the house where you can practice relaxation, you should separate relaxation periods of time from waking up or falling asleep periods of time as much as possible. DO NOT wake up in the morning, lay in bed, and start practicing relaxation. DO wake up in the morning (or whenever you normally awaken), do your waking up routine (getting out of bed to use the toilet, brush your teeth, and other morning hygiene, eat breakfast), and at a later time practice relaxation in bed.

DO NOT lay down at bedtime and do relaxation first and then drift off to sleep. You are teaching yourself to fall asleep when you are relaxing which is counterproductive for our ultimate purposes. DO lay down in your bed, do your relaxation exercise, and then get up. If near bedtime, do your evening routine rituals such as brushing your teeth, washing your face, taking evening medicine, or other evening hygiene or health habits. Then, lay down to sleep.

During relaxation, you may begin to experience certain feelings. Some people's arms and legs begin feeling unusually light, others unusually heavy. Some people's arms get numb and tingly while some completely lose sensation in their limbs. Some people begin to notice certain muscles twitching or moving involuntarily. Other people sometimes find they can't move at all. Your ability to move will gradually return as you ask it to. Some people experience that total body "jerk" like you sometimes do when you are dreaming and begin to fall in the dream or you literally fall out of your bed. For some people, sounds become keener or louder, while for others sounds become duller or they hear less. Some people notice the sound of their breathing or their heart beating or the sound of the blood rushing through their ears.

Sometimes as one group of muscles relax another group tense or go into spasm. Get up and move around if this happens. The idea is to get comfortable. Sometimes you might notice an itchy sensation; scratch it! In rare instances, people begin to visualize, dream, or have visual or auditory hallucinations or waking dreams.

All these phenomena are signs that you are being successful in relaxing. Enjoy! Compliment yourself on your exceptional abilities to relax.

"What if I can't get relaxed?" Keep practicing and experimenting with different phrases, images, or memories of times you did relax. When you first start doing this technique, your mind will drift off to other distractions or thoughts. When you notice this happening, don't beat yourself up or get frustrated. Just neutrally acknowledge the thought ("Oh, I was thinking about my boss or tomorrow's work or the kids" or whatever it might be) and focus back on the relaxation technique. As you get better, you will be distracted fewer times for a shorter duration. Eventually, you'll be able to remain focused on relaxing for longer and longer periods of time without any distractions in your mind or environment intruding.

You should also set yourself up for successful relaxation. Choose a time when you won't be interrupted for twenty to thirty minutes. If you can't find that time once a day, you need to look at the priorities in your life; make yourself a greater one! Unplug the phone, and have your partner manage the kids or the pets. Lock the door so you don't have to answer a door knock. Avoid caffeinated beverages or high-sugar foods for two to three hours before relaxing. They will have a stimulating effect or will contribute to a sugar crash that you will have to fight against to stay awake. Don't exercise right before relaxing. Exercise stimulates sympathetic arousal and will make relaxing more of a challenge.

If you are being treated for Bipolar Disorder or ADHD, understand that these conditions can make relaxing more of a challenge. Irritability, manic energy, or racing thoughts can make relaxing more difficult. Being easily distracted or having nervous energy from hyperactivity can do the same. These conditions do not mean you will not be able to relax. You and these conditions may ultimately benefit from learning to relax. It just may take longer to learn and present unique challenges for success. Do not give up! You can be successful doing it but recognize that hyper-activity, manic energy, racing thoughts, high distractibility, anger, and frustration aren't friends to relaxation. If their onset is recent, you might be better off letting these experiences pass, prior to practicing relaxation.

If you are being treated for an anxiety disorder, unipolar depression, chronic pain, or have an obsessive-compulsive, perfectionistic Type A, "driven" or controlling personality style, you NEED to learn to let go and relax! These exercises can and will benefit you greatly! These medical and psychological conditions and issues, however, might make relaxing somewhat more challenging for you. *You will need to persist in your efforts. Adopt an active pursuit, but paradoxically, a passive and "letting go" approach to the process.* I understand that this advice may seem contradictory in and of itself to you. This highlights a life lesson critical for you to learn, overcome, and master. So, keep the faith and keep up the effort! It will eventually pay off.

Also, if on antidepressants, anti-anxiety, anti-psychotics, or "nerve medicines," please avoid alcohol. Alcohol neutralizes the effectiveness of antidepressant medicines and can make them inactive or inert in your nervous system. It's like you are not taking them at all.

If you take anti-anxiety medicines, sleep medicines, or narcotic pain medicines, alcohol has a geometric multiplying effect (not an additive effect) on the impact of those medicines on your brain and nervous system. This means taking a medicine "like" Valium, Xanax, or Oxycodone and then drinking a single shot, beer, mixed drink, glass of wine, wine cooler, or hot toddy makes the medicine four to six times stronger (not twice as strong) as if you took the medicine normally, without alcohol. Please be safe!

A note to individuals being treated with medicines for

hallucinations or delusions: relaxation can sometimes influence your perception of reality and make reality seem even more tenuous by blurring intra-psychic boundaries. You should not do this type of relaxation. Practice yoga or do some of the other coping techniques I discuss to desensitize your fight-flight response. Avoid this type of relaxation!

A Formal Relaxation Script

Finally, *please see Appendix B*. With the exception of what you see in bold square parenthesis [....] representing instructions on how often to repeat the relaxing phrase, the rest of this text can be read into a tape recorder (dating myself), or some form of a digital recorder at a pace and vocal style that is comfortable for you. You now have your own custom relaxation tape! You can then simply play this guided relaxation induction for an even more passive approach to relaxing. I have done the same in **Appendix C** for the next relaxation technique I will teach you: **Progressive and Progressive Differential Relaxation.**

Performing **progressive relaxation** means beginning by relaxing the muscles in the "top" of your body (scalp, temples, cheeks, jaws, and tongue). Once these have begun to relax, continue "**progressing**" onto the next large group of muscles on your body (your neck and shoulders) until they begin to relax. Next, "**progress**" on to the next large group (shoulders arms, hands, chest, and upper back) and the next (stomach and lower back). **Progress** to the next (buttocks, thighs, knees, and calves) and the next (ankles, feet and toes). Some people prefer an **upward progression** rather than a **downward progression.** Some people divide the muscle groups into smaller clusters or components (scalp, forehead, and cheeks; jaws, neck, and shoulders; arms and hands; chest and upper back; stomach and lower back; buttocks and thighs; calves and ankles; feet and toes) or even smaller groups. Use your imagination!

It can be combined with imagery such as *"a white cleansing relaxing light flowing from the muscles of your scalp into your temple muscles and eye muscles, where that river of relaxation pools into a deeper vortex of calm before gently flowing into the muscles of your cheeks and jaws and chin, slowly drifting into your neck and shoulder muscles where you're just shrugging off the cares of the day and going deeper into a pleasant state of relaxation. Deeper pools of calm and tranquility, peace and quiet slowly drifting down into the muscles of your chest and upper back, just like laying back in your most comfortable chair or couch or bed as the gentle ripples of relaxation roll over your growing raft of peace that continues to drifting down the river of calm into your stomach and lower back bending effortlessly as it flows over a smooth rounded ridge of warm comforting earthy goodness. And as Mother Earth provides goodness for us all, so do the sensations of flexible goodness growth tumbling into the muscles of your hips and buttocks, unwinding into a whirlpool of peace as the warm relaxing sensations of pleasantness and peace are meandering into the muscles of your thighs and hamstrings, and knees and calves. And as this gentle river of cleansing warmth and light are making their way into your feet and toes, you're realizing your connection to yourself and your own powers of relaxation. Wellness and goodness connecting and rooting you to the goodness of mother earth as that meandering stream of relaxing calm is flowing out of your feet and returning to its source from which it blossoms and bubbles to the surface.*" Now use your own words to create your own journey.

In order to revive oneself, you can simply begin to move the muscles in the opposite order in which you relaxed them. Other people prefer to reverse the relaxing flow, and change it into "an invigorating river of energy entering through the soles of the feet and toes into your arch and instep lightly yet briskly floating higher up into the ankles and calves where it's sparkling into greater brightness and light! Alive with energy surging into your thighs and hamstrings, into the muscles of your hips and buttocks! Here a generator fueled by your true personal awakening is multiplying that energy to even higher levels and greater heights into your stomach and lower back, pushing away any remaining darkness as it's soaring up your body into your chest and upper back. Becoming more alive and alert, refreshed and revived, ready to shrug off the rest of the day as it is flowing into your shoulders and arms to embrace the wonderful life and day ahead of you! Refreshed, revived alert, and awake, functioning normally as you're moving toward the peak of your abilities to enjoy the day and life! That sparkling, refreshing, invigorating energy rushing into your neck and head, your jaws, your cheeks, eyes, and scalp, and then lighting the atmosphere like beautiful personal power that you and only you can generate to fuel your life. Completely refreshed and revived, alert and awake; ready to go on with the rest of your day at the peak of your highest level of experience! Again, you only need to use your imagination and by now should get the idea!

Progressive Differential Relaxation Exercise

Differential relaxation simply means tightening a particular muscle group in your body to the count of seven (while keeping the rest of your body relaxed) and then letting go of the tightness in the limb you just tightened. Repeat that on the same muscle group a second time, while keeping the rest of your body relaxed. Move on to the contralateral (opposite side of your body) muscle group if you performed a unilateral (one side of your body) contraction. If you performed a bilateral (both sides) contraction/tightening, then progress to the next lower muscle group on your body and repeat twice. *See Appendix C.*

In **"progressive differential"** *relaxation we follow the same "river of relaxation progression" as above, but add the process of* **tightening** *and* **relaxing** *each muscle group. It can "begin with your scalp and temples, tightening then relaxing them two times. Then progressing down to your eyes and cheeks and tongue and jaw, tightening to the count of seven and then releasing and letting go! Tightening to the count of seven and releasing and letting go. Shifting the focus to the muscles of your neck and shoulders and tightening to the count of seven and letting go, tightening to the count of seven, and letting go. Progressing on down into your arms, chest, and upper back tightening to the count of seven and letting go, tightening to the count of seven, and letting go. On to the stomach and lower back, hips and buttocks, tightening to the count of seven and letting go ... tightening to the count of seven and letting go, etc., etc. to your thighs,* *calves, and ankles, and toes and then reversing for the awakening sequence.*

Again, practice this a minimum of three times a week, preferably once a day five times a week. Even more preferably, twice a day every day to quickly learn to achieve a deep state of relaxation. You will want to enjoy a **deep state of relaxation** to override your sympathetic excitement and arousal. That's the same physiologic arousal that comes with the fight-flight response. *You use that deep relaxation to counter-condition that arousal when confronting Bigfoot (in your mind's eye and maybe in reality).* On to stress inoculation!!!

Stress Inoculation

I have taught you a variety of relaxation strategies and techniques. Prior to having any hopes of counter-conditioning your fight-flight response, you need to master relaxing *and be able to maintain a deep state of relaxation* for 20-30 minutes. *If you cannot accomplish this, you need to go no further in this chapter.*

In order to master relaxing, you should expect to practice a minimum of three times a week for three or four weeks. You get out what you put in. As such, the more frequently you practice the better you will become at deeply relaxing. Eventually, you should be able to get deeply relaxed within five to ten minutes of doing an exercise.

Even a faster-relaxed state can be achieved by getting into a deep state of relaxation and then using a "Key" or "Trigger" word, image, or posture. This is why you see Yogi masters sit with their legs folded together, resting their arms in their lap with their thumb and forefingers (index fingers) touching in a way that forms a circle. By pairing that circular touch of their index finger and thumb repeatedly with a deep state of relaxation, they condition their nervous system to enter that deep state *immediately* through that touch. The implications and risks of being able to do this, especially when in the presence of a Bigfoot should be self-evident, but will be discussed in an advanced techniques chapter. A word, phrase, or image, paired in the same fashion will have the same effect.

An Overview Steps of Stress Inoculation

The steps in a stress inoculation procedure include:

1. Learn to achieve a state of deep muscle relaxation. Done!
2. Develop a stress inoculation hierarchy, ranking the stressors from weakest/least evocative to strongest/most evocative.
3. Starting with the lowest or weakest of the stressful events you want to inoculate yourself against, follow the appropriate steps of the actual inoculation process (to be discussed below) until you can successfully calmly experience the least evocative/weakest stressor during mental rehearsal **three times in a row.**
4. Move on to the next strongest stress provoker and follow the actual inoculation procedure until you can calmly experience it **three consecutive times in a row.**
5. Keep moving up the chain of stress evokers until you are at least tolerating (if not relaxing through) the most stressful provoker **three consecutive times.**
6. Consider "in-vivo" (real life) or "digitally removed in-vivo" (video or movies) exposure experiences along the way when appropriate and possible.

We will now proceed in developing a stress inoculation hierarchy. I will first develop my own Bigfoot Stress Inoculation Hierarchy, as an example. Yours may end up being similar or different from mine. Either way is fine as long as it's tailored to what you think or anticipate will happen.

Developing the Hierarchy

Step One in developing a hierarchy is **brainstorming Bigfoot scenarios** *you have already encountered or anticipate encountering. Brainstorming means you simply write down any possible scenario that pops into your mind but* *in doing so, are uninhibited, uncensored, and uncritical in your thoughts. You are generating ideas **uncritically**.*

I'll make my list: Finding a fresh track. A tree or landslide sounds coming down on top of me and around me, while myself and my expedition partners all scatter, except one who turns to "face the music" (this actually happened). Hearing a Bigfoot roar or howl in the distance (happened). Hearing the very nearby (20 feet away) bushes rustle at night while not seeing what was making the rustling sounds and movement, but then hearing a deep guttural growl emanating from those bushes (happened). A loud breathing, tree moving, and ground shaking bluff charge at close quarters, without an actual sighting. Same bluff charge scenario with an actual sighting. Hearing an unidentified slap/pounding on my trailer exterior (happened and turned out to be a human). Hearing footfalls and Bigfoot-like breathing outside my trailer. Seeing red "eye shine" at a 50-yard distance (happened). Seeing red "eye shine" at a 50-yard distance when by myself. Seeing red eyes shine at a twenty-foot distance. Walking into a habituation site on a moonless night that had activity earlier that night or the previous night. Walking into a habituation site that had activity the previous expedition. Entering habituation site that I had a previous experience in (knock, roar, or growl). Getting nuts or pebbles thrown at my feet when entering an area known for Bigfoot activity; having pebbles and rocks thrown at my body and hitting me. Walking down a "Bigboy" trail at night and hearing Bigfoot breathing. Walking down a "Bigboy" trail as dusk transitioned into the night and seeing unidentified dull white lights blinking (happened). Walking down a "Bigboy" trail and hearing nearby knock, distant knock, nearby growl/howl or whoop. Hearing a distant growl/howl/whoop or knock. Staring a Bigfoot in the face; staring a teeth-bearing, roaring Bigfoot in the face. Returning to a gifting area and finding food taken and a print nearby; returning to a gifting area and finding my gift gone and new gifts left. Being aggressively picked up or drug off by an adult male Bigfoot.

This is my partial list, not a comprehensive review of every person's fears, fantasies, concerns, or wishes for a Bigfoot encounter/experience. It is not meant to be, nor should it be in order to create a stress inoculation hierarchy. It is my own personal list. As such and to avoid writing a thousand-page book entitled *My Fears and Fantasies of a Bigfoot Encounter,* I have truncated my list. In making your own, you should make it as long and detailed as accurately reflecting your fears, fantasies, and true desires for a Bigfoot encounter. If it is your hope to be adopted by a Bigfoot clan or tribe, write it on your list no matter how silly it may seem to yourself or others. **The list has to have true and deep meaning to you, and no one else!**

Now that your list of potential threats or exposure to a Bigfoot experience has been made, the next step in this process requires us to "**rate**" the *emotional or other sensory intensities* of those experiences in order, then "**rank**" them from lowest (weakest reaction, most benign experience) to highest (greatest intensity, most threatening experience). We will do so using a **Subjective Units of Distress Scale (SUDS)** for "ratings."

The SUDS scale was developed by Joseph Wolpe (1969).[3] It has been used in cognitive-behavioral treatments for anxiety disorders (e.g., exposure practices and hierarchy) and for research purposes.[4] Modified for our purposes, it will range from a "**rating**" of the number one (meaning a stress-producing event causes no to very little emotional distress or reaction in your body) to a number of ten (meaning the fight-flight reaction has kicked in and is overwhelming you as a result of the event)! Each experience in your list needs to be assigned a SUDS "**rating.**"

I will do so with mine, below. Also note, however what I might rate as a "10" might be rated as a "5" by someone else. *This is not a pissing or bravery contest and competitiveness should in no way enter the process.* Different people have different levels of fear associated with the same experiences based on their lives. You just need to be honest with yourself and not be concerned about how anyone else might "**rate**" it.

- Finding a fresh Bigfoot track (I close my eyes and **imagine** this happening and rate how much excitement, anxiety, or fear it brings to my body, mind, or awareness): I give it a SUDS *rating* = 1

- A tree or landslide sounds coming down on top of me and around me, while myself and my expedition partners all scatter, except one who turns to "face the music" (I close my eyes, **remembering** this happening and how my heart was beating and my respirations increased afterward): I give it a SUDS *rating* = 5
- Hearing a Bigfoot roar or howl in the distance (I imagine or remember that): SUDS *rating* = 2
- Hearing the very nearby (20 feet away) bushes rustle near me in the night, while not seeing what was making the rustling sounds and movement, but then hearing a deep guttural growl emanating from those bushes: SUDS *rating* = 8
- Loud breathing/tree moving/limb tearing and ground shaking bluff charge at close quarters without actual sighting: SUDS *rating* = 8
- Same bluff charge scenario with actual sighting: SUDS *rating* = 10
- Hearing an unidentified slap/pounding on my on my trailer exterior: SUDS *rating* = 8
- Hearing footfalls and Bigfoot-like breathing outside my trailer: SUDS rating = 9
- Seeing red "eye shine" at a 50-yard distance with a group of 15 other people around me: SUDS *rating* = 2
- Seeing red "eye shine" at a 50-yard distance by myself: SUDS *rating* = 4
- Seeing red eye shine at a twenty-foot distance by myself: SUDS *rating* = 7
- Walking into a habituation site on a moonless night that had activity the previous night with three other people: SUDS *rating* = 3
- Walking into a habituation site that had activity the previous (last year's) expedition: SUDS *rating* = 1

- Entering habituation site that I had a previous experience in (knock, roar, or growl): SUDS *rating* = 3
- Getting nuts or pebbles thrown at my feet when entering an area known for Bigfoot activity: SUDS *rating* = 6
- Having pebbles and rocks thrown at/hitting my body in an area known to have Bigfoot activity: SUDS *rating* = 8
- Walking down a "Bigboy" trail at night and hearing Bigfoot breathing: SUDS *rating* = 7
- Walking down a "Bigboy" trail at dusk into the night and seeing unidentified dull white lights blinking throughout the woods: SUDS *rating* = 3
- Walking down a "Bigboy" trail and hearing a distant knock: SUDS *rating* = 5
- Walking down a "Bigboy" trail and hearing a nearby knock: SUDS *rating* = 7
- Walking down a "Bigboy" trail and hearing a nearby growl: SUDS *rating* = 8
- Walking down a "Bigboy" trail and hearing a nearby howl: SUDS *rating* = 9
- Walking down a "Bigboy" trail and hearing nearby whoop: SUDS *rating* = 7
- Staring a Bigfoot in the face: SUDS *rating* = 9.
- Staring a teeth-bearing/roaring Bigfoot in the face: SUDS *rating* =10
- Returning to a gifting area and finding food taken and a print nearby: SUDS *rating* = 5.
- Returning to a gifting area and finding my gift gone and new gifts left: SUDS *rating* = 5
- Being aggressively picked up or drug off by an adult male Bigfoot: SUDS *rating* = 10

After "**rating**" each with SUDS, the next step is to "**rank**" them from lowest to highest. There are a few considerations to review before you do.

You'll want to ensure that you not only have high (8-10) and moderate (4-7) SUDS *ratings* but that your scenarios contain plenty of low (1-3) SUDS *ratings*. "Why do I need to have those?" you may ask, "I can already tolerate my fight-flight response in scenarios that mild, why do I need to include them in my hierarchy?" Good for you, but we're hoping to go beyond a minimal level of tolerance with these scenarios and want to learn to exercise a modicum of true control or "mastery" over these. Therefore, the lower SUDS *ratings* are important to use for practice. Let's explore this further.

Controlling ourselves and our own "hard-wired" bodily functions can be, at times, a challenge. Indeed, when discussing the **autonomic nervous system's** role in controlling fight-flight responses, they were traditionally considered beyond or out of our control **until** the relaxation response was discovered. *As such, stress inoculation is a technique combining thoughts, images, and feelings with a deep state of relaxation to recondition our automatic fight-flight responses by bringing them under our* **voluntary control.**

While this is an undeniably effective technique for most people in many or most scenarios, it ultimately has its limits in the physiology of our body. That is to say that everyone (with perhaps the exception of the true sociopathic or psychopathic killers or expert Yogis) will eventually encounter a scenario in which they either lose control of or cannot control their fight–flight responses. As such, *we need to be able to achieve a* **very deep** *state of relaxation* and become an expert at reconditioning even the mildest or minor of physiological changes. Thus, our inoculation hierarchy needs to include a substantial number of low evocative scenarios. This serves multiple purposes.

It gets us in touch with the milder and more subtle aspects of these reactions. Panic attacks by definition "occur out of the blue" while anxiety attacks are triggered by an external stimulus. The physiological changes associated with them often slowly build within our nervous system, below our threshold of awareness. We need to become increasingly aware of these subtle but very real changes and use that awareness to begin to counteract them early on in the process. Our weaker, less evocative scenarios and even pleasant scenarios that give us pleasure or excitement of a positive sort all begin to educate us. *They make us more aware of those subtle signals. Forewarned is forearmed!*

Additionally, like relaxation, stress inoculation is a skill. Any skill requires skill building. When training for a marathon race, you can't immediately go out and run twenty-three miles and expect a successful experience. You need to gradually train at shorter distances in a systematic fashion to gradually build your physical tolerance and endurance limits up to the longer distances required of a marathon. Small successive approximations of your ultimate goal allow you to properly condition your body and nervous system. They also allow you to have successes whereas failure and discouragement would most certainly follow if you immediately "go for broke." *Going for broke is the most certain way to get broken. This is even truer to reconditioning the fight-flight response.*

If you start with your most intense scenarios/experiences, you will most certainly not have gained the required **voluntary control** over your autonomic nervous system. You will be unable to stay relaxed in those intense scenarios; instead experiencing panic and other fight-flight reactions. You will end up conditioning yourself to greater rather than lesser levels of fight-flight reactions.

By starting with lower evocative stimuli, you set yourself up for successfully controlling those automatic reactions. This keeps the stress reaction under the control of deep relaxation. It also produces fertile soil for an emotional substrate upon which to sow the seeds of calmness and control in the face of minor arousal.

Stress inoculation uses successive approximations of high and higher levels of stress scenarios leading to physical reactions you'll want to bring under control. If you do not give yourself success experiences over mild or minor ones, you will most certainly fail at moderate or high ones. You need to learn to crawl before you can stand up. You need to learn to stand up before you can walk. You need to learn to walk before you can run. You need successive approximations of a skill in order to master that skill and become an expert in that skill. Thus, you need low-level evocative scenarios to create those successes upon which to build greater levels of autonomic control that will be needed for more intense scenarios.

If you have been detailed enough in generating scenarios, the odds are very good you will have more than one scenario at most SUDS levels. For example, examining my SUDS *ratings* reveals I have given two scenarios with SUDS *ratings* of "1." I have two scenarios with SUDS *ratings* of "2," and three scenarios with SUDS *ratings* of "3." There is one scenario with a SUDS *rating* of "4;" and four scenarios with SUDS *ratings* of "5;" etc., etc. *In order to rank our scenarios from weakest/lowest/least evocative to strongest/ highest/most evocative we now need to "break the ties" at each SUDS level.*

In order to break the tie or split those fine hairs between multiple scenarios with the same SUDS ratings, we simply need to focus more closely on each scenario and determine which is the least or most evocative. For example, at the SUDS level of "1," I have two scenarios: Finding a fresh Bigfoot track (SUDS *rating* = 1); Walking into a habituation site that had activity in the previous expedition (SUDS *rating* = 1). For me, the weaker/less evocative of these two scenarios is: Walking into a habituation site that had activity in the previous expedition. As such, my personal Bigfoot inoculation hierarchy begins as follows.

John S. Baranchok's Bigfoot Stress Inoculation Hierarchy

1. Walking into a habituation site that had activity the previous (last year's) expedition: (SUDS *rating* = 1).
2. Finding a fresh Bigfoot track: (SUDS *rating* = 1).

Note I keep the original SUDS rating attached to the scenario. This will become relevant a little later.

Next, we need to break the tie for those with SUDS *ratings* of "2:" Seeing red "eye shine" at a 50-yard distance with a group of 15 other people around me: (SUDS *rating* = 2); Hearing a roar or howl in the distance (SUDS *rating* = 2). For me despite the adage "there is comfort in numbers," the "roar or howl" scenario is the weaker of the two. *My rankings* now become:

John S. Baranchok's Bigfoot Stress Inoculation Hierarchy

1. Walking into a habituation site that had activity the previous (last year's) expedition: (SUDS *rating* = 1).
2. Finding a fresh Bigfoot track: (SUDS *rating* = 1).
3. Hearing a Bigfoot roar or howl in the distance: (SUDS *rating* = 2).
4. Seeing red "eye shine" at a 50-yard distance with a group of 15 other people around me: (SUDS *rating* = 2).

Next, we need to split some finer hairs.

Ranking SUDS: At this point (if not earlier), the process becomes tedious and redundant. It nonetheless remains of the utmost importance to complete if you wish to successfully recondition your fight-flight response.

1. You need to break ties or split hairs between multiple scenarios with the same SUDS **ratings** to appropriately **rank** them.
2. You then perform a "reality check" of those **ratings** and **rankings** and rearrange them accordingly if they don't seem to fit currently.
3. Finally, you further refine **rankings** in a more graduated fashion. It is only **then** that you are ready to proceed with actually following the core steps of the Stress Inoculation process.

Rather than bore disinterested readers further with those redundant processes and details in the main body of this book, I have appended these under Appendix D. IF YOU ARE AN INTERESTED READER WHO HOPES TO PERFORM THIS PROCEDURE, HOWEVER, PLEASE DO NOT SKIP OVER OR IGNORE THIS APPENDIX. TO DO SO WILL MOST CERTAINLY

COMPLICATE YOUR STRESS INOCULATION PROCESS AND MAY LEAD TO THE FAILURE OF IT.

So you're picking up from Appendix D?: Yes!! After completing this process, my original 27 ranked scenarios now include 32 ranked scenarios.

John S. Baranchok Bigfoot Stress Inoculation Hierarchy

1. Walking into a habituation site that had activity the previous (last year's) expedition: (SUDS *rating* = 1).
2. Walking down a "Bigboy" trail in the daylight and not having any Bigfoot activity experience during that walk: (SUDS *rating* = 1).
3. Hearing a Bigfoot roar or howl in the distance: (SUDS *rating* = 1).
4. Entering habituation site that I had a previous experience in (knock, roar, or growl): (SUDS *rating* = 2).
5. Walking down a "Bigboy" trail at night with no Bigfoot experience: (SUDS *rating* =2).
6. Walking down a "Bigboy" trail during the day and hearing a distant knock: (SUDS *rating* = 2).
7. Walking into a habituation site on a moonless night that had activity the previous night with three other people: (SUDS *rating* = 2).
8. Finding a fresh Bigfoot track: (SUDS *rating* = 3).
9. Returning to a gifting area and finding food taken and a footprint nearby: (SUDS *rating* = 3).
10. Returning to a gifting area and finding my gift gone and new gifts left: (SUDS *rating* = 4).
11. Walking down a "Bigboy" trail at dusk into the night and seeing an unidentified dull white light blinking throughout the woods: (SUDS *rating* = 4).
12. Walking down a "Bigboy" trail during the day and hearing nearby whoop: (SUDS *rating* = 5).

13. Walking down a "Bigboy" trail during the day and hearing a nearby howl: (SUDS *rating* =5).

14. Walking down a "Bigboy" trail during the night and hearing a nearby knock: (SUDS *rating* = 5).

15. Seeing red "eye shine" at a 50-yard distance with a group of 15 other people around me: (SUDS *rating* = 6).

16. Seeing red "eye shine" at a 50-yard distance by myself: (SUDS *rating* = 6.)

17. Walking down a "Bigboy trail and hearing a nearby howl: (SUDS

18. *rating* = 6).

19. Seeing red eye shine at a twenty-foot distance by myself: (SUDS *rating* = 7).

20. A tree or landslide sounds coming down on top of me and around me while myself and my expedition partners all scatter, except one who turns to "face the music: (SUDS *rating* = 7).

21. Hearing the very nearby (20 feet away) bushes rustle near me in the night, while not seeing what was making the rustling sounds and movement but then hearing a deep guttural growl emanating from those bushes: (SUDS *rating* = 8).

22. Getting nuts or pebbles thrown at my feet when entering an area known for Bigfoot activity: (SUDS *rating* = 8).

23. Walking down a "Bigboy" trail during the day and hearing Bigfoot breathing: (SUDS *rating* = 8).

24. Walking down a "Bigboy" trail at night and hearing Bigfoot breathing: (SUDS *rating* = 9).

25. Walking down a "Bigboy" trail during the day and hearing a nearby growl: (SUDS *rating* = 9).

26. Walking down a "Bigboy" trail during the night and hearing a nearby growl: (SUDS *rating* = 9).

27. Having pebbles and rocks being thrown at/hitting my body in an area known to have Bigfoot activity: (SUDS *rating* = 9).

28. Hearing an unidentified slap/pounding on my trailer exterior: (SUDS

29. *rating* = 9).

30. Loud breathing/tree moving/limb tearing and ground shaking bluff charge at close quarters without actual sighting: (SUDS *rating* = 9).

31. Hearing footfalls and Bigfoot-like breathing outside my trailer: (SUDS

32. *rating* = 10).

33. Same bluff charge scenario with actual sighting: (SUDS *rating* = 10).

34. Staring a teeth-bearing/roaring Bigfoot in the face: (SUDS *rating* =10).

35. Being aggressively picked up or drug off by an adult male Bigfoot: (SUDS *rating* = 10).

We're finally ready to proceed with the actual process of Stress Inoculation. If you followed all of my instructions (including those Appended), it should be a fruitful and rewarding process for you! If you have not meticulously followed my instructions and you hope to maximally benefit from this process, go back to square one, do not pass "Go" and follow those instructions meticulously. You will then pass "Go" and be rewarded!

The Stress Inoculation Process: Step by step.

1. Physically (in reality) go to the place where you've been practicing your relaxation successfully. Get into your most comfortable position to relax, take your three deep breaths, and go through your relaxation exercise until you are deeply relaxed.

2. Once deeply relaxed, begin to imagine, or otherwise create a mental movie or images or in some other fashion daydream or experience your weakest/least evocative

Bigfoot scenario ("*Ranking*" Number One) in your mind and/or body.

3. Allow this scenario to naturally unfold **until** you **just begin** to notice a **lessening** of your relaxed state (the scenario beginning to make you tense or anxious, or fearful).

4. **STOP** the mental movie, scenario, or experience immediately upon noticing that impact on your relaxation, and put it out of your mind by *focusing on and performing your relaxation exercise.*

5. *Re-engage in the relaxation exercise* and continue to do the exercise until you calm down or relax back down to that deep state of relaxation you were in **BEFORE** the scenario changed that feeling of calm and relaxation.

6. *Once calm and relaxed again,* **START** the scenario, mental movie, images, or experience **WHERE YOU LEFT OFF WHEN IT AFFECTED YOUR RELAXED STATE.** It is very critical that you *start the scenario where you left off when it affects your relaxed state.* **Do not** start all the way at the beginning or pick up the scenario further into the imagined future. *Start where you left off.*

7. *Starting where you left off,* run the mental movie, scenario, or imaginary experience forward until it either once again has a **lessening effect** on your relaxation or you run it to its natural conclusion.

8. If *it affects your relaxation again,* **STOP** the mental movie or imaginary scenario and focus back on performing your relaxation exercise.

9. *Re-engage in the relaxation exercise* and continue to do the exercise until you calm or relax back down to that deep state of relaxation you were in **BEFORE** the scenario changed that feeling of calm and relaxation the second time.

10. *Once calm and relaxed again,* **START** the scenario, mental movie, images, or experience *WHERE YOU LEFT OFF*

WHEN IT AFFECTED YOUR RELAXED STATE THE **SECOND TIME.** It is very critical that you start the *scenario where you left off* when it affected your relaxed state the **second time,** and not start all the way at the beginning. You **don't** start where you left off the first time you stopped or pick up the scenario. You **don't** pick up your scenario further into the imagined future. *Start where you left off the second time!*

11. *Rinse and repeat!* Starting where you left off, run the mental movie, scenario, or imaginary experience forward until it either once again affects your relaxation or you run it to its natural conclusion for a third or fourth or fifth or fifteenth time.

12. *Continue this process* until you can run the mental movie or imaginary scenarios from beginning to end and stay completely and deeply relaxed throughout its entirety one time.

13. *Continue to do this process* until you can stay completely relaxed through the scenario **three consecutive times** (three times in a row).

14. *Once you can stay relaxed three times in a row with your first* **"ranking,"** *move on to your second and repeat the procedure. Once you can stay relaxed* **three consecutive times** *through your second "ranking" move on to your third. Once you can stay relaxed through your third "ranking," move on to your fourth, etc., etc.*

Some general considerations warrant further comment. I cannot overstate the importance first and foremost of taking the time to ensure that you can get deeply relaxed using the relaxation techniques taught here or some other form of relaxation **before** *starting the inoculation process. Without deep relaxation as your basic foundation, the rest of the process will be fruitless and a waste of time. Take as much time as you need to master relaxation!!!*

If you hope to recondition your fight-flight response to your most evocative/strongest Bigfoot scenarios, it is **extremely** important to take your time and perform your low to moderate-ranking inoculations properly. *If you move ahead within a particular scenario by not restarting the mental movie where you left off, you will reduce the ultimate effectiveness of the entire process.*

Always pick up the scenario where you left off when it affected your relaxation. Some therapists would argue rather than picking up where you left off when the scenario "just begins" to affect your relaxation, you should restart the scenario at a point JUST BEFORE it started to affect your relaxation. For some people, this would simply represent a fine-tuning measure. For others, it may be necessary.

*You will also reduce the effectiveness of the inoculation process if you skip over rankings to move through the hierarchy quickly. You are counter-conditioning or reconditioning a "hard-wired," species-specific, atavistic, instinctual response in your nervous system. It's a physical thing! Literally a "mind over matter" thing! Not an easy thing to achieve as it's "hard-wired" to occur automatically, without the need to think about it. You are also using "**conscious**" thought to change that **automatic** or "**unconscious**" impulse or reaction. You are learning to override thousands of years of learning and conditioning of the human nervous system. You need to do it properly and not rush it!*

You should also note that ultimately most people will reach a point where they can't remain completely calm in an evocative "situation." That situation may be some of your more intense Bigfoot scenarios or it may be another situation in your daily life. The fight-flight response is an adaptive survival mechanism built into our nervous system. It serves a very important and very necessary function to our existence: SURVIVAL!! As such it is arguably necessary not to even bother to try to counter-condition or recondition this response to all situations in your life, be they social, work-related, or Bigfoot-related. We need to be able to "trust our instincts" to tell us when it's time to fight or flee, move forward or retreat, stand tall, defiant, and aggressive, or be timid, meek, withdraw, and hide. "Machismo" can get your ass kicked or get you killed! That's not always the appropriate or most adaptive approach!!

The landslide scenario stands as a good illustration of the

issue/debate on the value of doing such counter-conditioning. I was in a group of four expedition partners when we had what sounded like a landslide come down around us from about a 100-yard span of the ridge of the mountain above us. Three of us blindly scattered like cockroaches when the bright lights were thrown on in a dark kitchen. One of our group, who I subsequently nicknamed "Braveheart," simply turned, and faced up-hill. He reached for his "holstered" knife while looking to see who or what was coming down on top of us.

Although awesome to witness, it is truly debatable which these responses were most adaptive and appropriate in that scenario: fleeing or preparing to fight. You see the rest of that story reveals that the following day, a Bigfoot track was cast in the area of the road where the event happened. Additionally, a partial juvenile print was found near the adult print that was cast. Further exploration revealed another un-castable adult print on the precipice of the road, opposite the side of the upward slope where the event happened. Also discovered was what appeared to be a fresh tree bark tear 12-15 feet up on the tree next to that print. Further examination of that location revealed a level plateau on the down-slope (below the road edge) and what appeared to be multiple juvenile Bigfoot prints. *Could the "landslide" have been a Bigfoot charge by one or multiple clan members?*

The beginning of that story might be helpful to the reader. As the four of us hiked (*well, three hiked and I crawled*) up the forest road, the forest was dead silent of any animal life. No tree frogs, squirrels, or chipmunks scurrying in the leaves or underbrush. Just the sound of the trees blowing in the breeze and water from springs and rain run-off trickling. Otherwise, silence. I queried my more experienced colleagues if this was the silence I so often had heard about that signaled the presence of a Bigfoot in the area. The response suggested usually our sense of being watched/observed or followed/stalked would typically be associated with such silence when a Bigfoot was in the area.

We continued our hike and encountered no wildlife activity. Another group, however, approaching the same area from a different direction (behind and downhill from where we started our trek) spooked turkey on the ground and roosted in the trees. They also saw deer in the woods and hogs on the road with FLIR.

Upon returning down the way we came, I began to discuss how stage hypnotists use hypnotic suggestions. This caused George Wriggly, the person in the lead of our single-file line, to stop in his tracks, spin on his heel, and walk about five feet back to me to comment on how such phenomena might be involved in influencing Bigfoot experience stories told by multiple members of the same group. He got out the "J" consonant sound of my name when we all experienced an earth-quaking thud of what sounded to be a large tree falling (or being pushed) over, hitting the ground, and then rolling downhill, occasionally becoming airborne, before hitting the ground and tumbling some more. *George had an audio recorder running.* An audio recording of the event timed the tumbling landslide sounds as lasting 14 seconds. *The event was followed by particles of dust floating down on top of us from above. The air became replete with the smell of loam (musty-moist dirt). Despite the landslide sound, not a single pebble, rock, stone, log, tree branch, or other large debris could be detected as having recently fallen onto the road! Given the rain drainage and root rot, could a tree have naturally toppled? Could the rain drainage have produced a natural landslide or mudslide? Could a Bigfoot have pushed a tree and triggered a landslide? Could we have experienced a bluff charge from single or multiple members of the species?*

Our approximate twenty minutes of nighttime debunking efforts revealed no conclusive evidence and we began continuing our walk down the way we came. Observers below radioed up to us and asked if we were descending the forest road or the steep path we would take off the forest road to return to the cabin below. We responded we were still on the forest road. End of transmission. As we began to descend the steep slope/path towards the cabin, observers below once again radioed asking where we were in our descent. "On the downward steep path. Why do you keep asking?" "We're seeing red lights behind you" was the reply. This time we all pivoted on our heels and looked up the slope, our own red lights illuminating absolutely nothing. When we got down to the cabin, for the next 30 minutes we sat and watched "single red lights" appear and disappear in the woods.

Who was right and who was wrong in our initial response to the landslide sounds? None of us were right or wrong!!! We just "were." *Our instinctual and automatic, fight-flight response kicked in. There was no initial thought processing beyond that instinctual reaction.* Yes, perception, thinking, and reasoning entered into it seconds after that reaction and for those resulting actions, we could be judged right or wrong. Before that, however, it was *an automatic instinctual reaction, NOT a logical cognitive thinking process or decision. That is an important factor to understand.*

The "begged question" remains. *Were those reactions appropriate?* Fleeing is arguably an adaptive fight-flight reaction to the "landslide" situation in that scenario. So is turning to fight (or at least look).

Most of us (Mark Ogilbee, George Wiggly, and myself) reacted by fleeing to get out of the way of what sounded like trees and rocks tumbling down the hill above us and about to land on top of us. Fleeing seemed adaptive. Should the worst have happened and a landslide fell upon us it may have not been appropriate as *we most certainly hadn't fled far enough.* Barring a Glissando Illusion, the sheer breadth of the disturbance made it such that if the "landslide" had reached our location, our brief scurry would have most likely got us killed or injured. If the alternate worst had happened and we were being charged by a group or even a single Bigfoot with malintent, we certainly didn't flee far or fast enough!

Was Braveheart's (Dan Kegly) fight reaction more adaptive? Maybe, maybe not. If the worst of a true landslide had happened, he might have been in a better position to get to safety (dodge debris) given he was looking uphill rather than turning his back to the threat while running away from it. On the other hand, not running may have put him at greater risk of injury or death in the Bigfoot scenario.

If the mal-intended Bigfoot attack scenario had been realized and he turned to fight it, it would have most certainly been a losing proposition for him (adaptive, but not appropriate), while we ran even further to safety. *It just goes to show you that you don't have to be the fastest of the group running away from an assaultive Bigfoot chasing you. You just got to make sure you're not the slowest!* (What good friends, huh?)

In further discussing this scenario with Braveheart (months after the dust had settled), he commented that for him there **was** a cognitive/thinking process involved in his fight-flight reaction: curiosity. Characterizing it as a hierarchical level of reasoning/thinking, it inserted or created another layer of a behavioral response as part of his fight-flight reaction!

For me, this illustrates that there was a time, an event, or events in his life where he had already consciously or unconsciously reprogrammed his fight-flight response! This both underscores the potential power of the techniques I am teaching here, as well as the potential risks!

Returning to my point on the value (or lack thereof) in counter- or reconditioning our fight-flight response in our landslide scenario: I'm not sure there is much to debate, at least based on our responses above. *Although neither of the worst scenarios unfolded, we probably would have been screwed either way! Be careful what you ask for, you just might get it!*

The fight-flight response is an atavistic/species-specific reaction in humans and other species. It is purported to enhance the likelihood of survival of the species. *Our reactions highlight the limits of that reaction on various levels and beg the question if we would have been better or worse off if we had reconditioned that response for this scenario.* If we had counter-conditioned ourselves to stand relaxed and flaccid like a piece of cooked spaghetti, any outcome would most likely have been disastrous had the worst happened. In fact, there is a curvilinear relationship between arousal and performance.

Known as the Yerkes–Dodson law (1908) it reflects *the "empirical relationship between arousal and performance.*[5] It was originally developed by psychologists Robert M. Yerkes and John Dillingham Dodson in 1908. *The law dictates that performance increases with physiological or mental arousal, but only up to a point* (my emphasis).[6]

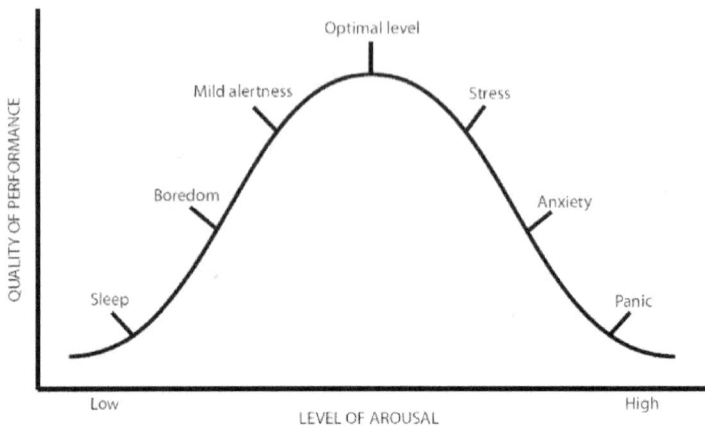

Source: Arousal Graph Figure.[7]

I believe most reading this book at some point in their lives had to study for a test. If your arousal level was very low, you probably didn't get much studying done as you were "**sleeping**." Test looming, pull yourself out of a state of "**boredom**" and become "**mildly alert**" that you need to study. As the final test deadline nears, hopefully, arousal increases, and motivation to study kicks in. On test day, you hopefully reach your "**optimal**" level of arousal. You're motivated to study and can remain optimally focused and absorb the material you need to learn. You'll likely get a good grade.

If you procrastinate studying too long, you don't give yourself enough time to absorb all the material. You might begin to feel "**stressed**," then "**anxious**" and possibly even "**panicky**" and your performance on the test will decline.

Although it will vary slightly depending on the task, this relationship not only applies to cognitive activity but to physical activity (sports and exercise) and emotional control/performance. Athletes try to "**peak**" game day. *At this point, I shouldn't need to point out that also applies to optimizing your fight-flight response and other reactions to a Bigfoot experience.*

Returning to my real-life example of the landslide sounds, I was actually cognitively focused on responding to the question posed:

"How might hypnotic suggestion apply to Bigfoot scenarios?" that came from the lead hiker at the very instant we heard the tree fall and milliseconds before the tumbling sound started. Although fully awake and alert, my arousal was engaged in a cognitive task that initially occupied my focus and subsequent reaction to the "tree fall." I was physically and emotionally only at a **mild level of alertness** which created a delayed and incomplete fight-flight physical reaction. A similar response was evidenced by the hike leader who was talking to me. We ultimately didn't scurry far enough had the worst happened. Those in the rear of our line hadn't gotten cognitively "caught up" in the conversation and displayed a stronger, quicker, and more immediate fight-flight reaction.

Braveheart was in the middle of the line when his fight-flight reaction put him in fight mode. He pivoted on his heel facing uphill as he simultaneously reached for his military capo blade and turned as white as a ghost. His eyelids were wide agape I assure you! Had we counter-conditioned our fight-flight reactions to a completely low level of arousal and the worst occurred, he and we wouldn't have stood a chance!

This suggests that not all scenarios are best reconditioned to the point of calm relaxation and inactivity in the face of threat. On the other hand, some counter-conditioning to avoid being "scared stiff" or "scared shitless" likely would have been adaptive and allowed us freedom of movement for avoidance and/or fighting.

So, there are reasons NOT to recondition this response, as well as reasons to recondition our fight-flight response in this and similar scenarios. Yerkes-Dodson's Law tells us there IS an optimal level of arousal for these scenarios which will vary from person to person. As such, if we recondition or counter-condition the fight-flight response, we need to be sure to insert other adaptive responses/reactions or behaviors, while maintaining some level of arousal as part of that reconditioning. This should serve to keep us safe. This can be done using guided imagery. But that is another chapter; the next chapter.

6

PROGRAMMING NECESSARY LEVELS OF AROUSAL AND APPROPRIATE BEHAVIORAL RESPONSES FOR A BIGFOOT ENCOUNTER

In the above title, programming necessary levels of arousal and appropriate behavioral responses are delineated as separate procedures or processes; they are in fact the same issue. They are also accomplished with the same broad psychological process/procedure/technique: **Guided Imagery**. *Guided imagery represents a variety of processes/procedures in which mental rehearsal of the desired outcome or behavior is practiced, often in a relaxed state, sometimes "under self-hypnosis" and other times simply in the imagination of your mind.* I will describe examples of all three of these processes/procedures so that the reader might determine and choose to utilize their own preference.

Develop "Appropriate Response" Guided Imagery Scenarios

We'll start just by getting into a deeply relaxed state just like you learned to do in Chapter Five. Do some deep breathing followed by autogenic relaxation or progressive relaxation. Once you are in a deeply relaxed state, use your imagination to create a scenario or mental movie or other mental story. A story of how you will "**ideally react**" (**Appendix E**) or respond in any of the various Bigfoot encounters you identified as you developed your stress inoculation hierarchy (**Appendix D**).

A few notes. What is an "appropriate" response is relative. In all likelihood what constitutes an appropriate response or reaction to this or any situation you encounter related to Bigfoot will largely be driven or dictated by your belief system associated with the phenomenon or species. If you believe it is an unidentified primate animal species representing an apex predator in the woods, you will likely react in a cautious or avoidant fashion. If you similarly believe it is a terrestrial species, but believe it is a protector of the forest and all those dwelling therein, you may react in a somewhat less anxious or avoidant fashion and remain in its midst longer and with less protective distance between you. If you believe it is a Nephilim demon, you may pray to God and recite protective biblical passages as you retreat. If you believe they are an inter- or intra-dimensional being or otherwise benign spiritual entity, you might visualize walking up and embracing or otherwise interacting with it. You must make your own script and visualization choices here, not adopt mine.

Nonetheless, based on my own biases, I feel the need to give **some general guidance** here. It is not my intention to encourage you to remain in place or try and make friends with Bigfoot during the throes of a bluff charge. If they are ape-like creatures, a bluff charge is a signal that the animal is upset, stressed, and likely feeling threatened personally, socially, or territorially. It wants you out of the area. My advice is to comply! In doing so, however, you want to react and move in a slow, controlled, and calm fashion. *Under no circumstances should you turn your back and run.* Many predators have a "chase instinct." Even after they stop their aggressive charge or attack, seeing their prey running will trigger or "throw a switch" to give chase in order to take their prey down. This is why I advise that you should remain stationary and calm when initially facing the source of the charge, and then slowly back out while continuing to face the direction from which the charge is coming. *Do not turn your back and run. Easier said than done!* Odds are you will be less likely to be successful in your retreat if you do.

My frank advice is to begin to do that (a controlled retreat) immediately, rather than stand in the open, stationary. If you feel the need to protect yourself, get a tree or a rock between you and the source of the sound. I'd advise against setting up your camp there. This represents a temporary protective step or measure and should not be thought of as a defensive position from which to mount an offensive attack or counterattack. You are just buying yourself some time and protection by putting distance between you and the source and then using it to slowly and safely retreat.

Regarding counterattack in any scenario, a friend's experience in these matters warrants reflection. When walking down a path in an attempt to locate the source of Bigfoot activity (howls) from the previous night, a group of four (two experienced investigators and two "rookies"' aka "newbie" researchers) initially encountered small nuts being thrown (from the right side of the path) in their general direction, landing harmlessly some distance from them. The group stopped and made verbal pleas for the creatures to show themselves or in some other way make themselves more visually obvious, clearly evident, or known. No response.

As they proceeded further down the path, the nuts next began to hit much closer to their location and occasionally very near their feet or legs. Once again verbal please and provocations failed to produce any audible or visual Bigfoot responses.

As they proceeded further, the nuts and small pebbles began to come at them with a higher velocity and hit them with some force. They decided to counterattack by throwing things back. Wrong decision!

One of the rookie group members developed a nosebleed and a little further down the path, lost sensation and some movement of his arm, which had all the hairs on it standing at attention. The two newest researchers "stayed put" while the experienced investigators moved on.

One of them felt "punched in the stomach so hard it felt like the fist went up under my ribs and I projectile vomited." The other proceeded further and was hit in the sternum "with what felt like a bat being swung at my chest so hard it knocked me back onto the ground. Then all hell broke loose ...and we started getting pelted by stones and nuts from all sides at the same time." *Counterattacks are ill-advised in my opinion. Avoidance would be the better wisdom and valor to follow.*

If you smell the animal or in some other way become aware of its presence before it becomes aware of yours, remain calm and still. Slowly move to concealment a safe distance from the source or strongest location of the odor. If you are an experienced, adventurous, and brave researcher, you might wish to linger a while to search out the source of the smell. Many (myself included) would argue against remaining there for any length of time. *In my opinion, the best way to survive a charge, be it a bluff charge or assault charge, is to prevent or avoid one to start with. You do this by getting out of the area before you are noticed or the creature feels agitated or threatened and develops a defensive posture or aggressive attitude.*

Self-Hypnosis Programming

Since we've got you doing visualization in a relaxed state, let's move forward with programming an appropriate response using self-hypnosis. A few preliminary notes on hypnosis are warranted. A hypnotic trance and trance behavior are natural phenomena within the brain and body of every human being. Think about that. It's within us! Every night as you become drowsy you naturally pass "down" through a number of levels of awareness with associated with distinct brain wave activity on your way to sleep. One of these levels is known as a "hypnogogic" level or awareness/trance. When you awaken from sleep, you once again pass "up" through the same levels of awareness including trance. When awakening, the trance level is called "hypnopompic" awareness. No stage or therapeutic hypnotist is required. No hypnotic induction is required! It happens normally and naturally! It is within you; you do it to yourself. As such all hypnosis in the strictest sense of the word is "self-hypnosis."

It is a power within you that you control. A hypnotist of any type or with any amount of training and experience cannot make you do something during a hypnotic trance, that given the correct or appropriate circumstance, you wouldn't do yourself. You are in control when you are in a hypnotic trance. If I put a person into a trance and tell them to take their clothes off and they don't want to, they won't. Additionally, in all likelihood, any request strongly contradicting a person's conscious character would bring the person out of their trance level of awareness. The conscious mind activates and trance consciousness is reduced.

Nonetheless, when you are in a trance, there are unique abilities, experiences, and behavioral potentials that you can access and utilize that are less available or totally unavailable to you in your normal waking state. Very deep states of relaxation can be achieved. So deep people lose their ability to move their muscles and feel all and any sensation or perception including physical and emotional pain. While the former example suggests a loss of physical control, on the contrary, it is due to increased control over the autonomic nervous system. *That is the part of our nervous system primarily responsible for our fight-flight response.* This is how Yogis, monks, and others who have mastered "mind over matter" techniques are able to control their respiration and heart rate. They can slow both down to one per minute and in doing so replicate death, and perform other amazing feats including being able to survive under extreme circumstances.

A person develops a heightened state of receptivity to suggestion (increased suggestibility). This allows for hypnotic and post-hypnotic suggestions to create or assist with behavioral change, as well as physiologic control and change used in medical treatment.

Anecdotally in single case studies, the use of self-hypnosis has been credited with cancer remission and tumor reduction. The patient is taught to imagine their immune system creating miniature warriors that are released into their bloodstream or other tissue to "fight" the cancer. Police officers are sent out to "slow or freeze" or "arrest" the abnormally accelerated cell growth. In severe pain patients, hypnosis is sometimes considered a treatment of choice (over narcotics and other pain medicines) for the wound debridement repeatedly required after receiving third-degree burns.

A hypnotic anesthesia is created to reduce the pain associated with this process, as well as dental surgical procedures.

While typically associated with feelings of relaxation, peace, and wellness, in rare cases "**abreactions**" or "the expression and consequent release of a previously repressed emotion, achieved through reliving the experience that caused it (typically through hypnosis or suggestion)" has been known to occur.[1] There are strategies to minimize this possibility and facilitate more successful hypnotic inductions and responses. You will be taught these!

By far, however, the majority of people utilizing hypnosis do not experience these. But, if you have a history of rape, physical, or sexual abuse, or other trauma, Acute Stress Disorder (ASD), Post-traumatic stress disorder (PTSD), Obsessive–Compulsive Disorder, other clinically diagnosed anxiety or mood disorders, or other mental health disorders, taking those protective steps would be well advised and will be discussed below.

A note to those diagnosed with or evidencing symptoms consistent with psychotic experiences and conditions (Schizophrenia, Schizoaffective Disorder, Psychotic Depressive Disorder, Schizophreniform Disorder) and/or certain emotional and personality disorders (Borderline Personality Disorder, Multiple Personality Disorder, Dissociative Disorders, Severe PTSD, Histrionic Personality Disorder, Antisocial or Sociopathic Personality Disorders), the use of hypnosis is not only ill-advised but is absolutely contra-indicated. Through the trance level of consciousness and awareness, general psychologic, intrapsychic, interpersonal, emotional, and consensus reality boundaries can become blurred, more permeable, and less existent. This therefore can be potentially harmful to the hypnosis user with these conditions. *You should seek the assistance of a trained professional familiar with these diagnoses and conditions and hypnosis if you wish to use hypnosis.*

To medical patients with seizures, diabetes, COPD, cardiac disease or illness, high blood pressure, thyroid dysfunction, and other metabolic disturbances, hypnosis is not contra-indicated and will likely help improve these conditions. *Nonetheless, the regular use of hypnosis and relaxation should be done under the supervision of your primary physician.* Because hypnosis and relaxation can be associated with reducing heart rate and blood pressure, increased oxygenation of the blood, production, and metabolism of insulin and natural sugars, improved thyroid efficiency, and the alteration of brain wave activity, their use should be medically monitored as appropriate medication and other medical intervention needs can change when these are used regularly (as in on a weekly basis).

The Steps in Self Hypnosis

For our purposes, the necessary steps in self-hypnosis include:

1. Narrowing your focus of attention.
2. Relaxing/Relaxation.
3. Relaxation Deepening.
4. Creating a "Safe Place."
5. Suggestion.
6. Post Hypnotic Suggestion.
7. Awakening.
8. Restoration to Normal Awareness, Normal Functioning, and Post Hypnotic Behaviors.

Narrowing Your Focus of Attention:

Some people would argue that the relaxation scripts I have written are nothing less than hypnotic inductions with only one suggestion: to relax. In these, the subject of the induction is asked to narrow their focus of attention to the pattern of their breathing (in deep breathing or pursed-lipped breathing relaxation techniques), repeating a single phrase (in autogenic relaxation) or tightening and relaxing successive muscle groups (in "progressive relaxation"). More traditional hypnotic techniques would ask the subject to focus on the sound of the speaker's voice, visually focus on an imaginary point 6 inches above the crown of their head, a swaying stopwatch, or a spinning pinwheel. *The common ingredient is using a narrowing of focus in attention and in doing so, minimizing other distractions.*

Relaxing/Relaxation:

At this point this process and procedure should be self-explanatory if you read the chapters on stress inoculation. *If you haven't, go back and do so before further learning about hypnosis.*

During relaxation inductions, especially if the person is highly distractible or has considerable control issues, it is often advised to use confusion or distraction techniques/suggestions. I believe I included some left/right confusion techniques in my autogenic induction. In essence: *"I'm not sure how much relaxing you're experiencing in your left arm. It may be just the right amount of relaxing left in the left arm or may be more relaxing that's right for the right arm. The right relaxing maybe left in the right, or what's left relaxing in the left is right for the left or the right or right for the right and the left. It doesn't matter which arms or limbs relaxing just right; if it's right for the left or left in the right doesn't matter all right because it's left just the right amount of relaxing left and right, right?* Such phrasing rambles on and on to overwhelm the conscious mind's attempts to follow the logic and eventually "give up that hunt."

Metaphorical Suggestions are another distraction technique. *"You see the conscious mind is like a big hungry guard dog posted at the gate of the unconscious mind. It's protective aggression causes it to bark at anything that approaches that gate hoping to get in, hoping to pass unnoticed. But that big old dog wants to hunt, it's hungry to hunt. And hungry dogs need to eat, don't they? So, let that big old hungry dog go on a hunt for something to eat, why don't you? It might hunt for something like that cat stealthily climbing over the wall behind the trees in the background, or that sound of scurrying over there might draw its attention to the acre behind that wall of trees, blocking its view from the gate. If all else fails you might just pack along a few big old juicy steaks or steak bones and throw them as faaaaaar as you can over that fence, over the head of the* dog, waaaayyyy over that tree line blocking the view of that gate and just watch that dog go hunting those bones and huge juicy steaks for hours on end, until they eventually find them and lay down in the shade and gnaw and gnaw and gnaw and eat and eat on and on them for even more hours on end, until the bones are bare and they go and spend hours and hours digging and burying those bones."

Relaxation Deepening:

Alert!!!!! *It can be done simply by recycling a second time on the relaxation procedure already used.*

Alternatively, metaphorical suggestion of "going deeper," "going down deeper or lower," "descending deeper" into anything can be used. For example: *"Now you are imagining yourself on a four-step staircase to begin deepening that present state of calm and relaxation. With each step down that staircase, you're becoming twice as relaxed as you were relaxing on the previous staircase or step. Taking that first step down now, from the fourth to the third step, you're feeling your body becoming more deeply relaxed and at ease, those muscles getting even more comfortably loose and pliable like a loose rubber band. The steps feeling cushiony or spongy under your feet as you safely descend from the third to the second step now, feeling your body getting even more comfortably loose and flexible, calm and quiet, safely relaxed and at peace, knowing that when you reach the bottom of the stairs you become completely relaxed and at ease. Now you're descending deeper into a relaxed state as you're stepping from the second level of relaxing and becoming twice as relaxed as you're reaching the level of the first step, your body relaxing more completely, your body relaxing more fully, your body relaxing deeply and peacefully safely on that first step. You're knowing that at the final step to base is you're feeling complete and utter comfort, complete and fully deep relaxing and calm. You're taking that final step down now into complete relaxation, completely and deeply and fully descending that last step into complete calm, deeply descending that last step into complete peace, fully descending onto the base, secure in your knowledge and experiencing complete relaxation. Your entire body now feeling completely relaxed and at ease, safe and secure in your knowledge you can give yourself this gift of complete and utter relaxation any time you want by descending that same four-step staircase; knowing you need only ascend back up it to reach a normal state of relaxation, back up on your way to normally enjoying the rest of your day.*

So, you are allowing yourself now to ascend back up those steps from the bottom level you take that first step up, becoming even more alert and aware. Twice as alert on the first step as you were before the first step. Enjoying a refreshing and reviving energy flowing back into your body as you're moving on from the first to the second step returning to your normal level of relaxing you enjoy whenever you are practicing relaxing your muscles of your arms and legs or any other parts of your body. Standing now on that second step, feeling your body returning twice as far towards that normal level of awareness, you're now stepping up higher to the third step, first stepping up with one leg becoming more alert and awake as the next leg and foot are finding firm footing on the third step, secure in knowing they are safely and strongly supported as they are safely and strongly supporting your body on the way up to the fourth and final step you previously descended! As you are ascending to that step landing on your feet and legs with the rest of your body returning to that pleasant relaxed and enjoyable state it was in before you went deeper. Becoming more aware of that pleasant natural feeling of comfort, that pleasant natural awareness of calm and ease; becoming more aware of continuing enjoying the security of relaxing the way you're relaxing the muscles of your body have been relaxing."

Some people will use elevators or escalators with more or fewer floors or steps depending on how quickly or slowly you relax. Some people enjoy slowly letting the air out of a balloon which allows them to magically descend into a pleasant pool of relaxing warmth, knowing any time the balloon can miraculously fill up with more air allowing them to rise and ascend to lighter states of relaxation. How will you use your imagination to push the elevator button to descend into your own deeper state of relaxation?

Creating A Safe Place:

The astute reader may have already noticed that in the deepening metaphors, I began to introduce the notion and words "safe" or "safety" and "security." This is intentionally done to ensure the person does not unintentionally lose body control or their sense of control. It is also done to prepare for the creation of a protective "**safe place.**"

As it sounds, the subject guides themselves into constructing a safe and secure place from which they can experience trance behavior. They can accelerate themselves into the future, take themselves back to the past, or do whatever their imagination will allow them to want to do to enjoy hypnosis and benefit from it. *It is especially important to take the time to create this safe place especially if you have been treated for depression, anxiety, or any other mental health condition or grief (in order to minimize the aforementioned chances of an abreaction).*

*What the person creates can vary. Some people have already established "a safe place" in their life, environment, or mind and just imagine themselves going there. Some people enjoy remembering a specific time or place in their life when they felt completely safe and secure, protected from even the most remote or extreme possibility of harm. Some people take themselves to a mountain peak where they can see all things surrounding them and only they know the secrets of how to scale the peak to get there. Some people imagine themselves in a vast ocean where they can see from horizon to horizon and know well in advance anything that approaches them from any side, safe and secure in their awareness that nothing can approach them without their knowledge. In the boat, they have everything they need to sustain and protect themselves and successfully defend themselves from any challenge. (**See Appendix F.**)*

Suggestion:

The astute and alert reader has no doubt noted the appended narrative contains "suggestions." Suggestions for safety and security are used throughout the construction process. That which is being constructed in its entirety is a metaphor for instilling a sense of security within oneself.

Suggestions can be made through such or similar metaphors, the telling of parables, or other stories. Forthright and obvious statements about a desired outcome or behavioral responses when the person is in a heightened state of suggestibility can also be used. *In short, they attempt to prescribe a desired symptom or outcome.*

Some general rules of guidance in forming suggestions are warranted. They should **not** simply be a restatement of the problem. *In fact, they should be a statement of the solution to the problem with little to no mention of the problem itself.* For example, if the problem is "I feel fear when I hear a Bigfoot growl near me" the suggestion **DOES NOT** become: "I don't feel fear when I hear a Bigfoot growl close to me." *The mention of the fear reinforces and suggests the fear itself and works against what we are trying to achieve through the suggestion.* It's like saying "Try not to think about the pink elephant in the room" after which all you can do is think about the pink elephant in the room.

The problem statement must be replaced with the opposite emotion or an affirmative action or behavior to overcome the problem: "Hearing what could be a Bigfoot growl near me, I'm increasing my vigilance and attention toward that location, while staying confidently calm and at the ready." In this suggestion, we distance ourselves from the possibility of it being produced by a Bigfoot by saying "... what could be ... ." Such psychological distancing assists with autonomic control and reactivity. We then prescribe the alternative and affirmative action and prescribe the alternate emotion: "... I'm increasing my vigilance and attention toward that location, while staying confidently calm and at the ready."

Suggestions need to be stated in the present tense whenever possible. When you add words like "if" you are suggesting a **hypothetical** *or* **potential** *situation, behavior, and reaction. Using the "when" or other future tense word/phrases (e.g., "I will ..."; I'm going to ...") places or stages the event and reactions sometime in the future. Using the past tense of verb stages and placing the response in the past. Suggestions using these words* *suggest the possibility of, the potential of, or the past process of behavioral and emotional actions and responses. Those will be of little use in a "here and now" reality. We are programming emotional and behavioral responses to be used in the present (the here and now) and as such they need to be stated in the present tense!*

To return to the above example of being in the near presence of possible Bigfoot growls, the suggestion is **NOT**: "**When** I hear a Bigfoot growl ..." "**I will**" ... or "I'm **going to** increase my vigilance ... and **try** to stay confidently calm ...". All those bold words suggest the **possibility** of action in the **future**. You don't want to have programmed in **potential** reactions of behavior or **future** reactions and behaviors when you are hearing a growl near you in the present. Trust me, I know as this has happened to me. *You want your behavioral responses and emotional reactions to occur immediately so they occur in a timely enough fashion to protect yourself should the need arise.*

The suggestions need to be repeated over and over again in a variety of ways. The unconscious mind likes repetition. Saying once or twice will not be sufficient even when properly phrased in the here and now. You are attempting to re-program genetically ingrained behavioral patterns and responses practiced throughout most of your life. If you believe in genetic memory, these have been practiced over thousands of years. This reprogramming does not and will not happen overnight and needs to be reiterated hundreds of times, in a variety of ways.

For example, the building of a safe place. The entire "construction project" is a metaphor for building safety. "Safe" and "secure" are repeated often not only in reference to the structure being built but in reference to relaxation, 'a safe and confident attitude,' 'confident and secure in the knowledge,' 'strength of the door bar,' the 'strength and impenetrable' nature of the construction materials, etc., etc. All these lend themselves to strength, safety, and security in one's self, one's environment and one's world.

Finally, suggestion work should be done when you are in your safe place and preferably when you are in your viewing room. This is of paramount importance to minimize risk of abreaction. It's the reason we created that safe place. There are other therapeutic hypnotic maneuvers built into this induction that I will not highlight as they contribute to layers of safety. Even if you don't have an emotional or personality issue, you are best doing your suggestion work from your viewing room. Imagine the desired outcome on your viewing screen or device for additional buffering.

Post-hypnotic Suggestion:

While the "suggestion" portion of the phrase "post-hypnotic suggestion" needs to follow all the rules for suggestions discussed above, the term "post-hypnotic" refers to programming those behaviors or emotional suggestions to occur as the person awakens from the hypnotic trance level of awareness. As such the post-hypnotic aspect of the suggestion **IS** phrased in the future tense. This ends up making for poor grammar and sentence structure as you are combining the future-tense post-hypnotic portion of the phrase ("**When** you awaken, you're continuing on going through your week" ...) with the present-tense hypnotic suggestion portion of the phrase ("... *you* **are** *feeling* safe, secure confident in the strength of the ever-present and growing safety experiences in life").

"As you are drifting back, you bring back that sense of safety with you and within you. Imagining putting it in a vault or safe within yourself, securely and firmly closing the door on that safety vault, secure in the knowledge you are the one and the only one who opens that door again, knowing you are carrying that safety and security where ever you go into the past, future, or present as you are returning to your body in the here and now, preparing yourself to go on with the rest of your day in a normal and natural fashion."

It is also preferable to begin post-hypnotic suggestion from the viewing room within the safe place and *continue with repetition after leaving the safe place and drifting back to the body and then through* reawakening the body into a normal and natural state. It is generally better to more deeply mask or hide the suggestions in metaphor the closer you get to a waking state to stave off the interfering nature of the conscious mind.

If you as the hypnotic subject (or another hypnotic subject) are easily hypnotizable simply **direct suggestion** or **prescribing the new skill or symptom** can be used. "Next time *(note future tense)*, when you're hearing what could be a Bigfoot growl near you, you are *(note present tense)* increasing your vigilance and attention toward that location, while staying confidently calm and at the ready." Repeat ad nauseam in a variety of scenarios or situations, be they with a Bigfoot or any other situation where this could be an adaptive response.

If you as the subject or another subject have an active and controlling conscious mind, you may need to be more indirect. Through storytelling for example. *"I know this person who enjoyed hiking and camping in the wilderness. He enjoyed doing this in many locations throughout the United States. We went camping together one weekend, and around the campfire he told me a story about this time he was supposed to meet a buddy on the trail. He walked and walked and walked all day. As he was walking, occasionally he would hear a sound rustling in the bushes. Being an experienced woodsman, he was always alert to such sounds and ready to respond in the event it could be a wild animal, rather than his bud- dy. He told me that the first few times it happened he got a little jumpy but as the day went on, settling into a confident calmness that eventually he would meet his friend without any harm befalling him. I commented that I'm not so sure I could remain calm hearing rustling in the bushes, maybe breath or a growl nearby me. He reminded me, however, about nature and made the valid point that most things in nature are more afraid of humans than we are afraid of them. Most animals' goals are to remain undetected from humanity and to avoid us at all costs. In fact, the most dangerous animal in the forest is the human animal and you are much more likely to be hurt by one of those animals than any of Mother Nature's creatures that growl or go bump in the night. You're keeping a fire going all night and most all (but humans) will keep their distance. He said it's most important just to stay calm and "keep your head" so that you're reacting appropriately. Ever since he told me this, it's easier for me to relax in the woods and react appropriately to every little noise and remain vigilant enough at the same time to stay safe."*

That's pretty obvious and direct. You could change the characters into mice and hear a lion growl that really had no interest in eating or killing the mouse but wanted help removing the thorn from its foot. You get the idea. Parables or stories with a moral or message.

Awakening:

These are simply suggestions to become more alert, awake, revived, and refreshed. If you used a deepening technique be sure to reverse it. *Note that at the end of "Deepening" induction above, you bring yourself back up the four stairs you went down to begin with.* You reverse the process which in and of itself becomes a metaphor or suggestion for lightening the trance and relaxation. *Yes?* If you fail to include this, it will take longer to awaken and restore functioning to normal. In effect some part of the person's unconscious will stay in a deeper level of trance and continue to influence waking behaviors. The worst that can happen is the person will fall asleep and awaken after that rest, but we all know that life doesn't always allow opportune times for two-to six-hour naps.

Some people enjoy remaining in the peace of the relaxed trance state and resist awakening. Building in suggestions to counter this enjoyment can be of benefit. *"And as you're lying there enjoying relaxing, your muscles becoming fuller and fuller of a flu- id relaxation meandering though out your body, you're beginning noticing fullness in those muscles and other parts of your body. I'm not sure where else in your body you're beginning noticing a fullness building and flowing or wanting to be flowing into other locations, but you might begin allowing yourself noticing not only those muscles full of relaxation, but those muscles that might enjoy letting the flow go to enjoy an even more relaxing fluid release of tensions. Releasing and letting go of those tensions in a fluid fashion that relieves the dis- comfort you might be noticing in some location of your body seeking relief, some part of your body seeking release, some part of your body wanting to enjoy relaxing comfort by releasing that which are needing to be*

JOHN S. BARANCHOK, PH.D.

release." You get the point that you can encourage awaken- ing without getting completely "pissy" about it! Extreme cold, extreme heat, getting splashed in the face with water (literally through suggestion, but not literally in real life) can also be effective awakening techniques for people enjoying being in a trance too much.

Restoration to Normal Awareness, Normal Functioning, and Post Hypnotic Behaviors:

On one level, this is more of the same as awakening techniques. Nonetheless, it is always best to also give suggestions of normal awareness and functioning to ensure the same when operating within consensus reality.

At this point, the main post-hypnotic suggestion I typically use with clients is to "Enjoy practicing new knowledge and learning from your trance experience." To directly restate post-hypnotic suggestions would be to make them conscious and vulnerable to interference of the conscious mind. I also repeat: "Refreshed, revived, and fully awakened, going on with the rest of your day in a normal and natural way!! Completely alert and awake now, refreshed, revived, and invigorated in your functioning!!! Ready to enjoy your day with your newfound skills and learnings in a normal and natural way!!!

So now it's up to you to create the scenario you are most likely to encounter. The one that you might need the most help with to respond appropriately when it comes to Bigfoot. Plan out that scenario, the problem it creates, the prescribed symptoms or suggestions to use as a solution, and write out your script or narrative. After that writing, record it on your cell phone, DVD recorder, or tape recorder. Create your own or use my suggestions for deepening and safe place development and then do your suggestion work from that place, having recorded it as well. Record the suggestions, post-hypnotic suggestions, and awakening and normal awareness and functioning tips. *In short, take the steps to reprogram your own appropriate reactions to the Bigfoot scenarios you want to respond to in a specific fashion!*

If that seems too much like hard work, I'll share a shorter method to do so next:

The SWISH Technique

I first learned of the SWISH technique when reading Richard Bandler's (1985) book *Using Your Brain for a Change*.[2] It is touted as a technique for behavioral change. The steps in the process are summarized in my own understanding and words below.[3]

1. **Identify a behavior you want to change and develop an image of it:** Once you've identified the unwanted behavior, create an image of *what you see through your own eyes* **just before** *you start that unwanted behavior.* It is important that this is an "**associated image**." An associated image is a picture "like or as if" you are in your own body, looking through your own eyes. You see your hands typing and the screen in front of you, but you can't see the front of your own face or your own expressions. It's only what you see through your own eyes **just before** you start doing the unwanted behavior. Remember that image, but set it temporarily aside.

2. **Develop your outcome image:** Now develop another image of **how you'll see yourself after** you change the unwanted behavior. *This is a "dissociated image."* This image is a picture "like or as if" *you have left your body and can observe yourself or are watching yourself* from another location, outside of your body. Now you can see the front of your face, your expressions, that balding spot on the top of your head. Remember this image, but set it temporarily aside.

3. **Construct the SWISH Image:** Now I want you to bring back up that first image (the image of what you see

through your own eyes just before you start the unwanted behavior) and make it BIG and Bright. Hold on to that image in your mind's eye. Now bring back the outcome image (the image of how you'll see yourself after you change the unwanted behavior) and make it small and dim and put it in the right corner of the first big bright image. Hold on to those images.

4. **SWISH:** Now as fast as you say or hear the word SWISH, allow the small dim image to become big and bright and cover the first image, which simultaneously dims and shrinks away! Say "SWISH." Next, blank out that screen or open your eyes. Do this entire process four more times, being sure to open your eyes and blank out the screen after each time.

5. **Testing the Results:** Now, try to bring up the first image and notice what's changed or different about that image. What has happened? If the technique has been successful, it may be difficult to bring up the first image at all. If it does come up it may quickly fade, get smaller, or dim away, while the second image phases in or in some other way takes its place.

Now let's run that through with an example of my own Bigfoot images. If I ever do have a face-to-face Bigfoot encounter, I **don't** want to run away in fear. Instead, I want to remain calm, hold my ground, and maybe even move forward (the reader should not feel encouraged to do the same and I would in fact discourage you from doing the same).

1. **Identify the behavior I want to change and create an image of what I see through my own eyes, just before I start the unwanted behavior:** I see a massive Bigfoot coming into view and my arms raising up with balled-up fists, my chest rising up in down at a faster pace, my

breathing gets more rapid and shallow, and my heart starts beating faster.

2. **The Outcome Image:** I'm looking down on myself from above my body. I see my breathing has slowed and steadied and now my arms are dangling by my side, fists unclenched and arms relaxed. I see my right foot coming up off the ground as I begin to step forward. I have a grin on my face without showing my teeth and my eyes are somewhat downcast, not looking directly into the eyes of the Bigfoot, but looking below his chin.

3. **Construct the SWISH Image:** Now I put the first image up, make it big and bright. I'm making it so large, it's like the full body of Bigfoot is on a movie screen and I've just turned up the "brightness dial" on the screen. The second image is small and dim and in the right corner of the first image.

4. **SWISH:** Now as fast I say the word SWISH, the small dim image becomes big and bright and covers the first image, which simultaneously dims and fades away. I open my eyes to "blank out the screen." I repeat this entire five-step process, four additional times, opening my eyes after each process to erase or blank out the screen.

5. **Test the Results:** I can't bring up the first image at all, but my heart is still beating in my chest. I will rinse and repeat until that beating lessens.

What is the Bigfoot experience you hope to have? How will you realistically react? Are you satisfied with that reaction? If the answer to that last question is "No," which of these techniques will you use to develop a more satisfying alternate response to that encounter? Have you had a Bigfoot encounter that has left you shaken? If so, which of the techniques in Chapters 5 and 6 will you use to reprogram that response, allowing yourself to once again be comfortable?

PART II

SCIENTIFIC RESEARCH STRATEGIES - THE CRITICAL CONCEPTS WE NEED TO DEPLOY!

7

EVIDENCE: WHAT FIELD RESEARCHERS GATHER AND SOME STICKY WICKETS IN THE KETCHUM DNA STUDY

The educated, informed, and prepared Scientific Bigfoot Researcher (SBFR) needs to understand and consider the type of evidence they are gathering in the hopes of understanding and hopefully protecting the species and its habitat. There is potential value in any form of evidence, but different types of evidence have different levels of such intrinsic, legal, and forensic value. Although the quoted definitions below speak to the value of specific forms of evidence in a court of law, their value seems to generalize well to the scientific Bigfoot area.

For one, such legal considerations offer a conceptual template to consider the potential scientific value and viability of the respective forms of evidence. A second, perhaps more important issue critical to the survival of the Bigfoot species exists. Previously endangered species living in natural settings (the spotted owl being a good example) have had to face and defend their legitimate need for habitat to be protected against legal challenges mounted by logging and other forest service industries. Based on **estimates** of their sheer numbers **and** theories speaking to the species' origins, it may ultimately be debatable whether Bigfoot truly represents an "endangered species." *Nonetheless on this topic, maintaining a legal* *mindset or bias filter regarding Bigfoot evidence would seem to come under the often cliched rubric of "An ounce of prevention, is worth a pound of cure."*

Analogical evidence: *"Telling a story that draws an analogy or parallel" between Bigfoot and other species thought to be similar to or otherwise possibly represent Bigfoot.*[1] *In my opinion (and despite using it in this book) this is of questionable to little value until we have studied the species with scientific or other forms of "certainty." Without such confidence, any analogous relationships between Bigfoots and humans, other known humanoids, great apes, other apex predators, and other wild species are strictly theoretical and hypothetical.*

Anecdotal Evidence: "Presents only anecdotes that support a particular conclusion. Consider it with skepticism, and in combination with other, more reliable, kinds of evidence."[2] Anecdotes are stories, be they "... short amusing or interesting stories about a real incident or person" ... or creatures.[3] "Although they can be factual and precise, they are often considered "an account regarded as unreliable or hearsay. They can also be imbued with analogical evidence and/or bolstered by testimonial evidence (see below)."[4] *As such, they can represent some of the most or least compelling Bigfoot evidence depending on the character and reliability of the storyteller and personal objectivity and validity versus bias or outright lies of the data/story.* (See Ray Wallace comments.)

Interestingly, this evidence also seems to represent the most common evidence communicated by texts/writings on the subject and is responsible for creating a plethora of what broader society calls "Bigfoot experts" in the field today. More often than not, this is a good thing for the writer, speaker, or "expert," but may or may not serve the species in a beneficial fashion. Witness internet sightings posted on any number of websites and pages online. Witness the increase in the number of people following that source and making a variety of "contributions" to them. Also witness the inevitable influx of trained/serious researchers, along with curiosity seekers, hoaxers, and plain old pedestrian traffic in and around the reported area of that sighting. *Intended or not, these later effects simply serve to harass the species and in my opinion, can be very detrimental to the species itself and any serious research attempts to assist them even when done in the name of science.*

Character Evidence: "This is a testimony or document that is used to help prove that someone acted in a particular way based on the person's character. (In legal settings) this can be used to prove that a person's behavior at a certain time was consistent with his or her character. It can be used in some investigations to prove intent, motive, or opportunity. This is a testimony or document that is used to help prove that someone [or something] acted in a particular way based on character. Also known as indirect evidence, this type of evidence is used to infer something based on a series of facts separate from the fact the argument is trying to prove. It requires a deduction of facts from other facts that can be proven and, while not considered to be strong evidence, it can be relevant in an … investigation …"[5]

Hopefully, it will not surprise the reader that it is my belief that we know little to nothing scientifically regarding Bigfoot's "character." Hypothetical theories have nonetheless formed based primarily on phenomenological fieldwork findings. "It's a previously unidentified species, a relict hominoid, an inter-dimensional being, an alien, a demonic spirit or Nephilim, an overseeing watcher and protector of Mother Earth and its creatures." Each of these hypotheses carries varying degrees of the weight of popular and scientific acceptance in the Bigfoot community. Each of these hypotheses presumes to ascribe a particular character (mental/behavioral characteristics and motives) to Bigfoot.

More relevant to Bigfoot's current unproven status in the scientific field, the character of the person providing or citing other forms of Bigfoot evidence would be well considered in evaluating the reliability and validity of that evidence. In short, "consider the source."

Demonstrative Evidence: "An object or document is considered to be demonstrative evidence when it directly demonstrates a fact. It's a common and reliable kind of evidence. Examples of this kind of evidence are photographs, video and audio recordings, charts, etc. In a(n)... investigation, this could be an audio recording ... or a photograph."[6]

This is an increasingly common form of demonstrative evidence seen in Bigfoot research with the prototype being the 1967 Patterson and Gimlin film. Photo and video evidence now include a plethora of both credible and non-credible examples. I will leave it to the reader and other experts to determine which is which, but add that the advent of the "smartphone" has greatly contributed to the explosion of this type of evidence, for better or worse.

Authenticated footprint casts could also be considered in this class of evidence. Although more open to debate, tree twists, bark tears, and other visually objective "recordable" findings are potentially attributable to Bigfoot.

*Bigfoot nonetheless remains unidentified to the general scientific community and zoological community. This identification may be a necessary prerequisite for taking steps to make it an official species thereby allowing it and its habitat to be protected by the US and other government agencies and programs. It indeed also represents something of a paradox and irony to have an increasingly large number and variety of experts weigh in on a "scientifically unidentified species." This may explain and highlight the **relative** weight given to the wide variety of different types of evidence of Bigfoot other than scientific evidence.*

Perhaps a broader reaching/encompassing classification of evidence (scientific vs subjective depending on its execution) is known as "**phenomenological evidence.**" It might be conceptualized to capture to subjective, observable, and seeming logically interpretable evidence of the species. It might include anecdotal, demonstrative, digital (audio, visual computerized), direct, forensic, and physical evidence.

"Phenomenology is a philosophical movement originating in the 20th century. Its primary objective is the direct investigation and description of phenomena as consciously experienced. This investigation and description should be without theories about their causal explanation and as free as possible from unexamined preconceptions and presuppositions."[7] It seems a particularly well-suited philosophy to use and context within which to study Bigfoot given its rarity, difficulty to "capture," and wide variety of often conflicting theories of existence. It would avoid many of the theoretical debates, bruised egos and heated arguments, as well as (what are considered by many) the "far-flung" notions concerning the origins of the species.

A personally objective review of the literature on Bigfoot might easily conclude that many of the best "experts" by process and possibly without conscious design have unknowingly been using this philosophy for some time. We are, after all phenomenologically bound creatures ourselves. By that nature, we must filter our world through our phenomenological perceptions. Problematic, to the Bigfoot field (in my opinion,) however, is that the phenomena are **not** allowed to exist **"without" theories** about their causal explanation and are as free as possible from unexamined preconceptions and presuppositions. *On the contrary, it appears to this writer that those observations have then been used to generate the Bigfoot Theory. The cart is now before the horse of hypothesis testing.*

Digital Evidence: "Digital evidence can be any sort of digital file from an electronic source. This includes email, text messages, instant messages, files, and documents extracted from hard drives, ... audio files, and video files. Digital evidence can be found on any server or device that stores data, including some lesser-known sources ... such as GPS and internet-enabled devices ... Digital evidence is often found through internet searches using open-source intelligence (OSINT). Investigators need to either develop specific technical expertise or rely on experts to do the extraction for them. Preserving digital evidence is also challenging because, unlike physical evidence, it can be altered or deleted remotely. Investigators need to be able to authenticate the evidence, and also provide documentation to prove its integrity."[8]

I find digital evidence to represent some of the best yet most problematic evidence available on Bigfoot. For example, digital versus digitized video images. An image that initially looks like what many researchers call a "Blob Squatch" (a blurry, amorphous, non-descript, unidentifiable image of what is thought or hoped to be a Bigfoot) is subject to projective "inkblot-like" interpretative biased procedures due to their vagueness. "But it can first be 'blown up' for clarity." Very often this only results in a larger image of the same "Blob Squatch." "Well, that's only because the camera wasn't stationary when the images were taken." Never fear, digital stabilization technology is here! Now the blob starts looking increasingly Bigfoot-like. But it still looks too non-descript to be sure. "We'll, just 'clean it up." "Well, that's only a profile shot, we don't know how it would appear if we captured the entire creature." "We'll use facial reconstruction/body reconstruction programming with a rotational enhancement that can help." By the time it's done, we've got a Bigfoot-looking image!!! *"The computer doesn't lie!"* Right? Yet, *we've just used it to make a Bigfoot out of our of a Blob Squatch!*

My problem is I don't know if the computer lies or not. I do believe that I, like many versus most Bigfoot researchers, only have a fundamental understanding of the technology and don't really understand what the human-conceived, designed, programmed, and constructed software and hardware is actually doing to the image. "Well, it's de-pixilating the image. Just taking out the blurred pixels and replacing them with clearer pixels." Oh really? And how does the computer decide which pixels need to be replaced and what to replace them with? Truly, I don't know the answers to these questions or even if they are the right questions to ask. I also have no doubt someone does understand it well enough to pose more valid questions and answer those.

My point, however, is researchers are making research decisions and drawing conclusions based on these stabilized and enhanced images. They are doing so without having an intimate/in-depth knowledge of the inner workings of the technology to know how the images are or could be altered. Without that level of understanding, it appears to me that we still risk the "inkblot effect" of seeing (or even creating) our own wishes and biases rather than knowing we're looking at objective data. Perhaps worst, we may be taking an image that is not a Bigfoot and using image manipulation technology to "construct" an image of a "Bigfoot." Why not just use a sketch pad, charcoals, and pastels to draw it?

Can you as a field researcher honestly say you understand the inner workings of your digitally enhanced data images or sound recordings to know how they are being manipulated by the computer program? Do you understand the software program well enough to be certain that it is not creating falsely constructed images, sounds, or graphic analyses of the same? Do you have an intimate enough understanding of FLIR and night vision to do the same? *How do you* **know,** if you haven't written the program or spoken the program's language to understand its influences?

Without that understanding, you are dealing with what is known as the **"black box" phenomenon.** In science, computing, and engineering, a black box "is a device, system or object which can be viewed in terms of its inputs and outputs (or transfer characteristics), without any knowledge of its internal workings. Its implementation is 'opaque' (black)."[9] *If we do not understand how the programming is analyzing, changing, and reconfiguring our data to produce the revised output, that output should be viewed with skepticism, at best, in my opinion.*

"It is a serious problem, but at the moment it is limited to **very large deep learning models and neural networks.** These neural networks break down problems into millions or even billions of pieces and then assemble them step by step in a linear fashion to solve them. Because the human brain doesn't work that way, we have no good way of knowing what exactly the algorithm is doing or what methods it is using. This has been called the 'black box problem' because during these times AI seems to emulate a black box that has no way of looking inside. This not only prevents us from gaining deep insight required to tweak the algorithms, but it causes all kinds of issues with trust."[10] *In my opinion, it should create issues with trust, but does not do so often enough in the Bigfoot field!*

Direct Evidence: "The most powerful type of evidence, direct evidence requires no inference. The evidence alone is the proof."[11]

While I personally find certain groups' plans to kill a Bigfoot repulsive, other than face-to-face personal sightings that are then relegated to other types of data discussed above, *the body of a Bigfoot* **may** *represent the only example of this type of powerful evidence to inform the issue.* This is certainly the opinion among scientists better versed in "Bigfoot" than myself (e.g., Grover Krantz (1999) in *Bigfoot Sasquatch Evidence* (p. 3) being one of many).[12] As such, no matter how distasteful or repulsive I personally find the idea and process of accomplishing that task, *it has potential merit.* I qualify that statement with the word "potential" as many conspiracy believers contend that our government already has bodies that they refuse to release for public purposes and open/unfettered scientific review, consideration, study, and research. I don't bring this question up to join or support any conspiracy theory or theorist. I raise this question to highlight a few hypothetical considerations to killing a Bigfoot for non-governmental research, should such conspiracies have any validity. Hopefully, the North American Wood Ape Conservancy (NAWAC) has already considered and addressed these through their protocols, which I hope and would imagine are already in place.

Of course, of great importance will be preserving the viability and integrity of the body itself. "Well, just freeze it or keep it chilled!" Noting that I am not a geneticist or a tissue pathologist, I can only imagine that the act of freezing such a creature intact or "field dressed" would carry multiple potential problems/hurdles that would need to be controlled. For DNA integrity and purity, my fantasy is a sterile field would be advantageous. Aside from having the hunters themselves garbed in medical gowns, gloves, and masks as they approach the kill and using sterile instruments if field dressing is part of the procedure, "dropping" an animal with a gunshot onto the forest floor would appear to present some challenges to preserving the purity tissue samples in and of itself. Water and other animal contaminants, both gross in size and microscopic in nature, would likely become potential issues.

Aside from the obvious logistical challenges of getting a recently killed body rapidly from the woods, swamps, or rocky cliffs of our forests into refrigeration, if the creatures' cells are fluid-based, freezing would appear to have potentially catastrophic effects on such cells and tissue samples. Could chilling (no, not the "Netflix and Chill" type of chilling, but the temperature-lowering type) be potentially less damaging? It would appear that transplant technology and organ transportation processes would be poised to inform integrity preservation issues. Again, I am a layman when it comes to these issues and I leave it to those with expertise in these areas to solve or otherwise address the importance of this topic in producing viable DNA and tissue samples for investigation.

Overlapping and interacting with the tissue integrity challenges is the issue of data security. In this case, the raw data is quite literally the body. If "men in black" reports or theories of other government interests and interference in Bigfoot phenomena have **any** inkling of validity, a significant security threat exists. The aspiring "Bigfoot harvester for the benefit of the species" would appear to have the need to mount defensive security strategies to protect the custody of the body itself against forces and factions of the US government who have the "rule of law" and "national security" behind them. It is not hard to imagine the well-intentioned Bigfoot harvester requiring a professionally trained and regularly drilled and practiced paramilitary-type "police force" to both guard and frequently shift locations of the data to avoid detection and subsequent confiscation by powers that wish to keep Bigfoot's existence "under wraps." To what extreme extent is the well-intentioned Bigfoot "harvest" group prepared to go to achieve this objective? A rather weighty and frightening thought to consider but an important problem to resolve, in my opinion. Likely one of many!

Forensic Evidence: "Forensic Evidence is scientific evidence, such as DNA, trace evidence, fingerprints ... and can provide proof.... [of Bigfoot]! Forensic evidence is generally considered to be strong and reliable evidence ..."[13] Of course, the most famous hotly debated forensic evidence associated with Bigfoot remains the Ketchum DNA study.

Scott Carpenter (2019), in his book, *The Nephilim Among Us Updated* provides a nice overview and addresses some of the criticisms challenging the scientific value of the study.[14] His more recent book on the subject [*Truth Denied-The Sasquatch DNA Study* (2020)] provides a more comprehensive overview/treatment that simultaneously highlights many of the strengths and scientific weaknesses of this pioneering and apparently painstaking work.[15] It is not my wish to join the debate on the merits or weakness of this very important, but nonetheless controversial work. In other words, my motives here are not to "pile on" (or for that matter support the study through my characterizations above). I raise these issues as they are more basic and fundamental "scientific" considerations warranting a reflective critique.

I will simply highlight two **relatively basic issues** as they relate to the potential scientific value of this work. The first of these is the fact that it was published in a journal bought by the primary investigator of the study (Dr. Ketchum). This was done ostensibly to move forward and publish the work in a timely fashion. The second issue is that of the data chain of custody.

Regarding the first issue, Dr. Ketchum (a veterinarian, forensic DNA expert for police investigations, and previously a "Bigfoot skeptic") purchased the very journal in which she hoped to publish her research findings. After reading Scott Carpenter's explanations of what led to this decision, I will admit that I have sympathy for her reasons and actions. *Nonetheless, one of the fundamental and "cornerstone" tenants of attempting to publish research in a* **"blind,"** **"peer-reviewed,"** *or* **"juried"** *journal is to minimize the development and proliferation of research influenced and biased by a "good ole boy (or girl) network."* In my opinion and with limited experience in psychological research, this remains more of an aspirational goal than a pragmatic reality.

There are a variety of factors contributing to and supporting my contention here. For example, prior to a study having any hopes of getting published, the study is often presented at a national professional association conference by the often young, attractive, enthusiastic, and aspiring doctoral candidate or academy climbing principle researcher. Here journal owners, editors, and "blind review" panelists interact with the researchers to examine and critique their studies. Through this process, they can become professional or social acquaintances, sometimes friends and, dare I point out, on rarer occasions, lovers. These same studies are then submitted to those very journals for "objective" and "blind" review. Need I go further to make my point on this topic? I hope not!

Perhaps somewhat less brow-raising and scandalous is another factor infringing upon true blind peer review: the reputation/renown of the principal investigator. Again, using the field of psychology for my example, in academic circles the rule of "publish or perish" for untenured assistant and associate professors still pervades as one of the criteria examined to obtain "tenure." Once achieved, tenure sometimes is to the detriment of the creative/divergent educational process through creating "bulletproof" job security. (Can a tenured professor do any wrong?) Combine those demands with many scientists' genuine drive and interest in certain areas of study and the result is a "research machine" housed within a university department or laboratory setting.

Here volumes of data can be generated on the backs of undergraduate and graduate assistant "technicians" working under the guidance and supervision of the principal researcher. If the quality of the work is good to excellent, after submission to a journal the research is subsequently published. This can become a repeated process to the point where certain research topics, studies, and experimental designs take on the "signature" qualities of a particular researcher/principal investigator. Like a "signature dish" from a world-famous chef becomes immediately identifiable to the educated and informed gourmand; certain research topics, studies, experimental designs, and even writing styles become easily identifiable to the "blinded" peer review panelists. These end up being published in particular journals at an increasing frequency or rate.

I highlight these processes to give the interested reader an "inside glimpse" of some of the pitfalls of the so-called "blind" or "juried" process of scientific publications and therefore research. More importantly and to the point: even within prestigious blind, peer-reviewed scientific journals, the potential for the review process to not be truly "blind" and objective exists. Such bias can be intrinsically built into the administrative review structure of the journal itself. This subsequently weakens the "unbiased" nature of the science disseminated by that journal.

To return to the Ketchum study, according to Scott Carpenter, it was published in a journal purchased by the principal investigator only after the previously blind review panelists for the journal (then owned by someone other than Dr. Ketchum) accepted the study for publication. Nonetheless "mysterious influences" (my characterization) apparently were brought to bear upon that owner/editor and the offer of publication was withdrawn. This was when Dr. Ketchum purchased the journal.

As such one might argue the study was in fact blindly reviewed and accepted for publication and therefore carries with it the weight of "scientific objectivity and validity." This is obviously scientifically problematic, after having glimpsed into the inner workings and behind-the-scenes processes involved in "blind" peer-reviewed scientific journals. *The reader should then be able to appreciate why her purchase obliterated any hope of the work being considered as subjected to a fresh, a priori, blind, peer review under the new journal owner/editor.* Even if such a review was performed, Dr. Ketchum's ownership would cast a jaundiced eye on the ultimate validity and value of the work to the broader scientific community. *It unfortunately became scientifically tainted by the purchase of the journal by Dr. Ketchum, no matter how honest or forthright her motives may have been. By default, when the lead investigator of a scientific work purchases a journal and then proceeds to publish her own work therein, the scientific objectivity and value attributed to that work becomes moot,* **justified or not!** This **does not** reduce/disprove the intrinsic value and validity of the work (in my opinion) but eliminates its value and potential use in scientifically proving the existence of the species.

The work becomes suspect to multiple levels of bias and therefore ill repute, *no matter how deserved or undeserved.* This is not meant as a statement or criticism of Dr. Ketchum but is a painfully objective assessment by the current author of the scientific value of the study, its potential to be accepted by the larger scientific community, therefore its ability to assist in any governmental or societal program to preserve the species and its habitat. Furthermore, it also potentially taints and hinders possible attempts to replicate Dr. Ketchum's work and findings so that they might be published in that journal or other blind, peer-reviewed scientific journals. *The design, procedures, and conclusions of the study are now simply too easily identifiable.* That is indeed unfortunate for the species!

The second issue to highlight is one that apparently Mr. Carpenter and Dr. Ketchum feel they have thoroughly addressed and dismissed: the Chain of Custody of the sample tissue/data. Mr. Carpenter writes "The relevancy of the chain of custody is a fallacy. The DNA is a research paper, not a criminal investigation. Where the hair came from and who has handled it is irrelevant when it concerns contamination."[16] He then proceeds to quote Dr. Ketchum's Facebook Page: "Somebody was told that the lack of chain of custody of our samples negated our scientific findings. This is not the case. ... Chain of custody is used in forensics to make sure the unknown samples from the crime scene are tracked from their recovery until they are tested and therefore not altered in any way. This ensures that nobody tampers with the sample. The samples themselves are often of unknown origin. ... however, this testing is a little different than a forensic case in that we are simply trying to determine the source of the samples, human, animal, or unknown. We're not trying to place an individual at a crime scene. In this type of scientific investigation, there is no crime and it doesn't matter where it's found, only what the DNA shows matters and DNA can't be altered with any kind of testing we did ... Therefore, it is nice to have a chain of custody since the DNA will tell you what sample it was from."[17]

"Research paper, not criminal investigation." "Chain of custody is used in forensics to make sure the unknown samples from the crime scene are tracked from their recovery until they are tested and

therefore not altered (current author's emphasis) in any way... [or] ... that nobody tampers with the sample."

"We're not trying to place an individual at a crime scene." Really?!! It may merely be a research paper, but one with potentially earth-shattering implications with greater and further reaching implications for humanity than any criminal investigation into "who done it!" True! You aren't trying to put a human at a crime scene. You are **merely** trying to prove the existence of a highly illusive "unknown" species that could influence what we know and how we think about the evolutionary versus biblical origins of humanity!

You are concerned about "tampering" with evidence and/or not altering the DNA evidence in a criminal investigation, but not worried about these issues in a scientific research paper? Really?! Dr. Ketchum's very words would suggest that Chain of Custody should be of **paramount** importance to such a research paper, if for no other reason than to counter the possibility of "human DNA contamination criticisms" of the study; not dismissed as a "fallacy."

"The term chain of custody refers to the **process of maintaining** (current author's emphasis) and documenting the handling of evidence. It involves keeping a detailed log showing who collected, handled, transferred, or analyzed evidence during an investigation."[18] In short, it refers to raw data security.

In my own experiences with psychological research, we indeed did not refer to a "chain of custody." We were nonetheless concerned about "the security" of our data and results. As such, we went to some lengths to protect our digital files, hard copies of computer analyses, and our writings, be they digitally recorded or handwritten.

Even at the level of university training and research where such information influences grades or professional promotions and job security; *piracy, destruction of data, surreptitious falsification, and/or contamination of data by highly competitive students was not uncommon.* So much so, that it warranted appropriate security protocols be developed and followed to protect the data. The design and implementation of Dr. Ketchum's research on Bigfoot should have most certainly engendered security concerns for said data.

Her task of proving the existence of such an elusive creature was highly challenging. There were and remain rumors of government interference in people's lives that have been discovered and attempted to share evidence in the past. She utilized a variety of field researchers, some of whom were conducting their own studies, hoping to accomplish similar or differing goals as herself. These are all compelling arguments for very tight security and closely monitoring the chain of evidence.

She highlighted the considerable oversight and training she exercised with these researchers to ensure the integrity of the DNA collection process remained consistent across researchers in order to guarantee the reliability of the collection process and maximize the purity of the DNA samples collected for analysis. Whether you call it "chain of custody" or "security measures," steps to ensure the integrity and preservation of the samples collected had to be considered and taken to ensure any hope of producing viable analyses of the same.

Such security concerns are glaringly underscored by the story of the "Smeja Steak."[19] A brief summary of the story highlights that Mr. Justin Smeja made claims of shooting an adult Bigfoot (which ultimately escaped) and an infant Bigfoot. Upon seeing the child-like humanity of the infant, fear of being charged with murder motivated him to reportedly bury the carcass, only to later return to recover it and maintain custody of it. A sample of this carcass or "steak" was submitted to and ultimately included in the Ketchum study (while Mr. Smeja maintained custody of the original carcass) and found to be of an unknown species thereby supporting the existence of Bigfoot. Mr. Smeja eventually became the object of disdain and scrutiny of a variety of members of the Bigfoot community and some genuinely curious researchers. Contacts with these individuals eventually rekindled his concerns regarding being charged with murder. Another "sample of the original carcass" was mysteriously submitted for DNA analysis (reportedly not by Mr. Smeja). The results came back that the sample was from a bear.[20]

One analysis produced results of an "Unknown species"

suggesting Bigfoot, and yet another DNA study of the same carcass finds Bear! How can the chain of custody be irrelevant or a fallacy?!! NOT!!

Mr. Carpenter's own review of Dr. Ketchum's research also highlights how samples were sent to laboratories that were kept blind as to their source of origin so as to not influence results or have results dismissed prior to sufficient analysis. He also highlighted how results were dismissed or negated when the true source of the DNA was revealed or discovered. *To suggest Chain of Custody or security was unimportant or not required or necessary because of the non-forensic/scientific nature of the study is simply inconsistent with these important factors and procedures implemented in the study. To not consider these factors or maintain a chain of custody would have and should have been unfathomable given the potential and anticipated/hoped-for conclusions possibly anticipated.* I am not just referring to the controversial Human hybrid finding/conundrum (not to mention the even more controversial gene-splicing finding), but to the broader hope to scientifically prove the existence of Bigfoot, which in and of itself would be controversial and literally unbelievable to many.

An even more basic issue refuting Mr. Carpenter's and Dr. Ketchum's dismissal of the Chain of Custody concerns revolves around nomenclature used for journals that include a blind review process/panel. They are also referred to as **"Juried Journals"** or using a **"juried review process."** *Again, this flies in the very face of the contention that a chain of custody was conceptually irrelevant or not needed due to the "non-forensic" nature of the research.*

I am not suggesting Dr. Ketchum or Mr. Carpenter are being disingenuous or lying. I do, however, believe these explanations represent what they are on their face value: attempts to refute criticisms challenging the validity of study data and procedures and therefore the scientific value of the study.

Physical Evidence: "As would be expected, evidence that is in the form of a tangible object, such as a firearm, fingerprints, rope purportedly used to strangle someone, or tire casts from a crime scene, is considered to be physical evidence. Physical evidence is also known as "real" or "material" evidence. It can be presented in court as an exhibit of a physical object, captured in still or moving images, described in text, audio or video, or referred to in documents."[21] *Bigfoot feces, hair, or other tissue comes to mind, as do foot and hand prints left on objects and the surface of the earth.*

Prima Facie Evidence: "Meaning 'on its first appearance,' this is evidence presented before a trial is enough to prove something until it is successfully disproved or rebutted at trial. This is also called 'presumptive evidence.'[22] This type of evidence doesn't seem all that relevant to Bigfoot evidence, but I remain open to any ideas or examples of same and would include them with appropriate citation credit in any subsequent reprinting of this book should I be lucky enough (if first printing runs out) to need a reprinting.

Statistical Evidence: "Evidence that uses numbers (or statistics) to support a position is called statistical evidence. This type of evidence is based on research or polls."[23]

Within the Bigfoot community little to sparse statistical evidence directly concerning Bigfoot exists. That which does is most typically in the form of **descriptive statistics**, one of the weakest forms of statistics for generalizability to the validity and reliability of the data itself and therefore the species. In short, descriptive statistics can easily be manipulated to the author's desires and a priori hypothesis or desired point. This is why these are so frequently used in politics and on the news. It's not unheard of for the same data descriptive analysis to be used to support conflicting views. The number of sightings, the frequency of sightings in a particular area, the frequency of the different types of evidence gathered, population estimates, and average size estimates are all examples of descriptive statistics.

A more reliable and valid type of statistical analysis is inferential statistics. These allow one to "infer" the meaning of a specific testable hypothesis or effect and get you closer to the true meaning of the data. *Problematic for Bigfoot research, this type of analysis most frequently requires an experimental manipulation to which the rarity of our target species presents a challenge.* Nonetheless, certain studies would not have to rely on the creature, but could ultimately be inferred to the creature. The zapping phenomenon is one of these and will be discussed in detail in a chapter to come on "zapping." (See Chapter 8.)

Testimonial Evidence: One of the most common forms of evidence is either spoken or written evidence given by a witness under oath. It can be gathered in court, at a deposition, or through an affidavit."[24]

In the Bigfoot community, this has actually been done to strengthen the voracity of a variety of other types of evidence. People reporting sightings have been known to swear to their account "under oath" or otherwise legally endorse their reports.

I have briefly defined each type of evidence and provided relevant examples to Bigfoot research. The concerned reader would do well to consider each type of evidence and come up with their own examples. More importantly, the concerned fieldworker/researcher or concerned future fieldworker/researcher would do well to consider the evidence they have already incorporated into their Bigfoot philosophy and belief system. They need to weigh that evidence based on the respective defining comments above for its relevance to the scientific and experimental value, or the validity and reliability of the evidence. They can then consider the value of that evidence and its impact on their own past or future experimental designs! If the meaning of these later terms (scientific and experimental value, validity, reliability, experimental design) is unfamiliar or only vaguely familiar to the reader, you would do well to carefully read through the remaining chapters in this book!!!

8

THE FIGHT-FLIGHT RESPONSE, THE HUMAN NERVOUS SYSTEM, AND BIGFOOT "ZAPPING"

Certain creatures (Elephants, Whales, Dolphins, Big Cats) produce infrasound (a supersonic, but subsonic to the human ear) sound to communicate, while apex predators use infrasound to stun their prey to increase the likelihood of a successful kill. It is believed and *considered factual by many that Bigfoots use infrasound in their defense against humans.* While many field researchers accept this as factual, *this has yet to be proven scientifically and arguably not even on a phenomenological level.* This last statement is important in its potential validity given the role of the human nervous system in the fight-flight reactions.

"The human nervous system consists of the **central nervous system** and the **peripheral nervous system.** ... (current author's emphasis) ... The central nervous consists of the brain and the spinal cord. Its [job] is to integrate and coordinate all bodily functions by processing all incoming and outgoing messages. ... The peripheral nervous system is the network of sensory and motor neurons that form the **interface** (my emphasis) between the central nervous system and the surface of the body. .... [It includes] the somatic nervous system ... that voluntarily controls the skeletal muscles of the body, ... while the **autonomic nervous system (ANS)** ... (current author's emphasis) ... governs activity not normally under an individual's direct control. [It consists of the] *sympathetic division [that] deals with emergency responding, while the parasympathetic division deals with the internal monitoring and regulation of a variety of functions*" (current author's emphasis).[1]

"The autonomic nervous system deals with the 'survival' matters of two kinds: Those involving a threat to the organism [fight-flight response] and those involving bodily maintenance. Its two divisions 'work together in opposition' to accomplish these survival tasks. The sympathetic division deals with emergency responding, while the parasympathetic division deals with the internal monitoring and regulation of a variety of functions [pupil opening size, degree of salivation and sweating, heart rate speed, breathing, digestive functions in the stomach, adrenalin regulation, digestion in the intestine, urine-elimination].

When you face an emergency or a stressful challenge the sympathetic division mobilizes the brain for arousal and the body for action. Digestion stops, blood flows away from internal organs to the muscles, oxygen transfer is increased, heart rate is increased, and the endocrine system is stimulated to facilitate a variety of motor responses. After the [threat] is over, the parasympathetic division takes charge to decelerate these processes so you can calm down and 'mellow out.' Digestion resumes, heartbeat slows, breathing calms, and so forth."[2]

The fight-or-flight syndrome "describes the sequence of activity regulated by the 'stress center of the brain;' the hypothalamus. The hypothalamus controls the autonomic nervous system and activates the pituitary gland [the master hormone secretion, growth, and regulation gland] ... *to prepare the body for combat and struggle or running away to safety.* The blood vessels in the skin, skeletal muscles, brain, and viscera constrict; the pupils dilate for far vision, sweating increases, and the bronchi dilate and produce more rapid, shallow breathing. Skin and body hair produce "goose pimples.' The heart accelerates the rate of beating, and increases the strength of contraction; the digestive tract decreases its internal contractions to reduce digestion, and secretions of digestive fluids decrease which can create stomach pain, nausea, or vomiting. The adrenal glands stimulate adrenalin secretion increasing blood sugar, blood pressure, and heart rate thereby giving our body an energy rush or surge and making us feel tense and shaky, the anal sphincter closes; the blood vessels in genitalia dilate causing genital discomfort, the liver releases sugar into the bloodstream."[3]

We integrate these processes into our language when we talk about being "scared stiff," or "frozen by fear." Sometimes we lose control of our bodily functions and we "get the piss scared out of us" or we are "scared shitless." Think of an anxiety or panic attack and recognize how many of these processes occur during one. *Physiologically there is no difference between fear and anxiety reactions. Psychologically, fear is those physiologic responses in reaction to a* **real and present threat.** *Anxiety is those same physiologic responses to an imaginary or not immediately present threat.*

A Bigfoot encounter can produce many of these same symptoms, whether we're being zapped or not. Friends who wish to remain anonymous have lost control of their bladder and bowels during close encounters (scared shitless or had the piss scared out of them). Others have been frozen in place and couldn't react or flee (scared stiff). Others have reported feeling like they've been punched in the gut, and double over to puke. One felt like he took a baseball bat to the chest. Some lose motor control of their arms; their hair stands on end or at attention. Nose bleeds black and blue marks on their flesh, abnormal swelling of parts of their body, electrical sensations, numbness and tingling, and extreme pain. Others find energy reserves and physical capacities previously unknown to them in order "to run like hell;" bumping into objects and pushing others away only later to discover pulled muscles and bruises not noticed or realized in the "heat of the moment." All these experiences can potentially be explained by sympathetic and parasympathetic reactions, but at least theoretically arguably could be a result of "zapping!"

All these experiences **can potentially** *be explained by sympathetic and* *parasympathetic reactions, but many are also **attributed** to being "zapped" by **Bigfoot infrasound**. How can we objectively know the difference?*

Is our body doing it to ourselves solely as a result of a fight-flight reaction in the presence of an apex predator? Is infrasound triggering that same reaction from our autonomic nervous system when we are in its presence and it is being emitted? Is infrasound creating that same reaction from our ANS, even when any animal producing it is a distant relative to our position? (Elephants reportedly sense infrasound through the pads on their feet from a distance of 10 miles). Is the effect a direct result of the infrasound itself, not requiring a receptive nervous system in which it provokes reactions?

In Bigfoots, is infrasound or "some other ability" creating a telekinetic force that can displace physical objects? Are ancestral memories (cellular collective unconscious) taking over on a cellular level in our body and creating archetypal behavioral responses? I do not have the answer to these questions, but each could represent a potential scientific hypothesis to test using scientific experimentation!

Infrasound is real! It has been well documented in the animal kingdom. According to Cornell Lab's *Elephant Listening Project*, we do know that African elephants can communicate over very long distances [using infrasound].[4] Other animals implicated in using it include whales, elephants, hippopotamuses, rhinoceroses, giraffes, okapis, peacocks, alligators, and human singers. Some vocalists, including Tim Storms, can produce notes in the infrasound range.[5]

Besides elephants, big cats, wolves, bears, and Bigfoot are cited within Bigfoot circles as creatures using infrasound. It is also contended that it has been weaponized by our military. To this last point, Nicole Chaves (2017), a CNN reporter tells a different story in her article on acoustic weapons.[6] She cites "a US government official [saying] an acoustic device may have been *used to attack State Department employees at the US Embassy in Havana*." Interestingly, she indicates: "Since the early 1990s, long-range acoustic devices—also known as LRADs—have helped authorities control crowds of people, especially protesters. They emit a loud, painful sound over a long distance and make people run away. ... In the US, police used such devices during demonstrations at the *2009 G20 Summit meeting in Pittsburgh*. They were also used more recently, during the *2014 protests in Ferguson, Missouri*, following the fatal shooting of Michael Brown."[7]

In addition to LRADS, her article goes on to detail other sonic stimuli/devices including "mosquitos," ultrasound devices, infrasonic devices, and "other sounds that hurt" ("a brown note" purported to induce loss of bowel control). Interestingly, James Parker, an expert in sound and law at the University of Melbourne in Australia is cited as indicating: "There are (sonic) devices that are used as weapons, *but none that I know of use infrasound, as infrasound is probably the hardest to weaponized* (my emphasis). Nonetheless, the article reports that since the 1990s, the US military and private companies researched infrasonic devices that could cause behavior changes at frequencies too low to be audible."[8]

Infrasound Experiments Proposed

Irrespective of weaponization, a variety of animals and even humans can produce infrasound. As such it would appear reasonably accessible for scientific studies. This is actually good news for scientifically biased Bigfoot researchers as it lends itself to an experimental design to investigate the phenomena and possibly answer some of the questions I proposed above.

No scientific investigation is easily accomplished, and investigating the issues noted above are no exception. Financial, time logistics and subject availability of resources issues abound. Any requirement of a human subject's safety review panel could represent a challenging obstacle to negotiate given the purported effects of infrasound on humans (people who work around elephants reportedly suffer these on occasion). Given that zoo work (cleaning, grooming, feeding) with elephants already happening on a necessary regular basis, however, appropriate human safety should not represent an insurmountable challenge. The hard-core scientific investigator is warned, however, that it is not my goal here to write a research proposal worthy of submission for a financial grant. My suggestions herein merely represent initial and tentative ideas toward a viable study. *It is meant to instruct on experimental designs to isolate the phenomena and their potential impact on humans.* It is not meant to be a definitive, air-tight, and infallible design. But...

The first obstacle would be to obtain an infrasound "generator" to produce infrasound in a predictable and reliable fashion, in short "on cue." Of course, based on my brief review above, the raw generation of infrasound could be accomplished using any number of animal species including apparently human vocalists. Problematic, even when using a "human generator" who could reliably INITIATE infrasound sonic stimuli on cue, would be the consistency of that stimuli or signature across multiple trials, over any given exposure time period, for different experimental human subjects. Variability in the depth of the breath used to produce the sound would impact its "sustain time." Vocal cord or other vocal apparatus used to produce the sound would be vulnerable to the effects of fatigue causing variability in volume, pitch, and tone consistency that need to be controlled.

The obvious and simple solution would be to use an audio recording shown to contain infrasound to generate and consistently control the aforementioned qualities of the infrasound. Indeed, my online search of infrasound revealed the website of the Cornell Lab's Elephant Listening Project to have an auditory and visually represented recording present on the first page of their site.[9] *The reader is encouraged to listen to this recording to fully appreciate the sonic intensity and other qualities of this stimulus. It is awesome!* Presenting the auditory stimuli of such a recording through a pair of headphone speakers of sufficient design to capture and accurately replicate the infrasound would also allow us to control for environmental factors in the "listening environment" or room. If needed, this room could further be acoustically insulated against extraneous or unwanted outside auditory stimuli infringing upon the listening environment and potentially contaminating study results.

The next goal would be to ensure the "purity" of the listening receivers or subjects. All would be required to submit to an ear wax cleaning to ensure no impediment or obstacle existed within the aural canal that might impact hearing ability. Of course, controlling for variable hearing abilities across subjects would be necessary. Each subject would need to undergo an Ear, Nose, and Throat consultation which included a hearing test to ensure that each subject could "hear" the infrasound and, in effect had "normal" hearing. What if (given how it is perceived in the elephant population) the infrasound phenomena were not a result of a "hearing" process? Elephants sensing it from the ground through their foot pads suggests a somatosensory perceptual process could also be instrumental in the phenomena. If so, a neurological examination including a somatosensory perceptual study would be required of all subjects to ensure "minimum" levels of sensory receptivity across all subjects.

Having exercised reasonable controls over the infrasound-generating device and receiving subjects, *a "double-blind, AB, counter-balanced" experimental design could be executed to test the influence of infrasound on humans.* Given the reported length of time this phenomenon has been being investigated and reports of the influence of infrasound upon humans, this seems unusual to me that this study hasn't already been conducted, with or without public discourse.

A "blind" experimental design requires the receiving subject to be kept ignorant, naive, or "blind" as to whether they are receiving the experimental manipulation (hearing the recording containing infrasound) or the control (placebo/non-active) manipulation (hearing an identical recording with the infrasound removed). A "double-blind" design requires the receiving subject, as well as the experimenter administering and/or recording the test/effects to both be unaware of the stimuli being presented. Neither knows if the subject is being given the infrasound or non-infrasound recording, minimizing bias or experimental demand characteristics on both of their parts.

An "**AB**" experimental design would involve presenting the control recording (A) followed by the infrasound recording (B). Making it a "**counterbalanced design**" would require some (50%)

subjects to participate in the testing protocol just described, while other subjects (50%) would participate in a "**BA**" testing protocol. They would be first exposed to the infrasound recording (B), then the placebo or control recording (A). Comparing similarities and differences in results between counter-balanced stimuli/groups (the AB versus the BA subjects) goes a long way to control for experimental bias and confounding influences/variables, especially the sequence of the presentation. That is, experiencing the non-infrasound condition (A) first, might predispose or sensitize the subject to the infrasound condition (B). A counter-balanced (BA) presentation, compensates for this when we statistically compare the AB condition to the BA condition.

Variables such as blood pressure, heart rate, respiration frequency, blood pressure, adrenal levels, cortisol levels, and other internal stress-dependent variables (variables influenced or not by the experimental manipulation) could be monitored and collected. Similarly, observations of the subject's behavior before, during, and after exposure to the recording by the experimenter or a "blind" panel of trained rating observers could be recorded and examined. Self-report tools such as emotional tests or symptom checklists or other self-rating tools could also be applied to the experimental subjects.

A further experimental manipulation could then be added: **Threat!** Herein lies the potential human subjects' panel sticky wicket! How do you get a panel looking out for the welfare of human subjects to agree to allow those subjects to feel threatened to provoke the fight-or-flight response? It might be a challenge.

Amusement park rides, as well as Halloween ghost or ghoul houses, do actually come to mind as options. *The pain cold-pressor test, in which a person is asked to hold their hand in a bucket of ice water up to the wrist, is a classic fight-flight pain manipulation that may or may not be generalizable to fight/flight from a predator.* "Candid Camera" television shows in which a trained bear or other apex predator suddenly appears come to mind.[10] Watching a scary movie might be more benign. Handling a benign large snake or being threatened to be forced to handle a snake should certain conditions not be met come to mind. After any of these threat conditions, cortisol levels could be drawn and analyzed. Controlling for Type C (thrill-seeking) personalities to eliminate the influence of their higher fight–flight activation thresholds would be required.

So, to complete the experimental design, we start with our original counter-balanced, double-blind, AB/BA design with two groups of people. In the AB condition, an infrasound recording is presented first, followed by a recording with infrasound components removed. In the BA condition, we would first begin with the recording without the infrasound, followed by the recording with the infrasound remaining in it. Including the cold-pressor test, each of these groups (simultaneous to the infrasound experimental condition or separate from it) would also be subjected to the AB threat test condition. Fifty percent of the AB condition would perform the threat test using a bucket of ice water first then the threat test with room temperature water), with the other 50% of the AB condition performing the threat test using the room temperature water test first then the bucket of ice water test. The same counter-balanced threat condition would also be applied to the BA threat test condition (room temperature water followed by ice water versus ice water followed by room temperature water).

Please note, that I have chosen the most scientifically established, apparently acceptable, and successful of the possible methods to induce the threat discussed above: the cold-pressor test. I personally like the snake handling or scary movie conditions, but each would require additional steps to measure and control for snake phobias or preferences to view scary movies.

The experimenter or a panel of trained experts would rate subjects' behavioral reactions in each of these conditions. Actual experimental subjects' self-ratings of their fear or stress response and objective measures of fight-flight (cortisol levels, heart rate, respiration rate, blood pressure, etc.) serve as the dependent variables (what's being influenced) in each condition. The independent variable (what's being tested) is the infrasound versus non-infrasound conditions and how they interact with the threat versus non-threat conditions.

So, where's the Bigfoot? There is none in this study! The elephant trumpet (with infrasound in it) represents the roar of the Bigfoot using infrasound (if it is the infrasound, rather than threat producing the reaction)! Other studies could use existing recordings of Bigfoot roars, howls, or other known output versus thought to contain infrasound. These infrasound samples could be compared to the elephant trumpets to show the similarity or correlation between them. Also, the inferential statistics used in the design of the hypothetical experiment described above would allow us to speak to the generalizability of the experiment to Bigfoot in the strengths and limitations portion of the study discussion. In short, there is more than one way to skin a Bigfoot without having a living or dead Bigfoot to study.

_____

9

EXPERIMENTAL DESIGN: HOW WE SCIENTIFICALLY "TRAP" BIGFOOT

G iven that the upcoming chapter entitled "Scientific Research and Numbers: The Necessary Evil Known as Statistics" is exquisitely tedious and painful, I hope to keep this chapter describing how to set up an experiment for the purposes of Scientific BF Research "simple" ... like my mind. *Nonetheless, if we want to truly call our field research "science," or "scientific," we would do well to think about what we are doing as an experiment and/or actually conduct experiments in the name of systematically discovering information on the species.*

Some definitions are required. In research, we first need to identify a research question, idea, or theory. These represent our "hypotheses." Our **hypothesis** is *the question we are hoping to answer through our study.* The pressing question most are still trying to answer through field research is *"Does Bigfoot exist from an objective, scientific perspective?"* For those who have had a definite, phenomenological visual sighting, no further research is needed!!! Not so for science! You have to prove it to the scientific community (and I might add to the general public).

In order to do so, we must first convert our research question into a testable hypothesis typically known as the "**Null hypothesis**."

Simply stated the null hypothesis is that there is **no difference** between our control and experimental groups or variables. Don't ask why we test to **disprove** "no difference," just take my word for it that it is the scientific thing to do. *We want to disprove that there is no difference between Bigfoot and other terrestrial species.*

Control and experimental groups are defined in Chapter 4. To briefly elaborate, the "**experimental group**" is the group of subjects or the variables we are attempting to observe or influence through our test or experimental manipulation. The "**control group**" is a "comparison group in a study whose members receive either no intervention at all or some established intervention."[1] *By comparing the "control group" to the "experimental group," we establish the differences between the two groups and their response to our test or manipulation.* The control group ensures the reaction of the experimental group is unique, and not influenced by some other issue, error, or extraneous variable. In doing so, it helps us answer our question or support our point.

In general, for our purposes, our experimental group will typically be Bigfoot; the species or group we are trying to prove exists or are trying to understand or influence through our experiment. For our specific purposes of proving Bigfoot exists, we would restate our question in the form of the null hypothesis: "*There is **no difference** between Bigfoot and other superficially similar species (such as great apes, chimpanzees, monkeys, or humans).* In science, we want to *reject or disprove the null hypothesis* (just to make it confusing). We want to accept what is known as the "**Alternative Hypothesis.**" In this case, the alternative hypothesis would be stated as: "*There **is a difference** between Bigfoot and superficially similar species.*" In less scientific wording; "*Bigfoot exists as a unique species.*"

Please note, in advancing these hypotheses and using the word "species," I am not making a judgment that Bigfoot belongs in the terrestrial animal kingdom or the extra-terrestrial/paranormal realm beyond the fact that we live on earth in this three-dimensional consensus reality. Bigfoot's exact origin or nature is an empirical (experimentally observable, definable, and testable) question to be researched in my opinion!

So now we have got our Null and Alternative hypotheses defined. *We next need to develop an experimental design to test those hypotheses.* In Psychology, one of the simplest experimental designs is the "AB" experimental design. "A" stands for our baseline. It contains no intervention/experimental manipulation. "B" stands for our experimental manipulation, "test" or intervention. In order to do that, however, we first have to define and operationalize our "**dependent**" and "**independent**" **variables.**

A **dependent variable** is an entity we are trying to intervene upon or manipulate. For our purposes, it will often be BF. Our **independent variable** will be the experimental manipulation or intervention through which we hope to influence Bigfoot. "Tree knocks," for example. We hypothesize proof that Bigfoots exist based on their response to tree knocks. No other animal commonly occurring in USA forests makes a tree knock sound, right? Well, none besides humans chopping wood or hitting a tree with a stick, beavers slapping their tails, rams butting heads, deer, and elk locking horns during the rut, and any primates escaping from zoos or traveling carnivals. **These** "extraneous" or "confounding" variables need to be controlled for or eliminated as contaminating variables in our study.

Assuming we can control or account for those (a **huge** experimental assumption), our **null hypothesis** then becomes: "If there is no Bigfoot in the area, there will be no sound after we make a "tree knock." Our **alternative hypothesis** would be, "If there are Bigfoot in the area and we make a tree knock, that knock will elicit a response identifiable as Bigfoot." Again, please note, that we are taking **a huge assumptive leap** if we cannot visually see the creature make the response. *With some notable exceptions (dermal ridges, mid-tarsal break), this factor is not too dissimilar, however, to the leap we take when we assume a Bigfoot made a track in the soil when we didn't see or have another objective record of BF making it.*

At this point, we could get fancy and compare tree knocks to howls. In doing so we subdivide our **independent variable** by renaming it "a provocation" rather than a tree knock. *We then test which provocation (howl vs knock) is more likely or effective in eliciting a BF response.* Although needed, that is a different study which we will not explore at this time in the spirit of keeping things simple.

An Expedition! It's a Habituation experiment!

Whether conceptualized as such or not, simply entering the field to hunt for Bigfoot is a loose "AB" experimental design. The **baseline** or "A" condition is the woods or wilderness undisturbed by human presence. The **manipulation or intervention** is the field researcher entering the field and introducing *their presence into the natural environment.* If you've been on a Bigfoot expedition, you quickly learn the hypothesis that: "BF knows we are here (in their presence) before we are certain that they are there in our presence. *True of Bigfoot or not, a human entering the undisturbed woods or wilderness creates an "unnatural" influence, intervention, or manipulation into nature. That influence needs to be controlled for and/or eliminated.* (See the Hawthorne effect and Heisenberg Uncertainly Principle definition in Chapter 2.) *Simply inserting ourselves into their environment has the potential to influence the natural behavior of any animal, species, or "being" existing there and needs to be considered for its influence on that species.*

It would be extremely difficult, if not impossible, to enter the field to conduct research on BF without having some influence on Bigfoot's natural environment and therefore potentially Bigfoot. The trained field researcher justifies/explains this influence away or more accurately **attempts** to minimize it through the notion of "habituation:" an attempt to make ourselves habitual or natural in their environment. In short, *through humanity's continuous presence in their environment, we believe they "get used to" us.*

Ron Morehead in making some of his recordings known as the Sierra Sounds, modified **an already existing dwelling** and **occasionally used it as a blind** to conceal his presence from BF and record. The following photo has become celebrated within Bigfoot circles.

Courtesy of Ron Moorhead.[2]

The astute reader might point out, that if they were truly **hidden** in a blind, a habituation process shouldn't have been necessary. I would submit that, at minimum, the habituation process began to occur when they entered the field, in addition to the labor-intensive activity it took to restore this shelter. This in no way represents or is intended as a criticism of their pioneering work in the field. My point is, that any animals' awareness of our presence in nature is pretty much unavoidable in any form of field research. If true habituation occurs, and allows the species to "act naturally," it is desirable. Nonetheless, please note that in any field research, *the lack of human presence represents the baseline or "A" portion of the design and our insertion into the environment represents the first experimental manipulation or intervention or "B."*

Another form of habituation is of equal importance as Bigfoot habituating to our presence to ensure "natural Bigfoot behavior." The **fieldworker** needs to "habituate" themselves to nature's sounds and silences. In effect, we need to habituate or desensitize ourselves to being in nature to minimize "reactive bias" also known as "freaking out." *We are the biggest disturbance and presence in most woods!* We need to recognize our own thoughts, feelings, and behaviors in response to the natural conditions around us. Most people are not familiar with nature sounds, let alone themselves when silent. *Knowing one's self-nature is critical to attempting unbiased interpretations of what you perceive around you.* We've got to know ourselves (our thoughts, feelings, behaviors, values, attitudes, etc.) to accurately know nature. *You have got to know yourself in your own sounds of silence.*

Assuming habituation occurs (it is not the purpose of this book to debate that issue), I will move forward with another example of an AB design commonly performed on expeditions: the night excursion with tree knocks and/or howls. Leaving base camp in small groups, we venture into the night in areas considered likely to have Bigfoot activity. When we arrive at the location, we establish our baseline ("A") by either sitting quietly or acting "natural" for a period of time. How long we do that is typically random depending on the group leader. If we were going to be systematic about that, we would do well to establish a time limit or time frame for that baseline ahead of time (a priori = in advance). For illustration purposes only, I will select 30 minutes of either "quiet as a possible baseline time" or "acting natural baseline time."

Those two activities for baseline time could be an experiment in and of itself to systematically determine if one or the other is most likely to illicit a Bigfoot response. Different researchers seem to have differing opinions on this (you should be quiet versus you should act natural versus you should "act the fool" [loud and boisterous to draw their attention]). *Simply systematically monitoring how much time elapses under any of those three conditions until a definitive Bigfoot response occurs in a given area would be important data to compare for significant differences (controlling for the area itself).* For our experimental example of an "AB" design, however, we will assume we will use baseline behavior (A) of "acting natural" and for 30 minutes. We will also establish an a priori "monitoring period" after "our experimental manipulation" for a response of five minutes. During this time, we will remain silent to maximize our chances of hearing an audible indicator should the BF knock or howl back or sneak in on us.

So, "by a stopwatch" at minute 31, we stop "acting naturally." One person designated as the official knocker for that night (the only person making knocks for all the sites/locations during that evening's excursion in your small group) would make a single tree knock (using the same stick or knocking device used by all the other "designated knockers" in the other expedition subgroups). This is then followed by five minutes of silence. (Of course, all the "designated knockers" would be trained in advance and outside the target field location to make the same sounding knock with the same force or propulsion as each other.) Results are meticulously recorded including the clock time of the knock and the clock time of any response and what type of response. If utilizing a howl, the duration of the howl is recorded. The knock or howl represents our experimental intervention or manipulation. The tree knocks or howl followed by five minutes of silence and appropriate recording is our "experimental condition" (B), thus our "AB" design.

"Well, hot damn! That's exactly what we do when I go on an expedition with my buddy! After having a burger and knocking back a few beers at the bar, we drive out into the woods, sit in the pickup truck, and down a few more beers. If we don't hear or see anything after those beers, we make a tree knock or two and listen for them to knock back. So, I guess we're doing science too! Ain't we?" No! Not if that is exactly how you do it!

You haven't established habituation by setting up a base camp and letting BF get "used to you" being in their general range of activity. You would need to establish an a priori (in advance) number of beers you'd drink and how fast you plan to drink them at your location. You'd need to record the time it took to drink them and the exact clock time when you make your knock. Only one of you would do the knocking with the same stick you use every time you go out. The knock should be done on the same kind and size of tree each time. You'd have to make the same kind of knock and the same number of knocks each time and record the time you made the knock. You would have already decided a priori (ahead of time) how many more beers you'd drink after the knock as you sat in silence, and how fast you'd drink them. You'd have to record those elapsed clock times to ensure you are "on pace." If you got a response (and were still awake,) you'd need to document the response as accurately as you could. This would include what type of response and how much time-lapse in between the knock and the response. If it was a howl or other vocal response, you'd need to time how long it lasted. If whoops, how many whoops, how long did each one last, and how long did the series of whoops go on, etc., etc.? Then you would have taken the first step down the path of science.

To make it the "truly rigorous science," you'd have to do the above "experimental protocol" initially at the same location at the same time of night, and then vary the locations and times systematically. Once you have gathered all that data, you then have to encode it into numbers. You'd then analyze those numbers statistically to detect differences and patterns. You'd then have to write up or publicly publish those results so that other researchers investigating the same hypothesis could replicate your study. Now we're talking science!

"Well, damn son! That sounds like a pain in the ass! That's a lot of work in the field just to do more work in an office on a computer and typewriter to make it science! Shoot, I just want to have a little fun on a Friday night! We'll stick to the bar, beer, and truck routine, if you don't mind."

In an "ABA" design, instead of remaining as silent as possible for an a priori period of time or until we hear a response, we'd develop an alternate design. During the second "A" in this alternate "ABA" design, we would simply return to our "acting natural baseline condition. In contrast, in the "AB" design we would simply leave the area after making our knock with no response.

Given the current scientific status of BF, we need to keep our research designs simple to establish fundamental data. Examples might include simply monitoring how long is it after entering an area before we detect a Bigfoot response without otherwise doing something to provoke one (other than our presence). This would potentially begin to inform BF habituation issues. What is that response when we enter an area? Is it a knock, howl, whoop, tree fall, etc.? How many tree knocks do they make when we arrive, if any? How do they announce their presence? Do they announce their presence at all or do they try to be surreptitious (secretive)? How often are knocks returned? *Forget about what that might mean for now. Opinions on these* **fundamental** *questions/issues already abound, but how well have they been systematically investigated and reported? If we allow untested theories (therefore opinions) to drive our fieldwork and research, we are already putting the proverbial cart before the horse and fail to establish the scientific foundation needed for good science to prove the existence of the species.*

*   **The above questions about tree knocks exist without known frequency data on what constitutes a "normal number" of tree knocks!** Form and standardize your knocking stick(s). Look at a map. Pick one area where you know Bigfoots live. Go make 50 single tree knocks in that area during a defined period of time and hours within a 24-hour cycle (i.e., 1400 = 2:00 am). Might not hurt to note weather conditions. Immediately record data in a numerically encoded fashion.*

*   Now, move on to a second location, where* **there may or may not be Bigfoot.** *Remain true to your best estimate of known Bigfoot activity when choosing this location. That is, the area* **should not** *have a reputation for Bigfoots or cryptids. It should also be at least 80-100 miles from your other locations. Go make 50 single tree knocks in that area during a defined period of time and hours within a 24-hour cycle (i.e., 1400 = 2:00 am). Might not hurt to note weather conditions. Record and immediately data numerically.*

*   Finally, pick another area where you're certain* **Bigfoot doesn't frequent or exist.** *Even if it is a town or city. Make 50 single tree knocks using the same knocking stick, preferably on the same type of tree as was used in the "Bigfoot area" condition. (Note, if you can't find a tree, a telephone pole will do.) Record and immediately data numerically.* **Be prepared to foam at the mouth and give a good roar at any crowds gathering around and staring at you!!**

*   Notice you have created three groups or conditions based on possible Bigfoot presence in the area. You made 50 knocks in strategic locations*

within each area and meticulously recorded responses (including delay times, and frequency) while digitally recording all these events on a separate audio or audio and visual recording system in real-time. Sustain time of knocks can be extracted on audacity and quantified (based on tonal qualities or other relevant factors).

We now have frequency data on three groups of tree knock samples (along with real-time audio recordings of the same): Bigfoot Presence, Possible Bigfoot Presence, and No Bigfoot Presence. We examine correlational versus causal relationships in the data and can test to see if any one of the three has a significantly stronger tree-knocking "effect" and what that tells us about its possible source.

*The calculations for these results could be done by hand by any reasonably practiced statistician, but easily run through a basic statistic package without spending their money on more advanced applications available in SPSS (formally known as Statistical Package for the Social Sciences).[3] Phenomenological studies have produced credible anecdotal evidence that there is not a scientifically established **causal** relationship between Bigfoots and tree knocks. That is there is not a 100% consistency between tree knock provocations and responses to those tress knocks. As such, the correlational analysis would be a targeted analysis to examine possible relationships between tree knocks and the "Bigfoot species" or if you prefer, "Bigfoot Phenomena."*

*Which of our three conditions (Bigfoot vs +/- Bigfoot vs No Bigfoot) should produce the most tree knock returns **if** tree knocks are representative of the presence of Bigfoot? What would you predict the results would be and why?*

Personally, having spent more money than I can afford on an insufficient number of expeditions, I hope for no less than the Bigfoot area producing a statistically significantly higher number of knocks than the other two groups!! Hell! It better come out that way!!!! I don't know about the rest of Y'all, but that's where I've been looking! But In Truth, I Have No Freaking Idea!! In truth, it hasn't been scientifically established. A potential research plumb for the novice or advanced ambitious Scientific Bigfoot Researcher?

This brings us back to the question of the "Bigfoot Joke" at the beginning *of this book. What if the Bigfoot areas aren't producing significantly more knocks!? That's where the damn research groups are looking! We've been looking for more than 60 years! That's where the lamp post is shining brightly. It's illuminating the sidewalk and the street. It's where the proverbial drunk and police officer are looking for the lost key!!!! We've been looking for that lost key pretty much in the same fashion and same location for more than 60 years without "scientific proof." We've done so because so few have championed the "scientific agenda," **not** because science is not up to the task. We've got to start looking where the light isn't shining so bright or maybe there is only darkness. We need to create a new light source to illuminate another path.*

At worst, this data represents a pilot study on the tree knock phenomenon. Results are arguably representative of "baseline data," irrespective of outcome and the deuced vs induced reasoning powers brought to bear on the data. Repeat this experiment in different locations geographically in the CONTUS. Once National Baseline Data on a phenomenon is established, you can then detect variations or differences between the three groups to bolster or refute your hypothesis.

We'd have also taken an initial step toward targeting a "Bigfoot Phenomena." Other types of Sonic Bigfoot Phenomena could be systematically identified, and further evaluated and studied. The Bigfoot evocativeness qualities of various provocations become scientifically standardized and an important control variable in the study. They also represent a potential variable to use in Bigfoot provocations (a scientifically standardized and proven one at that)!

Less basic, but very important, does Bigfoot respond "in kind" to provocations? If you make a howl are, they more likely to respond with a howl, whoop, or knock. If you make a knock, do they respond with a knock? Do they respond with the same number of knocks as you make? Do they respond with the same kind of howl or whoop or another vocalization that you make? Each one of these more basic questions begs for an experimental design to be developed to test out their respective hypotheses.

Given psychology's ability to operationally define, identify, test, and utilize the abstract (not concrete) **concept of intelligence**, these and other experimental designs and techniques certainly seem applicable to Bigfoot. If we cannot identify Bigfoot through consistent and frequent sightings, perhaps we can identify the concept of "Bigfootness" or "Bigfoot phenomena" through such experimental scientific avenues.

This leads me to the topic of **sample size** (the number of subjects you use in your study) in experimental design. By **sample**, I refer to taking a **representative measure** (amount) for the entire population or world of a concept or phenomenon to be investigated.

When you sample whiskey, you don't have to drink every ounce of every brand of whiskey in the world (although many have tried) to understand the **idea** or **concept** of whiskey. You can sample or taste a few blended whiskeys (each brand representing its own sample). Next, a few straight bourbon whiskeys (each brand representing their own sample). Then a few scotch whiskeys (each brand representing a unique sample). Finally, a few malted whiskeys to understand the concept of whiskey (not to mention the concept of hangovers). *We don't measure all the behaviors in the world, we take representative samples of them to know and understand "Whiskey."*

As a general rule of thumb, the larger your sample's size the better. We will, however, discuss exceptions to this rule. The number of samples you take influences the "power, strength, or likelihood" of your ability to detect the influence (the response) of the experimental variable you are trying to detect. Using our Bigfoot responses (the dependent variable) to tree knocking, if you go into the woods one time and make one tree knock, you have created a sample size of one for your independent variable (the tree knock). That is one tree knock. (Note in fact we are sampling Bigfoot responses to tree knocks [the dependent variable], not our knocks themselves. The knocks themselves have already been "standardized" so they remain consistent across time.)

If you don't receive a definitive response, it would certainly be premature to **accept** the null hypothesis (tree knocks do not illicit Bigfoot responses) and **reject** the alternative hypothesis (tree knocks do illicit Bigfoot responses). *You may be conducting your experiment in* *an area devoid of Bigfoots.* Bigfoots may be in the area but acting in a "stealth" mode. You may be in an area or region where these creatures respond more consistently to stone clacks or howls. You can only make educated guesses (hypotheses).

Following our protocol, you leave that area and move on to a new one. After a 30-minute baseline, at minute 31, you make your single knock. No response. Now your **sample** of Bigfoot responses to tree knocks is two. Rinse and repeat that evening, the next evening the next, etc., etc., until you have a reasonable **sample size.** Given the number of variables potentially influencing the result (besides if it is an actual creature that exists in the wilds), you'll want a high number of tree knock response attempts, let's say one thousand.

The more independent variables you add, the need for a larger sample size increases. For example, I earlier alluded to changing the independent variable (tree knocks) to the broader variable concept of "provocations" including knocks, howls, and let's add stone clacks. Now, in an ideal world, we need three times the number of provocations (one thousand tree knocks, one thousand howls, one thousand stone-clacking sequences). The disadvantage of this design is that means at least three times the work. The advantage of this design is you are killing three birds with one stone (no pun intended). It's also a more interesting and meaningful study given that many field researchers have hypothesized that not all provocations are equally provocative in certain regions, habituation sites, or around certain clans of the beast.

"Well, why wouldn't you collect considerably higher sample numbers than suggested in the example above? If a sample size of one thousand of each type of provocation is good, wouldn't ten thousand of each be ten times better?" Maybe, maybe not! There is the issue of practicality. That is, the time it would take to gather that many samples (a total of 30,000 provocations). Additionally, simply keeping count could become problematic without carrying a computer into the field.

The most important reason, however, revolves around the true strength or weakness of the effect (the response to the tree knock) you are attempting to elicit. That is the "strength" or "likelihood" of our dependent variable i.e., the likelihood of Bigfoot producing a response. On one hand, we do need our number high as it is unlikely that each time a Bigfoot hears a field researcher's knock (or that of another Bigfoot) they will respond. That is, for the field researcher who has been out in the field at a habituation site where you **know** Bigfoot lives and is in the area, you've already learned that they don't respond to every tree knock. There is not a 100% response rate to each provocation. Again, Phenomenological Research has already established that there is not a causal relationship between knock provocations and whatever is responding, be it a Bigfoot or something else!! We need to therefore subject our data to initial correlational analyses.

On the other hand, multiplying that factor by ten (ten thousand per type of provocation) **might** create an inflated likelihood of accidental or random responses just through the increased probabilities of some kind of response due to the higher sampling numbers. *In short, in terms of statistical probabilities, the more often you try to elicit a response, the more likely it becomes that you will eventually illicit a response, even if it's a very weak rather than robust phenomenon.*

*Paradoxically similarly, if your sample size is too small, you may miss robust influences or phenomena that do in fact exist in reality, but can't be identified or captured due to **limited sampling availability**. As such, the sample size is determined by the subject you are studying, the availability of the behavior or creature you want to sample, and the number of variables or interventions you hope to test.*

Low sample sizes also speak to the difficulty in identifying the effect, behavior, or variable you are trying to detect. *The illusiveness and low frequency of Bigfoot sightings highlight the challenge of using visual sightings as an indicator of the species' existence.* Footprints are more frequent, but *I would argue that vocalizations are even more common than footprints.* They (sonic data) therefore represent the most fertile soil to till in the hopes of proving the existence of the species. Of course, definitively identifying a Bigfoot auditory response from that of other creatures in the forest (including man) represents a technical challenge. *I would submit, however, that it is far from an insurmountable challenge, and earlier in this text outlined at least one path to accomplishing that.*

Understanding what a "**counter-balanced design**" is also seems critical. Simply stated, you reverse or alternate the order of your independent variable. Later in the text, I give an example of this based on the gender influences of the researcher on Bigfoot responses (p. 164). We will now use our provocation design to provide another illustration of a counter-balanced design.

In our provocation example, we have three levels of provocation: knocks, howls, and stone clacks. In the interest of efficiency (investment of time and "manpower"), presenting one stimulus (provocation) each night or outing may not be practical. Decades of time doing so might be required. It would be more time-efficient to do all three at each stop! Problematic in this, however, would be using the same sequence of presentation at each stop (i.e., knock, howl, then stone clack). If you get a response on a stone clack (in the sequence just noted), you won't know if it is the stone clack eliciting the response or if either the knock or howl is eliciting a **delayed** response. A counter-balanced order of presentation eliminates the order influences when later analyzed.

By counter-balanced, I mean that first you perform the knock, then the howl, and then the stone clacks at the first site. At the next site, you first perform the howl then the clacks then the knock. At the next site, you do the stone clack first, then the knocks then the howl. At the next, you are back to your original rotation (knock, howl clack). *By counter-balancing or systematically cycling the order of your provocations you effectively "equal out" or eliminate the confounding influence of one provoking delayed response that is attributed to another.*

Placebo control and Blind experimental designs also warrant further elaboration

The American Psychological Association Online Dictionary defines a "placebo" as "a pharmacologically inert substance, such as a sugar pill, that is often administered as a control in testing new drugs.

Placebos used in double-blind trials may be **dummies** or **active placebos.** Formerly, placebos were occasionally used as diagnostic or psychotherapeutic agents, for example, in relieving pain or inducing sleep by suggestion, but the ethical implications of deceiving patients in such fashion make this practice problematic ... [It is also defined as] ... any medical or psychological intervention or treatment that is believed to be 'inert,' thus making it valuable as a control condition against which to compare the intervention or treatment of interest."[4]

Stated more concretely, it's the "sugar pill" the old-time doctor who didn't want to cause addiction to pain pills would give grandma when she had a "sick headache."

*Of most importance to understand for our purposes is that the effect is not "just in your imagination." In medicine, at least, the sugar pill and other placebo interventions can and do actually create **physiological changes** in the body. The body reacts to the sugar pill in a similar way as it reacts to the pain pill! This is called the "placebo effect: a clinically significant response to a therapeutically inert substance or nonspecific treatment (placebo) deriving from the recipient's expectations or beliefs regarding the intervention.*[5]

It is now recognized that placebo effects accompany the administration of any drug (active or inert) and contribute to the therapeutic effectiveness of a specific treatment. For example, patients given a placebo to relieve headaches may report statistically significant reductions in headaches in studies that compare them with patients who receive no treatment at all. *"This term is also used more generally in nonclinical studies to indicate any effect arising from participants' expectations regarding the study"* (my emphasis).[6]

As such, a placebo control group is "a group of participants in a study who receive an inert substance (placebo) instead of the active drug under investigation, thus functioning as a **control group** against which to make comparisons regarding the effects of the active drug.[7] (See also **placebo effect.**[231])

In our earlier laboratory experiment on infrasound and "zapping," we developed a "placebo control group." You may recall we had one group exposed to a roar that contained infrasound to gauge the impact of infrasound on the body. Without any kind of control group, our experiment would not tell us if it was the infrasound creating any impact or if it was merely the intimidating aspects of the roar or human reactivity. *As such we needed to include a placebo control group in which the roar was presented, but without the underlying (inaudible to the human ear) infrasound.* If the "roar only" condition produced the same response as the roar and infrasound condition, we can then conclude that it's **not** the infrasound, but either the intimidating aspects of the roar or the human subject's mind and body producing the "Zapping effect."

Blind experimental designs are experiments or studies where the subject does not know if they are in the experimental or control group. They don't know if they are getting the experimental treatment or if they are getting no treatment at all. As in the above placebo design, the "no-treatment" control group allows us to more accurately identify or ensure that the intervention, test treatment, or experimental condition is creating the result and that the result is different from "normal." The subjects in the study are kept "blind" or not allowed to know which group they are in and whether they are receiving the active or "inert" intervention.

Unfortunately, because of the mere fact that we are corpuscular beings existing in a body (see Chapter 2 on Bias and Objectivity), we are biased. We can unintentionally communicate that bias through body language, tone of voice, or other nonverbal cues. Even the design of the experiment (a variation of demand characteristics) or the persons' participation in the experiment (see Hawthorne effect) can produce false results. This is why "**double-blind**" experimental designs are employed in such research.

In the "single-blind" experiment the subjects in the experimental and control group are not informed if they are getting the experimental manipulation or treatment versus the "inert" or control manipulation/intervention. In a "double-blind" experimental design, the subjects **and** the investigator conducting the experiment are kept blind or intentionally remain uninformed about what subjects are in the experimental condition and which subjects are in the control condition. Neither the experimenter nor the subjects know if they are receiving the active intervention or manipulation or not! *This eliminates any possible unconscious or unintentional communication of any bias between the experimenter and the study's participants that might influence the results.* (See experimenter bias.) It (the double-blind design) controls for unintentional, but nonetheless systematic errors entering and influencing the experiment.

Additional "academic" definitions follow for further clarity (or confusion) depending on your perspective. Blind "denotes a lack of sight. See **blindness** ... [It also denotes)] ... a lack of awareness. In research, a blind procedure may be employed deliberately to enhance experimental control. A 'single blind' is a procedure in which participants are unaware of the experimental conditions under which they are operating. A 'double-blind' is a procedure in which both the participants and the experimenters interacting with them are unaware of the particular experimental conditions. A 'triple-blind' is a procedure in which the participants, experimenters, and data analysts are all unaware of the particular experimental conditions."[8]

Returning to our infrasound experiment (Chapter 8), by not informing the subjects if they are in the "roar only" or "infrasound and roar" conditions, we have created a "single-blind" experimental design. Only the subjects are "blinded" to the nature of the manipulated or experimental conditions and which condition they are in. If we then also "blind" the experimenter running the experiment (the person actually interacting with, assessing the study impact and immediate results in real-time), we have then created a double-blind study. Now the experimental subject and the experimenter are "blind" (unaware of) the manipulation being administered. Keep the person doing the statistical analysis "blind" as to which condition is which by simply identifying each condition with a number, rather than a written or verbal description or classification. You have now created a triple-blind study.

Ohhh Yes!!! Yes!!! Yes!!!! I hope that was as good for you as it was for me!

10

SCIENTIFIC RESEARCH AND NUMBERS: THE NECESSARY EVIL KNOWN AS STATISTICS

S o, after suffering through the previous "waterboarding" read, do you still want to be a scientifically-based fieldworker/field researcher? Really!!!????

It's a lot easier, undoubtedly more fun to go "hunting and/or trapping;" applying basic scientific ideas and principles to the process of "capturing" Bigfoot! Once again, be careful what one you hope for as you just might get IT!

If you hope to report your results in any format other than storytelling or "show and tell," that "IT" will have to eventually involve numbers, math, and statistics. As such, I will tackle some of the basic statistical concepts in the hopes that the reader will better understand the importance of numbers, math, and statistics in communicating "data" from research studies. You will also hopefully understand the need to use numbers, math, and statistics in your own research if it is to be of scientific value and to assist in preserving the Bigfoot species. This information, along with the relevant section on the normal curve, can then be used by researcher to analyze the strengths and weaknesses of research related to Bigfoot for their value in informing issues and experimental designs involved in their own studies.

When you go into the field, if you are lucky, you *may* have a Bigfoot experience. You may find a tree structure, branch breaks, tree or limb twists attributable to Bigfoot. You might hear rustling in the bushes or leaves, nuts, branches or stone falls purported to be made by a Bigfoot. You may hear a tree knock, breathing, a growl, whoop, scream, or roar believed to be produced by a Bigfoot. You may find tracks thought to be made by a Bigfoot. They may be distinct enough to be photographable with a dollar bill included for perspective. Less frequently, the print may be castable using Plaster of Paris, Bakelite, or another substance. Sightings of red or green lights thought to be Bigfoot eye shine, ball light orbs, and other experiences more often associated with paranormal activity may occur during an expedition. It is indeed **very unusual** *to actually see a fleeting glimpse of what could be a Bigfoot!* It is **extremely rare** *to see one for consecutive seconds, yes seconds!* **Most unusual** *would be a sustained (minutes at a time) sighting and observation of a Bigfoot.*

Taken as phenomenological experiences, these make interesting and at times compelling stories and occasionally good "show and tell" presentations. If any of these events are to be of scientific value, however, they need to be **"coded"** into numerical data for closer analysis and exploration. Such a coding process, at its most fundamental level, involves either totaling the frequency with which these things occur or assigning a number (numeric value) to the event so they can be analyzed in some other fashion. *A descriptive statistical analysis and coding phenomenological experiences into numeric data is essential and typically an initial step in making data accessible to scientific analysis.*

If your only goal is to "hunt" or "trap" Bigfoot for your own experiential/phenomenological edification and/or profit (arguably the primary goal of many expeditions masquerading as having an interest in "the scientific study of Bigfoot"), numbers, math, and statistics have only minimal value to you. You will likely be satisfied with numbers and math that basically describe the creature, its habits and habitat, and your group's success in helping people make their desired "connection" with the creature.

Thirty-three percent (about one out of every three) of expedition attendees have a Bigfoot experience. Ninety-six percent of these experiences involve hearing a wood knock, howls, roars, or other sound or physical evidence possibly attributable to Bigfoot. Three percent involve finding concrete physical evidence consistent with Bigfoot (castable footprints, structures). Three-quarters of a percent involve seeing what is thought to be a Bigfoot and one-quarter of a percent involve actual confirmed Bigfoot sightings. Such percentages (*totally fictionalized by myself to protect the innocent and those guilty of this type of advertising*) describe the potential expeditioners experience and the likelihood of what kind of experience they might have. These are examples of "**descriptive statistics.**"

Descriptive statistics simply describe the frequency of the occurrence or the frequency of the qualities of certain phenomena. In my opinion, they are the weakest form of statistical analysis as they are highly vulnerable to biased presentation and interpretation. They can be twisted to mean just about anything. This is why TV news shows and political campaigns so often use them. I would argue that the vast majority of Bigfoot "research" seems to be anecdotal stories and possibly might include some descriptive statistics. My own survey of Bigfoot literature only occasionally revealed descriptive statistics.

Even rarer are "inferential statistics" as part of an experimental design or study. **Inferential statistics** help us infer or understand "the true reality" of the phenomena we are attempting to measure or what we are studying. An **experimental design** refers to how we set up or establish our research procedure to try and capture the phenomena or behavior or subject matter we want to examine. Rather than crudely and vaguely stumble through these descriptions, I will share/cite information from authors more adept at these explanations than I.

The **scientific method** has been earlier discussed in Chapter 2 within the framework of objectivity and bias. Again, for our purposes, I will borrow a psychological definition in that *much field research attempts to capture Bigfoot behaviors and inform Bigfoot attitudes thoughts, and emotions from same.*

As such a psychological definition of the scientific method

seems particularly suited to our studies. The **scientific method** is "a general set of procedures for gathering and interpreting evidence that limits sources of errors ... yields dependable conclusions ... and demands special attitudes and values of the scientist. These special attitudes and values include but are not limited to motives driven by a curiosity about the unknown and uncertain in which we seek to discover lawful, orderly patterns of relationships in the target phenomena, remain critical and skeptical of all conclusions while simultaneously maintaining a necessary open-mindedness that makes truth provisional, ready to be modified by new data and never absolute. A respect for data as the ultimate arbitrator of disagreements and as the cornerstone of basic knowledge is also a basic value. Secrecy is banned so that all data may be publicly verifiable—open to inspections, criticism, and replication by others. Scientific knowledge is built on the base of empirical evidence obtained by observation and measurement, rather than solely on the basis of "authority" beliefs and data-less experts. Data is collected using methods to eliminate or correct the subjective influences of the researchers, increasing their objectivity. Inferences and conclusions about the meaning of the evidence are kept distinct from the description of the data and methods for collecting them."[1]

"Basic to psychological research are (a) reliance on the empirical methods for investigating the 'mysteries of ...nature'; (b) systematic attempts to measure and quantify aspects of behavior and processes of the mind; (c) adoption of procedural safeguards to increase objectivity and reduce the ever-present danger of personal biases; (d) the keeping of complete record of observations and data analysis intact for other researchers to understand and evaluate; and (e) communication of one's feelings and conclusions in ways that allow independent observers to replicate (repeat) the findings-or to reject the conclusions."[2]

"Such research seeks to discover the **structure of behavior** *and* **psychological processes** *using correlational methods."*[3] It also "seeks to explore their **causes and determinants** through experimentation."[4]

It attempts to enhance objectivity by **operationally** defining variables, using standardized procedures and avoiding bias."[5]

"Defining variables 'operationally' means defining them in clearly observable terms. ... For example, aggressive behavior might be operationally defined as either a behavior that injures another person or by developing a test of aggressiveness."[6] An operational definition "defines a variable in terms of specific operation and investigator uses to determine its presence ... avoids the ambiguity of everyday descriptive terms and ensures that both stimulus variables and response variables are observable events."[7] "Even inner processes can be studied in observable terms. For example, hunger ... might be defined as '24 hours without food' or '15-percent loss of body weight over a given time period.'"[8]

Standardizing or using **standardized procedures** "employs uniform procedures to administer tests, interviews, [observations]/surveys, and experiments. It minimizes unwanted variability in the behavior of the research subjects ... by asking questions [or observing] in the same way, replicating conditions exactly and scoring responses in a uniform way so that all research participants experience exactly the same experimental conditions."[9]

In Chapter 2, I defined organismic perceptual bias, as well as other forms of bias including demand characteristics, the placebo effect, the Hawthorne effect, and experimenter bias. These and other forms of bias reflect errors in a particular direction "that may produce misleading or erroneous conclusions ... making a study scientifically worthless."[10]

One of the ways we must attempt to counteract such bias is through building **reliability** and **validity** in our study. **Reliability** refers to "our ability to generate behavioral data that are consistent and stable so that the same results will be found on repeated testing under the same conditions."[11] **Validity** means that "the information produced from research, [observation] or testing is an accurate measure of the psychological variable or quality it is intended to measure."[12] Are we actually measuring what we believe or are purporting to measure?

Validity and reliability!!! The bane of the Bigfoot "science" throughout the US and other countries. Does Bigfoot exist? When we see a video of a fleeting black, brown, or reddish-haired animal in the woods, how do we know if it is a Bigfoot or another animal? When we see a video of what clearly looks like a Bigfoot, is it a Bigfoot, a person in a suit, or a photo-shopped/other special effect? When we hear a tree knock or howl, is it a Bigfoot making it, another animal, an Army Ranger, other military personnel in training, or another researcher outside our group? When we knock or howl back and get a response, is it a Bigfoot responding at all, another researcher from another research group in the field, the same Bigfoot in the same or different location, or a different Bigfoot in the same or different location? When we find a Bigfoot track, is it a Bigfoot track, a bear track, a hoaxed track, or a human track? Contained within these questions lay the essence of validity and reliability.

"Are we actually experiencing or measuring (recording, video logging, etc.,) Bigfoot activity or Bigfoot behavior?" is the question that speaks to validity. Without a photograph or video or credible visual sighting of the creature actually performing the act that we are experiencing; raw validity is generally lacking.

Even when we have such evidence, scientific "proof" of the species remains allusive at best and illusive at worst. Witness the historical trials and tribulations of the Patterson Gimlin film. At first challenged as a hoax, but then considered valid. Then it was "definitively" debunked as "fake" based on a "character analysis" of the maker(s), as well as the opinions of other video, anthropological, and zoological experts. Currently, it has found "good favor" and is considered the "best video evidence of Bigfoot in existence" by many. Who knows what the future will hold for its authenticity, its representative foundation for the existence of the creature known as Bigfoot, and the science based on the same?

Are we measuring what we purport to be measuring? How do we know and how can we prove it? These are questions of validity. *Are we* **repeatedly** *measuring what we believe we are measuring without the* *interference of some other factor or variable?* How can we know and how can we prove this? These are questions of **reliability.**

According to the Oxford Languages Online dictionary, validity is defined as "the quality of being logically or factually sound; soundness or cogency" and "the state of being legally or officially binding or acceptable."[13] Formulated by Kelly (1927) who stated that "a test is valid if it measures what it claims to measure."[14] "For example, a **test of intelligence** (my emphasis) should measure intelligence and not something else (such as memory)."[15]

"A distinction can be made between internal and external validity. These types of validity are relevant to evaluating the validity of a research study/procedure."[16] "Internal validity refers to whether the effects observed in a study are due to the manipulation of the independent variable and not some other factor. In-other-words, there is a causal relationship between the independent and dependent variables. Internal validity can be improved by controlling extraneous variables, using standardized instructions, counter-balancing, and eliminating demand characteristics and investigator effects."[17]

Translated into our Bigfoot interests, is what we are claiming to be measuring what we are actually measuring? For example, when we arrive at a habitation site and immediately hear a tree knock, the assumed Bigfoot making the tree knock or the tree knock itself is the dependent variable (the variable we are trying to influence or investigate) and our arrival or presence is the independent variable (the variable being manipulated and assumed to be influencing the occurrence of a tree knock). Is our arrival "causing" a creature (assumed to be Bigfoot) to make a tree knock commonly thought to announce our arrival to the Bigfoots in the area?

Controlling for extraneous variables would include some process or technique to confirm that indeed a Bigfoot was making the knock and ruling out other creatures making the same knock (such as a human). Very tough to do unless you directly observe the Bigfoot making the tree knock. This is further complicated by the school of thought that these so-called "knocks" do not, in fact, represent tree knocks, but are Bigfoot teeth, jaw, or lip-smacking sounds. Interesting hypotheses, but considering we've yet to definitively scientifically prove the species' existence, clearly premature hypotheses if your focus is on "scientific objectivity." If your focus is on a subjective phenomenological experience, it's fun and interesting to consider.

Could the gender of the vehicle occupant make a difference in the initiation of a tree knock? Still fraught with a lack of a firm scientific foundation, counter-balancing to control for the notion that Bigfoots are more "attracted to or curious about women rather than men" (see definition for anthropomorphizing) could be empirically tested. This could be done by alternating the arrival of men and women to the habituation site. First, a woman would arrive, and after a designated delay, have a male arrive on the scene. Later (perhaps during the next expedition to the same site) counter-balance the gender arrival variable. Have a male arrive first and a standardized number of minutes afterward (the same as in the first expedition), and have a woman arrive on the scene. Other cyclical factors would need to be "controlled for."

Taking it one step further, what if the type of vehicle is what triggers or fails to trigger a "knock upon arrival:" Outfitted truck versus Prius? You could control for gender effects by using only male drivers, using only female drivers, or counter-balancing male and female drivers as just explained. The preferable technique would be the counter-balanced design as if you use only males, you have failed to investigate or control for the possibility of the gender of the vehicle driver having an effect.

Of course, the main extraneous or unwanted variable contaminating these results is that most of the habituation sites are not in locations isolated from public traffic. As such it would be hard to maintain constant knowledge of all vehicles with single or mixed-gender occupants arriving, and the influence this could play on the initiation of a tree knock. Statistically, this error can be hypothetically "**randomized**" across the sample. *In a database with large numbers of subjects, the error could be factored out to examine the resulting relationships.*

Demand characteristics were discussed in the chapter on

objectivity and bias. They are frankly a greater concern for the interpretation of the meaning of a tree knock than an influence on our creature/dependent variable. That is to say, Bigfoot **probably** doesn't know we expect or want to hear a tree knock signaling our arrival at a habituation sight. *Our own expectations and beliefs about the meaning of such a knock would, however, be influential in our interpretation of what it means.*

This becomes especially germane when a novice researcher is learning from an experienced researcher who has prematurely decided that such a knock is signaling our arrival. A valid hypothesis or not, that belief will be passed on to the trainee and quickly become a part of the accepted meaning of a tree knock when arriving at a habituation site. Again, phenomenologically such a hypothesis seems reasonable, but scientifically it remains far from proven. That then leads to *generations of investigator bias in the field* and is the next topic of discussion.

From a scientific perspective, it is my opinion that *investigator bias runs rampant* in Bigfoot Fieldwork. Unfortunately, phenomenologically it is accepted and has become part of much of what we **believe** we understand about Bigfoot. *That is important to let sink in. Bias, in the form of biased hypotheses, opinions, and observations have already become what is considered accepted and known behavioral characteristics of Bigfoot.* In addition to our earlier discussion on "**curiosity**," the tree knock is yet another example despite alternate countering theories including jaw, teeth, lip-smacking and vestige air bellows.

Although illustrations undoubtedly exist, how many firsthand visual accounts of Bigfoot hitting a tree with a stick are out there, let alone made credible by concurrent "live" audio recordings or video recordings? While undoubtedly less than comprehensive, my research for these writings revealed only a single eyewitness account (Janice Carter), with or without concurrent recording. **One knowledgeable person's account!!!** I am by no means an authority on the existence of such. I suspect there are few if any more, but welcome information or evidence contradicting this. In short, given that the existence of the species has yet to be scientifically definitively proven and accepted even by staunchly supportive scientific experts in the field; tree knocks, howls, roars, etc. remain unproven phenomenological experiences fraught with huge biased assumptions. *The strength of the "Tree Knock Bias" has become ingrained and institutionalized in Bigfoot culture. You will hear the phrase "tree knock" authoritatively spoken as a "fact" by many of the most famous Bigfoot fieldworkers/researchers and celebrities alive today.* And during an expedition ...

The same or similar could be said of a variety of purported Bigfoot lore and phenomena. "They recognize side arms are for personal protection, but know rifles can be used to kill them." "When they are in the area, the forest goes silent." "When they are in the area, you'll get that feeling you're being watched." "When they are in the area, you'll know it by their stinky smell." "Their fur is black." "Their fur is translucent." "Their fur is reddish brown." "They can cloak and disappear in the blink of an eye." "They disappear by moving from one dimension into another." "They can change their molecular vibration and disappear."

As researchers, we want to and do believe in Bigfoot. As such we are vulnerable to, if not likely to, filter our experiences through our own belief system (confirmation bias). Think about your drive to the expedition site. What do you think or talk about during that time? Speaking for myself? Bigfoot! Seeing Bigfoot. Hearing Bigfoot. Smelling Bigfoot! You arrive "primed for a Bigfoot experience!" I have filtered my biases through these writings. It is a rare fieldworker or researcher that hasn't done it unconsciously, if not at times by intent. As such, **investigator variables** remain *one of the biggest variables to overcome and control for in* **any** *scientific investigation,* let alone a scientific data-gathering process of Bigfoot phenomena.

Expeditions are especially vulnerable to investigator bias when a single or two-person investigative team is doing the research. *It is for this reason that any expedition team doing field research should be composed of at least three observers with a preferably an odd number (not odd personalities) of researchers constituting one field research team.* The odd number in the group will avoid "ties" on what the group experienced should it come down to the need for a vote, i.e., "Was that a Bigfoot we just saw?"

The staunchly objective researcher might counter: "If the phenomena or experience is so vague or fleeting that you have to vote on what you experienced, should it even be considered as part of the scientific database? Was it truly objective or observable, if we have to vote on it?"

Even deeper reflection on using a "tiebreaker" number of members in an outing also highlights the disadvantages of **forcing** the breaking of a tie when one exits in reality. *Are we altering our reality or the reality of our sample set by eliminating outliers?* Tie breakers or not? The expedition leader or primary researcher should decide.

Educational degrees in no way come to bear on the frequency or degree of experimenter, fieldworker, researcher, or investigator bias effects needing to be controlled. In my brief and limited experience in the field, I have met High School- and Bachelor-degreed graduates to whom I would unhesitatingly give a Ph.D. in "Bigfootology." I've also met advanced degreed field researchers (Master's degrees, PhDs, and MDs) to which I would not give a high school level diploma in "Bigfootology."

I do, however, believe a person's **ability** to be open, flexible, objective, and systematic in their observational and thinking skills is what makes for an excellent versus lousy Bigfoot field researcher. Having a reasonably thick or "calloused skin" to absorb or deflect "pseudo-experts" comments, opinions, and ideas regarding the field researcher also helps.

"**External validity** refers to the extent to which the results of a study can be generalized to other settings (**ecological validity**), other people (**population validity**), and over time (**historical validity**). External validity can be improved by setting experiments in a more natural setting and using random sampling to select participants."[18]

Ecological validity is an important consideration in Bigfoot research. Within experimental research, this refers to "the ability to generalize study findings to real-world settings. High ecological validity means you can generalize the findings of your research study to a real-life setting."[19] For example, In Chapter 8 on zapping, I proposed a laboratory study on infrasound. Whatever those results may come out to be, do they in fact reflect the actual experience of infrasound used as zapping by Bigfoot in a naturalistic field setting? Can our laboratory results be generalized to the real world?

Population validity refers to "the generalizability of our results from a study to other people,"[20] or in our case other Bigfoots within the "Bigfoot Population" (the entire population of Bigfoots in the USA and worldwide). Just within the US, names include: "the North American Wood Ape," "Sasquatch," "Skunk Ape," "Swamp Ape," the "Alabama Ape Man," the "Canal Creature of Alaska," "Hairy Men of the Old Mines," the "Hawaiian Menehune," "Kushtaka of Alaska," "Little Red Men of the Delta," "Mississippi Tusked Ape," and "Ohio's Gorilla."[21] "Sokqueatl," or "Sesquac" originates from a language spoken by several tribes of Pacific Northwestern Native Americans.[22]

These names represent only a partial list of names describing Bigfoot-like creatures. Outside the US, names such as "Yeti," "Yeren," "Yowie," and the "Orang-pendeck of Sumatra" are commonly cited in texts.[23] These names reflect varying descriptions of Bigfoot-like creatures located throughout the world and oftentimes living or existing in differing ecological environments. Consistent with evolutionary tenants, the size, body proportions, hair color, and other physical features of these creatures can vary *and suggest/are consistent with the notion that these beings/creatures or people may have evolved differently in different ecological environments.* As such we need to consider *the generalizability of our results from one Bigfoot-type creature to another.* Are our results of high ecological validity so that we can safely assume the findings on the North American Wood Ape from Area X in Oklahoma also apply to the North Western Sasquatch on the Olympic peninsula? Do these two creatures act or behave the same in identical circumstances?

To their credit, members of NAWAC maintain scientific objectivity in their reasoning during their podcast round table discussion and paper on Tag 7. They consider **population validity** without labeling it as such when discussing the "home range" implications of their tagged creature. That they tagged a Bigfoot is deduced through convergent and divergent validity reasoning processes; beginning at 1:23:35.[24]

To the point of population validity and ecological validity, however, they discuss the role of the gender and age of the specimen, its role within the Bigfoot social structure, and the impact that could have on its behavior (wide-ranging travels). Is it a male or female, youth or mature adult? Is it the Alpha of the tribe leading its group to prime feeding and climate territories seasonally? They even extrapolate from ape research and imply the possibility of it being a rogue member of the tribe wandering at its leisure or need (1:22:44-1:22:50).[25] In short, they pose the very important question and point, "How can we be sure this creature's movements are representative of and generalizable to the movements of other individual Bigfoots, its entire tribe, or regional, national, or worldwide species home ranging behavior. *They correctly conclude (from an objective and scientific perspective) that they cannot.* Bravo, NAWAC!! Bravo! We often assume our thoughts, ideas, and hypotheses are true and accurate and repeatable (valid), *but cannot know with scientific certainty until those hypotheses are tested in a systematically controlled, documented, and replicated fashion.*

"**Historical Validity**" refers to understanding how the results of a study might be generalizable across time or history.[26] Does the Bigfoot of today behave in the same way as the Bigfoots of Native American legend and lore? Potentially problematic from a scientific perspective is that such legend and lore have already been integrated into the Bigfoot culture to inform and hypothesize about the creature themselves. This creates the potential for unrecognized bias in our conceptualizations and the way we think about Bigfoot. *Phenomenologically, such legend and lore are interesting and thought-provoking. Scientifically, it is potentially problematic as such conceptualizations may reflect possible bias.*

Validity and Bigfoot

Saul McLeod (2013) further discusses other concepts of validity germane to our subject. "There are two main categories of external validity used to assess the validity of a test (i.e., questionnaire, interview, IQ test, etc.): **Content** and **criterion** ... **Content** validity refers to the content of the test appropriate to what is being measured/and includes face validity and construct validity. ...

... Face validity is simply whether the content of the test appears (at face value) to measure what it claims to. This is the least sophisticated measure of [content] validity."[27]

"Tests wherein the purpose is clear, even to naïve respondents, are said to have '**high face validity**.' Accordingly, tests wherein the purpose is unclear have '**low face validity**.'"[28] "*Having* **face validity** *does not mean that a test really measures what the researcher intends to measure, but is only reflected in the* **judgment of raters** *that 'it appears to do so.'* Consequently, it is a crude and basic measure of validity."[29]

"A test item such as '*I have recently thought of killing myself*' has obvious face validity as an item measuring suicidal cognitions, and may be useful when measuring symptoms of depression." ... "However, the implications of items on tests with clear face validity is that they are more vulnerable to **social desirability bias.** Individuals may manipulate their response to deny or hide problems, or exaggerate behaviors to present a positive image of themselves."[30]

"It is possible for a test item to lack face validity but still have general validity and measure what it claims to measure. This is good because it reduces demand characteristics and makes it harder for respondents to manipulate their answers ..." in a socially desirable direction.[31] "For example, the test item '*I believe in the second coming of Christ*' would lack face validity as a measure of depression (as the purpose of the item is unclear)."[32] This item appeared on the first version of The Minnesota Multiphasic Personality Inventory (MMPI) and loaded on/influenced the score of the Depression Scale."[33] Because most of the original normative sample of the MMPI were good Christians, only a depressed Christian would think Christ is not coming back. Thus, for this particular religious sample, the item does have general validity, but not face validity."[34]

Speaking for myself, the applicability of the concept of "**face validity**" to the study of Bigfoot was initially elusive. We're not using paper and pencil tests or interviewing Bigfoot, so how could it be applicable? When we reconceptualize the various "traps" used in Bigfoot research as "tests" of the presence of Bigfoot, however, their **face validity** became of paramount importance. *The test's "naturalness" or ability to blend into the environment in a multitude of ways so that its "unnaturalness" goes* **unnoticed** *by target species seems important. Its naturalness versus unnaturalness should figure prominently in its deployment and subsequent success or lack thereof in "capturing" the creature.* This is true for physically capturing it in a live or death trap, tissue sample trap, telemetry trap, audio trap, night vision or infra-red scope (visual and/or visual recording "trap"), or the ever-present and frequently used photographic or video trap. I will focus on the latter for further discussion of **face validity**.

The Trail Camera (TC): A potential blessing, more recently has been discovered to be a potential curse to the process of photographically "capturing" Bigfoot. In their initial advent and utilization, they were thought to be the panacea that would eventually capture the definitive photographic evidence of Bigfoot. Indeed, I have personally seen photographs from these cameras that are quite impressive and revealing. As time went on, these impressive photos seemed to become increasingly rare due possibly to the lack of the **face validity** of the tool. Initial versions and some current ones did little to "blend in" with the tree or natural setting they were affixed or mounted to. The adaptability of the target species may be another factor. Has Bigfoot learned to avoid them? Most recently, the possible combination of these and other factors has come to bear through the growing hypothesis versus consensus that Bigfoot can detect infrared radiation or light.

The trigger on the photographic mechanism on these devices is an infrared beam. Not visible to the unaided human eye, it must be "tripped" in order to take day or night photos. Night vision technology also uses infrared light to add illumination and increase nighttime visibility. FLIR devices have infrared-generating sources integrated into their function. **Infrared** has been hypothesized to be visible to numerous creatures, including Bigfoot. It therefore serves as a "non-face valid" variable in the test/trap function. It *acts as a "tell" or "tip off" to the creature that everything is not natural or right.* This of course changes the creature's behavior around these devices (see Hawthorne effect). It often results in a complete lack of success (warning and driving the target species away from the area). Some partial successes (catching what appears to be part of an arm, leg, head, or other part of the Bigfoot's body) are still evidently produced (assuming they aren't hoaxed).

As I understand it from individuals with vastly greater expertise in this than I, producers of this technology are either eliminating or otherwise altering the role that infrared technology has in these devices. This should at least temporarily increase their face validity as a test or trap for the presence of Bigfoot. *I hesitate to hypothesize a concomitant improvement in result, however, given the apparent adaptability of the target species.*

Another trap example is illustrative of issues of face validity and how it may or may not be a factor in "trap success" for testing or detecting the presence of Bigfoot: Tree traps. Trees are used in a **variety of fashions** by Bigfoot field researchers to gather evidence of Bigfoot. Trail cams are traditionally affixed to a tree in an area likely subject to Bigfoot activity.

Hair sample collectors will use double-sided tape wrapped around a tree trunk. Above the wrap, an item thought to be irresistible to Bigfoot will be placed so that the creature will rub against the sticky tape and leave hair in their attempt to gain the "bait." Tissue sample collectors use similar strategies containing sharp objects affixed to the tape or other material. These cause skin tissue or blood to be deposited on the sharps.

I simply pierce marshmallows, apples, or donuts onto a tree limb or branch. I also leave other tasty or non-food items on stumps or downed trees to serve them up or have the big guy's attention drawn to them. The NAWAC hung their "burr" telemetry trap from an elevated string or line draped across a likely trail, secured to a tree on each end.

All are examples of utilizing nature's natural structure (the tree) in the pursuit of "capturing" Bigfoot. The tree adds to the face validity of the trap. The natural versus unnatural qualities of the "bait" or other instrumentation add or detract from that face validity.

Jeff Carpenter, a bigfooting friend and likely one of the best and most objective field investigators I have encountered, showed me a relatively simple but ingenuous use of trees as an element of a "trap system" designed to "capture Bigfoot" among other questions. On top of a knoll (in a location that will remain untold), he discovered a widely spaced grove of trees located somewhat off of a path thought to be frequented by hikers and Bigfoot. Amidst the grove of trees was a tree with a hollowed-out knot hole (or broken branch scar) that created a deep vertical pocket/indentation in the trunk. It approximated an ill-formed bowl approximately 5 ½ feet up the face of the vertical trunk. This natural hollow of the tree trunk served as a receptacle to hold a variety of forms of "bait" to entice the animal to that specific tree (which had a footpath right next to it). A black sewing thread was strung at a height of about 9 feet across the path to ensure that if a creature taller than a human passed by, it would break the string.

Around this "bait tree" at varying distances and locations, he placed multiple tree cameras and video/photography traps shielded or camouflaged to minimize detection. They were positioned to gather converging/convergent evidence from a variety of angles and varying height positions. The multiple numbers of these also served the additional task of redundancy should Bigfoot identify one trap and disable it to avoid detection. This system was also set up/located in a fashion to avoid detection by casual hikers, explorers, or hapless wanderers entering the grove. This minimized detection and sabotage by the most dangerous creature in the woods: humans. *It is a highly face-valid system virtually impossible to detect in the dark, with human detection a significant challenge in the daytime without a concerted, intentionally focused search. This is true even with general knowledge of its location (i.e., "Sup thar on that hill").*

The **face validity** of the system could then be further manipulated by the type of bait contained within the "bowl." Grubs various insects, tree frogs, etc., have good face validity. Objects such as oranges, children's balls/toys, and marbles represent low face validity bait. *Low face validity items, however, might be advantageous!* That is, naturally occurring bait in the hollow might go unnoticed or passed by. Non-face valid bait (apples, oranges, marbles, and children's toys) might be more likely to capture a Bigfoot's attention and draw it to the trap! Would you rather eat a grub or an apple given a choice? Which would be more likely to draw your attention if casually noticed in a tree hollow? Face validity is not always an advantage in a test or trap!

Onward with the validity and reliability of statistical concepts. "**Construct validity**" was invented by Cronbach and Meehl (1955).[35] "This type of validity refers to the extent to which a test captures a specific theoretical construct or trait, and it overlaps with some of the other aspects of validity." ... "Construct validity does not concern the simple, factual question of whether a test measures an attribute." ... "Instead, it is about the complex question of whether test score interpretations are consistent with a nomological network involving theoretical and observational terms."[36] Does the test score actually capture the intended targeted concept or phenomena?

"To test for **construct validity**, it must be demonstrated that the phenomenon being measured actually exists. So, the construct validity of a test for intelligence, for example, is dependent on a model or **theory of intelligence.**" ... "Construct validity entails demonstrating the power of such a construct to explain a network of research findings and to predict further relationships. ... The more evidence a researcher can demonstrate for a test's construct validity the better. However, there is no single method of determining the construct validity of a test" ... "Instead, different methods and approaches are combined to present the overall construct validity of a test. For example, factor analysis and correlational methods can be used."[37] Correlational (co-relationships) statistics is covered in these writings. Factor analysis is beyond the scope of these writings, but can capture previously unidentified abstract "factors" (effects, influences, and concepts) within the data (e.g., intelligence).

"**Criterion validity**" (one form of construct validity) refers to "the test's relationship to other measures purported to measure or assess the same phenomena under consideration. It includes **concurrent** validity and **predictive** validity."[38] **Concurrent validity** (another form of construct validity) "is the degree to which a test corresponds to an external criterion that is known concurrently (i.e., occurring at the same time)."[39] *Orbs, anyone?*

"If the new test is validated by a comparison with a currently existing criterion, we have concurrent validity ... Very often, a new IQ or personality test might be compared with an older but similar test known to have good validity already."[40]

"**Predictive validity**" (the second type of concurrent validity) "is the degree to which a test accurately predicts a criterion that will occur in the future ... For example, a prediction may be made on the basis of a new intelligence test, that high scorers at age 12 will be more likely to obtain university degrees several years later. If the prediction is born out then the test has predictive validity.[41] Using a test to predict the future based on the theoretical underpinnings of the concept being investigated. Any better than Tarot cards? Hopefully, although I don't believe that study has been done!

To apply these concepts to Bigfoot, I remind the reader that above, I conceptually equated a variety of "trapping" techniques with a "test:" the test of Bigfoot's presence. Also, by way of reminder: "*To test for construct validity it must be demonstrated that the phenomenon being measured actually exists.*"[42] Uhh Ohhh!!! So, the construct validity of a test for Bigfoot's existence depends upon a model or theory of Bigfoot!!! Here we go again. Phenomenologically, many field researchers "believe in" Bigfoot and as such, or perhaps more accurately stated, because of this belief "know" it exists. This has not, however, been proven to the true scientists, even those who "suspect" and find supportive evidence that Bigfoot does exist. Let that sink in within the context of the **intelligence** example used by McLeod (2013) for construct validity.[43]

Ironically, **intelligence** (but not Bigfoot) is scientifically accepted as a valid and reliable construct. **Intelligence:** you can't see it or directly observe it (unlike Bigfoot)! "Yep! I know I saw intelligence dart between those two trees up on that hill. Did you?"

How often have you heard this? I doubt you ever have or will. "Yeah, we were driving around the corner on this dirt road and saw (insert name of a great thinker here; e.g., Albert Einstein, Andrew Wiles, Noam Chomsky) in the middle of the road. When he spotted us, he disappeared into the woods in the blink of an eye, but left a big pile of intelligence that smelled so sweet!!" Please note the aforementioned geniuses are very "**intelligent**" but are not "**intelligence**" in and of themselves. *Intelligence, you can see the end or byproduct of its influence (people's behavior, work product).* You can validly and reliably measure it, *but still can't directly observe or physically touch it.* Yet, it's accepted by **science** and the **general public!**

Bigfoot, on the other hand, has reportedly been seen thousands of times by credible and reliable witnesses. We have casts of footprints, hand prints, butt prints, fecal samples, hair and other tissue samples. *Despite this, the species isn't considered a proven species by science and is viewed as a legend, folklore, fantasy, or myth by the general public! Why? One reason is that intelligence has been repeatedly validated by other criteria concurrently associated with intelligence*; Bigfoot has not!

Can this concept of criterion validity therefore be applied to Bigfoot? Certainly, as an analytical process to enhance certainty, it can and should be considered and used, in my opinion. The challenge then remains: "Can we the measure ontological concept of "Bigfoot" phenomena or its "Bigfootness."[44] If successful, in doing so have we scientifically captured enough of "Bigfoot" to prove it is actual existence?

Creativity and inventiveness are and will continue to be needed. For example, we already have the technology to record infrasound and other qualities of sonically-based animal communication. Surely, with proper time, interest and capital, this existing technology could be experimentally employed to define and differentiate unique qualities of different animals' "sonic signatures," including infrasound. Creating a library, catalog, or sonic database on these signatures would allow us to compare "Bigfoot" sonic signatures to known species; validating the unique characteristics of those signatures. A computerized program could then be written to immediately compare a scream, howl, roar, bellow, or other sounds and identify the species, including possible Bigfoot producing them. *If we can capture the abstract concept of intelligence using psychological science surely, we can use that same science to capture Bigfoot or at least "Bigfoot."*

Predictive validity speaks to the issue of *whether the test accurately predicts future criteria* (Bigfoot behavioral responses). Consider tree knocks as a form of provocation. The "Bigfoot tree knock test" is already empirically employed in a quasi-experimental fashion on most Bigfoot expeditions. Problematic (besides the scientific proof of the species) is the lack of control within the laboratory (forest) setting. Arguably the more remote the location, the better control we have of systematic confounding variables (such as humanity and the interfering aspects of their technology).

Also problematic is the unsystematic, non-theory-driven, or variable theory-driven nature of their use. Some expedition leaders use them to announce the arrival of the Bigfoot in an area. Others will only respond with a tree knock after hearing a tree knock. Yet others will only use a tree knock when the forest has been silent of any Bigfoot sonic sign. Some investigators will deploy a single knock, others a double or triple. Some will wait a brief period of time before repeating the procedure, others long periods of time. Some will use a "native wood" knocking stick on any tree in the area. Some have crafted their own knocking sticks from axe handles; hammer handles, baseball bats, etc. Some will knock only on hardwood trees, others softwood trees. Others vary which type of tree they knock on by using the one closest to them.

The variances in the list can go on to include the resulting tonal qualities of the knocks, the force or pressure exerted by the velocity of the knock according to the strength of the person swinging the implement, and on and on with an almost infinite list of variables to control for by elimination, minimization, or randomization. *Yet, within the Bigfoot community, tree knocks are commonly accepted as evidence of Bigfoot's presence in the area without seeing a Bigfoot make the knock.*

Add to this that wood knock sound is just one theory. Other theories suggest these sounds are a result of hand claps, as well as teeth clacks or air sack bellows. Should anyone be surprised at the inconsistency and randomness that tree knocks elicit responses? *In short, a tree knock has poor predictive validity of the presence of the target species in the area, in my opinion.* They need to be systematically studied for their validity as a Bigfoot tool to reliably produce communication responses. This is true of other sonic techniques employed (howls, whoops, stone clacks, etc.).

Concepts of "**convergent**" and "**divergent validity**" are also of paramount importance to the scientific study of Bigfoot given the rarity and elusiveness of the quarry, the "official" lack of a flesh and blood "specimen" and the burgeoning number of "scientific" research groups and "experts" in the field. From this writer's perspective, **convergent validity** refers to other observations, logic/reasoning evidence, or data that supports and/or is consistent with the observed variable we are measuring.

Dr. Jeff Meldrum rests much of his research and database on **convergent** and **divergent** validity processes. He represents one of the few individuals to analyze casts of Bigfoot prints backed by **convergent** video evidence of the creature making them (Patty, from the Patterson Gimlin film, for example). The film of the creature leaving the prints serves as **convergent validity** for the authenticity of the casts of the prints themselves.

Additionally, he is also able to point to other factors in these prints that **converge** on or further support their authenticity, such as dermal ridges (aka dermatoglyphics) and a midtarsal break or pressure ridge often seen in Bigfoot prints/tracks and casts thereof. In his writings, studies, and talks on the subject, he then uses **divergent validity** to further support the authenticity of Bigfoot prints/casts. By comparing Bigfoot prints to bear tracks, big cat tracks, and human footprints (representing **divergent** or differing evidence), he further supports the authenticity of Bigfoot prints.

"**Reliability:**" According to the Oxford Languages Online dictionary, **reliability** is defined as "the quality of being trustworthy or of performing consistently well" and "the degree to which the result of a measurement, calculation, or specification can be depended on to be accurate."[45] From a psychological perspective, Saul McLeod (McLeod, S. A., 2007) once again covers the topic quite nicely.[46] "The term reliability in psychological research refers to the consistency of a research study or measuring test."[47]

"For example, if a person weighs themselves during the course of a day, they would expect to see a similar reading. Scales that measured weight [randomly] differently each time would be of little use" ... "The same analogy could be applied to a tape measure which measures inches differently each time it is used. It would not be considered reliable."[48]

"If findings from research are replicated consistently, they are reliable. A correlation coefficient can be used to assess the degree of reliability. If a test is reliable it should show a high positive correlation. ... Of course, it is unlikely the exact same results will be obtained each time as participants and situations vary, but a strong positive correlation between the results of the same test indicates reliability."[49]

"There are two types of reliability – "**internal**" and "**external**" reliability. **Internal reliability** assesses the consistency of results across items within a test. **External reliability** refers to the extent to which a measure varies from one use to another."[50] Do the individual questions within the test measure the intended concept they were designed to measure? Do the questions have a strong co-relationship (correlation) with each other? These are **internal reliability** questions.

When that same test is repeatedly administered over time to the same or similar people, do the results come out similarly? Are peoples' scores from taking the same test repeatedly close in their values or similar to each other? Is there a strong co-relationship (correlation) between those scores? These questions speak to **external reliability.**

He (McLeod, 2007) goes on to discuss how to assess or analyze reliability defining three types of reliability: **Split-half, Test-retest,** and **inter-rater reliability.**[51] "The *split-half method* assesses the internal consistency of a test, such as psychometric tests and questionnaires. There, it measures the extent to which all parts of the test contribute equally to what is being measured."[52]

"This is done by comparing the results of one half of a test with the results from the other half. A test can be *split in half* in several ways, e.g., by first half and second half, or by odd and even numbers. If the two halves of the test provide similar results, this would suggest that the test has internal reliability."[53]

The reliability of a test could be improved through using this method. For example, any items on separate halves of a test which have a low correlation (e.g., r = .25) should either be removed or re-written."[54]

"The *split-half method* is a quick and easy way to establish reliability. However, it can only be effective with large questionnaires in which all questions measure *the same* construct. This means it would not be appropriate for tests which measure different constructs."[55]

"For example, the Minnesota Multiphasic Personality Inventory has subscales measuring **different** emotions and behaviors such as depression, schizophrenia, and social introversion.[56] Therefore, the split-half method was not an appropriate method to assess reliability for this."[57] **Test-retest reliability** is the preferred method in "this" situation.

"A typical assessment [**Test-retest reliability**] would involve giving participants the same test on two separate occasions. If the same or similar results are obtained then external reliability is established. The disadvantage of the test-retest method is that it takes a long time for results to be obtained."[58]

"Beck et al. (1996) studied the responses of 26 outpatients in two separate therapy sessions one week apart.[59] They found a [very high] correlation of .93 therefore demonstrating high test-retest reliability of the depression inventory."[60] "This is an example of why reliability in psychological research is necessary, if it wasn't for the reliability of such tests some individuals may not be successfully diagnosed with disorders such as depression and consequently will not be given appropriate therapy."[61] That is, if their scores vary or change dramatically each time they take the test, the clinical diagnosis cannot be pinpointed and appropriate therapy is given. Without consistent results identifying the problematic condition, it would be impossible to know what condition needed to be treated!

"The timing of the test is important; if the duration is too brief then participants may recall information from the first test which could bias the results" ... "Alternatively, if the duration is too long it is feasible that the participants could have changed in some important way which could also bias the results."[62] They might evidence "practice effects" on the test. Gaining familiarity by repeatedly taking a test (i.e., "practicing") can influence subjects' responses to the test. Alternatively, they may have become more or less depressed. Each of these would influence their scores on a test of depression and its external reliability.

"The *test-retest method* (my emphasis) assesses the external consistency of a test. This refers to the degree to which different raters/researchers give consistent estimates of the same behavior. **Inter-rater reliability** (my emphasis) can be used for interviews."[63]

"Note it can also be called **inter-observer reliability** (my emphasis) when referring to observational research. Here researchers observe the same behavior independently (to avoid bias) and compare their data. If the data is similar then the raters are reliable."[64] *The observation skills or "powers of observation" of observers are reliable with each other.*

"Where observer scores do not significantly correlate then reliability can be improved ... Training observers in the observation techniques being used and making sure everyone agrees with them and ensuring behavior categories have been operationalized. This means that they have been objectively defined."[65]

"For example, if two researchers are observing 'aggressive behavior' of children at nursery, they would both have their own subjective opinion regarding what aggression comprises. In this scenario, it would be unlikely they would record aggressive behavior the same and the data would be unreliable."[66] "However, if they were to operationalize the behavior category of aggression, this would be more objective and make it easier to identify when a specific behavior occurs."[67] "For example, while "aggressive behavior" is subjective and not operationalized, "pushing" is objective and operationalized. Thus, researchers could simply count how many times children push each other over a certain duration of time."[68]

Applied to Bigfoot research, the use of sonic provocation once again comes to mind. Does a tree knock evoke a Bigfoot response as reliably as stone clacks? Do stone clacks or tree knocks evoke a Bigfoot response as reliably as a howl/whoop/roar/scream? Do howls, whoops, roars, and screams all produce BF responses with equal reliability? Does this vary within localized home ranges or between localized home ranges?

Is each type of sonic provocation reliable within itself? For example, does a branch from an Ash tree struck against an Ash tree provoke BF response as reliably as a Pine tree branch stuck against a Pine tree? Does a one-and-a-half-inch thick branch provoke a BF response as reliably as a three-inch-thick branch? Does a high-velocity strike provoke BF response as reliably as a low-velocity strike?

Turing to vocalizations, do certain types of vocalization more or less reliably produce Bigfoot responses? For example, does a roar produce a BF response as reliably as a howl as reliably as a scream as reliably as a whoop provokes a BF response? Given a specific type of vocalization, does one researcher's roar more reliably evoke a BF response than another? **Within the person emitting** the roar, do they make it reliably from one instance to the next in tone, pattern, or duration? **Within** the **roar pattern,** is one portion of the pattern more important than another portion to eliciting a BF response (ending in a drawn out, rising "oooooOOOOOH" inflection, for example)?

A few examples warrant reflection. During a recent BFRO expedition, we had a **Bigfoot calling contest.** Relative to test-retest reliability, I would note that a number of members participated. Not one person's call seemed to resemble another member's call. So much for reliability across calls! This is not a criticism of the calls or callers. It more likely speaks to ontological considerations associated with each person's schema (notion or idea) of "a Bigfoot call." In effect, each person had a different Bigfoot called "blueprint." Each was unique in its own right including volume, tone, and duration. A scientific investigation was not the point of this "for a prize" contest. The winner was chosen based on applause, cheers, and jeers of the group. It was good fun!!

These individual differences in calls (which are likely utilized during our nighttime expeditions) do, however, highlight a likely lack of reliable provocation techniques between research groups. Although we purport to do "scientific research" on these outings, we have yet to systematically investigate the influence of calls on provoking BF responses. We are clearly not controlling for call variables and tracking their influences on responses as would be needed if we had hopes of identifying the most effective calls to use on our expedition settings and subsequent experimental designs. Without such controls, we don't know (for example) if a woman's call is more effective than a man's call. We have also not investigated issues of volume, tone, or duration of the call to determine which are more effective. Perhaps more accurately, we need to determine which calls or call qualities are more effective, under what circumstances, in what areas or locations, and during which seasons!

Interestingly, about a week later one of our expedition co-leaders (who had audio-taped the contest) detected what could have been BF responses to some of the calls. This was totally unexpected and unplanned but sets an example of how a simple experiment could be designed to begin to investigate call qualities and their reliability in provoking responses.

A similar "Bigfoot call" experimental contest could be a regular part of each expedition. Specific quality variables associated with presumed "effective calls" would be identified/defined in an a priori fashion using existing *external criterion validity* call examples. These are calls considered to be "validated" or "proven" recordings of authentic Bigfoot calls. BFRO's "Ohio Howl,"[69] Ohio Night Stalker Ohio Call,[70] or Ron Morehead's "Sierra Sounds"[71] for example, could be used.

By listening to such recordings, a panel of judges would first participate in a training protocol. This training is done to ensure the **inter-rater reliability of the judges**. "Inter-rater reliability of the judges" refers to the reliability or consistency of judging between different judges. This would create an entire panel of judges that "are on the same page" in identifying the a priori established qualities of authentic and high-quality Bigfoot calls (to which the contestants are kept "blind). Again, this increases the objectivity of the contest by using the previously validated call recordings as an **external criterion validity** measure of what constitutes an "authentic call." Keeping the **contestant callers** "blind" or ignorant of those qualities minimizes practice or preparation effects.

The contest can now commence with each "**contestant caller**" making their call twice (**test-retest reliability**). Judges rate each call on the identified variables defined in a Likert scale: (0 = none of the particular quality being judged, 1 = A low amount of the defined quality, 2 = A moderate amount of the defined quality, 3 = A high amount of the defined quality). Also included would be a rating on the "consistency scale" between the roars (1 = Inconsistent, 2 = Consistent) for each individual caller's **test-retest measure**. Consistency could be used as a "multiplier" for each identified call variable. At the end of the multi-person contest, rather than subjective votes (applause, cheers, and jeers), the judges' quality ratings would define the winner.

The **calls** represent the **independent variable** in the experimental contest. They are the intervention or variable being tested (eventually to provoke the ultimate **dependent variable: Bigfoot**). For the contest, however, the **dependent variable** is the outcome of the contest decided by the judges' ratings. **Eliminating** subjective votes as an outcome-dependent variable controls for any one contestant's popularity or social desirability influence within the expedition group. It's no longer a popularity contest! **Using trained judges' ratings** as the **dependent variable** further increases objectivity in choosing an "authentic" winner and *of greatest scientific value the* **validity** *of the call itself.*

The winner then sets the group standard or "criterion" to which other members should train themselves if they are intent on doing calls in the field for their group. This in turn establishes and controls for caller reliability between each "mini"- expedition group. This process could be repeated for each type of vocalization (howl, scream, whoop, etc.) establishing "group vocalization experts" trained within each group.

More labor-intensive than the contest we did on the BFRO expedition I alluded to earlier. Absolutely! As much good fun as the earlier BFRO contest? Maybe not or maybe! It's likely that the judges will become the object of the applause, cheers, and jeers rather than the contestants! Better "science" than the other? Yes!! More beneficial to the scientific status/reputation of the research group! Absolutely!! Ultimately more beneficial to Bigfoot Science to assist the species? Absolutely!! Imagine a research group armed with scientifically validated procedures and processes. But only if consistently used on every outing. On each night expedition, it must be systematically applied, recorded, and encoded into numeric data. That data must then be statistically analyzed, and the results written up and published so that they can be shared with other expedition groups for further study. Those groups must meticulously **replicate** the process to either confirm or refute previous findings and repeat the cycle.

Honestly, the "burger and beer approach design" seems a lot more fun to me!!! It doesn't, however, help advance the science needed to advance the cause of the species! *It all boils down to choices of priorities. The belly or the beast?*

To that end, you can have your cake and eat it too! I recently watched Charlie Raymond finish his Glenn Williams BBQ'd Ribs having just completed about 3/4ths of his presentation. He literally cleared the room by playing an example of what I would characterize as an "unusual" Bigfoot call. At least it wasn't one I had ever heard! Not a second after his recording tapered off—dare I say it?—an almost identical or "mimicked" return call was heard by 26 people, 22 of whom rushed out of the presentation room to "investigate further." It was an awesome experience. The resemblance between Charlie's recorded call and the apparent spontaneous return call was so similar, that it was kind of Twilight Zone eerie. They followed similar to often identical pitch, tone, and melody patterns. (Of each other, not the Twilight Zone theme.)

"Tree knocks" would also need to be similarly systematically investigated. On my first three BFRO expeditions, I heard numerous tree knocks produced by researchers and investigators. Some found a hardwood branch, some a softwood branch, some a large thick branch, some an even thicker club-like branch. Some had even constructed their own "knock sticks" from native woods or commercial baseball bats, and a variety of wooden handles (claw hammer, ball peen hammer, small sledgehammer, large sledgehammer, hatchet, axe, etc.).

An "appropriate" tree would then be selected upon which to strike the knock stick. Some chose soft-wood trees, some chose hard-wood trees, some chose standing trees, and some chose downed or fallen trees.

The knock was then made. Some made one knock, and some made two knocks in rapid succession. Some made two knocks with multiple, but random seconds in between while others made three knocks. In rare instances, a few even made rhythmically patterned knocks.

We'd await a response and when none was forthcoming, the knock cycle might be repeated or not. Depending on response or lack thereof, we'd eventually move on down the trail where the previous or differing knock cycle may or may not be repeated. Clearly, reliability with and between knockers (split-half reliability, test-retest reliability) was missing. I never heard a knock returned over three expeditions!

Finally, on a "private" expedition (just some friends getting together outside of an official BFRO event), I heard one of these knocks returned. John Eaves (aka in BF circles as "The Deranged Gnome") and the guide for the very first *"Finding Bigfoot* show, took me to "the front porch" of Bigfoot's home. He looked upon the ground and picked up a broken stick he felt appropriate to the task. He then made soft taps against a few standing trees until he heard (or felt) the appropriate tonal or vibratory response. He then made a single knock, swinging the stick at maximum velocity against the designated tree.

Seconds later, we heard a somewhat distant, but crystal-clear knock returned from the hollow below us. Having heard a variety of different tones produced by a variety of "production knocking sticks" on trees, I was shocked to note that the returned knock tone was crystalline and moderate to high frequency in its timbre (like a home run hit out of the park). This was a tone I had come to associate with knocking sticks made from kiln-dried, commercial-grade wood handles. (John insisted this was a BF knock and I believed him.) Another member of our group, some 200 yards distant from us, made a return knock using his commercial grade/production light-sledge handle knock stick. It sounded distinctly different from the one we had just heard in response to John's knock. I became increasingly convinced of the authenticity of that returned knock!

The phenomenologist within me is certain I heard a "Bigfoot tree knock" in response to John's knock. He certainly identified it as one and has infinitely more experience and background on the subject than I do. I trust him and have no reason to doubt him. The human-generated knock in response to the "Bigfoot knock" did sound tonally different than the original "Bigfoot knock" (in response to John's). The more objective and stringent scientist side of my "split personality" can't be sure. We didn't see a BF make the knock. The army uses the area for its Ranger stealth training. Why would a BF knock presumably using native wood materials sound so much like a knock made by a commercially modified wood handle? Investigators who are less secure and certain in their BF knowledge base and experience might take this as an attack on their character or expertise. It is not a challenge to John's credibility or expertise in any form or fashion. Hopefully, it does, however, highlight the "split personality" struggle or schism in the field between phenomenological techniques versus more stringent and standardized/experimental "scientific approaches" and interpretations thereof, during an expedition.

In response to his knowledge that I was writing this book after only one year in the field at the time, an investigator suggested I was arrogant and audacious to write such a book with so little field experience. "It's a mistake to trust and imbue value into scientific technology if you don't trust the people you're going out on expeditions given their years of knowledge and experience." Wow! Wanting to bring science to the Bigfoot table means I don't trust field researchers with years more experience than me? Not the case!! We need each other!

All science begins with one person's phenomenological observation, thought, or experience. When those experiences, observations, and thoughts repeatedly occur in the same person or a variety of people, that constitutes a hypothesis to be tested scientifically. When empirically validated scientifically and replicated, the next logical scientific step becomes experimental validation. *Trusting other people's experiences and observations in fact serves as the beginning foundation of all science. If I didn't trust John's reports and my experiences with him, there would be no need to or value in subjecting them to scientific hypothesis testing!*

On the other hand, to once again paraphrase Dr. Jeff Meldrum (2006), "...trust involves a leap in faith. Faith has no place in the world of science where factual, tangible data and evidence are brought to bear to take us beyond faith and into the realm of scientific validation ..." and arguably consensus reality.[72] (Please note, Dr. Meldrum makes no comment on consensus reality.) *As such, it is **because** I trust John's observations and experiences that I want to bring the light of scientific technology to bear on the subject. It illuminates it and validates it for all to see, hear, smell, (I'll pass on tasting BF), feel, and understand.*

To return to tree knocks, I would remind the reader that not all agree that the sound we call a "tree knock" is made by Bigfoot hitting a tree with a stick. It is also hypothesized that it is BF clacking its teeth together, hand claps, stone clacks, and some or lip smacking. Some hypothesize that air sacs extending from the larynx (like exist in great apes) are instrumental in this sound production.

The reader should also note that Dr. Meldrum, based on BF hand print casts examined and discussed by Grover Krantz (1971) echoes the hypothesis that the thumb does not work in opposition as it does in humans.[73,74] While not precluding "brandishing sticks or lobbing stones" he also highlights the consistency of this "... with the universal lack of observations of tool use by Sasquatch... ."[75] While not precluding BF from holding a stick and hitting it against a tree to make "tree knock" sounds, such "compromised" opposable thumb use could serve as a complicating factor when doing so.

Let's rinse and repeat with "Tree Knocks"

A more systematic study and possible standardization of tree knock technology would appear of some potential value. Is there test-retest reliability with the same stick and tree combination? That is, in the field, does using the same scavenged branch of wood for a single knock produce the same sound when that branch is used for an immediate second knock? Does that same stick used three hours later to make either a single or repeated knock produce the same sound as the original knock(s)? Might the initial impact disrupt the molecular and structural stability of the device sufficiently to change the sound of the second strike? Might the drying of that stick hours later, when propelled against a tree "on down the trail," be reliable in its tonal reproduction? Would the structural stability disruption resulting from repeated use make it a more OR less valid replication of a BF tree knock? In short which are more likely to produce a returned knock?

Again, consensus audio recordings of alleged BF tree knocks could be used as a criterion against which to compare man-made tree knocks. We would do well to control for the geographic region as the resource for the utilized wood due to differing moisture levels would differ in the BF home ranges across the US. That is, a moisture-laden wooden stick propelled against the existing trees of the Pacific Northwest might reasonably be expected to produce a different tone than a less saturated stick propelled against a lodge pine in middle or Northern GA. Alternatively, that in and of itself is an empirical question left to be preliminarily investigated using sound technology highlighting volume, pitch, and other sonic qualities generated by the act.

We'd also need to control for the velocity of the propulsion against the tree to ensure equal force is being applied each time. I imagine, baseball bat or axe swinging devices exist or could be constructed along the lines of a clay pigeon launcher. These could be employed as a consistent measure of impact force for these purposes. Greater funding might employ hydraulic systems to allow for more consistency of force slowly lost in a spring-like mechanism. Thickness and length of the branch would also need to be systematically investigated and controlled for.

Of course, the major obstacle in using a returned knock as the dependent variable is how to validate the origin of that returned knock. I remain optimistic, however, in our ability to investigate and devise sonic signature technology. Sonar, for example, has long been used to identify the signature of certain types of ocean vessels by submarines. "Audacity" recording technology monitors and displays a variety of sonic qualities graphically. Our ability to detect infrasound already exists. I've also heard of meow and bark machines being used to translate cat and dog sounds into human communication. *Surely discovering the sonic signature of Bigfoot should not represent an insurmountable challenge!*

Once the test-retest reliability is established within one wood/tree combination, this can be replicated for other types of wood throughout the different regions of the USA. Reliability between differing wood types and regions can be established to guide tree knock technology deployment for any given expedition. Training group members within and across various expedition groups could then produce increased tree knock reliability within and between expedition groups. This would further "tighten" the reliability of tree knocks as a scientific investigative tool. This would, in turn, increase the value of scientific data generated on commercial BF expeditions.

That seems like a lot of work, time, and energy invested in something that could be as simple as smacking two 2x4s together in the woods. *I cannot debate that valid point. Without systematic investigation and control of extraneous variables (some not explored above), however, tree knocks remain an unreliable and invalid tool.* Their current deployment only serves phenomenological value without contributing an improved benefit to the species. Are our priorities for fortune and fame via commercial expeditions developed to produce Bigfoot experiences or in assisting the species? *There is no reason that these would have to be mutually exclusive!*

Although dealt with in Chapter 2, we will revisit "**coincidence**," "**correlation**," and "**causality**."

"**Coincidence**" is defined by Merriam-Webster's Dictionary as "the act or condition of **coinciding**, as well as the occurrence of events that happen at the same time by accident but seem to have some connection."[76] **Coinciding**, happening at the same time by **accident**, but **seem to** have some connection." *There seems to be a connection or a relationship between two things, but in reality, they have just randomly occurred together!*

Without adequate scientific controls and/or objectivity, there might not be any coincidences in Bigfoot research. Many researchers' propensity to attribute anything and everything to Bigfoot effectively eliminates coincidences. Alternatively, that propensity relegates that evidence to the status of scientifically insufficient to make the scientific leap to proof! Without controls for objectivity, only coincidence can occur with scientific certainty. The evidence is then relegated to unusable as it fails to advance the cause with such certainty. Government influence or not!

A lighting bug uncharacteristically quickly zig zags and loops to the ground and its light dies out upon hitting the ground. "It must have been zapped by a Bigfoot" or "it must have been mini-orb." During the fall of the year, a nut falls on to the leaf blanketed floor of the forest. "It was a Bigfoot throwing a pebble at us!" These are random events occurring at the same time we are thinking about and hunting for Bigfoot. Without calm logic, emotional control of excitement, fear and fantasy, the hunt itself biases our observational powers and creates **causality** *out of* **random coincidence.** *THIS represents just one example of why a fully developed sense of SELF-KNOWLEDGE is an essential characteristic of any good Bigfoot fieldworker!*

"**Correlation**" is defined by Webster's as: "a relation existing between phenomena or things or between mathematical or statistical variables which tend to vary, be associated, or occur together in a way not expected on the basis of chance alone."[77] They often, but not always **co-relate** to or with each other.

In Chapter 2, I used the example of the correlation between rising temperatures and ice-cream melting. In Bigfoot fieldwork, a prime example might be hearing a nearby howl, tree knock, or even landslide sounds; subsequently finding an authentic Bigfoot track in the general vicinity of the origin of sounds. "Well, that represents scientific proof that Bigfoot **caused** or made the noise!" *"That proves causality." "That's a causal relationship, right!?" Wrong!!!!!*

If you've been out in the field, think about how often you have heard a whoop, howl, scream, and wood knock you were sure was produced by a Bigfoot yet never found the first footprint anywhere in the area. *There's not a 100 percent* **causal** *relationship between a Bigfoot being in a particular area and finding Bigfoot prints in that area.* Our phenomenological foundation informs us of this factual gem of evidence. *Similarly, there is no causal (100%) relationship between hearing these sounds and finding a print.*

It can validly be argued this could be coincidental! It could be a random event! Perhaps Bigfoot (or a hoaxer) walked through the area hours or days ago. Later, while you happen to be in the "general vicinity," a Bigfoot researcher from an expedition group not associated with your larger expedition organization makes an audible provocation. It's a howl. Hearing the howl, you move toward the sound and find the footprint. This does not mean a Bigfoot made the sound. The print just happened to be in the general vicinity/direction form where the unknown researcher made their provocation. This does not mean a Bigfoot left the print. It could have been a hoaxer or another species of animal. Even if a Bigfoot left the print, you have no way to know that a Bigfoot made the sound. Even if a Bigfoot made the print and a Bigfoot made the sound, these "signs" might not have been made by the same creature. Even when the same Bigfoot that left the print, made the sound, you have no way to make that correlational or causal link or connection, either. *No definitive correlational or causal relationship exists in such an example, except the presence of two or more humans in a Bigfoot habituation area! In order to make the connection in the final example, you would need to have actually observed the Bigfoot stub its toe, leave a print from jumping up and down while howling in pain!*

Correlations can be either **negative** or **positive**. When **negative**, one variable increases in frequency or intensity as the other variable decreases or lessens in frequency or intensity. The frequency of one variable's occurrence moves in the opposite direction of the other variable. As one goes up the other goes down, and vice versa. For example, as air temperature goes up, the number of daytime Bigfoot sightings going down would be a negative correlation. The number of Bigfoot sightings goes down, as the number of researchers carrying high power rifles into woods goes up. These are considered **negative correlations** due to the "opposite" or "negative" relationship between each variable.

*In a **positive correlation**, both variables rise and fall in intensity or frequency together. As the number of Bigfoot TV shows increase, the number of reported Bigfoot sightings also increase. As the amount of food available in an area goes down, the number of Bigfoot living and competing in that area for that food goes down, as well. These are considered **positive correlations** because the corresponding relationship between the variables makes them rise or fall together. (Please note, the positive and negative relationships exemplified above are fictitious in nature. I used my own logic/reasoning to create them. The relationships may not be accurate in their dynamics or influences. As such, they represent specific hypotheses to further explore through careful and systematic Scientific Bigfoot Research (SBFR) in and of themselves. They should not be taken as proven or established facts and assumed to be accurate. I included them only help the reader understand the concepts they exemplify!)*

"**Causality**" *in science can only be proven through repeated and replicated experimentation, not by solely relying on coincidence or correlation.* To facilitate scientific discovery and informational findings, we need to conduct **experimental** scientific research. The field psychology (by definition) tends to focus on behavioral and emotional phenomena and processes. As such, psychological research strives to **experimentally** measure behavior and emotional phenomena *which, in my opinion, makes it particularly well suited for Bigfoot research.*

Bigfoot research appears to focus on the behavioral and thinking processes/characteristics of the species. Given the increased potential for subjective bias involved in such field research, Bigfoot research should also focus on the researchers themselves, in my opinion. Research methods ripe to be influenced by investigator bias include "**observational methods**," "**verbal reports**," "**longitudinal studies**" (monitoring across time), "**archival research**" (investigations done in the library or other informational archives), "**testing**," and "**experimentation**" (my emphasis).[78]

"**Observational methods**" include "**direct**," "**naturistic**," and "**automated**" observation. If you have been able to follow and understand (not to mention stay awake) through this chapter so far, definitions for "**direct**" (with the human eye) and "**naturalistic**" (conducted in the natural environment of the target species) warrant no further definitions.

By "**automated**" observation, I am referring to the use of "automated" technology to do the observation for us. This can be something as simple as a voice-activated recording device or trail camera. It might also include more sophisticated, remote computer-driven, real-time viewing cameras, recorders and other technological advances (the NAWAC Tag 7 tracking device comes to mind). I envision the utilization of nano-technological devices in the near future given their extremely small size and lack of detectability. The mind boggles with the numerous observational AND hunting/trapping applications possible simply by combining nano-technology with variations of the NAWAC Tag 7 general trap design.

Irrespective of the research technique used, raw data will need to be converted into **numbers** for data analysis. This is one of the necessary evils identified in the title of this chapter. Again, data that simply sits in a large database and is used primarily for commercial ventures does not constitute "scientific data" or science, in my opinion. There's that dead horse, again. It **may** have scientific potential.

Ideally, however, it is the scientific hypothetical questions (hypotheses) asked (not financial or commercial concerns) that should drive data collection and subsequent analysis. *It is ultimately statistical data analysis techniques that make the turn and begin to complete the scientific circle of discovery and knowledge.* As such, we need to trudge another big step down that path to better "outfit" ourselves to **understand statistics.**

Statistics allow us analyze our own data. Of equal importance, by understanding statistical results reported in other scientific investigations, we are able to judge their scientific meaning and value. They tell us the true utility of the study results to guide, assist, and inform our own research plans for the species and phenomena of Bigfoot. Take an oxycodone and a good stiff drink to steel yourself against the pain, because here we go!

Statistics

According to the American Psychological Association's Dictionary of Psychology a "**statistic**" is "a number that represents a measurement of some characteristic, construct, variable or other item of interest ... [and] ... any function of the observations in a **sample** that may be used to estimate the unknown but corresponding value in the **population.** Examples include measures of central tendency (e.g., the **mean, median, mode**), measures of dispersion (e.g., **standard deviation, variance**), and distributional attributes (e.g., skewness, kurtosis) ... ."[79]

Stated less technically for our purposes, it is a **number** that represents a phenomenon, observation, behavioral or emotional activity or other research variable used for research analysis (statistical data analysis) related to Bigfoot. For example, if I was observing "tree knock sounds" the number "1" would stand for one tree knock sound, the number "2" would represent two tree knock sounds, "3" three knock sounds, etc..

If I was also observing vocalizations in my database (in addition to knocks: two variables now included in the study) tree knocks would be coded as "1" and vocalizations as "2." The numeric code "1: 2" would then mean I observed (heard) a tree knock with two consecutive strikes. The code "2: 2" would mean I observed (heard) two distinct vocalizations.

Vocalization could be further refined by type. A howl equaling "1," a scream equaling "2," a whoop equaling "3." "2: 2:1, 3" would then be translated to mean: I heard two vocalizations, one being a howl followed by another being a whoop. "2: 2:3, 1" would translate into I heard two vocalizations, this time the whoop first and the howl second. *Please note I have chosen these numeric codes in totally arbitrary fashion. In practice, the design of your survey or experiment and the statistical analysis program you are using would figure largely in driving or dictating your coding scheme.*

The more technical definition nonetheless contains other words important to define and understand if we hope to analyze and judge the value of research results. The **population** *represents "the entire world or all of what you are studying."* For example, if you are studying characteristics of human beings (say shoe size), to truly "test" the "population's" shoe size you would have to measure the shoe size of literally every person on the planet! Not a very practical thing to do given that there are a lot (billions) of people in the world. **Even** within the world population, there are subgroups of people that wear shoes, and others that don't. *Nonetheless they all still have a measurable shoe size!* Do you have the time, energy or financial resources to spend finding out every persons' shoe size? Not likely!

So rather than try to get the shoe size for everyone in the world (those that do and don't wear shoes i.e., the "population"), you will first narrow the focus of your study to only people that wear shoes. You will then measure *shoes from a small group of people from each country in the world. That small group of people represents your "**sample**."*

Performing this in each country in the world insures you are not **biased** in measuring shoe sizes using on only one ethnic group. If we only measured the shoe sizes of Mexican people, who we know are generally/overall smaller in stature than US citizens, our sample would be **biased**. By measuring shoe sizes from each country in the world and taking measurement from all races and/or geographically distributed groups within those countries, you ensure your "**samples**" accurately reflect the shoe sizes of groups of people in that country. The shoes size measurements you get then accurately represent (**are representative of**) of the shoe sizes in that country. *By performing that process in all countries in the world, you ensure those "samples" are also then representative of the entire "population" of the world.*

Relating it to Bigfoot, **most** BF sightings haven't reported the creature wearing shoes. As such we don't need to measure shoes sizes. But the species is called "BIG" "FOOT" for a reason. They've got unusually big feet compared to humans. So, it may be both interesting and of scientific value to measure their **foot sizes** represented through **shoe sizes**.

Taking out an ad in the paper promising two smoked salmons to every Bigfoot willing to have their shoe size measured at the local "Shoe Rack" store probably wouldn't draw too many Bigfoots into town to get their feet measured. Even going into the woods with a Brannock Device (the name of the device to measure shoe sizes) in one hand and two smoked salmon in the other wouldn't produce much better results. So, given we aren't likely to be able to directly measure a Bigfoot's shoe size anytime soon, we are forced to do "second best;" measure "**samples**" of their "foot-print size."

It warrants reflecting on the fact that when we measure an imprint of a supposed Bigfoot footprint in the terraform substrate (as in we didn't actually visually observe Bigfoot make it in real time), we **aren't** measuring Bigfoot's **foot size**. *Similarly, when we cast that footprint and then measure it, we still are not getting an actual measurement of Bigfoot's foot size.* Seeing the creature make the imprint changes none of this beyond our certainty that it was made by a Bigfoot! Scientifically these are "**samples**" that may be **reasonably representative** (but not an "actual" measure) of a single Bigfoot creature's foot size taken "cooperatively." It does not likely represent the entire "**population**" of Bigfoot footprints, let alone actual Bigfoot foot sizes. I highlight this only to further differentiate between the concepts of a "**sample**" versus a "**population.**" *It is not meant as a criticism of footprint or foot cast studies in any fashion, which in my opinion represent some of the best scientific evidence available of the existence of Bigfoot.*

The difference between these two concepts nonetheless points out why basic frequency research on the subject is still needed and why databases like John Green's and the acclaimed large BFRO database continue to have potential scientific value if appropriately exploited for scientific purposes and if containing such information. Contained within those databases or not, however, it remains not only impractical, but likely impossible to assess the entire population of Bigfoot prints within the USA, let alone the entire planet. As such systematic "sampling" studies of new imprints and existing casts seems needed within the US borders and within and between other countries. Given the pioneering work and hypothetical understandings based on Dr. Krantz's and Dr. Meldrum's work, such samples and sampling studies likely represent one of our best hopes for generating truly representative data and information on the species population (at least within the US for now, but worldwide in the future).

Measures of central tendency refer us back to our normal curve and are statistical terms describing the "average" score on the normal curve. In a broader sense they are "the middle or center point of a set of scores. The central tendency of a sample data set, for instance, may be estimated by a number of different statistics (e.g., **mean, median, mode**)."[80]

The "**mean**" is one method of describing or defining the concept of "average." In statistics, it symbolizes "the numerical average of a set of scores, computed as the sum of all scores divided by the number of scores. For example, suppose a health researcher sampled five individuals and found their numbers of hours of exercise per week to be 3, 1, 5, 4, and 7, respectively. The mean number of exercise hours per week thus would be (3 + 1 + 5 + 4 + 7)/5 = 20/5 = 4. The mean is the most widely used statistic for describing **central tendency**. Also called the 'arithmetic mean;' 'arithmetic average.'"[81]

The "**median**" is "the **midpoint** in a distribution. That is the score or value that divides the entire list of scores it into **two equal-sized halves**. The **median** is a measure of central tendency that is particularly useful when analyzing data that have **skewness** (i.e., lopsidedness), because it is more resistant to the influence of extreme values."[82] Using the numbers from above (1, 3, 4, 5, 7), the median is the number "4." Given we have a series or string of five numbers listed above, the number that "splits those scores into two even groups" of two numbers (in this case) is "4," the median.

The "**mode**" is either "a characteristic manner of behavior or way of doing things, as in a technique" ... [or if speaking statistically] ... "the most frequently occurring score in a set of data, which is sometimes used as a measure of <u>central tendency</u> ... [Let's add one more score to our above string of values (another number "5").] Our hypothetical data set is now 1, 3, 4, 5, 5, 7. The most frequently occurring score in that set (it occurs twice) is "5." The number five, in this case, is also called "**mode**" or "**modal value**."[83]

The difference between these three measures of central tendency is critical to understand if doing detective work on understanding the value of a particular data set or type of research. Television surveys/polls, political statistics, (and most disturbing recently) COVID-19 data are most typically reported using graphic statistics based on percentages, means and other basic **descriptive statistics**. When this is being done, it is typically being done to over-simplify the picture or to manipulate the message. It will often be "dumbed down" because they are hiding something in the numbers or the true numbers are inconclusive or meaningless and literally tell us nothing. Alternately, keeping it simple allows the analyst or the people using the data to manipulate the message or otherwise try "to make a mountain out of a molehill." I have given concrete examples of this elsewhere in this text and will not belabor those generalities further.

To speak to **mean, median,** and **modal** definitions however, the "statistically purest" measure of central tendency (or stated less technically) the purest measure "of average" is the **mean.** We first potentially bias our reality by eliminating outliers (data so extreme or unusual it would create a false or otherwise skewed result or picture of the data). We then compute the sum of all of the scores in the data set. Then dividing that obtained numeric value by the number of scores reflecting that variable in the data set gives you the **mean.** It represents the most valid and accurate measure of "what is the average" or most accurately reflects that phenomena. This occurs and is the appropriate statistic to use when there is a symmetrically shaped hump reflected in the distribution of the data. This means the phenomena we are measuring is "Normally distributed." This guides our choice of statistical formulas and analyses to use.

Note that the "**median**" is used when the distribution of scores is skewed or lopsided. The **median** is then calculated because other calculation techniques (i.e., mean and mode), would be less accurately or truly reflective of "average" or the norm (normal) within that **skewed** or lopsided distribution of scores. Unfortunately, its use reflects that the underlying distribution of scores measuring the phenomena itself varies from the shape of the normal distribution (which typically has the "hump" in the center of the distribution). In a **skewed** distribution, that "hump" is closer to either end of the graph, rather than in the middle. See the figures below to get a better visual understanding of the point and its implication.

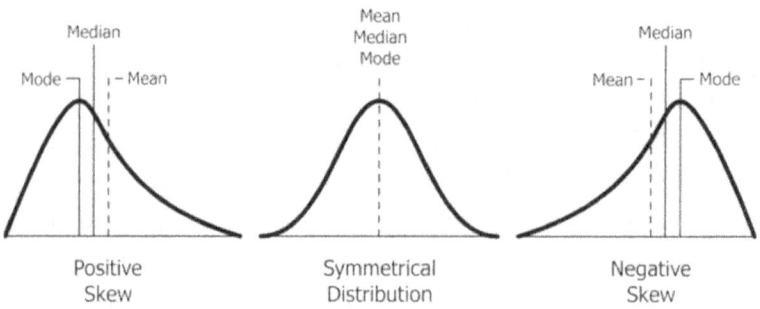

| Positive Skew | Symmetrical Distribution | Negative Skew |

Source: https://en.wikipedia.org/wiki/Skewness.[84]

Note that in a **symmetrical distribution**, numeric value or number for each measure of central tendency (mean, median, mode) is identical. When the underlying distribution (under the dark curved mountain-like line) is **positively skewed**, this produces three different numerical values (numbers). The **mean** value remains in the center of the distribution (from left to right) and is unchanged in its value. The **mode** value shifts furthest to the left (as we look at the figure), is reduced to a smaller number or value, but continues to bisect the peak of the hump. The median (now on the down slope) has decreased in value or size, and shifts to the left of the **mean** to a lesser degree than the **mode**.

On the **negatively skewed** distribution, the **mean** remains in the center of the distribution (from left to right as we look at the figure) maintaining the same numerical value. The values of the median and mode have increased in value (gone up). The **mode** continues to bisect or split the peak of the hump which now has shifted to the right. The mean and median are now on the upslope. Once again the **mode** value has changed (increased in this case) the most, the median increase in value the second most, while the mean remained the same number. Confused? You're probably not alone! The meanings of new words are difficult to grasp for most folks! Let me try to make it real and meaningful!

A concrete example of a **negatively skewed** data set or distribution of scores would be "retirement age" (the number of people that retire according to age range). Look at the shape of the hump or dorsal fin in the negatively skewed distribution above. The older you get the more likely you are to retire up to a certain age (63-65 years old). At that point the distribution of scores or numbers rapidly decline (to the right of the hump peak). They drop off as most have people have retried by this point.

A concrete example of a **positively skewed** distribution would be number of days stayed in a hospital following surgery. Only a few people stay one to three days, with the **modal** (most frequent occurring number represented by the peak of the hump) number of days being 6, the average number of days being 10 days. The median (splitting the middle between the mode and mean) being 9 days. It's all crystal clear now, isn't it? NOT!

The important concept to remember is that the underlying distribution (or shape) of the mountain, hump, or dorsal fin influences which measure of **central tendency** represents the most accurate or valid measure of what is "normal" or "usual." Scientists or reporters advancing a particular biased agenda might inappropriately report one measure of central tendency because it suits their agenda better than the most accurate or appropriately used measure of central tendency. In doing so, they "spin" or "twist" what constitutes "normal" in the data to fit the needs of their agenda.

More specifically when a researcher fails to report the mean, there is likely a meaningful reason why the median or mode are being reported. If the **mean** is not reported, it likely reflected a skewed underlying distribution in the data. Reporting the mean might somehow not support the argument being made. Using the median or mode numbers might be more impressive due to their larger or smaller values depending on the topic at hand.

Perhaps even more importantly, when these basic descriptive statistical numbers (percentile/percent, mean, median mode) represent the totality of the data presented/reported from a study, *be cautious of the implications of meaning and generalizability of that study.* In effect it may not be able to be applied to your ideas, theories, or models that are **symmetrical** in their distribution. If there were **true** or **meaningful** differences to report, a relatively simple z-score or t-test would been calculated to prove or reflect that difference.

For example, on June 8th, 2020 MSNBC reported an NBC/Wall Street Journal Poll showing Joe Biden had 49% of "key voters" voting for him compared to 42% of "key voters" that would vote for Donald Trump. Biden was leading by 7 points.[85] Biden fans should have been should have **been** celebrating, right? Wrong!!! Re-examine the properties of the normal curve illustration.

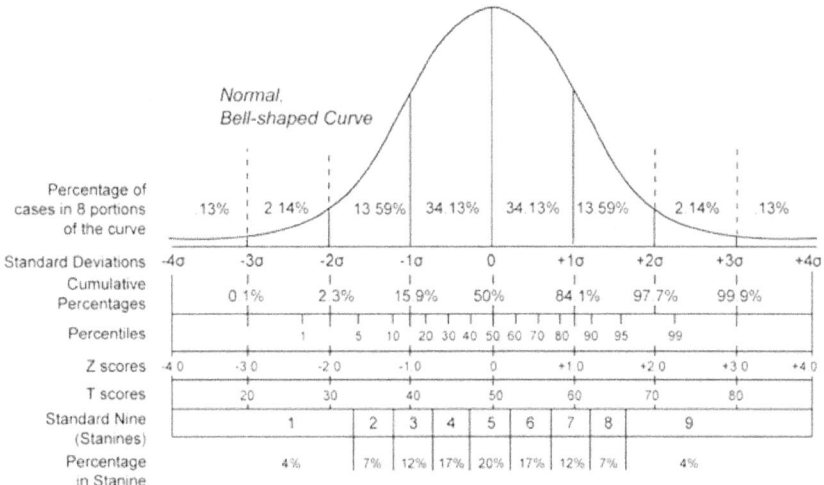

Source: Normal Curve.[86]

Examine the cumulative percentages and/or the percentile lines. Forty-nine percent (49%) and 42% fall in the same distribution between zero and one step down (one standard deviation). In short, they are not statistically different from each other merely by visual inspection. We really need to go no further. There is no story here. There is no true statistical difference between polling at 49% or polling at 42%. It could be due to random error!!! Scientifically (statistically), it is simply inaccurate to interpret this data as meaning that Biden was leading Trump in the polls! (Also note, the sample included only "key voters," whoever they were.)

The most scientifically accurate interpretation of this data would be that: "*There is no statistically significant difference between Biden and Trump in the polls in a sample of 'key voters.'*" A less scientific interpretation might state: "*Biden and Trump are virtually locked in a tie in the polls,*" but I guess that wouldn't be as seemingly big of a headline or perhaps not support the network agenda!

Unfortunately for our political system, this is not unique to Trump or Biden biased news sources. Nor was this new to this election cycle. It has been true for as long as I can remember and a good example of how statistics can "be interpreted or twisted to make any point you wish." Had z-scores or t-tests been run and reported, this twisting would be more difficult to achieve! *Be leery of any information on any topic that only reports percentages, percentiles or measures of central tendency! It could reflect either weak results that aren't statistically significant and not of value or the process of hiding significant differences the writer would prefer you ignore.*

It's now time to bring this back to Bigfoot related research (or lack thereof). A somewhat recent post on YouTube entitled "Great Apes, Trail Cameras, and The Bigfoot Implications" was "shared" by a Bigfoot enthusiast genuinely hoping to help Bigfoot fieldworkers.[87] It **seemed** to have specific findings that would inform Bigfoot research. Some Bigfoot Sonic research friends that I "follow" posted it on their Facebook page. *Aside from taking what may or may not ultimately prove to be the logical leap from Great Ape research to the Bigfoot species; this study reported only descriptive percentages. If a t-test or other analysis was run, the authors certainly did not report it. After watching the video this was my spontaneous reply.*

"...First and foremost, thanks for a thought-provoking summary! Very interesting with POTENTIAL implications for Bigfoot! I say "potential" as the bulk of your discussion (based on citing this research) is based on the assumption that the Bigfoot is closest to a great ape. Great and valid if that is the case, but not so much if the Human/Hybrid Bigfoot theory camp or any other theory is right. Secondly, I correctly use word "potential" as (unless you left out the most critical analyses from the experiment/study), it appears the study and your analysis/summary of and conclusions based on same are based totally on descriptive statistics. Very dangerous scientifically!!! IF that is the case, this is a prime example/parallel to why the "scientific status" of Bigfoot research remains light years distant from acceptance in the true scientific community: Descriptive statistics have VERY LITTLE true scientific value/meaning as they represent the most basic/crudest form of data analysis and as such lead to and leave open possible endless interpretations and theories based on the readers (YOURS AND MINE AND EVERYONE ELSE'S) biases. For example, you draw conclusions and develop hypotheses (albeit tentative ones) based on 85% versus 58% verses a smaller number (I already forget after my one viewing; maybe 13%) comparisons without discussing or citing any t-test run on these data to understand if these numbers represent and are truly different from each other (represent true behavioral differences between the three sub-species) and/or could be due to random error or reflect sampling error or any number of other types of environmentally-based or statistical analysis-based error detectable by further statistical analyses. (FWIW, it's likely there is a true statistical difference between 85% and the 13% data, but maybe not between 85% and 58% or 58% and 13% data. We can't know without further analyses.) IF AND ONLY IF your conclusions and hypotheses are due to such error, your genuine attempt to enlighten and refine Bigfoot field research and our knowledge of the creature based on same simply has created red herrings for researchers to spin their wheels on and waste their time and resources on as they are scientifically flawed and therefore scientifically meaningless (despite how valid or appealing they may seem to our own preconceptions/biases). Not criticizing or trying to offend/provoke/put down you personally; just stating a scientific fact that we all need to understand if we are critically analyzing and reviewing such research in the hopes of informing our own and what we do. Thanks to Sheila TJ for sharing! Baiting or not, I certainly rose to the bait! (Lol)."[88]

As stated, and suggested above, while intriguing to reflect on, it was essentially scientifically meaningless for drawing definitive scientific conclusions on primates, let along being generalizable to the Bigfoot species, **should** they prove to be similar primates as those cited in the article. *This is not because the research is invalid, but because their analysis appeared based totally on describing their results in terms of percentage comparisons. It was without any tests for true differences between the groups and was devoid of other inferential statistics.* I did attempt to speak to true differences in a cursory fashion (without consulting the normal curve or doing a statistical analysis of my own). Emphasizing that I used a "casual" approach when reacting on Facebook, let's see how I did.

"... (FWIW, it's likely there is a true statistical difference between

85% and the 13% data, but maybe not between 85% and 58% or 58% and 13% data. We can't know without further analyses) ... ."[89] Let's break out our normal curve once again!

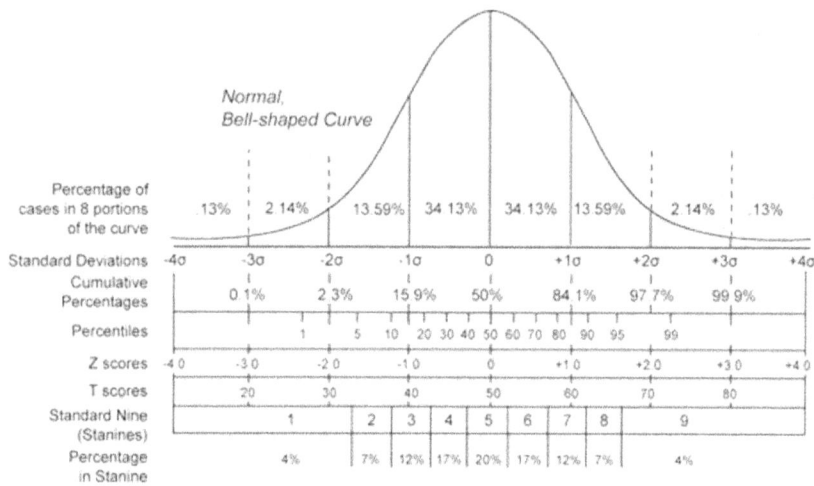

Source: Normal Curve.[90]

Examining the "Cumulative Percentages" line re-levels that "85%" falls into the very beginning of the +1 - +2 standard deviation range on the curve (just past the "84.1%" designation). The "13%" would be located just below the -1 to -2 standard deviation range on the curve. This would appear consistent with at least a two standard deviation difference between the two percentages and would be consistent with a **significant difference** between these two statistical numbers and the **great ape species** they represent.

Again, examining the "Cumulative Percentages" line re-levels that "85%" falls into the very beginning of the +1 - +2 standard deviation range on the curve (just past the "84.1%" designation). The "58%" would fall just below the number "60" on the "Percentiles" line. As such, it would appear there is slightly less than one standard deviation gap or difference between "85%" and "58%' and the great ape species represented therein. *There is not statistically significant difference for the great ape species they represent.*

Luckily, I did pretty well in my "guestimate." Reflecting back on the video, the interested viewer might more seriously consider/give greater credence to the difference between the subspecies represented by the thirteen percent classification and eighty-fifth percent classification, but not so for the other comparison. This has some validity, however, *only for the great apes being compared! Regarding generalization to Bigfoot behavior, however, we are left to our ink-blot test-like fantasies/personally biased projections and interpretations as no inferential statistics are presented upon which to base an opinion!* Field researchers using camera traps beware of how you allow this data to influence your camera trap placement and utilization!

TO SHOW A RELATIONSHIP, WE NEED TO LOOK AT CORRELATIONAL STATISTICS. TO SHOW CAUSALITY, WE NEED TO USE EXPERIMENTAL DESIGN. If the research you are reviewing provides only summary descriptive statistics, there ultimately may not be much there. You've got to read and apply this knowledge to understand it's value to you and the field. BE A DISCRIMINATING CONSUMER OF RESEARCH PAPERS AND MORE POPULAR SOUND BITE VENUES. What it really means is in the numbers!

So far, most of my description has focused on descriptive statistics. These are "procedures for depicting the main aspects of sample data, **without** necessarily **inferring to** a larger "**population**." Descriptive statistics usually include the **mean, median,** and **mode** to indicate **central tendency,** as well as the **range** [of scores] and a **standard deviation** that reveals how widely spread the scores are within the sample. Descriptive statistics could also "include charts and graphs such as a **frequency distribution** ... among others."[91]

A chart, for example might be a **frequency distribution** refers to "a tabular representation of the number of times a specific value or datum point occurs. The left column lists the different categories of a [phenomenon] or ... variable(s) ... and the right column lists the number of occurrences of each. When a frequency distribution is plotted on a graph, it is often called a frequency curve, frequency diagram ... [or] a frequency table.[92]

Inferential statistics are "a broad class of statistical techniques that allow **inferences** about characteristics of a population to be drawn from a sample of data from that population while controlling (at least partially) the extent to which errors of inference may be made. These techniques include approaches for testing hypotheses ... and selecting among a set of competing [theories]/models."[93]

An inference is a **conclusion** derived from an earlier premise or premises according to valid rules of [inductive and deductive] reasoning or the process of drawing such a conclusion. Some hold that "an inference, as contrasted with a mere conclusion, requires that the person making it actually believe that the inference and the premises from which it is drawn are true. ... In statistical analysis, a conclusion about a population is based on logical reasoning from data gathered about a smaller sample ... The most common example of this type of inference is statistical hypothesis [or theory] testing."[94]

In short, descriptive statistics speak to only what you have actually measured, but inferential statistics speak to the entire population that you don't have the time or resources to measure. Descriptive statistics simply describe the characteristics of the variable you are measuring in your sample (the actual single or group of Bigfoots or knocks or vocalizations you are measuring). Inferential statistics allow you to infer, generalize, or extend your estimation about how true or accurate that may be for your population (all Bigfoot knocks, or vocalizations, including ones you have never seen or heard)! Did that tree make a sound in the woods when Bigfoot pushed it over but no one was around to hear it? *Think about what your answer to that question means about your beliefs and biases about Bigfoot.*

"**Statistical significance**" is another very critical concept to understand and differentiate from **effect sizes** and **likelihood ratios**. I read a book written by a respected BF author that interpreted a less than ("<") .01 level of significance to mean *there was a 99% chance that Bigfoot created the data or effect being measured.* Wrong! A "< .01" level of significance means there is less than a one in one hundred chance that the result was *due to random error.* It is an **error statement** that in no way speaks to Bigfoot influences or effects on the data. Bigfoot's influences (on the data) are spoken to statistically by **"effect sizes"** or **"likelihood ratios."** A more technical analysis might help (or hurt).

"The level of statistical significance symbol is "α" in **significance testing**, a fixed probability of rejecting the **null hypothesis** of no effect (no difference between groups) when it is in fact true. It is set at some predetermined (a-priori) value, usually .001, .01, or .05, depending on the consequences associated with making a **Type I error (a false positive)**. When a particular effect is obtained experimentally, the **probability level** (*p*) associated with this effect is compared to the significance level. If the *p* value is less than the α level, the null hypothesis is rejected. Small *p* values suggest that obtaining a statistic as extreme as the one obtained is rare and thus the null hypothesis is unlikely to be true. The smaller the α level, the more convincing is the rejection of the null hypothesis. Also called alpha level."[95]

Yep! That hurt!!! Let's see if I can ease the pain (simplify it) while discussing a few other concepts relevant to our purposes in this chapter. Any time you have a hypothetical question you must do an experiment or take a test to answer that question. At the time of this writing, "Do I have COVID-19?" is a question on many peoples' minds. If you have even a passing interest in Bigfoot, the most pressing question is "Does Bigfoot exist?" But these questions must be transformed into hypotheses for experimentation or testing purposes. This is done simply by restating them in their affirmative "alternative hypotheses" form: "I do have COVID-19" and "Bigfoot does exist;" versus their negative or "null hypothesis" form: "I do not have COVID-19" and "Bigfoot does not exist." Let's run with the COVID-19 hypothesis first.

Any time you are trying to answer a question by testing the hypothesis, the test result can have one of four possible outcomes. They are represented below:[96]

REALITY

	Positive (You Have It)	Negative (Don't Have It)
Positive (You Have It)	True Positive (Hit)	False Positive (Miss) Type I Error
Negative (Don't Have It)	False Negative (Miss) Type II Error	True Negative (Hit)

TEST RESULTS

300. Normal Curve. (n.d.). Wikipedia. Retrieved from https://psychology. wikia.org/wiki/Bell_curve_grading

To the left side of the square you find the results of the test (**TEST RESULTS**) which may be "**Positive**" (meaning the **test** indicates you have COVID-19) or "**Negative**" (meaning the **test** indicates you don't have COVID-19). Above the square you have the consensus reality of the situation (**REALITY**) which includes the "**Positive**" of the reality (meaning you have COVID-19) or the "**Negative**" of the reality (meaning you don't have COVID-19).

The four possible outcomes of the test are a "True Positive," "False Positive," "False Negative," or a "True Negative." A "**True Positive**" is a correct test result (a "Hit"). This means that "**in consensus reality**" you **do** have COVID-19.

A "**False Positive**" means the test result was **incorrect** (a "Miss") and created a specific type of error known as a "Type I Error." The **test result** says you have COVID-19 when **in reality** you don't have it.

A "**False Negative**" means the **test result** was **incorrect** (a "Miss") and created a specific type of error known as a "Type II Error." The **test result** says you don't have COVID-19, but you do.

A "**True Negative**" is a **correct test result** (a "Hit") and means that "**in consensus reality**" you **don't** have COVID-19. The test says you don't have COVID-19 and you really don't have COVID-19.

Again, a "**True Positive**" is defined as when the test **correctly** indicates you do have COVID-19 and in consensus reality you do have COVID-19. A "True Negative" is when the test **correctly** indicates you don't have COVID-19 and in consensus reality you don't have COVID-19.

A "Type I Error" (a "False Positive Test Result") is when the test **incorrectly** indicates you do have COVID-19 because, in reality, you don't have COVID-19. A "Type II Error" (a "False Negative Test Result") is when the test **incorrectly** indicates you don't have COVID-19 because, in reality, you do have COVID-19.

Get ready to take another Oxycontin and a second drink because now were going to insert Bigfoot into the model! Ohhhhh Nooooo! The **TEST RESULTS** are **Positive** indicating Bigfoot **Does Exist** and the **REALITY** of the situation is **Positive** indicating Bigfoot **Exists. In Reality**, we then have a "**True Positive**" or a "Hit." *Bigfoot exists in consensus reality!!!!*

When the **TEST RESULTS** are **Negative** indicating a Bigfoot **Doesn't Exist,** but the **REALITY** of the situation is **Positive** indicating Bigfoot exists in reality, that puts you in the **false negative** quadrant meaning the test has **missed** and creates a "Type II error." Bigfoot actually exists, but your test is telling you the species doesn't.

When the **TEST RESULTS** are **Positive** but the **REALITY** of the situation is **Negative;** this means the test has created a "**False positive,**" another **miss** known as a "Type I Error." Bigfoot doesn't exist even though the test is telling you it does.

Finally, when the **TEST RESULTS** are **Negative** and the **REALITY** of the situation is also **Negative**, that is a "True Negative," also known as a "**Hit.**" The test is telling you Bigfoot doesn't exist and, *Bigfoot doesn't exist in consensus reality!*

The purpose of scientific testing is to maximize the probability of **hits** (true findings) and minimize the chances of **error.** To return to the point of level of significance, it refers to the consequences of a Type I error; that is the consequences of obtaining a "false positive" result. This is the consequences of a test telling you there is a difference or experimental effect, when there is not. The level of significance is usually decided and set or established ahead of time (a-priori) based on the probability of this error. You will see a variety of numbers used to reflect the level of significance (.001, .01, .05, and .15). Numbers **greater than** .05 (.15 for example) are considered to have too high of a frequency of risk of a "Type I error." This is a scientifically **unacceptable result.**

Please note that in an article stating a "statistical finding is significant at a .01 level (p < .01)" means: there is less than a 1 in 100 chance (.01 means 1 in a hundred) that the result was due to a Type I error. *THE LEVEL OF STATISTICAL SIGNIFICANCE SPEAKS TO THE CHANCES THAT THE EXPERIMENTAL RESULTS ARE DUE TO ERROR.* Subtracting the value of a Type I error from 1 does not give you the "effect size" or probability that the result is due to "Bigfoot," but actually tells you the probability that there is no difference between Bigfoot and the control group. Nor does subtracting the "Type II" error rate from one tell you about Bigfoot. It tells you the power of the test.

It is your experimental design and ability to account for systematic error/extraneous influence that speaks to Bigfoot influences. **Effect size** would be a more accurate statistic use to explain the **influence** or **effect** of Bigfoot. Significance or probability levels speak only to error. A point .01 or less level of significance doesn't mean there was a 99 % chance it was Bigfoot. It means there was only a one in one hundred chance the result was due to error or that there is a 99 out of 100 chance that the result is not due to error. *It speaks only to error, not "Bigfootness!"*

A final important consideration in statistical analysis is the difference between **statistical significance** and **clinically meaningful significance** (clinical significance). Assuming the study reveals a statistically significant difference between variables or groups, that difference may or may not be **meaningful** in the real world. It may or may not be **clinically significant.** Let's return to our earlier ice cream experiment and set it in the Arctic environment. Do you know how to sell an ice cream freezer to an Eskimo?

In that experiment, we discovered that although there is a relatively strong relationship (correlation) between temperature rising and ice-cream melting, it is not, however, a causal relationship. It does not occur invariably 100% of the time. This is because temperatures well below freezing can rise to 32 degrees Fahrenheit and still not melt ice cream! This also comes to bear on **statistical** versus **clinical** significance.

So, if you live in the Arctic "January, February, and early March you experience uniform conditions with mean temperatures of about –35°F (–3°C) in the central Siberian Arctic and –30° to –20°F (–34° to –29°C) in North America. The lowest extreme temperatures in the winter are between –65° and –50°F (–54° and –46°C)."[97] No need for a freezer! Arctic average July temperatures range from about –10° to 10°C (14° to 50°F), with some land areas occasionally exceeding 30°C (86°F) in summer."[98] You want a freezer for those temperatures during that time period!

Turning from debunking some of my childhood (potentially racist) jokes, to clinical versus statistical significance, given that the average winter temperature ranges from -30°F to -20°F (10 degrees of variability), it seems safe to assume that a 30-degree increase in temperature (-30°F to 0°F) would be a statically significant increase. (Let's pretend it is for this example, even if it's not.) In terms of melting ice cream, is that **statistically significant** difference meaningful in reality or **clinically significant**? No!! The ice cream is frozen solid at 0°F and at -30°F! When we have that same 30°F statistically significant increase from 31°F to 61°F, that **statistically significant increase** now also becomes **clinically meaningful** and relevant in reality and provokes the need for a freezer. Without that freezer, the ice cream would melt in the Arctic! Go figure! Even Eskimos need a freezer to store ice cream in the summer! The thirty-degree increase now is not only statistically significant; it is also **clinically relevant** or **clinically significant**.

Here is yet another wrinkle. *A phenomenon or variable can be* clinically relevant or significant *even when it's not* statistically significant. Take depression for example. Someone who is severely clinically depressed (also known as a severe major depression) would likely have suicidal ideation (thoughts of suicide) and might score a t-score (mean of 50, standard deviation of 10) of 88 on the MMPI-II, a measure (test) of emotional and personality functioning. They are put on antidepressant medicines and enter therapy and their suicidal ideation goes away. They are retested on the MMPI-II and their score goes down less than a full standard deviation to 79. That would **not** be considered a **statistically significant reduction** or decline in their Depression scale score on the test but **would be** considered a **clinically significant improvement** or a clinically significant difference. That is, they would likely look less depressed. *(Please note, that the depressed patient in this condition is at an increased risk of successful suicide. They now have enough energy and focus to act on their thoughts!)*

Let's get to a hypothetical (pretend or scientifically uninvestigated) Bigfoot example: Bluff Charges versus True Charges/Attacks. First off, let me say I have never experienced either, so I can only imagine! ...

Although documented in numerous other writings (e.g., Meldrum, 2006;[99] Gerhard, 2019;[100] and Native American oral lore to name but a few), assault and abduction charges by Bigfoots would appear relatively rare in frequency. "More than a few" experienced field researchers and random sighting witnesses have reported bluff charges in which the creature "pulls up short" or stops its charge before approaching close enough for assault or abduction. It is therefore not uncommon that the Bigfoot *is not visibly seen* by it's intended "victim of intimidation." Although I have not personally experienced this, even given my limited number of outings, I have been a member of a larger expedition group where other group members have been bluff-charged. The actual Bigfoot was never visually seen or identified by the field researcher(s) being charged. Scott Carpenter (2019) has also documented one such example in his book *The Nephilim Among Us Updated*.[101] Although these two behaviors apparently have not been systematically and scientifically investigated beyond documenting them, based on that documentation, it would appear a reasonable conclusion that Bluff Charges happen at a higher frequency or rate than True charges.

Hypothetically assuming that is the case, if these two behaviors were systematically recorded for frequency, we would expect a **significant difference** between Bluff charges and True Charges. If this happened, however (hypothetically speaking) there would most certainly be a **clinical difference** between the two. The worst that might happen to a person from a Bluff charge would be the emotional trauma (not to minimize the severe emotional trauma and possible PTSD associated with a Bluff charge). Any physical injury would be unintentional, likely incurring when fleeing the scene or location of the Bluff charge.

I am aware of details from two documented abduction reports: one by Albert Ostman (documented in Ken Gerhard's 2019 book "*The Essential Guide to Bigfoot,*" pp. 54-56)[102] but documented by others (Meldrum, 2016[103] and Redfern[104]). This reported abduction failed to result in physical harm beyond some dehydration. There was also apparently no reported emotional harm.

Mary Green and Janice Carter, however, documented the abduction and rape of an unidentified young woman who remained hospitalized in a "sanitarium" for an extended period of time.[105] Even dehydration, but most certainly an emotional breakdown resulting in hospitalization are examples of **clinical significance**, irrespective of statistical differences between the two types of behavior. *Clearly, more systematically documented scientific investigations are needed on these behaviors to better understand them and their consequences.*

11

HUNTING/TRAPPING VERSUS FIELD RESEARCH VERSUS SCIENTIFIC BIGFOOT RESEARCH (SBFR): WHERE DO WE GO FROM HERE?

If you do Bigfoot Field Research (BFR) research and I haven't pissed you off yet, this should do it! In my opinion, going into the woods and systematically hunting for Bigfoot (research) in the hopes of seeing them or "gathering evidence" of their existence (BFR) does not constitute "scientific" field research, or Scientific Bigfoot Research (SBFR). Remember, phenomenological/experiential evidence forms the foundation for scientific research and serves as a blueprint for scientific investigations into Bigfoot. It's fun! It's even fun, interesting, and informative, especially when you experience some form of evidence. But "science," in my opinion, it is not! Before you cuss me any further and tear up this book, please allow me to explain!

Hunting is defined as "the activity of hunting wild animals or game, especially for food or sport."[1] "There are probably as many reasons to hunt as there are hunters, but the core reasons can be reduced to four: to experience nature as a participant, to feel an intimate, sensuous connection to a place, to take responsibility for one's food, and to acknowledge our kinship with wildlife."[2] **Trapping** is defined as "catching (an animal) in a trap."[3] A **trap** is "a device for taking game or other animals."[4]

The successful hunter or trapper will study their target species in order to understand their distribution within the intended area to be hunted or trapped. This typically includes seasonal migration, food preferences, eating, and mating habits. Most hunters and trappers will have an awareness of the differences in appearance based on the gender of the species, their varying size, as well as the sounds and meanings of their calls or vocalizations. Signs such as foot or paw prints, hair, flesh, blood, and scat (shit) become important in stalking or tracking the species. Bedding habits, design, locations, and territorial signs or boundaries enter into the formula. The species' sensory and behavioral strengths and weaknesses are understood intimately and exploited during the stalk and ultimate capture or kill. The truly dedicated hunter/trapper will take notes in the field and log them either into a database or journal. These will then be used for analysis and reflection to better understand their quarry, and recall specific successful versus failed hunt locations and times from hunting season to hunting season. The trophy hunter/trapper searches and targets only the largest most unique or impressive of the species, while the food hunter is less selective regarding size. The ethical and moral hunter/trapper makes efforts to not over-exploit the species and preserve the resource.

Now, re-read the above paragraph, and wherever I used the words "hunter/trapper," substitute the words "fieldworker" or "Bigfoot researcher." With the possible exception of hunting/trapping including a food target priority, the description seems to apply equally to the hunter/trapper and the fieldworker/researcher (at least the field research I have been involved in, which I considered "phenomenologically" exemplary). Phenomenologically exemplary, but where is the "science" that distinguishes field research from hunting and trapping?

Field research is defined as a **"qualitative method of data collection** that aims to observe, interact and understand ... (a variety of species) ... while they are in a natural environment. For example, nature conservationists observe the behavior of animals in their natural surroundings and the way they react to certain scenarios. In the same way, social scientists conducting field research may conduct interviews or observe people from a distance to understand how they behave in a social environment and how they react to situations around them. ... Field research typically begins in a specific setting although the end objective of the study is to observe and analyze the specific behavior of a subject in that setting. The cause and effect of a certain behavior, though, is tough to analyze due to the presence of multiple variables in a natural environment. Most of the **data collection** is based not entirely on cause and effect, but mostly on correlation. While field research looks for correlation, the small **sample size** makes it difficult to establish a **causal relationship** between two or more variables."[5]

"Field research encompasses a diverse range of social interaction including direct observation, limited participation, analysis of documents and other information, informal interviews, <u>surveys,</u> etc. *Although field research is generally characterized as qualitative research, it often involves multiple aspects of quantitative research in it*" (my emphasis).[6] "**Quantitative** research is defined as a systematic investigation of phenomena by gathering **quantifiable data** and performing statistical, mathematical, or computational techniques" (my emphasis).[7]

"Observe, interact, and understand;" "analyze the specific behavior of a subject in that setting;" "**data collection;**" "cause and effect;" "direct observation, limited participation, analysis of documents and other information, informal interviews, <u>surveys.</u>" Be honest with yourself. But for your knowledge that these are from a definition of "field research," could you actually tell if it was referring to hunting/trapping strategies/procedures or field research? Again, what is the difference?

"Although field research is generally characterized as qualitative research, it often involves multiple aspects of **quantitative analysis** in it." "... Performing statistical, mathematical, or computational techniques."[8] Uhhh Ohhh! Be careful! It looks like some hard-core science might be sneaking in here! Actually, converting qualitative/phenomenological/observational information into numeric data! Analyzing it!!!! My goodness, that sounds and looks like "science?" Or does it?

In these days of computer technology, miniaturization, and capitalistic profit motives, competition between wildlife guides (fishing guides for example) for client bookings is keen. The successful fishing guide must be able to put their clients within range of their targeted quarry and produce results at virtually any time of year, under any conditions, on any type or body of water. It should not therefore be surprising that the industry sees an increasing number of guide services carefully cataloging ("logging") their daily outings.

Information maintained may include the time of year/season, specific location by GPS, water conditions, weather conditions, hatch, or bait activity. Tackle used. Reel, rod, line type, and diameter, bait used by fishermen including coloring, size of the body, size of hooks, not to mention the skill of the client which can influence the entire schmear!

This information is then numerically coded and loaded into a statistical analysis fishing database program and analyzed in the hopes of maximizing success. An example of software serving this purpose is FishStatJ.[9] The "Marine Recreational Information Program (MRIP), NOAA Fisheries and its state, regional, and federal partners use in-person, telephone, and mail fishing surveys to measure the number of trips saltwater anglers take and the number of fish they catch."[10] *So, is that hunting/trapping or field research?* Or might they be the same processes and procedure with yet another variable distinguishing the between field research and the remaining two? *Could there be a co-relationship influencing things?*

Revisiting the definition of "science" would suggest they may be the same, or part of the same, process and procedure. Science is knowledge or a system of knowledge covering general truths or the operation of general laws especially as obtained and tested through scientific method. The scientific method is defined as: "principles and procedures for the systematic pursuit of knowledge involving the recognition and formulation of a problem, the collection of data through observation and experiment, and the formulation and testing of hypotheses."[11]

The 6 traditional steps of the scientific method are:

1. **Make an observation:** "The fish aren't on the land; the fish are in the water!"
2. **Ask a question:** "Do I want to catch a fish? Am I more likely to catch a fish if I put my bait next to the log in the water, or next to the log on the land?"
3. **Form a hypothesis or testable explanation:** "I'll catch more fish from the water than I will from the land."
4. **Make a prediction based on the hypothesis:** "I hypothesize that if I make 500 casts that land next to the log in the water with my bait, I will be more likely to catch a fish than if I make 500 casts that land next to the log on the terra-firma (land).
5. **Test the prediction:** Make 500 cast to the log in the water, and let your live bait sit for 20 minutes (while you drink a beer) each time. Count how many fish you catch. Make 500 casts to the log on the land, and let your live bait sit for 20 minutes (while you drink a beer) each time. If you can still count past zero, count how many fish you have.
6. **Iterate [and/or reiterate]:** Use the results to make new hypotheses or predictions [and/or (current authors addition) have someone else repeat the experiment to independently confirm results].[12] Go to another lake with a buddy. Have him make the 500 casts with live bait and beer to the log on the land (wait 20 minutes each time), while you make 500 casts with live bait and beer, to the log in the water (wait 20 minutes each time). Count the fish.
7. **Experimental Protocol Addendum:** Completely consuming an entire beer while waiting the 20 minutes after each cast **is not** mandatory. Water and food would be permissible and well-advised substitutes for the beer given

the time involved in waiting 20 minutes after each of 500 casts! But if you're a **real** fisherman ...

Hunting/trapping (e.g., fishing), science, and the scientific method sound the same! So, does that mean Bigfoot field researchers are doing SBFR? Based on definitions and despite my contentious statement at the beginning of this chapter, I fear I am forced to respond with an unequivocal "Yes... in part."

Congratulations, grab a couple of cases of beer, food, and friends, go into the woods, cook a meal, get drunk, sit around the campfire, and if you hear something "Bigfoot-like," write it down on a piece of paper, or audio record it. You have your database for analysis. Repeat this process informed by the "analysis" of your database. By the definitions above, you are now a Bigfoot Field Researcher, not to mention "a Scientist!!" Yippee!

Want to be a "hard-core" Bigfoot Field Researcher? Stay overnight and when the effects of alcohol allow you, walk around in the woods on a trail or forest road. Occasionally hit a tree with a stick and wait and see if someone not in your group responds in kind. Scream or roar loudly to make a sound that you "think is similar to a Bigfoot" and wait and see if there is a response. Record (audio or written) your actions and any response in military time (makes it more "governmental"). Save the paper for the next night or next trip to use as a reference. *Geez, to think of the time and money I wasted getting my Ph.D. studying the scientific aspects of psychology!!*

Despite my above sarcasm, I would respectfully suggest that there is more to being a fieldworker/researcher, scientist, and specifically a Bigfoot research scientist, than applying elements of the scientific method to the hunting and trapping process. The most important of these differences is the conscious intent or goals engendered in the process. Hunting and trapping's goals are for the purposes of sport and food. True scientifically based/driven field research's primary purpose or goal is the understanding of a particular species including their anatomy and physiology, the function of same, social and feeding habits, their habitat or environment, and the interaction of these. A Bigfoot scientist should have the same goal or intent but may conduct their research and "analysis" in the field or in a laboratory using statistical procedures. The goal (in my opinion), however, is to gain knowledge to benefit the species, not ourselves, our bank accounts, or our taste buds and stomachs.

This latter point (the dead horse) warrants further reflection (whipping). Developing a database to inform future hunting/trapping success does not and should not be considered scientific and does not make hunting/trapping scientific field research, in my opinion. *When the sole or primary "analysis" of the database is to increase the "hit rate" of the target species for purposes of commercial gain, I call that a commercial business venture or capitalism, not science!* True (or at least "truer") science should utilize a numeric encoding process to convert raw data to statistically analyzable data and then subject said data to descriptive and inferential statistical analysis. The analysis should not stop at percentage descriptions or charts that do nothing to speak to true differences or inform scientifically testable hypotheses and theories. These analyses (in the form of a paper or article) should then be presented to the scientific community and public for wider review, critique, and replication.

Any organization that maintains a database for the primary purposes of commercial gain does not (in my opinion) constitute a scientific organization and should not represent itself as such. *The goal of Bigfoot Scientific Research should be using a database primarily to enhance our knowledge and understanding of the Bigfoot species in the hopes of preserving that species and its habitat for further scientific investigation; not commercial exploitation and personal gain.* Any resemblance of any organization to these comments is completely coincidental and not meant as a commentary on that organization or the staff and personnel therein. On the other hand, if the shoe fits, you might want to consider if you want to continue to wear it!

This leads me to reflect on future directions implied or suggested through these writings. In short, what can be done to create a "scientific shoe" that can be worn by any number of existing or aspiring Bigfoot groups that will benefit the species?

As I noted in my initial chapter, I am far from being a Bigfoot expert. I had about a year and a few months of field experience at the time I started these writings. I start my third year participating in expeditions as I conclude these writings. I have never had a Class A Bigfoot encounter. At a recent regional Bigfoot conference, I was surprised to note that the panel of "conference identified experts" consisted of people with brief through decades of Bigfoot field research. As best as I could tell, *only one had a Class A experience.* The rest had simply put varying amounts of time into "the search" in the field and had been lucky and fortunate enough to somehow record or document their Class B or Class C encounters. During my now nine BFRO expeditions, I too have had Class B and C encounters. I count myself blessed to have learned from field researchers (such as Lori Wade, Jeff Carpenter, Rick Reles, John Eaves, and Glenn Williams) all of whom have had Class A encounters/experiences upon which to draw upon in forming their opinions. As such, I feel my experiences have put me "in as good company" as any conference-identified or self-proclaimed expert.

Please note, without exception based on their presentations at the conference, my impression is that none of the panelists would consider or proclaim themselves as "Bigfoot experts," although some did classify themselves as "Cryptozoologists" in their conference biographies. Indeed, it might be considered a bit of an oxymoron (or just being a plain old moron) to call oneself an expert on a species that remains scientifically unidentified and unclassified, largely undocumented beyond volumes of anecdotal evidence and relatively little true objectively verifiable and reproducible "scientific evidence." As such, I do not know, nor have I ever considered myself a Bigfoot expert.

I do, however, have expertise in the fields of Clinical and Counseling Psychology, Neuropsychology, and Psychological Test development. To that latter point, my dissertation involved developing a statistically and linguistically equivalent Spanish-language imagery test and doing a cross-cultural comparison between Mexican and Southern USA Cultures.

In **this** text, I have attempted to bring this information to bear on the hunt for Bigfoot by sharing what I consider critical concepts and knowledge from the fields of psychology. I have illustrated the importance of many (not all) of these ideas, concepts, and principles by sharing my own and the field research of others in our search for Bigfoot. I have also attempted to highlight how the science of psychology may still have untapped technology essential in the Bigfoot scientific research process. I have loosely proposed experimental designs and rudimentary research protocols in the hopes of demonstrating and inspiring how psychological research may be of value to the scientific exploration of Bigfoot. In my opinion, some specific ideas and concepts warrant repetition and somewhat closer reflection.

WHERE DO WE GO FROM HERE?

We need to get the horse out from behind the cart and reposition it in front of the cart. As such, the major challenge facing all Bigfoot research is validly and reliably identifying the creature itself. In the absence of visually being able to do so, we need to reliably and validly identify a Bigfoot sign, activity, or a "Bigfoot Signature."

Indeed, through improved technology and re-analysis, researchers of the Patterson Gimlin film have taken great strides (no pun intended) in identifying the species without having a "hard specimen." Dr. Jeff Meldrum has taken up the mantle of Dr. Grover Krantz and other seminal field researchers through his cast analysis combined with his in-depth understanding of human, bear, and Bigfoot feet and locomotion, anatomy, physiology, and kinesiology research. In doing so, he has set a reproducible standard and has arguably identified a "Signature Bigfoot Footprint." It can be used to verify the passing of the creature known as Bigfoot or Sasquatch in the soil substrates in a particular area of the world or North American continent. The work of Dr. Krantz and others mentioned in this text have borne similar fruit.

Although remaining highly controversial from an objective scientific perspective and dismissed by many scientific advocates, Dr.

Ketchum's DNA research provides interesting reported evidence and has influenced ideas as to what the creature known as Bigfoot may be.

Finally, the NAWAC needs to be congratulated for their efforts on behalf of the species primarily manifested through their Tag 7 study (even if one disagrees with or views their intent to "harvest a specimen" as premature). I believe it to be premature, at the least. It may be unnecessary!

What remains needed, however, is a valid and reliable method to unequivocally identify Bigfoot signs/activity in the field. We need to be able to do this without harvesting a specimen or requiring expert opinions or the subjective biases engendered by current field research procedures. To this end, audio recordings of Bigfoot vocalizations seem to hold fertile promise. I discussed how convergent and divergent validity and reasoning studies might be brought to bear to identify Bigfoot vocalization signatures and/or infrasound signatures. These could then stand as a normative database or even as a graphic signature against which to compare recorded vocalizations in real-time in the field.

Indeed, at the conference I recently attended, I discovered research along similar lines is already being advanced within certain circles which I will not identify for the sake of propriety. I also discovered that the Night Stalkers have already had their own recordings analyzed by an audio expert to prove the standing validity of these recordings as being representative of a "previously unidentified species." *This is a necessary initial step for creating such a valid and reliable audio signature.*

Once validly and reliably identified, integrating that or an infrasound signature into an application used either on a cell phone or other portable recording device in order to compare recordings in real-time in the field appears to be just a step away.

I would also highlight my comments regarding psychology's ability to identify, quantify, and scientifically prove the existence of intelligence. When you think about it, intelligence can't be seen, heard, touched, tasted, smelled, or felt. It is an intangible construct with no substantive material in our three-dimensional world. We can, however, measure the results of intelligence (such as visual and verbal thinking including verbal similarities/reasoning abilities, visual spatial and visual perceptual problem-solving abilities, ability to define words) without intelligence being a concrete entity unto itself. We see it **reflected in** various forms of art, the logic and reasoning in certain arguments or ideas, inventions, and theories of the intellectual elite (a group of which I am NOT a member). We see a lack of it reflected in political and personal debate leading to violence, division, war, ethnic cleansing, and other authoritarian processes.

Now think of the illusiveness of BF. It is very difficult to see, even more difficult to physically touch or feel, but somewhat easier to hear (vocalizations and "knocks"). Confirming these experiences as Bigfoot experiences, however, seems just as illusive and non-concretized as intelligence. Yet psychology has been successful in "capturing" intelligence, so why not Bigfoot!

Albeit an admitted bias of this psychologist, it seems to me Psychology's ability to capture the concept of intelligence reflects a significant potential to "capture" Bigfoot. If not the creature, at least the sign, concept, or ontological idea of Bigfoot Phenomena or "Bigfootness." Surely, through the experimental designs, techniques, and statistical analysis methodologies commonly employed by psychological science to capture emotions, attitudes, and non-concrete concepts such as intelligence, we can capture Bigfoot phenomena, "Bigfootness," and eventually Bigfoot. Psychology science will allow us to accomplish this without the need to kill a Bigfoot. We didn't need to kill intelligence to scientifically prove its existence!

To that end, the experimental design I suggested to study infrasound in the laboratory would seem to represent a potentially promising start. I would additionally point out, however, that we are missing fundamental basic information on Bigfoot behavior that field research databases if properly developed and documented, should be able to inform.

At the recent conference for example, there were debates with

very firm and **unequivocally conclusive opinions** on telepathy or mind speak in Bigfoot and other "Woo" phenomena, such as the association of Bigfoot with UFOs. Yet, when I asked the simple and basic question as to what was the most common number of tree knocks produced by a Bigfoot (be that sound actual tree knocks or produced in another fashion), the panelists had no answer. Think about that! *"Tree knocks" are one of the phenomena most frequently cited by field researchers as being consistent with and attributed to the existence of Bigfoot. Yet no one has thought to study or calculate simple frequency data on the most common number of tree knocks produced by Bigfoot and under what conditions!!* All but one panelist also struggled with how many tree knocks the field researcher should use in response to a knock sound. *Something IS wrong with that picture!* We're discussing telepathy in Bigfoot, but have grossly understudied and have inadequate scientific knowledge of tree knocks. *The cart is in front of the horse!!*

*My question nonetheless generated brief comments regarding the "**purpose**" of tree knocks. It appears to this researcher that developing **any** theory on the meaning of tree knock sounds is premature. It represented a spontaneous example of **how quickly** we go from **phenomena** to **untested theory**, puffing out our chest and patting our backs! Without performing experimental investigation between the phenomena and the theory, we're "putting the cart before the horse!!" We have no reason to "puff and pat" ourselves based on our "insightful theory" on the subject of tree knocks!! Although most are "very sure" of themselves on this topic, we haven't even scientifically established that the sound truly is a "wood on wood" phenomena. We don't even have fundamental frequency count data on the number of "knock" sounds most commonly produced!! Why are we puffing and patting?*

This brings me to my closing point. It seems to me that most (not all) Bigfoot fieldwork/research is biased, disorganized, and/or in a scientifically unsystematized/unanalyzed state. Again, we've put the cart before the horse!

Through our phenomenological field research process, we have encountered and experienced possible Bigfoot evidence or even Bigfoot.

Scientific principles demand systematically statistically analyzing the data from these encounters and experiences to prove their validity, generate/test hypotheses, AND THEN generate Bigfoot theory. It appears to this writer that most "Bigfoot researchers," "Bigfoot Scientists," and "Scientific Bigfoot Research Groups" have simply moved forward developing theories about Bigfoot based on those untested and unanalyzed observations and experiences. Developing theories based on untested and statistically unanalyzed observations and hypotheses creates one thing: a biased database due to inadequate research design, inadequate recording of data, and most damning, little to no analysis of statistical data beyond how it informs where the next expedition should be.

On these expeditions, plans on where and when to go are a first step. What is done at those specific locations and times, however, is either not or incompletely systematized ("I'll go over somewhere on north ridge above the river and maybe make some knocks or howls or stone clacks and see what happens"). To control for scientific analysis purposes, specific or exact times and locations are needed. Specific provocation techniques need to be determined ahead of time, and deployed identically by all members at designated times, with predetermined intervals between provocations and for how often done. The tools used (tree knock sticks, rocks for stone clacks, pre-recorded howls or other pre-recorded vocalizations) need to be developed, tested and standardized in advance. They can then be deployed at all locations visited by different reliably trained research sub-groups on the same night. Audio, visual, and written recording of all events should be undertaken. A priori standardized numeric data encoding systems will have been developed for activities, pilot tested and responses then entered into a database for statistical evaluation and comparison that address the questions at hand. To complete the "scientific" field research, results should be published by the research group and then either replicated by that group or an independent group.

These work-like, tedious, time consuming, labor intensive, and fun robbing processes merely scratch the surface of what needs to be done to transform an *excellent phenomenologically-based BF fieldwork expedition into a Scientific Bigfoot Research Fieldwork Expedition.* That does not seem to be happening on commercially and experientially driven expeditions, currently. This, in my opinion, is one reason why despite decades of BF fieldwork/research findings and evidence, the scientific community continues to reject its existence. *Most of the existing research has put the cart before the horse! The validity of coercion theories not-withstanding, the status of Bigfoot research simply has not risen to baseline requisite scientific standards through its focus and implementation scientific methods. An observation, not a criticism.*

Most of the existing research has been conducted like the proverbial drunk looking for his key in the dark with the police officer. The processes of obtaining the "hard" BF evidence out there (foot casts for example) shines a bright light for us to look under and we are doing so. But we continue to do that (and often less than that) because that is where the light allows us to see. There are likely other keys to prove BF existence out there, but we seem so caught up in our current process and its rewards that we are not thinking to look for an unilluminated key proving Bigfoot's existence in a different darkened location. The keys are there, but were so caught up looking where the light is that we can't see those keys laying in the dark even when we tread on them on our way to lamp post. *We simply need to develop our own illumination technology and start looking in other places! You got a flashlight or a lighter?*

"They are an unknown hominid. They are inter-dimensional; they are alien; they are Nephilim." It would appear in the (strictest sense), many commercial Bigfoot Expedition Field Research Groups sprouting up with the intention of "scientifically investigating Bigfoot to protect the species and preserve its habitat" **are** attempting to "do science." Scientifically admirable, much needed ideals and aspirations until … the financial realities of funding Bigfoot field research rear their ugly head. Those financial realities, in concert with potential commercial benefits and social recognition (fame), may contribute to those scientific aspirations falling by the wayside in favor of charging sometimes exorbitant amounts of money to go out with "Bigfoot experts and celebrities" and participate in the hunt.

This reflects the "split personality" of many Bigfoot researchers and much of Bigfoot science. Phenomenologically, we want to have a Bigfoot encounter so we can prove to ourselves they exist. For many, this process leads to pimping the Bigfoot species and whoring ourselves for profits, while losing site of the aspirational and scientific goals for the species. This book (and therefore myself) is **not** an exception to that pimping and whoring process.

This book was written to inform interested individuals first and foremost, but also done for personal gain. Like many before me and no doubt after me, I am not exempt from the pimping and whoring exploitation of Bigfoot phenomena. Nor are many, if not most, expedition groups or merchandisers of Bigfoot paraphernalia exempt. Nor are Bigfoot researchers or scientist that lecturer at conferences or conference organizers themselves exempt. There is plenty of pimping and whoring guilt to be spread around. So, before you cuss me, you may want to look in the mirror. Scientifically, we want to be objective, prove the species existence and honor and protect it. We **can** have it both ways (phenomenologically and scientifically) *but it will require lots of patience, hard work, and nationwide cooperation!*

To move forward with the goal of "**proof**," serious and dedicated fieldworkers and other researchers need to first recognize and strive to minimize bias within themselves. They should learn behavioral and emotional regulation techniques to minimize the potentially traumatic and bias contaminating aspects of this work. They also need to increase and expand their psychological and scientific knowledge base of illusions and other key concepts and issues detailed within these current writings. Such knowledge should, can, and needs to inform their fieldwork.

While admittedly potentially boring and most certainly tedious, a fundamental shift in fieldwork and other types of research on Bigfoot is necessary. Researchers need to shift their data gathering work from collecting anecdotal, analogical, and demonstrative evidence *to creating research designs generating experimental data that can be statistically analyzed thereby informing BF behavioral and mental processes, as well as their causes and determinants.* The research then needs to be subjected to public and peer review, replication for purposes of confirmation or contradiction, and finally disseminated to the larger Bigfoot, scientific, and public communities. Researchers need to stop protectively guarding their databases so they might be examined for their scientific rather than commercial value.

Through this text, I have attempted to provide important preliminary techniques and knowledge needed for this process of change. Given Bigfoot's elusiveness (they are hard to see, touch, taste, and smell), it seems to this admittedly biased psychologist that the field of psychology sits poised to be a substantial (but not sole) contributing force in this process of change. Through more closely examining the techniques and processes utilized by psychological science to prove the existence of Intelligence (a concept even less concrete and more elusive than Bigfoot), the field offers up a possible "blueprint" or path to follow to scientifically prove the existence of Bigfoot.

This represents a personal realization on my part through the process of writing this book. As such it was not accomplished through these writings. Maybe that could be the next book. In truth, such writing would only have value if Bigfoot fieldworkers, researchers, organizations, and the larger Bigfoot community are able to set aside their own pride, prejudices, and financial interests sufficiently to accept and embrace the knowledge contained in **this** book. Indeed, some preliminary feedback I have received suggests this book may serve to strengthen that pride and prejudice though activating a defensiveness in the reader. If such acceptance doesn't or can't happen, moving forward with that additional manuscript would simply serve the purpose of mental masturbation!

We need some way or perhaps some organization to transcend this process (research process that is, not masturbation)! Within the very messy, less messy, and good field research already completed lay the cornels of questions that need to be scientifically tested and explored. They serve as the foundation for the future directions of our research! I propose a planning/steering committee be formed. Its purpose would be to investigate the possibility of those who still aspire to benefit the species joining forces to create an over-reaching research society to standardize, prioritize, and direct Bigfoot research efforts. This admittedly may represent an insurmountable challenge given research interests, reputations, as well as commercial and financial interests in the field already well established, if not entrenched. I nonetheless remain an idealist and believe it is possible for people to set aside or at least suspend commercial, financial and ego investments/interests long enough to identify common goals for the benefit of the species. It won't be easy, but the eventual outcome could represent a Bigfoot Research Society.

This organization could raise money to distribute via research grants designed to standardize research protocols, procedures, and tools and implement field and laboratory research and experimentation to benefit the species and preserve their habitat. While "harvesting a species" **may** eventually be necessary to prove Bigfoot's existence, my cover art suggests we should first weigh the utility of the psychological sciences to achieve that goal.

Call me an idealist; I am. But if you are too or aspire to be, email me at johnsbaranchok@yahoo.com to discuss the possibility of becoming a member of a planning or steering committee to develop such a research society. Let's try to strengthen Bigfoot science by bringing philanthropic and scientific interests together to come to bear on the process of Scientific Bigfoot Research!!!

Thank you for your purchase of this book. I hope you have found it thought provoking, informative, and occasionally funny and entertaining. I hope you have found some tidbit of information or inspiration to use to better inform your own research into Bigfoot. It is my sincere hope that you will take that tidbit, apply it, and use it to benefit the species.

Sincerely,
John S. Baranchok, Ph.D.

APPENDICES

APPENDIX A

UNDERSTANDING THE NORMAL CURVE

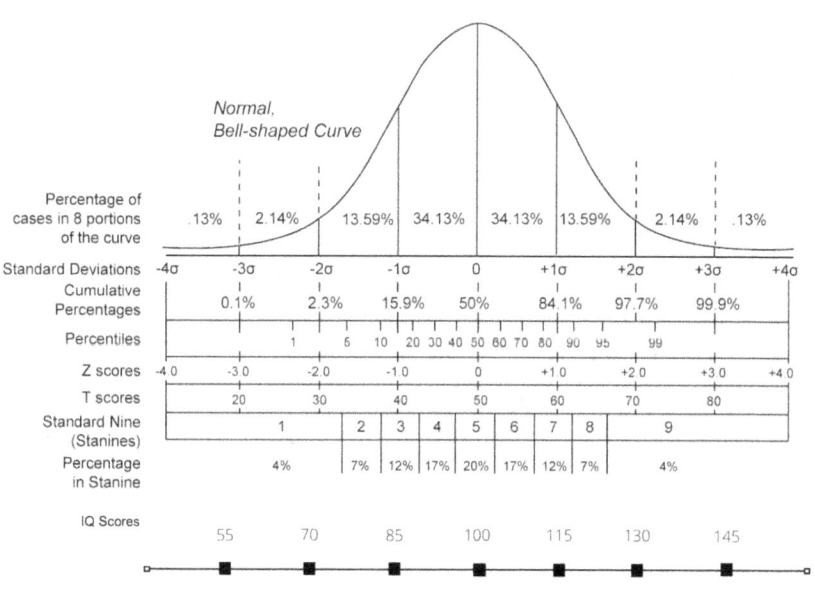

Adapted and modified from Wikipedia.[1]

On that curve, the most "normal" or average score has a value of "0." Any score occurring between zero and one full step above zero is "average or normal." Notice that this includes or captures 34.13% of the world or normally distributed scores. A score one step up represents a mild strength (+1). An additional 13.59% of the world population or distribution of scores then falls between one and two steps up. Two steps up is a moderate strength (+2) with an additional 2.14% of the world population or normal distribution of scores falling between two and three steps up. Three steps up is a high strength (+3), with an additional .13% of the world population or normal distribution of scores three and four steps up. Four steps up (+4) is an extreme strength with the additional percentage of the world population or normal distribution of scores occurring beyond this so small as to traditionally not be noted.

The same is true for scores descending below average or normal and are called "weaknesses" or impairments. Any score occurring between zero and one full step below zero is still "average" or "normal." Notice that this includes or captures 34.13% of the world population or normally distributed scores. A score one step down represents a mild weakness or impairment (-1). An additional 13.59% of the world population or distribution of scores falls between one and two steps down. Two steps down is a moderate weakness/impairment (-2), with an additional 2.14% of the world population or normal distribution of scores falling between two and three steps down. Three steps down is a high weakness/severe impairment (-3), with an additional .13% of the world population or normal distribution of scores falling three to four steps down. Four steps down (-4) is an extreme weakness/impairment. The additional percentage of the population below this (-4) is so small that the scores occurring beyond it are to not noted in illustrations of the normal curve.

Each of these steps up or down is also called a "standard deviation." The word "standard" in this case refers to equally or commonly occurring in a standard fashion. The word "deviation" refers to deviating, changing or varying. So, a standard deviation is a standardly occurring change up or down from normal or average. Depending on the test scale or statistic used, that step (the raw number of cases contained within) will be different, but always remains the value of "1" on the normal curve itself. That is, the normal curve has an average score of "0" and each step up or down is one step or deviation.

By examining the illustration above, you will note z-scores. These are a statistical transformation or conversion process of raw numeric research data that allows us to compare oranges to oranges across different tests, scales, measures, or disparate phenomena/experiences. The z-score does this by creating a common "yard stick" on which we measure them. A z-score also has an average numeric value of "0" and a step up or down of one. T-scores are a conversion of disparate data serving a similar purpose as a z-scores. They have an average or "mean" score or value of "50" and each step up or down is ten points.

The percentage portion of the illustration is frankly more confusing and difficult to understand, but nonetheless important if you hope to understand statistical results of any scientific paper. I have already discussed the percentage of the population within each standard deviation in paragraphs above. Please re-read that now and repeat that reading until you thoroughly understand it as the statistical shit is about to get deep. If you don't understand that illustration, you are likely to become lost from here on in. When we start comparing percentages, percentiles, and percentile ranks to T, Z, and other scores, it can get confusing. Again, however, being able to make such comparisons is the key to understanding statistical research results. Without understanding statistical research results, you cannot judge the value of research findings and know if it's even worthwhile to consider their meaning or implications to use to guide your own research!

Let's walk through it slowly. You might want to put a mouth guard over your teeth (to reduce the "gnashing" of teeth) and ear plugs in your ears (to protect yourself from losing your hearing as you scream and wail in pain and agony) through this discussion. A roll of paper towels to wipe up the tears also wouldn't hurt!!!

On the left-hand side of the illustration, you will note the words "Percentages of cases in 8 portions of the curve" and below that five other sets of words or classifications. We have already defined the first one below "Percentages of ... 8 ..." as a "standard deviation" in the above paragraphs. It represents one step up or down from normal and will be a different number depending on what statistical analysis/transformation and/or test is being used or what experience is being measured. Note the standard deviation symbol beside each number. Note that each number has a "-" (minus) sign or "+" (plus) sign depending on if it is below or above average or normal.

A few more comments warrant reflection. This curve, its percentages and standard deviations conceptually represent the world population and a variety of "normally distributed" qualities of the people within that population. Height, shoe size, birth weight, and intelligence are examples of qualities that are "normally distributed." As such these qualities fit this "normally distributed" conceptual model within the world population of human beings. Interestingly within the world of Bigfoot, Dr. Henner Fahrenbach (1997-1998) found a sample of Bigfoot track lengths were primarily consistent with the normal distribution.[2] (As such if Bigfoot's wore shoes, their shoes sizes would be normally distributed similarly to humans.) Interestingly, BF growth rate and step length did not appear normally distributed in Fahrenbach's findings.

These later Fahrenbach's (1997-1998) findings highlight another important point to understand and remember about the normal curve. It is a "conceptual and theoretical model" to which not all phenomena adhere. It is a model that not everything in the world fits. Some phenomena are skewed or slanted in one direction or another (BF growth rate, step length). Additionally, some phenomena are "'bimodal' (having two peaks or humps rather than one) or 'multimodal (having multiple peaks).'"[3] "For example, book sale prices would represent a bimodal distribution (regular book versus textbook prices), while restaurant peak sales hours (Breakfast, Lunch, and Dinner) would represent a multimodal distribution."[4] The most important point here is when a phenomenon is not normally distributed (as in the data do not come out looking like this bell-shaped model with one peak or hump) the statistics to be discussed below do not apply and cannot be used for the analysis of the data. For example, we are currently embroiled in a bimodal political process (Republican vs. Democrat; Conservative vs. Liberal). You can't use statistical techniques based on the normal curve (unimodal or single hump) and expect a valid outcome when the underlying distribution of the population you are measuring is bimodal. Statistical validity and reliability fly out the window if you do! *This could be important in analyzing "clock times" of BF sightings as being representative of the timing of Bigfoot activity. Day-time versus nighttime. Possibly bimodal!*

The next line below "Standard Deviations" on the illustration is "Cumulative Percentages." The percentages noted in between the standard deviation on the curve reflect how much of the population exists between those standard deviations. In contrast, the cumulative percentages reflect the total percent of the population starting at -3 standard deviations and increasing, moving left to right along the line until you reach +3 standard deviations. Note that less than .1 percent (one tenth of a percent) of the world population occurs between -4 and -3 standard deviations. Note that the cumulative percentage at the "0" standard deviation captures 50% of the population and that 99.9% of the population is captured at +3 standard deviations.

The combination of cumulative percentages and percentile statistics are two of the most frequently used and abused descriptive statistics due to their misleading (and at times) meaningless nature. This is why it is frequently used in popular media including newspapers and television and is regularly exploited in political campaigns, and more recently pandemic information.

For example, from the CDC website: the morning of 7/20/2020: "Nationally, the overall percentage of respiratory specimens testing positive for SARS-CoV-2 decreased slightly from week 27 (9.4%) to week 28 (9.2%) but increased in four regions."[5]

"Nationally, the overall percentage of respiratory specimens testing positive for SARS-CoV-2 decreased slightly from week 27 (9.4%) to week 28 (9.2%) but increased in four regions." Great! It looks like COVID-19 is declining and then the bomb that it actually increased in four regions. So, what the hell does that mean? Let's break it down.

"Nationally," means the entire "population" of the United States of America. Pretty clear... so far. Relative to our illustration they are referring to the Nation which lives or is contained between -4 standard deviations and +4 standard deviations. Or is it that clear?

Consider the statement "the overall percentage of respiratory specimens testing positive for SARS-CoV-2." "Overall percentage" refers to the cumulative percentage column in our model. "...of respiratory specimens testing positive for SARS-CoV-2." ... [Here we go with having to pay closer attention to details!] "... of respiratory specimens." What this means is they are only testing specimens (samples) taken using respiratory (breathing) tests, which is not the only way CoV-2 is tested (it can be tested using blood plasma samples, as well). So, we're not looking at ALL CoV-2 cases across the nation (despite them starting the sentence with "Nationally.") Next, "...testing positive for SARS-CoV-2": Now were looking only at the cases testing positive for the virus. That excludes the results testing negative. We're examining only the number of positive tests without considering the number of negative tests. We're only being shown part of the total picture here.

The overall picture of the population of COVID-19 tests is now further reduced. On one hand it's not unreasonable to look at positive tests, after all we're tracking the virus, not the lack of it. On the other hand, wouldn't it be nice to know the negative test results to provide an overall context or back drop for these results? How does only looking at one half of the overall testing process (the positive test) help? It not only doesn't include negative tests results, but also fails to include false positive and false negative tests! It appears to skew or provide a bias to the picture and the analysis! Not a statistical theorist here, but logic would suggest it also influences the underlying distribution of the data.

Now here comes the BIG ONE: "... decreased slightly ..." It's going down, right? POSSIBLY correct for positive respiratory COVID-19 tests. But how representative are COVID-19 test results of the entire population of the COVID-19 virus? We are only being given an incomplete/limited/restricted "glimpse" or test sample of the entire COVID virus population! We can't know its true degree of represented accuracy! It could be validly argued that "decreased slightly" is operationally defined as "from week 27 (9.4%) to week 28 (9.2%)." A .2%. decrease (two tenths of a percent decrease). It takes five of those to make a one percent change. Scientifically (statistically) is that a true significant change? We can at least get a darn good estimate or actually discover the answer by examining our normal curve!

When discussing the normal curve and change (**significant** decreases or increases) a one standard deviation (one step) difference or change is required to be considered statistically significant. Let's say you took a Bigfoot IQ test (pre-test) then studied hard, reading every book in existence on Bigfoot. After that extensive reading/studying, you take a second Bigfoot IQ test (post-test). Was your last score on your Bigfoot IQ test (118) significantly higher than the one before it (108)? Well, it went up 9 points so it must be true (real) improvement, correct? You'd need only to plot that IQ score on the above Bell-shaped curve illustration and note if it improved (or declined) a full standard deviation. *If it hadn't or even only came close to a one step (standard deviation) improvement, scientifically (statistically) that would not be considered a true or real change. It would represent normal variability or other factors contributing to the change in the numeric value which is a* **symbol** *of your Bigfoot IQ. If it had improved a full step then your studying would have truly paid off.* As to the best of my knowledge, a standardized (normed) Bigfoot IQ test does not exist (there's a project for an aspiring scientific BF researcher), we'll use the existing concept of an Intelligence Quotient (IQ) and existing tests of same for this example.

IQ scores have a mean or average score of 100 and a standard deviation (step up or down) of 15 points. Plotting your 108 BFIQ score on the IQ line of our illustration reveals it falls in the average range of intelligence (between "0" and "1" standard deviation on the normal curve). Plotting your apparent higher score of 118 reveals it to be in the high-average range in the next step (standard deviation) higher than your 108 scores. Yes, it's a significant improvement or change, correct? Wrong!!!!!

Even when two scores exist or fall in two different step ranges (standard deviation ranges), those two scores are not considered statistically significantly different unless there is a full (complete) step in between the two numbers! For IQ scores, a full step is 15 points. The difference between 118 and 108 is 10 points, not fifteen. As such, even though 108 falls in the average range of intelligence and 118 falls in the high-average range of intelligence; these two scores representing your Bigfoot intelligence are not statistically significantly different from each other.

Although the 118 score appears to represent a higher score than the 108 score, that 10-point improvement falls short of a full standard deviation (one full step) improvement. As such, the 118 score does not represent a significant improvement!! It (the symbolic number) certainly appears bigger. But it only represents/reflects the underlying concept of your Bigfoot intelligence. Your Bigfoot intelligence score has not increased significantly in spite of all your reading and studying. In reality, you are not significantly smarter about Bigfoot than before you read and studied! What a bummer! You can still console yourself if you remember, numbers are symbols representing IQ scores, not the intelligence itself!

Let's now return to our real life (and unfortunately much more obvious/easy to figure out) COVID-19 example. Looking at the percentile line in the Bell curve figure above reveals that both the 5 and 10 percentile scores to fall between -2 and -1 on the cumulative percentage line. The COVID-19, week 27 score (9.4%) and the week 28 score (9.2%) are not even graphically represented. One only need estimate where these two scores could be plotted on the cumulative percentage line to see that both scores fall within the same standard deviation range (-2 to -1) and as such do not represent a significant (true or real) decline or change. Although different scores, there was no significant decline in respiratory COVID-19 test results, suggesting (not proving) there was no significant decline in the COVID-19 virus between week 27 and 28.

Why did I emphasize "suggesting?" Because we are not drawing from the true overall sample of COVID-19 test results, only the positive respiratory specimen ones. As such, these data may not be a true representation of the COVID-19 virus. It is a model, not reality. THAT is imperative to remember. Additionally, believe it or not, with high enough sample numbers collected on another phenomena, it is also possible that the two tenth percent decline in our example could represent a significant change if we go beyond simple descriptive statistical analysis! Statistical results can be manipulated not just by the words used to interpret the data, but by the statistical formulas used in the analysis!

*Thus, it is imperative when reading Bigfoot research, especially when research is taking the conceptual leap from monkey, chimp or great ape studies/data and **extrapolating** to Bigfoot, that the informed scientist consider these and other factors in order to understand the true generalizability of the data to their own conceptualization of and research for Bigfoot!*

(Excuse me while I yawn.) Next is "Percentiles" which by necessity, I have already integrated into the above discussion. It is defined as "each of the 100 equal groups into which a population can be divided according to the distribution of values of a particular variable."[6] "The percentile rank of a score is the percentage of scores in its frequency distribution *that are equal to or lower than it*. For example, a test score that is greater than 75% of the scores of people taking the test is said to be at the 75th percentile, where 75 is the percentile rank."[7]

The next two terms below percentiles are z-scores and t-scores. From this author's perspective both are statistical formulas that allow you to transform or convert disparate (different) data from different phenomena to the same yards-stick of measurement. You can then compare them directly to each other. In effect, this allows you to compare apples and oranges by converting or transforming one of the two fruits to the other. You can then compare "apples to apples" or "oranges to oranges."

"A z-score is defined as "a statistical measurement of a score's relationship to the mean in a group of scores … it is measured in terms of standard deviations from the mean. If a z-score is 0, it indicates that the data point's score is identical to the mean score."[8] The z-score is positive if the value lies above the mean, and negative if it lies below the mean."[9]

"Technically, z-scores are a conversion of individual scores into a standard form. The conversion allows you to more easily compare different data; it is based on your knowledge about the population's standard deviation and mean. A z-score tells you how many standard deviations from the mean your result is. You can use your knowledge of normal distributions … "to determine what percentage of the population will fall below or above your result. The z-score formula doesn't say anything about sample size; the rule of thumb applies that your sample size should be above 30 to use it."[10]

"Regarding a t-score, it represents the number of standard deviations, or a unit of measurement, (a) score is above or below the average score. The score formula enables you to take an individual score and transform it into a standardized form; one which helps you to compare different scores. You'll want to use the t-score formula when you don't know the population standard deviation and you have a small sample (under 30)."[11] "Like z-scores, t-scores are also a conversion of individual scores into a standard form. T-scores, however, are used when you don't know the **population** standard deviation; you make an estimate by using your **sample** of that population. If you have a larger sample (over 30), the t-distribution and z-distribution look pretty much the same. Therefore, you can use either. That said, if you know the **population** standard deviation, it doesn't make much sense to use a **sample estimate** instead of the "real thing," so just substitute the **population** standard deviation into the equation in place of the **sample** standard deviation."[12]

The next two classification lines represent stanines (standard nines) and the percentage of the population between each stanine score. I have included them as they are a traditional part of the normal curve within psychology research as there are a few psychological instruments that use stanine scores. I have personally rarely found the need for or benefit from using stanine scores. Stanines have a mean of "5" and a standard deviation of two. It allows you to compare two scores on the normal curve much as do z –scores and t-scores. Conceptually, the entire normal distribution is subdivided into eight vs ten portions. Frankly, even in consulting references on this topic, I failed to find statistics that don't perform the same function in a much more meaningful way, beyond some tests using them as a scoring system. As such I will not belabor the reader further with this measure.

Finally, IQ scores refer to scores on test purporting to measure intelligence. IQ tests scores have an average of 100 and a standard deviation (a step up or down) of 15 points. An IQ score of 115 is one step above average, while a score of 130 is two steps above average. A score of 145 is three steps above average and an IQ score of 160 is four steps above average. An IQ score of 85 is one step below average and an IQ score of 70 is two steps below average. An IQ score of 55 is three steps below average and an IQ score of 40 is four steps below average.

Although I stop my description at +4 and -4, this theoretical normal distribution goes on to infinity on the high end (+5, +6, +7 to infinity) and on the low end (-5, -6, -7 to infinity). It's called the bell shape curve because it has a big hump in its center which curves quickly/relatively steeply to look like a bell shape.

PLEASE RETURN TO PAGE 80 TO CONTINUE YOUR STATISTICAL JOURNEY!

APPENDIX B

AUTOGENIC RELAXATION SCRIPT

Find a chair, couch recliner, or mattress of any kind to sit or lay with your arms and legs uncrossed. *"First allow yourself to be taking three deep cleansing breaths using pursed lip breathing. Taking a deep breath in now through your mouth, nose, or mouth and nose at the same time ... Holding it for a second or two and then exhaling slowly through pursed lips. Now taking a second, deep cleansing breath in ... Holding it for a second or two and exhaling slowly through pursed lips, noticing how your body releases tightness and tension on the exhale. And now ... taking your third and final deep breath in ... holding it for a second or two, and then slowly exhaling through pursed lips and enjoying your body beginning letting go and relaxing on that exhale. Continuing breathing naturally now, I'm next asking you to be focusing your awareness on the muscles in your right arm ... your right-hand muscles including the muscles connecting each joint in your fingers, the palm of your hand, your right wrist, forearm, elbow, bicep, triceps, and shoulder ... simply repeating out loud or to yourself the following phrase: "Now I am relaxing my right arm, feeling more calm and feeling more peace!"* [repeat this phrase four to eight times for your right-arm], *then shifting your awareness and focus to your left arm ... your left hand and finger muscles connecting each joint of your fingers ... The palm of your left-hand, your left wrist and forearm ... your left elbow muscles, biceps and triceps and left shoulder repeating: "Now I am relaxing my left-arm, feeling more calm and feeling more peace"* [four to eight times for your left-arm]. *Next shifting your focus and awareness to your right leg ... Your right-foot and toes and the muscles connecting the joints of your toes, the sole and arch of your foot ... your instep of your right-foot, the muscles of your right-ankle, calf, your thigh muscles and hamstring muscles and the muscles of your right-hip while repeating: "Now I am relaxing my right-leg, feeling more calm and feeling more peace"* [four to eight times] *prior to shifting to your awareness to your left leg .... Your left-foot and ankle, the muscles of your toes, the sole, arch and instep of your left-foot, your left ankle muscles, calf muscles, your left-knee muscles, thigh, quadricep muscles ... Your left-hamstring muscles and your left-hip muscles and repeating: "Now I am relaxing the muscles of my left-leg ... feeling more calm and feeling more peace"* [four to eight times]. *Now shifting your awareness and focus once again, back up to the muscles in both your arms ... repeating: "Now I am relaxing the muscles in both my arms, ... feeling more calm and feeling more peace"* [for two to four repetitions]. *Shifting your awareness once again back down to the muscles of both your legs repeating: "Now I am relaxing both my legs ... feeling more calm and feeling more peace"* [two to four times]. *Just allow your awareness to scan the muscles of your legs and arms, noticing which muscles are relaxing and which muscles might enjoy even more relaxing ... relaxing is a skill and just like any other skill, the more you practice the better you become at relaxing the muscles of your arms and legs and the other muscles of your body. Sitting in silence for a few minutes, enjoying the relaxation you are noticing in your body and allowing that comfortable feeling or sensation flowing into other areas of your body. Breathing naturally and enjoying your relaxing comfort.*

When you are ready, then allow your awareness to shift once again to the muscles of your toes, beginning allowing a refreshing and reviving energy flowing back into the muscles of your toes and feet, up the muscles of you calves into your knees and thighs and hips. Saying out loud or to yourself: "I'm beginning noticing a refreshing and reviving energy flowing back into the muscles of my toes and feet, becoming more alert and awake, refreshed and revived. Allowing the refreshing and reviving energy to be flowing from my ankles into my calves and knees, feeling more alert and aware more awake and revived so I'm moving on with the rest of my day in a normal and natural fashion! That invigorating and awakening energy flowing from my thighs and hamstrings into the muscles of my hips, becoming more alert and awake, more refreshed and revived, going on with the rest of my day in a normal and natural fashion." Now shifting your awareness once again from your legs to the muscles of your arms ... Your fingers, the muscles connecting each joint of your fingers to each other and to your hands, the palms of your hands, your wrists and forearms, your elbows and biceps and triceps and shoulders. Say out loud or to yourself: "Now I am allowing a refreshing and reviving energy flowing back into the muscles of my hands and arms. It's starting in the tip of my fingers becoming more and more aware, more refreshed and revived, moving up through my fingers in the palms of my hands and into my wrist and forearms becoming more alert and awake, more energized and refreshed, more awake and alive. That refreshing energy flowing from my forearms in to the muscles around my elbows, into my biceps and triceps becoming more alert and awake, more refreshing and reviving so I'm going on with the rest of my day in a normal and natural fashion ... now it's flowing into my shoulder muscles becoming more refreshed and alert, revived and energized. Now that energy is moving the muscles of my arms and legs, wiggling my toes and fingers, ankles and wrists allowing that refreshing and reviving energy flowing throughout my entire body now becoming more awake and alert so that I'm going on with the rest of my day in a normal and natural fashion!! Now I am moving my arms and legs normally and naturally, opening my eyes if I've closed them, taking in the wonderful feelings of calm and peace, refreshed, revived and invigorated and going on with the rest of my day in a normal and natural fashion. Completely alert and awake, refreshed and revived ready to go through the rest of my day in an energized and productive fashion!!!"

This latter half is the "awakening" portion of the relaxation exercise and can and should be repeated until your feel normal and ready to move on in an alert and aware and normal fashion. Some additional tips or explanations or highlights seem warranted at this time.

As you begin learning to relax, you may initially find it difficult to remain focused on relaxing for the entire time. You may find yourself easily distracted by activities going on around you. You would therefore do well to arrange up to 35 minutes of uninterrupted time for yourself to perform the exercise. Unplug the phone, have someone take care of the kids and pets (if you got them), lock the outer doors and windows. Set yourself up for successfully not being interrupted for 35 minutes.

Even after controlling for environmental distractions, you may still be distracted by your own thoughts. You may notice the air-conditioning or heat cycling on and off. You may get an itch. Scratch it. You may get uncomfortable in the position you are situated in. Change that position until you are comfortable. You may find it hard to keep your mind on relaxing and begin to think about what you just got done doing or what you're needing to do after you are done relaxing. If this happens, stay calm and don't beat up on yourself or punish yourself. Passively and in a neutral or pleasant emotional tone tell yourself: "You've gotten distracted. Just focus your awareness back on the exercise wherever you left off." Do so. Relaxation is a skill and like any other skill the more you relax, the better you will become at relaxing and the less frequently you will be distracted when relaxing. Cut yourself some slack. It's not a race or a competition. Eventually it will only take you ten minutes to get just as deeply relaxed as it used to take you 35 minutes to achieve.

As you relax, most people have some experiences. Your arms or legs may get unusually light or heavy. They may go numb and if they stay numb long enough, they may become difficult to move. Just gradually begin to move your shoulder then your arm and then your fingers and sensation will gradually return to your limbs and you'll be able to move them again normally.

You may get an itch, need to cough, pass gas, or change body positions or move your arms or legs. These sensations are your body's way of telling you or guiding you about what you need to do next to get even more relaxed. Listen to your body and do what it is asking you to do.

If you've ever been falling asleep, you may have experienced a "myoclonic spasm." This is like the experience you have when you fall out of bed and your whole body suddenly jerks or spasms awake. It can be scary, but it is a sign you are being successful in relaxing.

You might also actually fall asleep. Congratulations you have been successful in relaxing. You would have gotten even more deeply relaxed, however, if you had stayed awake. We are using our conscious mind to relax your body. If you fall asleep half way through the exercise, your body simply will not get as deeply relaxed as if you had stayed awake and focused on relaxing through the entire exercise. If falling asleep becomes a repeated problem, listen for the word "Now" and tell yourself that hearing or thinking that word in your mind tells you are still awake.

As you begin to getting better at relaxing, I advise you to make your own tape or another type of recording by reading this script into or onto a recording device. Or make up your own script. The advantage of doing this now is that you know more about which parts of your body relax faster or slower than other parts. You can therefore slow down or speed up the induction accordingly. Repeat the relaxing phrases more times for the areas you know are slow to relax and fewer times for those that are quicker to relax. Make up your own relaxing phrase focusing you on relaxing your arms and legs. In short, make your own custom relaxation tape tailored to your own needs. It will be a more effective and powerful tool for you.

Enjoy relaxing!

APPENDIX C
PROGRESSIVE RELAXATION SCRIPT

Find a chair, couch recliner, or mattress of any kind to sit or lay on with your arms and legs uncrossed. "I'll first ask you to focus your awareness on the muscles of your upper body. Your head, neck and shoulders. When I say the word 'Now,' I am asking you to tighten the muscles in both your shoulders and your arms at the same time, your right and left shoulder, biceps (the big muscle on the top or front of your upper arm), triceps (the big muscle on the back of your upper arm), forearm muscles, wrist muscles and hand and finger muscles. So, I'll ask you NOW! to tighten the muscles in both your arms, making them tighter and tighter to the count of seven ... 2 ... 3 ... 4 .... tighter to ... 6 ... and 7 ... and ... letting go and releasing those muscles ... letting go of all of the tightness and tension in your arm muscles ... relaxing the muscles of both your shoulders ... both your biceps and triceps ... letting go of the tension from both your forearms ... wrists and both your hands and all your fingers letting go and relaxing completely. And I am asking you once again NOW! ... tightening the muscles in both your arms to the count of seven ... 1 ... making them tighter to 2 ... even tighter than before ... 3 ... 4 ... even tighter to 5 ... 6 ... 7 ... and release all the tightness in both your arms!! You're allowing the muscles of your shoulders, biceps and triceps let go and relaxing.

You're allowing comfort and calm flowing into the muscles of your forearms and wrists ... releasing and letting go of the tension in your hands and fingers. And I'm asking you once again now to shift your awareness to the muscle of your right and left legs ... Both sides of your hips and buttocks muscles, ... both quadriceps and hamstrings, ... your knee muscles connect to the muscles of your calves connecting to the muscles of your ankles, ... into the muscles of your feet and toes, ... each individual muscle connecting each joint of your toes to the next joints of your toes ... And I am asking you NOW! to tighten the muscles in both your legs NOW to the count of seven ... tightening to the number 1 ... making them tighter to 2 ... and 3!!! ... and increasing that tightness to 4!!!! And tighter to 5!!!! Even tighter to 6 ... and tighter to 7!!! ... and letting go of the tension in your hips and buttocks muscles, ... allowing your back and butt and hips to drop completely into the mat or mattress or cushion upon which it's resting ... allowing that comfortable relaxation to be flowing into your hamstring and quadricep muscles filling completely with calm, filling completely with a comfortable quiet as the relaxing is flowing into the muscles of your calves pooling like whirlpool of peace and relaxation draining down through your ankles into your feet and toes becoming more relaxed and at ease, becoming more calm and quietly comfortable...and relaxing. And one more time NOW!!! ... Tightening the muscles of your hips and buttocks to the count of seven now... making the thigh and quadricep muscles tighter and tighter to the count of 3 ... and tighter to 4 ... as those calf and ankle muscles are tightening to the count of 5 while the muscles of your feet tightening even tighter to the count of 6 and the count of 7 and ... letting go of all the tightness in your hips and legs and feet, allowing that stream of relaxation flowing from your hips into your buttocks, into your thighs and hamstrings letting go and becoming even more deeply relaxed and quiet, like deep calm pool of a relaxing stream, so smooth and still, so calm and relaxing as its flowing through your knees into your calves and shins letting go and flowing into your ankles and feet and toes becoming more completely relaxed, becoming more completely and deeply comfortable ... enjoying those peaceful sensations of relaxing."

"And just siting or laying or reclining in whatever position you're finding yourself relaxing or in some other way enjoying peace and calm, ... it doesn't matter what position your body enjoys relaxing in or what place your body is continuing deepening the pleasant sensations of quietly relaxing those arm and leg muscles ... because relaxing is a skill and just like any other skill the more your practicing relaxing the better you're becoming relaxing more deeply, relaxing more fully and completely and the more your body is learning relaxing. So, enjoying those learnings and lessons in peace and calm and quiet comfort, enjoying those learnings knowing you are already learning relaxing by giving yourself the gift of relaxation, giving yourself the gift of calm and peace, you're already learning relaxing and deepening relaxing as much as you are deepening your relaxing. So, once you learned what you've learned about what you're discovering about your relaxing abilities and skills you begin to allow yourself to become more refreshed and revived alert and awake, so you're going on with the rest of your day in a normal and natural fashion. Allowing a refreshing and reviving energy to be returning to the muscles of your toes and ankles, your calves and knees, drifting lightly up through the awakening muscles of your thighs ... up through your quadriceps and hamstrings becoming energized and alert, more aware and awake as a refreshing and reviving energy continues flowing into the muscles of your buttocks and hips, becoming more energized and alert. Allowing that invigorating energy to be flowing into the tips of your fingers and hands ... lightly awakening the palms of your hands and drifting even lighter and more awake and energized into the muscles of your wrists and forearms becoming more energized and awake and moving your life on to bigger and better and more enlightening fulfilling experiences ... Allowing those triceps and shoulders to be moving on to new heights of awareness so that you are going on with the rest of your day in a normal and natural fashion! Becoming completely refreshed and revived, energized, alert and aware so that you go effortlessly through the rest of your day in an awakened and alert fashion!!!!"

APPENDIX D

COMPLETING SUDS RATINGS AND RANKINGS

In order to break the tie or split those fine hairs between multiple scenarios with the same SUDS *ratings*, we simply need to focus more closely on each scenario and determine which is the least or most evocative. For example, at the SUDS level of "One" I have two scenarios: Finding a fresh Bigfoot track (SUDS *rating* = 1); Walking into a habituation site that had activity the previous expedition (SUDS *rating* = 1). For me, the weaker/less evocative of these two scenarios is: Walking into a habituation site that had activity the previous expedition. As such my personal Bigfoot inoculation hierarchy begins **ranking** as follows.

John S. Baranchok's Bigfoot Stress Inoculation Hierarchy

1. Walking into a habituation site that had activity the previous (last year's) expedition: (SUDS *rating* = 1).
2. Finding a fresh Bigfoot track: (SUDS *rating* = 1).

Note I keep the original SUDS rating attached to the scenario. This will become relevant a little later.

Next, we need to break the tie for those with SUDS ratings of "Two:" Seeing red "eye shine" at a 50-yard distance with a group of 15 other people around me: (SUDS *rating* = 2); Hearing a roar or howl in the distance (SUDS *rating* = 2). For me despite the adage "there is comfort in numbers," the "roar or howl" scenario is the weaker of the two, my *rankings* now become:

John S. Baranchok's Bigfoot Stress Inoculation Hierarchy

1. Walking into a habituation site that had activity the previous (last year's) expedition: (SUDS *rating* = 1).
2. Finding a fresh Bigfoot track: (SUDS *rating* = 1).
3. Hearing a Bigfoot roar or howl in the distance: (SUDS *rating* = 2).
4. Seeing red "eye shine" at a 50-yard distance with a group of 15 other people around me: (SUDS *rating* = 2).

Next, we need to split some finer hairs between my three SUDS *ratings* of "Three:" Walking into a habituation site on a moonless night that had activity the previous night with three other people (SUDS *rating* = 3); Entering habituation site that I had a previous experience in (knock, roar or growl) (SUDS *rating* = 3); Walking down a "Bigboy" trail at dusk transitioning into night and seeing unidentified dull-white lights blinking throughout the woods (SUDS *rating* = 3). For myself the previous experience of a knock, roar, or growl seems more removed and distant than knowing there had been activity the previous night. As such the more distant of these events is weaker and ranked lower. I have also actually had the experience of the dull white light, making it more vivid and powerful for me than the other two. Accordingly, *my ranking* hierarchy becomes as below.

John S. Baranchok's Bigfoot Stress Inoculation Hierarchy

1. Walking into a habituation site that had activity the previous (last year's) expedition: (SUDS *rating* = 1).
2. Finding a fresh Bigfoot track: (SUDS *rating* = 1).
3. Hearing a Bigfoot roar or howl in the distance: (SUDS *rating* = 2).
4. Seeing red "eye shine" at a 50-yard distance with a group of 15 other people around me: (SUDS *rating* = 2).
5. Entering habituation site that I had a previous experience in (knock, roar or growl: (SUDS *rating* = 3).
6. Walking into a habituation site on a moonless night that had activity the previous night with three other people: (SUDS *rating* = 3).
7. Walking down a "Bigboy" trail at dusk into night and seeing unidentified dull white lights blinking throughout the woods: (SUDS *rating* = 3).

You may take exception to some of my *rankings* and *ratings* and my stated rationale for them. Likely that is because they don't "make sense" to you and your reality and experience. It is fine for you to disagree with my reasons for splitting a hair or my SUDS *rankings* themselves. You may even potentially assign different SUDS *rating* values to these experiences based on your history and reality. The issue, however is moot and not to be debated as my own feelings, thoughts, and realities need to be represented in the hierarchy for it to be relevant and powerful for me. Although we are using numbers *ratings* and *rankings* to lend an air of objectivity to the process, this is *nonetheless a totally subjective process*! It is **my** fight-flight response I am reconditioning, **not** yours. As such rather than continue to explain each hair split and decision I make regarding my *rankings*, I have completed them below so that we might move on to the next step in this process.

John S. Baranchok's Bigfoot Stress Inoculation Hierarchy

1. Walking into a habituation site that had activity the previous (last year's) expedition: (SUDS *rating* = 1).
2. Finding a fresh Bigfoot track: (SUDS *rating* = 1).
3. Hearing a Bigfoot roar or howl in the distance: (SUDS *rating* = 2).
4. Seeing red "eye shine" at a 50-yard distance with a group of 15 other people around me: (SUDS *rating* = 2).
5. Entering habituation site that I had a previous experience in (knock, roar or growl: (SUDS *rating* = 3).
6. Walking into a habituation site on a moonless night that had activity the previous night with three other people: (SUDS *rating* = 3).
7. Walking down a "Bigboy" trail as dusk transitions into night and seeing unidentified dull white lights blinking throughout the woods: (SUDS *rating* = 3).
8. Seeing red "eye shine" at a 50-yard distance when by myself: (SUDS *rating* = 4).
9. Walking down a "Bigboy" trail and hearing a distant knock: (SUDS *rating* = 5).
10. Returning to a gifting area and finding food taken and a print nearby: (SUDS *rating* = 5).
11. Returning to a gifting area and finding my gift gone and new gifts left: (SUDS *rating* = 5).
12. A tree or landslide sound coming down on top of me and around me, while myself and my expedition partners all scatter, except one who turns to "face the music:" (SUDS *rating* = 5).
13. Getting nuts or pebbles thrown at my feet when entering an area known for Bigfoot activity: (SUDS *rating* = 6).
14. Seeing red eye shine at a twenty-foot distance when by myself: (SUDS *rating* = 7).

15. Walking down a "Bigboy" trail and hearing a nearby knock: (SUDS *rating* = 7).

16. Walking down a "Bigboy" trail and hearing a nearby whoop: (SUDS *rating* = 7).

17. Walking down a "Bigboy" trail at night and hearing Bigfoot breathing: (SUDS *rating* = 7).

18. Walking down a "Bigboy" trail and hearing nearby growl: (SUDS *rating* = 8).

19. Having pebbles and rocks being thrown at/hitting my body in an area known to have Bigfoot activity: (SUDS *rating* = 8).

20. Hearing the very nearby (20 feet away) bushes rustle near me in the night, while not seeing what was making the rustling sounds and movement, but then hearing a deep guttural growl emanating from those bushes: (SUDS *rating* = 8).

21. Hearing an unidentified slap/pounding on my trailer exterior: (SUDS *rating* = 8).

22. Loud breathing/tree moving/limb tearing and ground shaking bluff charge at close quarters without actual sighting: (SUDS *rating* = 8).

23. Walking down a "Bigboy" trail and hearing nearby howl: (SUDS *rating* = 9).

24. Hearing footfalls and Bigfoot-like breathing outside my trailer: (SUDS *rating* = 9).

25. Same bluff charge scenario with actual sighting: (SUDS *rating* = 10).

26. Staring a teeth-bearing/roaring Bigfoot in the face: (SUDS *rating* = 10).

27. Being aggressively picked up or drug off by an adult male Bigfoot: (SUDS *rating* = 10).

Now for a reality check of the SUDS ratings and rankings. By reality check, I mean do they make sense to me (or when you are doing your own, you).

Simply starting with *ranking* number one, read each scenario and see if it "feels right" or "makes logical sense" in its placement relative to the next *ranking* below it and/or the *ranking* above it. For example, speaking for myself, the juxtaposition of *ranking* numbers Two and Three do not make sense to me! Finding a "fresh" Bigfoot track means one could be in the immediate vicinity, whereas hearing a distant howl, could mean one may be around, but not in the immediate vicinity. In my final *rankings*, I will also switch their SUDS *ratings* so that the fresh track is *rated* higher than the distant howl. The same with *ranking* numbers Four and Five.

John S. Baranchok's Bigfoot Stress Inoculation Hierarchy

1. Walking into a habituation site that had activity the previous (last year's) expedition: (SUDS *rating* = 1).
2. Hearing a Bigfoot roar or howl in the distance: (SUDS *rating* = 2).
3. Finding a fresh Bigfoot track: (SUDS *rating* = 1).
4. Entering a habituation site that I had a previous experience in (knock, roar or growl: (SUDS *rating* = 3).
5. Seeing red "eye shine" at a 50-yard distance with a group of 15 other people around me: (SUDS *rating* = 2).
6. Walking into a habituation site on a moonless night that had activity the previous night with three other people: (SUDS *rating* = 3).

In doing so the reader will note that we now have a SUDS rating of "2" in a lower ranked position of Two relative to my number three ranking with a SUDS rating of "1." Similarly, I have a SUDS rating of "2" ranked higher (number Five ranking) than a SUDS rating of "3" (ranking number Four). This is the reason I continued to carry the SUDS rating forward. These inconsistencies further allow me to "reality test" or test the accuracy of my SUDS ratings. I should now either raise or lower those SUDS ratings appropriately.

John S. Baranchok's Bigfoot Stress Inoculation Hierarchy

1. Walking into a habituation site that had activity the previous (last year's) expedition: (SUDS rating = 1).
2. Hearing a Bigfoot roar or howl in the distance: (SUDS rating = 2).
3. Finding a fresh Bigfoot track: (SUDS rating = 2).
4. Entering a habituation site that I had a previous experience in (knock, roar, or growl): (SUDS rating = 3).
5. Seeing red "eye shine" at a 50-yard distance with a group of 15 other people around me: (SUDS rating = 3).
6. Walking into a habituation site on a moonless night that had activity the previous night with three other people: (SUDS rating = 3).

After reassigning a SUDS *rating* of "2" to my "fresh track" scenario (previously *rated* as a "1"), it now feels even more intense than *ranking* number Four above it (entering a habituation site...) due to the current visible presence of the creature in the vicinity, so I'll switch the *rankings*.

John S. Baranchok's Bigfoot Stress Inoculation Hierarchy

1. Walking into a habituation site that had activity the previous (last year's) expedition: (SUDS *rating* = 1).
2. Hearing a Bigfoot roar or howl in the distance: (SUDS *rating* = 2).
3. Entering a habituation site that I had a previous experience in (knock, roar, or growl): (SUDS *rating* = 3).
4. Finding a fresh Bigfoot track: (SUDS *rating* = 2).
5. Seeing red "eye shine" at a 50-yard distance with a group of 15 other people around me: (SUDS *rating* = 3).
6. Walking into a habituation site on a moonless night that

had activity the previous night with three other people: (SUDS *rating* = 3).

This *re-ranking* not only puts a SUDS *rating* of "3" (entering habituation site ...) below a SUDS *rating* of "2" (fresh track), but also (for me for the first time) forces me to notice that *ranking* number Six feels less intense than *rankings* Four and Five. Oh boy! Here we go again!

John S. Baranchok's Bigfoot Stress Inoculation Hierarchy

1. Walking into a habituation site that had activity the previous (last year') expedition: (SUDS *rating* = 1).
2. Hearing a Bigfoot roar or howl in the distance: (SUDS *rating* = 2).
3. Entering a habituation site that I had a previous experience in (knock, roar, or growl): (SUDS *rating* = 3).
4. Walking into a habituation site on a moonless night that had activity the previous night with three other people: (SUDS *rating* = 3).
5. Finding a fresh Bigfoot track: (SUDS *rating* = 3).
6. Seeing red "eye shine" at a 50-yard distance with a group of 15 other people around me: (SUDS *rating* = 3).

Please note I not only switched *rankings* (number Six to number Four, number Four to number Five, and number Five to number Six), but also changed the SUDS *rating* for the fresh track scenario from "2" to "3!" Although tedious and possibly seeming somewhat redundant, *this is important to do with the entirety of your numeric rankings and SUDS ratings so they make logical sense in the numeric rankings and have an "appropriate feel" in the SUDS ratings.* Hopefully you understand the process. As such, I will not go on ad nauseam describing the process. I have made appropriate adjustments to the entirety of my *rankings* and *ratings* below.

John S. Baranchok's Bigfoot Stress Inoculation Hierarchy

1. Walking into a habituation site that had activity the previous (last year's) expedition: (SUDS *rating* = 1).
2. Hearing a Bigfoot roar or howl in the distance: (SUDS *rating* = 1).
3. Entering a habituation site that I had a previous experience in (knock, roar or growl): (SUDS *rating* = 2).
4. Walking down a "Bigboy" trail and hearing a distant knock: (SUDS *rating* = 2).
5. Walking into a habituation site on a moonless night that had activity the previous night with three other people: (SUDS *rating* = 2).
6. Finding a fresh Bigfoot track: (SUDS *rating* = 3).
7. Returning to a gifting area and finding food taken and a footprint nearby: (SUDS *rating* = 3).
8. Returning to a gifting area and finding my gift gone and new gifts left: (SUDS *rating* = 4).
9. Walking down a "Bigboy" trail at dusk into the night and seeing unidentified dull white lights blinking throughout the woods: (SUDS *rating* = 4).
10. Walking down a "Bigboy" trail and hearing a nearby whoop: (SUDS *rating* – 5).
11. Walking down a "Bigboy" trail and hearing a nearby knock: (SUDS *rating* = 5).
12. Seeing red "eye shine" at a 50-yard distance with a group of 15 other people around me: (SUDS *rating* = 5).
13. Seeing red "eye shine" at a 50-yard distance by myself: (SUDS *rating* = 6).
14. Walking down a "Bigboy" trail and hearing a nearby howl: (SUDS *rating* = 6).
15. Seeing red eye shine at a twenty-foot distance by myself: (SUDS *rating* = 7).

16. A tree or landslide sound coming down on top of me and around me while myself and my expedition partners all scatter, except one who turns to "face the music:" (SUDS *rating* = 7).

17. Hearing the very nearby (20 feet away) bushes rustle near me in the night, while not seeing what was making the rustling sounds and movement, but then hearing a deep guttural growl emanating from those bushes: (SUDS *rating* = 8).

18. Getting nuts or pebbles thrown at my feet when entering an area known for Bigfoot activity: (SUDS *rating* = 8).

19. Walking down a "Bigboy" trail at night and hearing Bigfoot breathing: (SUDS *rating* = 9).

20. Walking down a "Bigboy" trail and hearing nearby growl: (SUDS *rating* = 9).

21. Having pebbles and rocks being thrown at/hitting my body in an area known to have Bigfoot activity: (SUDS *rating* = 9).

22. Hearing an unidentified slap/pounding on my trailer exterior: (SUDS *rating* = 9).

23. Loud breathing/tree moving/limb tearing and ground shaking bluff charge at close quarters without actual sighting: (SUDS *rating* = 9).

24. Hearing footfalls and Bigfoot-like breathing outside my trailer: (SUDS *rating* = 9).

25. Same bluff charge scenario with actual sighting: (SUDS *rating* = 10).

26. Staring a teeth-bearing/roaring Bigfoot in the face: (SUDS *rating* = 10).

27. Being aggressively picked up or drug off by an adult male Bigfoot: (SUDS *rating* = 10).

Notice, not only have some of the SUDS *ratings* changed dramatically, but so have some of the *rankings*. Some have not. Indeed, as you practice the actual inoculation practice, SUDS *rating* saliences and/or relative *ranking* values will begin to change. That's fine, it's appropriate to the process and means the process is already beginning to change your perspective/perception which ultimately is part of reconditioning your fight–flight response. Now on to the **core** of the inoculation process!!

You mastered relaxation and are able to achieve a state of deep muscle relaxation. You may have even noticed there are times when your mind "slips into neutral," goes blank or just stays still! That is great! You've also created your stress inoculation hierarchy as we did above. You are certain you have enough low and moderate rankings to "set yourself up for success" by remaining very relaxed as you run the mental movie of the scenario or otherwise mentally imagine or rehearse the scenario while in a relaxed state. That is the next step in the process. I will now describe that process in more specific detail. You next need to further refine or systematically break your differences between rankings. The more systematic and graduated or gradual the differences are between rankings, the more likely you will be successful in the process. For example, my "Bigboy" trail scenarios (*rankings* Four, Nine, Ten, Eleven, Fourteen, and Twenty) represent an example of this principle. Personally, for me a "Bigboy" trail in and of itself is intimidating. It signals an area Bigfoots frequent and has broken off branches high up on the tree to allow ease of passage for themselves without their bodies being battered by low-hanging branches (or so the theory goes). As such, when I am on one, my sense of vigilance is heightened, which is my reason for including so many of those scenarios. I start with the innocuous experience in ranking number four of "hearing a distant knock when walking down one." In fact, it might be a good idea to create an even more innocuous scenario of "walking down a 'Bigboy' trail in the daylight and not having any Bigfoot activity experienced during that walk" (SUDS *rating* = 1). I could then add only a slightly higher scenario of doing the same thing "Walking down a 'Bigboy' trail at **night**" (SUDS *rating* = 2) to add the fear element of darkness to it. As a concrete example of my point, I will break it down further:

Appendix D

John S. Baranchok's Bigfoot Stress Inoculation Hierarchy

1. Walking down a "Bigboy" trail in the daylight and not having any Bigfoot activity experience during that walk: (SUDS *rating* = 1).
2. Walking down a "Bigboy" trail at night with no Bigfoot experience: (SUDS *rating* = 2).
3. Walking down a "Bigboy" trail during the day and hearing a distant knock: (SUDS *rating* = 2).
4. Walking down a "Bigboy" trail at dusk into the night and seeing unidentified dull white lights blinking throughout the woods: (SUDS *rating* = 4).
5. Walking down a "Bigboy" trail during the day and hearing nearby whoop: (SUDS *rating* = 5).
6. Walking down a "Bigboy" trail during the day and hearing nearby howl: (SUDS *rating* = 5).
7. Walking down a "Bigboy" trail during the night and hearing a nearby knock: (SUDS *rating* = 6).
8. Walking down a "Bigboy" trail during the day and hearing Bigfoot breathing: (SUDS *rating* = 9).
9. Walking down a "Bigboy" trail during the night and hearing Bigfoot breathing: (SUDS *rating* = 9).
10. Walking down a "Bigboy" trail during the day and hearing nearby growl: (SUDS *rating* = 9).
11. Walking down a "Bigboy" trail during the night and hearing nearby growl: (SUDS *rating* = 9).

The more graduated or broken down into smaller steps, the more effective the inoculation process will be. Yes, the smaller the steps and the more graduated or slight change from one step to another the longer the process will take. That is true. It is equally true, however, that the more graduated the process, the more effective it will ultimately be when you get to your more intense scenarios. That should, however, also highlight for the reader the importance of those more intense scenarios having even finer graduated steps; smaller steps in between rankings! Note that although ranked from One to Eleven, these have yet to be integrated (Re-SUDS and Re-ranked) into the larger inoculation hierarchy. I have done so below.

John S. Baranchok's Bigfoot Stress Inoculation Hierarchy

1. Walking into a habituation site that had activity the previous (last year's) expedition: (SUDS *rating* = 1).
2. Walking down a "Bigboy" trail in the daylight and not having any Bigfoot activity experience during that walk: (SUDS *rating* = 1).
3. Hearing a Bigfoot roar or howl in the distance: (SUDS *rating* = 1).
4. Entering habituation site that I had a previous experience in (knock, roar, or growl): (SUDS *rating* = 2).
5. Walking down a "Bigboy" trail at night with no Bigfoot experience: (SUDS *rating* =2).
6. Walking down a "Bigboy" trail during the day and hearing a distant knock: (SUDS *rating* = 2).
7. Walking into a habituation site on a moonless night that had activity the previous night with three other people: (SUDS *rating* = 2).
8. Finding a fresh Bigfoot track: (SUDS *rating* = 3).
9. Returning to a gifting area and finding food taken and a footprint nearby: (SUDS *rating* = 3).
10. Returning to a gifting area and finding my gift gone and new gifts left: (SUDS *rating* = 4).
11. Walking down a "Bigboy" trail at dusk into night and seeing an unidentified dull white light blinking throughout the woods: (SUDS *rating* = 4).
12. Walking down a "Bigboy" trail during the day and hearing nearby whoop: (SUDS *rating* = 5).

13. Walking down a "Bigboy" trail during the day and hearing a nearby howl: (SUDS *rating* =5).

14. Walking down a "Bigboy" trail during the night and hearing a nearby knock: (SUDS *rating* = 5).

15. Seeing red "eye shine" at a 50-yard distance with a group of 15 other people around me: (SUDS *rating* = 6).

16. Seeing red "eye shine" at a 50-yard distance by myself: (SUDS *rating* = 6.)

17. Walking down a "Bigboy: trail and hearing a nearby howl: (SUDS *rating* = 6).

18. Seeing red eye shine at a twenty-foot distance by myself: (SUDS *rating* = 7).

19. A tree or landslide sounds coming down on top of me and around me while myself and my expedition partners all scatter, except one who turns to "face the music:" (SUDS *rating* = 7).

20. Hearing the very nearby (20 feet away) bushes rustle near me in the night, while not seeing what was making the rustling sounds and movement but then hearing a deep guttural growl emanating from those bushes: (SUDS *rating* = 8).

21. Getting nuts or pebbles thrown at my feet when entering an area known for Bigfoot activity: (SUDS *rating* = 8)

22. Walking down a "Bigboy" trail during the day and hearing Bigfoot breathing: (SUDS *rating* = 8).

23. Walking down a "Bigboy" trail at night and hearing Bigfoot breathing: (SUDS *rating* = 9).

24. Walking down a "Bigboy" trail during the day and hearing a nearby growl: (SUDS *rating* = 9).

25. Walking down a "Bigboy" trail during the night and hearing a nearby growl: (SUDS *rating* = 9).

26. Having pebbles and rocks being thrown at/hitting my body in an area known to have Bigfoot activity: (SUDS *rating* = 9).

27. Hearing an unidentified slap/pounding on my trailer exterior: (SUDS *rating* = 9).
28. Loud breathing/tree moving/limb tearing and ground shaking bluff charge at close quarters without actual sighting: (SUDS *rating* = 9).
29. Hearing footfalls and Bigfoot-like breathing outside my trailer: (SUDS *rating* = 10).
30. Same bluff charge scenario with actual sighting: (SUDS *rating* = 10).
31. Staring a teeth-bearing/roaring Bigfoot in the face: (SUDS *rating* =10).
32. Being aggressively picked up or drug off by an adult male Bigfoot: (SUDS *rating* = 10).

Compare my original 27-step inoculation hierarchy to my now 32-step inoculation hierarchy. *Note not only are there more rankings, but some of the SUDS ratings have changed from the original to the "final step."* I have written the words "final step" in quotation marks to denote that ultimately, *there is no truly "final step" in the inoculation hierarchy. As you begin to inoculate yourself to the lower evocative scenarios, it will often change the salience or strength of those above it.* Sometimes you'll end up downgrading their evocativeness, sometimes upgrading their evocativeness. It is a flexible, dynamic list that will change as your reconditioning of your fight-flight response changes.

APPENDIX E
PROGRAMMED RESPONSE

Allow yourself to imagine yourself (for example) during a bluff charge. "See you're standing in the woods and beginning to hear a roar or growl or grunt and footfalls in the near distance. See yourself remaining relatively calm, but preparing yourself to take up a defensive post in behind a tree or rock where you can still see the beast coming toward you should it decide to show itself. Notice how your body moves silently, yet quickly and efficiently to that position. Note how although your breathing and heart rate may quicken in the excitement of the moment, your heart rate remains regular and steady and under comfortable control. Notice how your breathing remains deep and regular and under your comfortable calm control. You are preparing yourself and your body for that optimum level of arousal to perform perfectly and effortlessly and efficiently in response to whatever comes your way, always protecting your own welfare, spending the time facing the source and direction of the footfalls you hear coming closer. The animal's breathing may become more audible and trees and branches may begin to snap and break loudly and rustle or be parted in a dramatic fashion, moving aside or back and forth almost as if in a hurricane wind. All the time you are remaining well aroused, calmly aroused, but steady and prepared to react appropriately whatever that appropriate reaction might be, but always facing the origin of the sound. You may wish to stand firm, or you may wish to more thoroughly conceal yourself or hide yourself or slowly walk away from the source of the sound, talking calmly to it, telling it you are a friend and want to enjoy your experience with it and wish it peace and love and kindness. You may want to project images or thoughts or love and comfort, sharing a meal or gently shaking hands, depending on your desires. As the bluff charge and commotion in the forest subside or stop, you see yourself calming even more and reach your thoughts and mind out further to the creature. You are feeling confident in your ability to continue to safely take care of and guard yourself using only safe and cautious behaviors, never turning and running with your back to the source of the sound, but if you are leaving slowly and in a controlled fashion walking or stepping backwards down an obvious path or if no path is immediately available, even more carefully backing up slowly and calmly, projecting kindness and understanding, love and respect. Should it occur that you see the creature, avoid direct eye contact, and lower your body posture in a respectful and submissive posture. Imagine the encounter playing out peacefully with you always aware of your own safety and welfare knowing you will instinctively do whatever you need to protect yourself from harm. You are noticing footfalls receding back into the forest in a hurried fashion, leaves or branches or trees rustling more and more distant away from you and your breathing becomes even more deep and regular and your heart rate begins to slow in a gradual and controlled fashion. You're beginning to relax some of the tension in your muscles as you are slowly backing away from the retreating sounds in front of you, projecting images and words of graciousness and thanks for the exciting and unique experience you just had."

PLEASE RETURN TO PAGE 136 TO MOVE FORWARD WITH THIS PROCESS.

APPENDIX F
CREATING YOUR HYPNOTIC SAFE PLACE

The safe place I was first introduced to involved: "Imagining yourself floating out of your body and through the air to a location you discover, whether you know it or not, that contains all the supplies, skills, and knowledge you needed to build a safe house or castle and enjoy experiencing trance. It doesn't matter where this house is located. It may be located at the beach, or on a mountain, next to a river, or in a forest. You might build it in the sky, under water, on another planet, in another universe, in another dimension or someplace else you and only you are aware of. You already have everything you need. You already know how to build this dwelling of safety and peace. You already know how to build this dwelling of relaxing security, confident in your abilities to create whatever you want or need so that everything is within your reach to build whatever your desire or need. Now you are allowing yourself to think about what that safe and secure dwelling will look like. Is it big or small? What materials will you build it with: brick and mortar, tall and strong wooden beams, rocks, stone, cement. Perhaps you'll build the wall underground or of a yet to be discovered and invented material stronger than anything else on earth. Perhaps its diamond corrugated fibrous panels of gold or silver or platinum or carbon. It's not important what materials you consider, it's only important the materials you use to build the place of relaxing safety. What is the foundation made of and how deep will you dig it? Will it have a basement, a first floor, second floor, how high and glorious and impenetrable will you build it? Will you want to put windows in it? What will those windows look like or resemble? Will they be shaded or tinted or have storm shutters on the outside or in? Will they have blinds or louvers on them to close or open at your will? Will they be square, or rectangular or round or oblong or some other shape, composition and appearance that only you create and are aware of. They can be magical and let only pleasant, healing, warming, and relaxing light in, blocking out the sun's harmful UV rays and destructive particles and energy. Are the windows on the front of the house, the sides of the home, the back for your security or did they exist all round and at all levels on all floors or your structure of security and calm. You'll want to include two doors. Most people include and front door and a back door, while others include a front door and a hidden exit door only they know about. What are these doors made of and how are they constructed? Do they have a door knob, a door handle, a latch, and entrance button? What is on the door? Windows, a buzzer, a door bell, a door knocker and intercom system, a peep hole? You can make it any color or appearance you enjoy creating your doorway, the security within and without your dwelling. Where are the doorways located? Are they at ground level or are stairs required to enter your safe house? Some people build a moat or draw bridge to approach the doors, others use escalators or elevator. Some use a magical password or phrase or motion or activity to move within the comfortable distance to open and close these doors. Is there a lock, a key hole, a dead bolt, a bar across the inside or outside of the door for added security? Now you're stepping inside your safe place. What does the inside of it look like, how does it appear? What materials are the walls made of, and what shade or color are they decorated with? Is there art on the walls, shelves with curios or books on the walls? How many rooms are in this dwelling? What is the purpose of these rooms? Is there a reception area or vestibule? Is there a kitchen, bathroom, dining room, bedroom, a recreation room or area, a TV room, a library or office space, a greenhouse or garden? Move about all the rooms in your safe place, exploring all the floors or levels you are creating for yourself from which within you enjoy relaxing your mind and body, relaxing the muscles of your head, neck, shoulders and arms. Letting go and allowing pleasant sensations to flow into your chest and upper back, stomach, and lower back becoming more comfortable, secure in your ability to bring a certain comfort to your hips and buttocks, thighs and hamstrings, calves and shins, feet and toes. How are your rooms furnished? Are there tables, chairs, couches, carpets, throw rugs, a stereo or entertainment center? Add whatever you want, wherever you want to make this place your perfect escape to comfort. Making this place whatever you want or need it to be for your comfortable security in knowing it is yours where only pleasant learnings and experiences occur to you, its impenetrable to outside influence you don't or won't allow."

"It is good to create some form of a viewing room where you can sit and look at a TV screen, movie screen, a magical projection wall or something else only you can imagine. Place comfortable chairs or other sitting or lying or resting furnishings into this viewing space. Add anything else you might like to have within an arm's reach to sit and enjoy watching things on this surface. This surface and the room it's contained within is your trance room, the place you go to when you want to enjoy a safe and certain deep level of relaxing trance and hypnosis. You can then use your viewing screen or surface like a time recorder or computer or DVD player to watch yourself go backward in time, back to experiences you're already experiencing or experienced. You can push fast forward and go forward in time by seconds, minutes days, years, decades, centuries, millenniums to see what future you might create for yourself. Add some speakers or other sound devices so you can immerse yourself in the sounds of these experiences wherever or whenever they may occur. Add a "smell or taste a vision" feature so you're allowing yourself to experience the flavors of those lives, tasting the sweet smell of success and enjoyment or whatever reality you're wishing to create for yourself. What are the feelings and tactile sensations that are installed into this experience, installed into this device, the device of your own creation and making to safely enjoy trance work and hypnosis? Add whatever features you're wanting to enjoy this experience in the calm security of this place and time wherever it may be. Enjoy as much time as you want here, knowing you can speed up or slowdown that time passage and space passage at your will. You're making things as fast or as slow as you want or need to thoroughly learn and experience what you're learning

and experiencing about safety and security, calm, peace, tranquility and any other experiences you may wish to have in this place, whenever you're wishing having them."

"Finishing the ultimate creation of the place now as you're preparing to leave this place and bring back security and safety with you, knowing fully and confidently that you can safely return to this place any time you want or need to experience anything you want to safely and securely experience in any way. Knowing it is your secret refuge from any and all distractions from which you wish to retreat or face. It is for you and only you for whatever wants or needs you may fulfill here from a place of impenetrable safety, strong, and unbreakable security and strength. Your safe place and only your safe place accessible to you any time by allowing yourself to relax, feel at ease, and go deeper down into yourself as you have today."

"And now you are continuing enjoying relaxation and processing any learnings you may be experiencing constructing your safe place you're leaving for now knowing you can return any time you wish, bringing back feelings of calm and security. You're imagining yourself safely drifting back to the place where you began experiencing your experiences, while bring back any safe, secure, and relaxing feeling you're continuing enjoying. You're continuing enjoying peaceful calm and security as you're returning to the time and place the experience began. Bringing bring back confidence and feelings of safety, feeling of strength and knowledge you are where you need to be now and, in the future, enjoying a quiet calm confidence and knowledge of your strength and security. Easily returning to the place where you left your body, all the time knowing it remains where it remains and remained as is and peacefully relaxed awaiting your return. You bring back strength and security, bring back a safe calm peace, return yourself to your body with the knowledge that you're going on with the rest of your day in a normal and natural fashion. As you are drifting back, you bring back that sense of safety with you. Imagining putting it in a vault or safe within yourself, securely and firmly closing the door on that safety vault, secure in the knowledge you are the one and the only one who opens that door again, knowing you are carrying that safety and security wherever you go into the past, future, or present as you are returning to your body in the here and now, preparing yourself to go on with the rest of your day in a

normal and natural fashion. Functioning normally in every way, but functioning even better with your confident strength and resolve, your undeniable sense of carrying safety and security in to the rest of your day, carry safety and security in to the rest of your week, carry safety and security and confidence into the rest of your life. You, now fully back in your body, enjoying bringing back any pleasant and comfortable learning and prepare to go on with the rest of your day with a new found confidence and certainty of security and safety."

PLEASE RETURN TO CHAPTER 146.

SELECTED BIBLIOGRAPHY

Bandler, R. (Author), Andreas, S and Andreas, C. (Editors). (1985). *Using your brain for a change*. Real People Press.

Benson, H. (Author). Klipper, M. Z. (Author). (August 1, 1976). *The Relaxation Response*. Mass Market Paperback.

Bowman, Jr., P.; Capparella, Angelo, P.; Colyer, Daryl, G.; Higgins, Alton; McClurkan, Mark;& Perry, John. (January 2017). Tracking a Self-Tagged Unidentified Species in the OuachitaHighlands. NWAC.

Carpenter, S. (2019). *The nephilum among us updated*. Self-published.

Gerhard, K. (2019). *The Essential Guide to Bigfoot*. Self-published.

Gordon, S. (2010). *The silent invasion*. Stan Gordon Productions.

Green, Mary and Carter Coy, Janice. (2002). *50 Years with Bigfoot: Tennessee Chronicles of Co-Existence*. Self-Published.

Kimbro, Charles & Monongahela. (March 3rd, 2020). *Squatchin 101*. [Self-Published Edition].

Krantz, Grover. (1999). *Bigfoot sasquatch evidence. The anthropologist speaks out*. Hancock House Publishers, LTD (Canada) and Hancock House Publishers (USA).

Meldrum, Jeff. (2006). *Sasquatch: legend meets science*. Forge Book. Published by Tom Doherty Associates, LLC.

North American Wood Ape Conservancy (NWAC) Online Podcast. (2017 Dec 24th). *Apes Among Us: Tag 7*. [Audio Podcast].

Piaget, Jean in Gruber, Howard E.; Vonèche, J. Jacques. (eds.). *The essential Piaget*. (1977) London: Routledge and K. Paul. ISBN 978-0710087782. OCLC 3813049.

Powell, T. (2003). *The locals*. Hancock House Publishers, LTD (Canada) and Hancock House Publishers (USA).

Raymond C. (9/1/2018). Bluegrass Bigfoot: Encounters with the Kentucky Wildman. Independently Published.

Redfern, N. (2016). The bigfoot book: the encyclopedia of sasquatch, yeti, and cryptid primates. Visible Ink Press. Index

INDEX

E

Eaves, John: v, 71, 235, 271

ecological validity: 215

effect size: 256-257

Einstein, Albert: xxi, 224

Elephant Listening Project: 180-182

empirical: 73-75, 133, 208, 238

empirical knowledge: 74

empirical method: 17, 74

empirical validity: 75

empiricism: 75

evidence: 5-8, 13-14, 16-22, 30, 40, 42-48, 91, 159-168

expedition: v, 8-14, 59-65, 70-74, 87, 116-118, 122-125, 190-193, 206-207, 212-215, 231-240, 276-278

experimental design: 10

AB: 183-185, 189-194

ABA: 194

blind: 169, 183-185

counter-balanced: 185, 201

double-blind: 183, 185, 203-204

experimental group: 76, 188

experimenter expectancy bias effect: 26

external reliability: 227-228

external validity: 215

extraneous variables: 21, 239, 182

eye shine: 50-51, 116-118, 122-125

F

face validity: 218-222

Fahrenbach, Henner Dr.: 286

faith: 12

Festinger, Leon: 71-72

field research: 264-267

fight-flight response: 24, 58, 98-103, 111, 114, 120-123, 128-135

fight-or-flight syndrome: 178

figure - ground phenomena. See illusions

Finding Bigfoot TV show: xvi, 8

Franssen, Nico Valentinus: 43. See also illusions: Franssen effect

frequency distribution: 255

Freud, Sigmund: 67

functional analysis: 17

G

genetic memories: 77

Totherow, Wayne. See Mannimalresearch.com
trail camera: 219
trapping: 205, 223, 242, 264–267
tree traps: 220
Trinity County, California: 90
triple blind experimental design: 204
t-score, t-test: 80, 285, 291-293
Turner, Lucian Seth: Dedications, vii
Type I Error: 257
Type II Error: 258

V

validity: 75, 170, 209-211, 215-226, 232-233, 255. See also construct validity; concurrent validity; convergent validity; criterion validity; divergent validity; external validity; face validity; historical validity; internal validity; population validity
variable(s): 20-21. See also confounding variable; dependent variable; extraneous variables; independent variable; stimulus variable; response variable
video evidence: 6
vigilance: 54, 60, 147-150, 315

W

Wade, Lori Copeland: Dedications, v
Wallace, Ray: 18, 22, 160
Wall, Marc: Dedications, vi
wildlife laws: 7
Wiles, Andrew: 224
Williams, Glenn: Dedications, v, 71, 223, 271
Woo phenomena: 66, 78, 83-87, 94-97, 275
Woo theorists: 32
Wrigley, George: Dedications, v

Y

Yerkes-Dodson law: 135

Z

zapping: 57, 81, 97, 176, 177-179, 202-203, 216
Zimbardo, Phillip: 24
Zorc, Kevin: Dedications, vii
z-score: 80, 250-251, 285, 291-292

ABOUT THE AUTHOR

Photo credit: Sedona A. Baranchok

Recently, John Baranchok closed his Neuropsychology practice after 17 years and spent 2 years working at the Rome Veteran's Administration Outreach Clinic as a Clinical Psychologist. Now medically retired, he continues to live life as a cancer survivor.

He continues to enjoy his affiliation with Mannimalresearch.com/Southeastern Sasquatch Investigations, as well as the Georgia, Tennessee, and Kentucky BFRO Expedition Teams. He was honored to join Doug Hajicek's Untold Radio Network and is thrilled with his YouTube Channel and Podcast, "Grasping Bigfoot".

He is scheduled to be featured in the upcoming documentary "Sasquatch: Legend Meets Science II". Despite many "Class B" experiences, he has not yet had a "Class A" encounter, even after starting his sixth year of Bigfoot Fieldwork. He is looking forward to that Class A encounter and is excited to see where his Bigfoot journey leads him.

AFTERWORD

Go to hangaripublishing.com to learn more about the Authors and stay up to date with their newest releases.

NOTES

Disclaimers

1. Kimbro, C. & Monongahela. (March 3rd, 2020). Squatchin 101. [Self-Published Edition].
2. Powell, T. (2003). The locals. Hancock House Publishers, LTD (Canada) and Hancock House Publishers (USA).
3. Finding Bigfoot (May 29,2011 - May 27,2018). Animal Planet/Discovery. Produced by Keith Hoffman, Brad Kuhlman, Casey Brumels.

Introduction

1. Kimbro, C. & Monongahela. (March 3rd, 2020). Squatchin 101. [Self-Published Edition].

1. Yes!! There Is a Santa Claus and I Believe in Bigfoot: These Are My Biases!

1. Biography.com Editors. Saint-Nicholas. (Dec 12, 2019). biography.com. Retrieved from https://www.biography.com/religious-figure/saint-nicholas.
2. Green, M, and Carter Coy, J. (2002). 50 Years with Bigfoot: Tennessee Chronicles of Co-Existence. Self-Published.
3. Meldrum, J. (2006). Sasquatch: legend meets science. Forge Book, Published by Tom Doherty Associates, LLC., pp. 73-88.
4. Redfern, N. (2016). The bigfoot book: the encyclopedia of sasquatch, yeti, and cryptid primates. Visible Ink Press.
5. Gordon, S. (2010). The silent invasion. Stan Gordon Productions.
6. Carpenter, S. (20019). The nephilim among us updated. Self-published.
7. Meldrum, J. (2006). Sasquatch: legend meets science. Forge Book, Published by Tom Doherty Associates, LLC.
8. Patterson, R, Gimlin, R. (1967). Patterson Gimlin Film. Roger Paterson, Bob Gimlin. [Motion Picture]. USA.
9. Meldrum, J. (2006). Sasquatch: legend meets science. A Forge Book Published by Tom Doherty Associates, LLC. p. 271.
10. Meldrum, J. (2006). Sasquatch: legend meets science. A Forge Book Published by Tom Doherty Associates, LLC. p. 271.
11. Meldrum, J. (2006). Sasquatch: legend meets science. A Forge Book Published by Tom Doherty Associates, LLC., p. 276.
12. Meldrum, J. personal e-mail communication. (12:03, July 14, 2020).
13. Debczak, M. (October. 21.2016). Is it-legal-shoot-bigfoot. Mentalfloss.com. Retrieved from mentalfloss.com/article/87148/.

14. Michelle Dennehy in Debczak, M. (October. 21.2016). Is it-legal-shoot-bigfoot. Mentalfloss.com. Retrieved from mentalfloss.com/article/87148/.
15. Ibid.
16. Mountain Monsters Television Show (June. 22.2013 Premier). Travel channel, Destination America. Produced by American Chain Saw.
17. Finding Bigfoot (May 29, 2011 - May 27, 2018). Animal Planet/Discovery. Produced by Keith Hoffman, Brad Kuhlman, Casey Brumels.
18. Faith. (n.d.). In Oxford Languages Online Dictionary. Retrieved from https://en.oxforddictionaries.com/definition/faith.
19. Meldrum, J. (2006). Sasquatch: legend meets science. A Forge Book Published by Tom Doherty Associates, LLC. p. 271.

2. Scientific and Personal Objectivity vs. Bias? The Body Dictates the Answer!

1. Science. (n.d.). Merriam Webster's Online Dictionary. Retrieved from https://www.merriam-webster.com/dictionary/science.
2. Scientific method. (n.d.). Merriam Webster's Online Dictionary. Retrieved from https://www.merriam-webster.com/dictionary/scientific method.
3. Zimbardo, P. G. (1988). Psychology and life (12th Edition). Scott, Foresman and Company, Boston, p. 28.
4. Ibid., p. 29.
5. Ibid.
6. Ibid., p. 30-37.
7. Ibid., p.33.
8. Co. (n.d.). Merriam Webster's Online Dictionary. Retrieved from https://www.merriam-webster.com/dictionary/co.
9. Relationship. (n.d.). In Oxford Languages Online Dictionary. Retrieved from https://en.oxforddictionaries.com/definition/relationship.
10. Zimbardo, P. G. (1988). Psychology and life (12th Edition). Scott, Foresman and Company, Boston, p. 34.
11. Ibid.
12. Zimbardo, P. G. (1988). Psychology and life (12th Edition). Scott, Foresman and Company, Boston, p. 36.
13. Redfern, N. (2016). The bigfoot book: The encyclopedia of sasquatch, yeti, and cryptid primates. Visible Ink Press. p. 308-309.
14. Ibid.
15. Warhol, A. (1968). Program for work. The Moderna Museet in Stockholm, Sweden.
16. Redfern, N. (2016). The bigfoot book: The encyclopedia of sasquatch, yeti, and cryptid primates. Visible Ink Press. p. 309.
17. Zimbardo, P. G. (1988). Psychology and life (12th Edition). Scott, Foresman and Company, Boston, pp. 141-182.
18. Zimbardo, P. G. (1988). Psychology and life (12th Edition). Scott, Foresman and Company, Boston, pp. 143-144.
19. Ibid., p. 144.
20. Ibid., p. 185.

21. Ibid., pp. 31-32.
22. Ibid.
23. Ibid.
24. Ibid.
25. Dear, W. (Producer). (1987). Harry and the Henderson's {Motion Picture]. USA.
26. Zimbardo, P. G. (1988). Psychology and life (12th Edition). Scott, Foresman and Company, Boston. p. 400.
27. Heisenberg Uncertainty Principle. (n.d.). Merriam Webster's Online Dictionary. Retrieved from https://www.merriam-webster.com/dictionary/heisenberg.
28. North American Wood Ape Conservancy (NWAC) Online Podcast. (2017 Dec 24th). Apes Among Us: Tag 7. 01:50:55. [Audio Podcast].
29. Bowman, P. Jr., Capparella, A. P., Colyer, D. G., Higgins, A., McClurkan, M., Perry, J. (January 2017). Tracking a Self-Tagged Unidentified Species in the Ouachita Highlands. NWAC.
30. Ibid.
31. North American Wood Ape Conservancy (NWAC) Online Podcast. (2017 Dec 24th). Apes Among Us: Tag 7. [Audio Podcast]. 01:50:55.
32. Ibid., 1:20:25.
33. Ibid., 1:21:11.
34. Ibid.
35. Ibid., 1:21:56.
36. Heisenberg Uncertainty Principle. (n.d.). Merriam Webster's Online Dictionary. Retrieved from https://www.merriam-webster.com/dictionary/heisenberg.
37. Incredulous. (n.d.). Lexico Online Dictionary. Retrieved from https://www.lexico.com/en/definition/incredulous.
38. Incredulous. (n.d.). Dictionary Definition. Retrieved from vocabulary.com.
39. Incredulity. (n.d.). Oxford Languages Online Dictionary. Retrieved from https://en.oxforddictionaries.com/definition/incredulity.

3. Illusions: If It Looks and Sounds like Bigfoot, It May Not Be a Bigfoot!

1. Illusion. (n.d.). Oxford Languages Online Dictionary. Retrieved from https://en.oxforddictionaries.com/definition/illusion.
2. Zimbardo, P. G. (1988). Psychology and life (12th Edition). Scott, Foresman and Company, Boston. 190.
3. Ibid.
4. Clear Eyes. (n.d.). TYPES OF OPTICAL ILLUSIONS. Retrieved from https://www.cleareyes.com/eye-care-blog/201610/types-optical-illusions/.
5. Cognitive illusions. (n.d.). Optical Illusions. Retrieved from https://fac.coloradocollege.edu/optical-illusions/.
6. Physiological Illusions. (n.d.). Optical illusions explained. Everything you need to know. feeldoppel.com. Retrieved from https://feeldoppel.com/blogs/news/optical-illusions-explained.
7. Cognitive illusion. (March 16, 2016). What are optical illusions? Definitions and types. Retrieved from https://study.com/academy/lesson/what-arle-optical-illusions-definition-types.htm.

8. Nierenberg, C. (Nov. 19, 2008, 12:19 PM). Optical Illusions: When Your Brain Can't Believe Your Eyes (abcnews.go.com).

9. The Müller-Lyer illusion. (n.d.). Sourced from merriam webster online dictionary. Retrieved from https://www.merriam-webster.com/dictionary/illusion.

10. Müller-Lyer illusion. (n.d.). Wikipedia, the free encyclopedia. Retrieved from https://en.wikipedia.org/wiki/M%C3%BCller-Lyer_illusion.

11. Figure-ground illusion. (n.d.). Figure-ground illusion. Retrieved from https://www.britannica.com/science/figure-ground-illusion.

12. Carroll, R. T. (Monday January 9, 2012). Pareidolia. Unnatural Acts That Can improve your thinking.

13. Pareidolia. (n.d.). Wikipedia, the free encyclopedia. Retrieved from https://en.wikipedia.org/wiki/Pareidolia.

14. The Face on Mars and Other Martian Tricks. (September 03, 2015). Mars Illusion Photos:. Space.com Staff. Retrieved from https://www.space.com/11947-photos-mars-illusions-martian-face-images.html.

15. Carroll, R. T. (Monday January 9, 2012). Pareidolia. Unnatural Acts That Can improve your thinking. Retrieved from http://59ways.blogspot.com/

16. Carroll, R. T. (Monday January 9, 2012). Apophenia. Unnatural Acts That Can improve your thinking. Retrieved from http://59ways.blogspot.com/.

17. Pareidolia: Coincidence or Meaningful Coincidence. (n.d.). Retrieved from https://enigmose.com/paredoilia.html.

18. Carroll, R. T. (Monday January 9, 2012). Apophenia. Unnatural Acts That Can improve your thinking.

19. Gerhard, K. (2019). The Essential Guide to Bigfoot" Self-published. p. 135.

20. Carroll, R. T. (Monday January 9, 2012). Apophenia. Unnatural Acts That Can improve your thinking. Retrieved from http://59ways.blogspot.com/.

21. Macpherson, F. and Baysan, U. (July 2017). Binaural Beats in F. Macpherson (ed.). The Illusions Index. Retrieved from https://www.illusionsindex.org/i/binaural.

22. Macpherson, F. and Baysan, U. (July 2017). Binaural Beats in F. Macpherson (ed.), The Illusions Index. Retrieved from https://www.illusionsindex.org/i/binaural#mp-pic-1-mod.

23. A Constant Spectrum Melody. (n.d.). wikimedia.org. Retrieved from https://en.wikipedia.org/wiki/Constant_spectrum_melody.ogg.

24. AConstantSpectrumMelody. (n.d.). wikimedia.org. Retrieved from https://commons.wikimedia.org/w/index.php?title=File%3AConstantSpectrumMelody.ogg.

25. Deutsch scale illusion. (n.d.). wikipedia.org. Retrieved from https://en.wikipedia.org/wiki/File:Deutsch_scale_illusion.ogg.

26. Ibid.

27. Hartmann, W. M., & Rakerd, B. (1989). Localization of sound in rooms IV: The Franssen effect. Journal of the Acoustical Society of America, 86(4), 1366-137.

28. Franssen Effect (n.d.). Psychoacoustic Phenomenon's all Audio Engineers should know. Retrieved from gearslutz.com. http://www.parmly.luc.edu/parmly/franssen.html http://www engr.sjsu.edu/~duda/Duda.R.B.7.3.3.html.

29. Deutsch, D., Hamaoui, K., and Henthorn, T. (2007). "The Glissando Illusion and Handedness". Neuropsychologia. 45(13): 2981–2988.

30. Illusory continuity of tones. (n.d.). Wikipedia, the free encyclopedia. Retrieved from https://en.wikipedia.org/wiki/Illusory_continuity_of_tones.
31. Illusory discontinuity. (n.d.). Wikipedia, the free encyclopedia. Retrieved from https://en.wikipedia.org/wiki/Illusory_discontinuity.
32. Ibid.
33. McGurk, H.; MacDonald, J. (1976). "Hearing lips and seeing voices." Nature. 264 (5588): 746–748. doi:10.1038/264746a0. PMID 1012311.
34. Deutsch, D. (1974). An auditory illusion. The Journal of the Acoustical Society of America. 55 (S1): S18–S19. doi:10.1121/1.1919587. ISSN 0001-4966.
35. Jaekel, P. (2017-01-29). Why we hear voices in random noise. Nautilus. Retrieved from https://nautil.us/blog/why-we-hear-voices-in-random-noise.
36. Pareidolia. (n.d.). Wikipedia, the free encyclopedia. Retrieved from https://en.wikipedia.org/wiki/Pareidolia.
37. Rosen, R, J. (2012). Pareidolia: A Bizarre Bug of the Human Mind Emerges in Computers. The Atlantic. August 7th, 2012.
38. Shepard, R. N. (December 1964). Circularity in Judgements of Relative Pitch. Journal of the Acoustical Society of America. 36(12): 2346–53. doi:10.1121/1.1919362.
39. Deutsch, D. (1986). A musical paradox. Music Perception, 3, 275-280.
40. Deutsch, D. (1995). Musical Illusions and Paradoxes. La Jolla: Philomel Records.
41. Kirby, J. (May 16, 2018). Why you hear "Laurel" or "Yanny" in that viral audio clip, explained. Vox. Archived from the original on May 16, 2018. Retrieved May 16, 2018.
42. Kimbro, C. & Monongahela. (March 3rd, 2020). Squatchin 101. [Self-Published Edition].

4. More "Critical" Definitions and Discussion

1. After images. (n.d.). Psychology & Mental Health. Retrieved from www.britannica.com› Psychology & Mental Health.
2. Ibid.
3. Zimbardo, P.G. (1988). Psychology and life (12th Edition). Scott, Foresman and Company, Boston. p. 156.
4. Ibid., p. 157.
5. Ibid., p. 165.
6. Anthropomorphism (n.d.). Oxford Languages. Retrieved from Google.com/search?q=anthropomorphism&ei=QAVaYj_ZAdaqNoP38Gr-mAE&og=Anthro[pom&gs_Icp=Cgdnd3mtd216wAEB&sclient=gws_wiz.
7. Paulides, D. (April 3, 2012). Missing 411- Western United States and Canada: Unexplained disappearances of North America that have never been solved. CreateSpace, North Charlston, South Carolina. Copyright 2011, David Paulides.
8. Powell, T. (2003). The locals. Hancock House Publishers, LTD (Canada) and Hancock House Publishers (USA).
9. ABC News. (Nov. 18, 2016). Wild Polar bear pets dog. [Video]. Retrieved from https://www.youtube.com/watch?v=J_3tdkaEX8g.
10. FirstscienceTV. (Oct. 24, 2007). Polar bears and dogs playing. Youtube. [Video]. Retrieved from https://www.youtube.com/watch?v=JE-Nyt4Bmi8.

11. Vigilance. (n.d.). Oxford Languages Online Dictionary. Retrieved from https://en.oxforddictionaries.com/definition/vigilance.

12. Vigilant. (n.d.). Merriam Webster Online Dictionary. Retrieved from Retrieved from https://www.merriam-webster.com/dictionary/vigilant.

13. Curiosity. (n.d.). Oxford Languages Online Dictionary. Retrieved from https://en.oxforddictionaries.com/definition/curiosity.

14. Curiosity. (n.d.). Merriam Webster Online Dictionary. Retrieved from https://www.merriam-webster.com/dictionary/curiosity.

15. Pursuit Predation. (n.d.). Online Wikipedia. Retrieved from https://en.wikipedia.org/wiki/Pursuit_predation.

16. Ibid.

17. Ambush Predation. (n.d.). Online Wikipedia. Retrieved from https://en.wikipedia.org/wiki/Ambush predation.

18. Instincts. (Sep 19, 2012). Human Instincts. Copyright Eric R. Pianka. Retrieved from www.zo.utexas.edu› courses Human Instincts› Thoc.

19. Awareness. (n.d.). APA Online Dictionary of Psychology. Retrieved from https://dictionary.apa.org/awareness.

20. Self-awareness. (n.d.). APA Online Dictionary of Psychology. Retrieved from https://dictionary.apa.org/self awareness.

21. Serling. R. (creator). (1959). Twilight Zone (Original series). CBS Television Show.

22. Moneymaker, M. (n.d.). BFRO policies and procedures on debriefing. BFRO Leaders Manual.

23. Confirmation bias. (n.d.). APA Online Dictionary of Psychology. Retrieved from https://dictionary.apa.org/confirmation-bias.

24. Control. (n.d.). Oxford Languages On line Dictionary. Retrieved from https://en.oxforddictionaries.com/definition/control.

25. Ibid.

26. Ibid.

27. Ibid.

28. Zimbardo, P. G. (1988). Psychology and life (12th Edition). Scott, Foresman and Company, Boston. p. 89.

29. Ibid.

30. Zemeckis, R. (Director). Roth, E. (Writer). (1994). Forest Gump. [Film]. Paramount Pictures.

31. Franklin, B. (1789). In a letter to Jean-Baptiste Le Roy.

32. Festinger, L. (1957). A Theory of Cognitive Dissonance. California: Stanford University Press.

33. Cognitive-dissonance. (n.d.). APA Online Dictionary of Psychology. Retrieved from https://dictionary.apa.org/cognitive-dissonance.

34. Dissonance reduction. (n.d.). APA Online Dictionary of Psychology. Retrieved from https://dictionary.apa.org/dissonance-reduction.

35. Empirical. (n.d.). Online APA Dictionary of Psychology. Retrieved from https://dictionary.apa.org/emperical.

36. Empirical Knowledge. (n.d.). APA Online Dictionary of Psychology. Retrieved from https://dictionary.apa.org/emperical knowledge.

37. Empirical Method. (n.d.). APA Online Dictionary of Psychology. Retrieved from https://dictionary.apa.org/emperical method.

38. Empirical Validity. (n.d.). APA Online Dictionary of Psychology. Retrieved from https://dictionary.apa.org/emperical validity.
39. Empiricism. (n.d.). APA Online Dictionary of Psychology. Retrieved from https://dictionary.apa.org/empericism.
40. Ibid.
41. Ibid.
42. Experimental Group. (n.d.). APA Online Dictionary. Retrieved from https://dictionary.apa.org/experimental group.
43. Knowledge. (n.d.). APA Online dictionary of Psychology. Retrieved from https://dictionary.apa.org/knowledge.
44. Jung, C. (1916). The Structure of the Unconscious. (pp. 437–507). In Jung, C. (1953). Collected Works Vol. 7. pp. 263–292.
45. Ibid.
46. Collective Unconscious. (n.d.). APA Online dictionary of Psychology. Retrieved from https://dictionary.apa.org/collective-unconscious.
47. Llinas, R. R. (2001). I of the vortex: from neurons to self. MIT Press. pp. 190–191. ISBN 0-262-62163.
48. Norms. (n.d.). Oxford Languages. Retrieved from Https://en.oxforddictionaries.com/definition/norms.
49. Normal Curve. (n.d.). Wikipedia. Retrieved from https://psychology.wikia.org/wiki/Bell_curve_grading.
50. Duignan, B. (Last Updated Aug 5, 2020). Occam's-razor. Retrieved from https://www.britannica.com/topic/Occams-razor.
51. Outliers. (n.d.). APA Online Dictionary of Psychology. Retrieved from https://dictionary.apa.org/outlier.
52. Parameter. (n.d.). APA Online Dictionary of Psychology. Retrieved from https://dictionary.apa.org/parameter.
53. Outliers. (n.d.). APA Online Dictionary of Psychology. Retrieved from https://dictionary.apa.org/outlier.
54. Parameter. (n.d.). APA Online Dictionary of Psychology. Retrieved from https://dictionary.apa.org/parameter.
55. Reason. (n.d.). Online APA Dictionary of Psychology. Retrieved from https://dictionary.apa.org/reason.
56. Inductive reasoning. (n.d.). Online APA Dictionary of Psychology. Retrieved from https://dictionary.apa.org/inductive reasoning.
57. Deductive reasoning. (n.d.). Online APA Dictionary of Psychology. Retrieved from https://dictionary.apa.org/deductive reasoning.
58. Sentient. (n.d.). Definitions from Oxford Languages. Retrieved from https://en.oxforddictionaries.com/definition/sentient.
59. Sentience. (n.d.). Definitions from Oxford Languages. Retrieved from https://en.oxforddictionaries.com/definition/sentience.
60. Sentient beings; Jane Kotzmann. (Apr 8, 2020). Sentience: What It Means and Why It's Important. Sentient Media. Retrieved from sentientmedia.org› sentience-what-it-means-and-why-its.
61. Marc B. (September 06, 2013). After 2,500 Studies, It's Time to Declare Animal Sentience Proven (Op-Ed). Retrieved from https://www.livescience.com/39481-time-to-declare-animal sentience.html.

62. What beings are not conscious? (n.d.). Animal Ethics. Retrieved from www.animal-ethics.org› animal-sentience › beings-consci.
63. Marc B. (September 06, 2013). After 2,500 Studies, It's Time to Declare Animal Sentience Proven (Op-Ed). Retrieved from https://www.livescience.com/39481-time-to-declare-animal-sentience.html.
64. Qualia (n.d.). Definitions from Oxford Languages. Retrieved from https://en.oxforddictionaries.com/definition/sentience.
65. Piaget, Jean in Gruber, Howard E.; Vonèche, J. Jacques. (eds.). The essential Piaget. (1977) London: Routledge and K. Paul. ISBN 978-0710087782. OCLC 3813049.
66. BFRO Report Classification System. (n.d.). BFRO Database History and Report Classification System. Retrieved from bfro.net/GDB/classify.asp.
67. Ibid.
68. Ibid.
69. Ibid.
70. Ibid.
71. Ibid.
72. Ibid.
73. Ibid.
74. Ibid.
75. Ibid.
76. Ibid.
77. Stamey, J. (May 15, 2019). Bigfoot Column: To Woo or Not To Woo? It's not even a question. Grey Area News. Retrieved from https://greyareanews.com/category/feature/strange/.

5. How to Control Your Fight-Flight Response During a Bigfoot Encounter

1. Benson, H. (Author), Klipper, M. Z. (Author). (August 1, 1976). The Relaxation Response. Mass Market Paperback.
2. Marilyn Mitchell M.D. (Posted Mar 29, 2013). "Dr. Herbert Benson's Relaxation Response: Learn to counteract the physiological effects of stress. Psychology Today.
3. Wolpe, J. (1969). The Practice of Behavior Therapy, New York: Pergamon Press, ISBN 0080065635.
4. Ibid.
5. Yerkes R. M., Dodson J. D. (1908). The relation of strength of stimulus to rapidity of habit-formation. Journal of Comparative Neurology and Psychology. 18(5): 459–482.
6. Ibid.
7. Arousal Graph Figure. (n.d.). Yerkes Dodson law. Modified and retrieved from https://www.google.com/url?sa=i&url=http%3A%2F%2F5zakob9gi.youdontcare.com%2FYerkes-dodson-law-anxiety-disorders.html&psig=AOvVaw3zVYUsjvYadzHpH-6K7bj-&ust=1599395597826000&source=images&cd=vfe&ved=0CAIQjRxqFwoTCKCn4ZCDousCFQAAAAAdAAAAABAO.

6. Programming Necessary Levels of Arousal and Appropriate Behavioral Responses for A Bigfoot Encounter

1. Abreaction. (n.d.). English Oxford dictionaries. Retrieved from englishoxforddictionaries.com/abreaction.
2. Bandler, R. (Author), Andreas, S and Andreas, C. (Editors). (1985). Using your brain for a change, Real People Press. chapter 9, pp. 131-152.
3. Ibid.

7. Evidence: What Field Researchers Gather and Some Sticky Wickets in the Ketchum DNA Study

1. Lomeron, D. (Posted by April 6th, 2016). 15 Types of evidence and how to use them. i-sight.com. Retrieved from resources/15-types-of-evidence-and-how-to-use-them-in-investigation/.Analogy. (n.d.).
2. Lomeron, D. (Posted by April 6th, 2016). 15 Types of evidence and how to use them. i-sight.com. Retrieved from resources/15-types-of-evidence-and-how-to-use-them-in-investigation/.Anecdote. (n.d.).
3. Anecdote. (n.d.). Oxford Languages On line dictionary. Retrieved from https://en.oxforddictionaries.com/definition/anecdote.
4. Lomeron, D. (Posted by April 6th, 2016). 15 Types of evidence and how to use them. i-sight.com. Retrieved from resources/15-types-of-evidence-and-how-to-use-them-in-investigation/.
5. Ibid.
6. Ibid.
7. Phenomenology. (n.d.). Oxford Languages. Retrieved from http://english.oxforddictionaries.com/phenomenology.
8. Lomeron, D. (Posted by April 6th, 2016). 15 Types of evidence and how to use them. i-sight.com. Retrieved from resources/15-types-of-evidence-and-how-to-use-them-in-investigation/.
9. Black box phenomena. (n.d.). Wikipedia, the free encyclopedia. Retrieved from https://en.wikipedia.org/wiki/Black box.
10. Cress, Matthew. (January 10, 2019). The black box problem. Artificial Intelligence Mania. Retrieved from http://artificialintelligencemania.com/2019/01/10/the-black-box-problem/.
11. Lomeron, D. (Posted by April 6th, 2016). 15 Types of evidence and how to use them. i-sight.com. Retrieved from resources/15-types-of-evidence-and-how-to-use-them-in-investigation/.
12. Krantz. G. (1999). Bigfoot sasquatch evidence. The anthropologist speaks out. Published simultaneously in Canada and United states by Hancock House Publishers LTD and Hancock House Publishers, p. 3.
13. Lomeron, D. (Posted by April 6th, 2016). 15 Types of evidence and how to use them. i-sight.com. Retrieved from resources/15-types-of-evidence-and-how-to-use-them-in-investigation/.
14. Carpenter, S. (2019). The nephilim among us updated. (Scott Carpenter, Publisher). pp.77-122.

15. Carpenter, S. (2020). Truth denied-The sasquatch DNA study. (Scott Carpenter, Publisher).
16. Carpenter, S. (2019). The nephilim among us updated. (Scott Carpenter, Publisher), p. 88.
17. Ibid.
18. Chain of custody. (March 9, 2019). Legal Dictionary. Content Team. Retrieved from https://legaldictionary.net/chain-of-custody/.
19. Smeja steak quote (Carpenter vs Meldrum vs Powel).
20. Final Report on the Analysis of Samples. Submitted by Tyler Huggins, Wildlife Forensic DNA Laboratory, Case File 12-019.
21. Lomeron, D. (Posted by April 6th, 2016). 15 Types of evidence and how to use them. i-sight.com. Retrieved from resources/15-types-of-evidence-and-how-to-use-them-in-investigation/.
22. Ibid.
23. Ibid.
24. Ibid.

8. The Fight-Flight Response, The Human Nervous System, and Bigfoot "Zapping"

1. Zimbardo, P. G. (1988). Psychology and life (12th Edition). Scott, Foresman and Company, Boston, pp. 122-123.
2. Ibid., pp. 499-500.
3. Ibid.
4. Cornell Lab. (June 9, 2017). Cornel Lab's Elephant Listening Project Deep into Infrasound. The Cornell Lab. Retrieved from https://elephantlisteningproject.org/about-elp/team-elp/.
5. Infrasound. (n.d.). Wikipedia, the free encyclopedia. Retrieved from https://en.wikipedia.org/wiki/Infrasound.
6. Nicole, C. (Wed September 27, 2017). Using sound to attack: The diverse world of acoustic devices. cnn.com. Retrieved from https://www.cnn.com/2017/08/10/health/acoustic-weapons-explainer/index.html.
7. Ibid.
8. James Parker University of Melbourne in Australia. in Nicole, C. (Wed September 27, 2017). Using sound to attack: The diverse world of acoustic devices. cnn.com. Retrieved from https://www.cnn.com/2017/08/10/health/acoustic-weapons-explainer/index.html.
9. Payne, K. of the Elephant Listening Project (ELP). (n.d). Elephant Listening Project. Center for Conservation Bioacoustics. Retrieved from https://www.birds.cornell.edu/ccb/elephant-listening-project/.
10. Candid Camera TV Show. (1949). NBC Television. Produced by Alan Funt.

9. Experimental Design: How We Scientifically "Trap" Bigfoot

1. Control group. (n.d.). APA Online Dictionary. Retrieved from https://dictionary.apa.org/control group.

2. Morehead, R. (n.d.). Sierra Sounds Shelter Photo. Courtesy of Ron Moorhead.
3. IBM. (n.d.). SPSS Statistics. Retrieved from ibm.com/products/spss-statistics.
4. Placebo. (n.d.). American Psychological Association Online Dictionary of Psychology. Retrieved from https://dictionary.apa.org/placebo.
5. Placebo effect. (n.d.). APA Online Dictionary of Psychology. Retrieved from https://dictionary.apa.org/placebo.
6. Ibid.
7. Placebo control group. (n.d.). APA Online Dictionary of Psychology. Retrieved from https://dictionary.apa.org/placebo control group.
8. Blind, double blind. (n.d.). Online APA Dictionary of Psychology. Retrieved from https://dictionary.apa.org/placebo blind.

10. Scientific Research and Numbers: The Necessary Evil Known as Statistics

1. Zimbardo, P. G. (1988). Psychology and life (12th Edition). Scott, Foresman and Company, Boston, p. 28.
2. Ibid., p.29.
3. Ibid.
4. Ibid.
5. Ibid., p. 30.
6. Ibid.
7. Ibid., pp. 30-31.
8. Ibid., p. 31.
9. Ibid.
10. Ibid.
11. Ibid., p. 33.
12. Ibid.
13. Validity. (n.d.). Oxford Languages Online Dictionary. Retrieved from https://en.oxforddictionaries.com/definition/sentience.
14. Kelley, T. L. (1927). Interpretation of educational measurements. New York: Macmillan, p.14. In McLeod, S. A. (2013). What is validity? Simply Psychology. Retrieved from https://www.simplypsychology.org/validity.html.
15. Ibid.
16. McLeod, S. A. (2013). What is validity? Simply Psychology. Retrieved from https://www.simplypsychology.org/validity.html.
17. Ibid.
18. Ibid.
19. Ecological Validity in Psychology: Definition & Explanation. (October 1, 2015). Study.com. Retrieved from https://study.com/academy/lesson/ecological-validity-in-psychology-definition-lesson-quiz.html.
20. McLeod, S. A. (2013). What is validity? Simply Psychology. Retrieved from https://www.simplypsychology.org/validity.html.
21. Halls, K. M., Spears, R., & Young, R. (n.d.). Bigfoot by Any Other Name (n.d.). Directions Retrieved from https://www.frontiercsd.org/cms/lib/NY19000265/Centricity/Domain/218/Bigfoot.pdf, 208025P, pp. 18-20.
22. Ibid.

23. Redfern, N. (2016). The bigfoot book: The encyclopedia of sasquatch, yeti, and cryptid primates. Visible Ink Press. p. xvi.

24. North American Wood Ape Conservancy (NWAC) Online Podcast. (2017 Dec 24th). Apes Among Us: Tag 7. 01:50:55 [Audio Podcast].

25. Ibid.

26. McLeod, S. A. (2013). What is validity? Simply Psychology. Retrieved from https://www.simplypsychology.org/validity.html.

27. Ibid.

28. Nevo, B. (1985). Face validity revisited. Journal of Educational Measurement, 22(4), 287-293.

29. Ibid.

30. Ibid.

31. Ibid.

32. Ibid.

33. Hathaway, S. R., & McKinley, J. C. (1943). Manual for the Minnesota Multiphasic Personality Inventory. New York Psychological Corporation.

34. Nevo, B. (1985). Face validity revisited. Journal of Educational Measurement, 22(4), 287-293.

35. Cronbach, L. J., and Meehl, P. E., (1955). Construct validity in psychological tests. Psychological Bulletin, 52, 281-302.

36. Ibid.

37. McLeod, S. A. (2013). What is validity? Simply Psychology. Retrieved from https://www.simplypsychology.org/validity.html.

38. Ibid.

39. Ibid.

40. Ibid.

41. Ibid.

42. Ibid.

43. Ibid.

44. Cosby, K. A. (2020). Cultural history and the ontological. Examining the relationship of scientific knowledge and communities researching relict hominoids in North America. The Relict Hominoid Inquiry, Ontology, (9) 3-24.

45. Reliability. (n.d.). Oxford Languages Online Dictionary. Retrieved from https://en.oxforddictionaries.com/definition/anecdote.

46. McLeod, S. A. (2007). What is reliability? Simply Psychology. Retrieved from https://www.simplypsychology.org/reliability.html.

47. Ibid.

48. Ibid.

49. Ibid.

50. Ibid.

51. Ibid.

52. Ibid.

53. Ibid.

54. Ibid.

55. Ibid.

56. Hathaway, S. R., & McKinley, J. C. (1943). Manual for the Minnesota Multiphasic Personality Inventory. New York: Psychological Corporation.

57. McLeod, S. A. (2007). What is reliability? Simply Psychology. Retrieved from https://www.simplypsychology.org/reliability.html.
58. Ibid.
59. Beck, A. T., Steer, R. A., & Brown, G. K. (1996). Manual for the beck depression inventory. The Psychological Corporation. San Antonio, TX.
60. McLeod, S. A. (2007). What is reliability? Simply Psychology. Retrieved from https://www.simplypsychology.org/reliability.html.
61. Ibid.
62. Ibid.
63. Ibid.
64. Ibid.
65. Ibid.
66. Ibid.
67. Ibid.
68. Ibid.
69. Moneymaker, M. (1994). Ohio Howl.mpg. Retrieved from youtube Nov2201/youtube.com/watch?V=TPCcLddBekY.
70. Ohio Night Stalkers. (n.d.). The Ohio Calls. Retrieved from facebook.com/OhioNightStalkers2016.
71. Morehead, R. (1996). The Bigfoot recording. A true High Sierra wilderness story. (Volume I). Produced by Ron Morehead.
72. Meldrum, J. (2006). Sasquatch: legend meets science. A Forge Book Published by Tom Doherty Associates, LLC. pp. 108-109.
73. Krantz, G. (1971). Sasquatch Handprints. Northwest Anthropological Research Notes, 5(2):145-151. In Meldrum, J. (2006). Sasquatch: legend meets science. A Forge Book Published by Tom Doherty Associates, LLC., p. 108-109.
74. Meldrum, J. (2006). Sasquatch: legend meets science. A Forge Book Published by Tom Doherty Associates, LLC., p. 109.
75. Ibid.
76. Coincidence. (n.d.). Webster's' Merriam Dictionary. Retrieved from https://www.merriam-webster.com/dictionary/coincidence.
77. Correlation. (n.d.). Webster's Merriam Dictionary. Retrieved from https://www.merriam-webster.com/dictionary/correlation.
78. Zimbardo, P. G. (1988). Psychology and life (12th Edition). Scott, Foresman and Company, Boston, pp. 37-47.
79. Statistic. (n.m.). American Psychological Association's Dictionary of Psychology. Retrieved from https://dictionary.apa.org/statistic.
80. Central tendency. (n.d.). Online APA dictionary of Psychology. Retrieved from https://dictionary.apa.org/central tendency.
81. Mean. (n.d.). Online APA Dictionary of Psychology. Retrieved from https://dictionary.apa.org/mean.
82. Median. (n.d.). Online APA dictionary of Psychology. Retrieved from https://dictionary.apa.org/median.
83. Mode. (n.d.). Online APA Dictionary of Psychology. Retrieved from https://dictionary.apa.org/mode.
84. Skewness. (n.d.). Wikipedia. Retrieved from https://en.wikipedia.org/wiki/Skewness.
85. June 8th, 2020 MSNBC reported at NBC/Wall Street Journal Poll.

86. Normal Curve. (n.d.). Wikipedia. Retrieved from https://psychology.wikia.org/wiki/Bell_curve_grading.

87. "Great Apes, Trail Cameras And The Bigfoot Implications." (n.d.). Youtube. Retrieved from (https://www.youtube.com/watch?v=B-CS4tUVlvw&feature=share&fbclid=IwAR2p93nBbK2CGTglsvSoZQRdPI5MyIZt28Pygfx7VagtIf LFVyOYrvo6DBg).

88. Ibid.

89. Ibid.

90. Normal Curve. (n.d.). Wikipedia. Retrieved from https://psychology.wikia.org/wiki/Bell_curve_grading.

91. Descriptive statistics. (n.d.). Online APA Dictionary of Psychology. Retrieved from descriptive statistics.

92. Frequency distribution. (n.d.). Online APA Dictionary of Psychology. Retrieved from https://dictionary.apa.org/frequency distribution.

93. Inferential Statistics. (n.d.). Online APA Dictionary of Psychology. Retrieved from https://dictionary.apa.org/inferential statistics.

94. Inference. (n.d.). Online APA Dictionary of Psychology. Retrieved from https://dictionary.apa.org/inference.

95. Statistical Significance. (n.d.). Wikipedia. Retrieved from https://en.wikipedia.org/wiki/Statistical significance.

96. Hypothesis testing. (n.d.). Online APA Dictionary of Psychology. Retrieved from https://dictionary.apa.org/hypothesis testing.

97. Artic climate. (n.d.). Britannica. Retrieved from https://www.britannica.com/place/Arctic/Climate.

98. Polar climate. (n.d.). Wikipedia. Retrieved from en.wikipedia.org/wiki/Polar climate!

99. Meldrum, J. (2006). Sasquatch: legend meets science. A Forge Book Published by Tom Doherty Associates, LLC.

100. Gerhard, K.. (2019). The essential guide to bigfoot. Self-Published.

101. Carpenter, S. (2019). The Nephilim among us updated. Self-Published.

102. Ostman, A. in Gerhard, K. (2019). The Essential Guide to Bigfoot. Self-Published. pp. 54-56).

103. Meldrum, J. (2016). Sasquatch: legend meets science. A Forge Book Published by Tom Doherty Associates, LLC., p 187.

104. Redfern, N. (2016). The bigfoot book: the encyclopedia of sasquatch, yeti, and cryptid primates. Visible Ink Press. pp. 144-146.

105. Green, M. and Carter Coy, J. (2002). 50 Years with Bigfoot: Tennessee Chronicles of Co-Existence. Self-Published.

11. Hunting/Trapping versus Field Research versus Scientific Bigfoot Research (SBFR): Where Do We Go from Here?

1. Hunting. (n.d.). Oxford Dictionary. Retrieved from http://english.oxforddictionaries.com/hunting.

2. Why hunt. (n.d.). Centers for Humans and Nature. Retrieved from https://www.humansandnature.org/why-hunt.

3. Trap. (n.d.). Oxford dictionary. Retrieved from http://english.oxforddictionaries. com/trap.
4. Ibid.
5. Field research. (n.d.). Question Pro. Retrieved from https://www.questionpro. com/blog/field-research/.
6. Ibid.
7. Field research. (n.d.). Question Pro. Retrieved from https://www.questionpro. com/blog/field-research/questionpro.com/blog/quantitative-research/.
8. Ibid.
9. Fisheries and aquaculture software. FishStatJ - Software for Fishery and Aquaculture Statistical Time Series. In: FAO Fisheries and Aquaculture Department [online]. Rome. Updated 21 July 2016. [Cited 23 July 2020].
10. National Oceanic and Atmospheric Administration. (n.d.). fao.org. Retrieved from(http://www.fao.org/fishery/) and https://www.noaa.gov/.
11. Scientific method. (n.d.). Merriam Webster's Online Dictionary. Retrieved from https://www.merriam-webster.com/dictionary/trap.
12. Khan (article). (n.d.). The scientific method. How the scientific method is used to test a hypothesis. Retrieved from www.khanacademy.org/science/high-school-biology/hs-biology-foundations/hs-biology-and-the-scientific-method/a/the-science-of-biology.

Appendix A

1. Normal Curve. (n.d.). Wikipedia. Retrieved from https://psychology.wikia.org/wiki/Bell_curve_grading.
2. Fahrenbach, W.H. (1997-1998). Sasquatch: size, scaling and statistics. Cryptozoology 13:47-75.
3. 5 Examples of Bimodal distributions (None of which are human Height). (n.d.). Graph Paper Diaries. Retrieved from https://graphpaperdiaries.com/2016/08/28/5-examples-of-bimodal-distributions-none-of-which-are-human-height/28.
4. Stephanie Glen. (n.d.). Bimodal Distribution: What is it? Retrieved from StatisticsHowTo.com: Elementary Statistics for the rest of us! https://www.statisticshowto.com/what-is-a-bimodal-distribution/.
5. SARS-CoV-2 decreased. (7/20/2020). CDC website. Retrieved from https://www.cdc.gov/.
6. Percentile. (n.d.). Oxford Languages On line Dictionary. Retrieved from http://english.oxforddictionaries.com/percentile.
7. Percentile rank. (n.d.). Wikipedia, The Free Encyclopedia. Retrieved from https://en.wikipedia.org/wiki/Percentile_rank.
8. Hayes, A. (2020, June 2020). Z-Score. Corporate Finance & Accounting. Retrieved from https://www.investopedia.com/terms/z/zscore.asp.
9. McLeod, S. A. (2019, May 17). Z-score: definition, calculation and interpretation. Simply Psychology. Retrieved from https://www.simplypsychology.org/z-score.html.
10. Glen, S. (n.d.). T-score vs. z-score: What's the difference? StatisticsHowTo.com: Elementary Statistics for the rest of us! Retrieved from https://www.

statisticshowto.com/probability-and-statistics/hypothesis-testing/t-score-vs-z-score/.

11. Glen, S. (n.d.). T-score formula: Calculate in easy steps. StatisticsHowTo.com: Elementary Statistics for the rest of us! Retrieved from https://www.statisticshowto.com/probability-and-statistics/t-distribution/t-score-formula/.

12. Glen, S. (n.d.). T-score vs. Z-score: What's the difference? StatisticsHowTo.com: Elementary Statistics for the rest of us! Retrieved from https://www.statisticshowto.com/probability-and-statistics/hypothesis-testing/t-score-vs-z score/.